MRS CHRISTIAN:
'BOUNTY' MUTINEER

Glynn Christian

Other books by Glynn Christian
FRAGILE PARADISE
– The Discovery of Fletcher Christian, BOUNTY Mutineer

......

REAL FLAVOURS – *The* Handbook of Gourmet and Deli Ingredients
WINNER 2007 Food Guide of the Year - Le Cordon Bleu World Food Media Awards

HOW TO COOK WITHOUT RECIPES

THE DELICATESSEN FOOD HANDBOOK

For others, see www.glynnchristian.com

oooOooo

Copyright © 2011 Glynn Christian
The right of Glynn Christian to be identified as the author of this work is hereby asserted

All rights reserved

The Long Riders' Guild Press
ISBN: 1-59048-050-3

Enquiries about serialisation, dramatisation or reproduction in any other form should be directed to the author:
www.glynnchristian.com
Author available for press, radio and TV interview

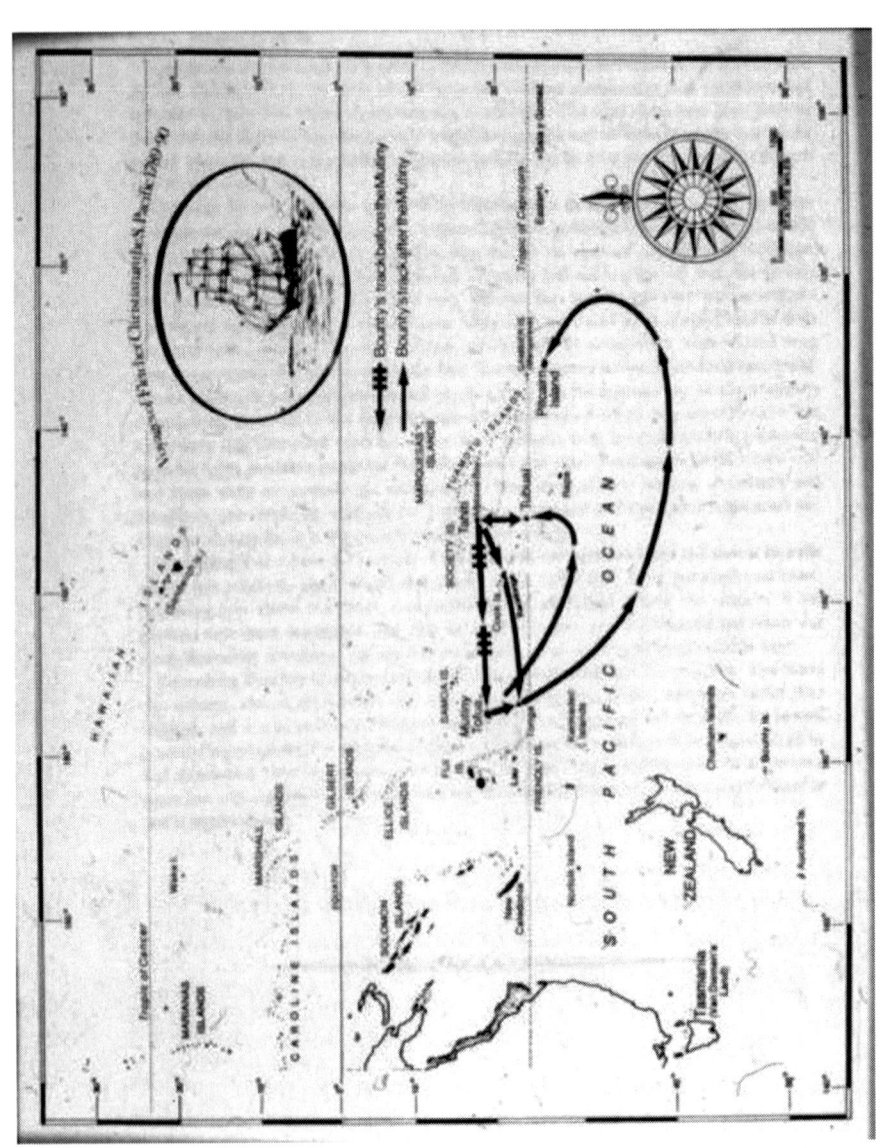

AUTHOR'S NOTES ON COLOUR, NAMES AND WORDS

What colour is black?

At the time of their discovery in 1808 Pitcairn Islanders called Ma'ohi men 'blacks'. Most had never seen such a man. Their Tahitian foremothers, some still living, knew what these men looked like and appear to have used this word, yet curiously they never described themselves as black. At the time words like native and black were used indiscriminately by Europeans for anyone not strictly Caucasian and Pitcairn's women must have followed suit.

Black is used appropriately for Ma'ohi men and women throughout the book because I feel the pejorative sense it gives is a better picture of how even the lowest white men of the time thought all coloured races inferior.

The Ma'ohi of Polynesia

I have used Ma'ohi as the collective for the men and women of Tahiti and neighbour islands throughout as this was the only unifying word at the time. Polynesia and Polynesians are later constructs by Europeans.

The Ma'ohi/Polynesian culture and language are the most geographically widespread on the globe, forming a vast triangle with points in Hawaii (*Havai'i*), New Zealand (*Aotearoa*) and Easter Island (*Rapa Nui*). These people are thought to have originated in South East Asia, particularly from Taiwan and close mainland areas. The variations between the languages of the many islands of the Polynesian triangle are so simple that men and women from thousands of miles apart can soon converse fluently. For instance Hawai'ian uses a 'k' where Tahitian uses a 't', so *tapu* (meaning something forbidden) becomes *kapu*.

Maimiti

Maimiti is widely thought to be one of the names of Fletcher Christian's Tahitian consort Mauatua, but she was never called Maimiti in her lifetime.

The most usual name found in contemporary papers is Mrs Christian, which she continued to use until she died even though she also had three children by Ned Young. The next most common is Mainmast (because she was so tall and straight-backed), and then Mauatua, her Tahitian name when Fletcher met her. For a while he also called her Isabella, after his cousin, Isabella Curwen of Workington Hall and Belle Isle, Cumbria.

The name Maimiti was popularized by Nordhoff & Hall in their 20th century trilogy of books about BOUNTY and Pitcairn Island. Research by eminent BOUNTY scholar Rolf DuRietz shows where Nordhoff and Hall might have found their inspiration. He told me:

'Among their sources ... is Harry L. Shapiro's anthropological monograph, Descendants of the Mutineers of the Bounty, published in Honolulu 1929 as no. 1 of vol. XI in the Bishop Museum's quarto Memoirs. At the end (pp. 98-106), there are several genealogical tables, and there Fletcher's (and then Young's second) wife (Isabella) is mentioned as 'Mimitti', followed in round brackets by the explanation 'Main mast, mai-mast' (pp. 99 and 105).'

Mi-mitti must have been heard by Shapiro on Norfolk Island, the island where the Pitcairners were shipped in 1856 and where most BOUNTY descendants live; this is where he did most research and this raises questions about how faithfully he was able to record the unique vowels and pronunciation of Norfolk Islanders – for instance, were the 'i' sounds in Mi-mitti long or short or a mixture of the two? And were they correctly transcribed anyway?

Some Norfolk Island families later returned to Pitcairn and when I first visited Pitcairn Island in 1980 Mainmast had become 'Mummas', as in 'Mumma's pool'. Yet during the childhood of the oldest living Pitcairners, the pool had been 'Maimas' pool'. In just three 20th century generations it had changed so much not one younger Pitcairners associated the pool with their foremother Mainmast/Mauatua. With no written Pitcairn or Norfolk language, many a truth has been buried under such linguistic evolution. On Pitcairn, for instance, The Other Side has become Tedside, and it is not only visitors wondering who Ted might be.

So, although Nordhoff & Hall didn't entirely invent Maimiti, it's clear they found the early 20th century degeneration of Mainmast to their liking for a character in their largely fictitious trilogy about the mutiny and Pitcairn Island. They added a vowel to Mi'mitti to make it sound like a genuine Tahitian name. Maimiti is prettier and easier to say and remember than Mauatua, and more romantic than Mainmast.

Once Maimiti was used in the famous Gable/Laughton movie based on their books it became accepted as genuine.

Nordhoff and Hall also included a character called Moetua, who is given much of the grace, gravity and wisdom of Mauatua. From one amazing woman they created two.

Today more and more girls are being called Maimiti among Mrs Christian's descendants and this can only be a good thing, for it helps preserve the memory of one of history's most successful revolutionaries and forward-thinking heroines.

Tahitian personal names

The men and women of pre- and immediately post-European contact in Tahiti regularly changed their names or exchanged their old names with new friends. BOUNTY's men also gave their Ma'ohi women European names. I have kept name changes to a minimum and except for Jenny (once Teehuteatuaonoa) the other Ma'ohi women of BOUNTY keep their original names in this book.

Alexander Smith/John Adams

Mutineer John Adams signed on BOUNTY as Alexander Smith, a false name. He reverted to his real name soon after his hideaway on Pitcairn Island was rediscovered in 1808. In this book he is John Adams from start to finish.

Tapa cloth

Tapa is a cloth made by beating the treated inner bark of several tropical trees. This beating thins and felts the inner bark and different techniques then give cloth thick enough to be a floor covering, thin enough for a bed sheet or something gossamer like, just as there are many grades of silk or cotton or wool. At the time of this story it was more usually called *'ahu* but gradually the Hawaiian word *kapa* replaced it during the 19th century. Eventually it became known universally as *tapa* cloth. I have used tapa throughout as this is the name by which it is most recognised and displayed in museums around the world, whenever or wherever it was made.

Museums around the world have early Pitcairn Island tapa that demonstrate the unique designs of Pitcairn's foremothers and their daughters, which have no equivalents elsewhere. The British Museum currently displays a small piece of tapa made by Mauatua/Mrs Christian, and Pauline Reynolds' excellent small book 'Pitcairn Tapa' (www.anaanapublishing.com) illustrates many other examples and tells you where they might be found.

The Tahitian Language

Singular words in Tahitian are the same as their plural. *Vahine* can mean one woman or any number of women. *Ma'ohi* is the generic name for all Polynesians and also used for just one man or woman. The apostrophe anywhere in a Ma'ohi word indicates a glottal stop.

A wonderful curiosity is the equivalence between Tahitian and Greek. If you ask a man in Athens called Panos to tell you his name, he will say 'Opanos', meaning in broad terms 'It is/I am Panos'. Tahitians did and do the same. The Tahitian so famously painted by Joshua Reynolds was not Omai but Mai. The island was Tahiti, not Otaheite.

Modern speakers of Tahitian might not recognise some language used throughout the book. They are the correct words but now archaic and thought old-fashioned, more often encountered today in a Tahitian-language Bible. This was the language used by BOUNTY'S Ma'ohi women, who took almost untouched pre-European custom and language to Pitcairn. Soon after they left in 1789 English and French missionaries arrived in Tahiti and erased Tahitian belief, burned virtually all artefacts and banned everything that might not have been found acceptable in an English village or European society.

The little-known massacre of Tahitian culture is one of the most disgraceful crimes of Christian proselytism and European colonisation. No other South Pacific nation was so erased.

Pitcairn Island's language

Pitkern, the language of Pitcairn Island, is a true Creole language, with its heritage in both English and Tahitian.

It is wrong to call it a 'pidgin' English.

Just as its English origins include regional words with roots from Cornwall to the Orkneys and the West Indies, Pitkern includes Ma'ohi variations from Tahiti, Raiatea and Huahine. But whether English or Ma'ohi in origin many words have been adapted. It's easy to see that *dudwe,* the Pitkern word for candlenut, is a simplification of the Tahitian *tutu'i.* The glottal stop in Tahitian words has been abandoned on Pitcairn.

For the sake of clarity and speed of reading I have not transcribed the Pitkern language.

THE WOMEN

Mauatua/Mrs Christian: (Isabella, Mainmast) Tahitian consort of Fletcher Christian and later of Ned Young

Mary Ann Christian: Only daughter of Mauatua and Fletcher Christian

Faahotu: Tahitian first consort of John Williams

Jenny (Teehuteatuaonoa): Tahitian consort of John Adams and then of Isaac Martin

Mareva: Shared Tahitian consort of Manarii, Teimua and Niau

Puarei: First Pitcairn consort of John Adams. Tahitian

Sully (Sally): Arrived on Pitcairn as a baby, daughter of Teio and an unknown Tahitian father; married Mauatua's second son, Charles, known as Hoppa

Teatuahitea: Tahitian consort of William Brown

Tee: see Jenny

Teio: First Tahitian consort of McCoy and later of John Adams

Teraura: First Tahitian consort of Ned Young and then of Matt Quintal. Married Mauatua's oldest son Thursday October when she was over 30 and he was 16

Tevarua: First Tahitian consort of Matt Quintal

Tinafanea: Tubuaian, shared consort of Titahiti and Oha, then given to John Adams

Toofaiti: From Huahine. She was first the consort of Tararo but then given to Williams. After Massacre Day she was one of Ned Young's consorts

Vahineatua: First the Tahitian consort of John Mills and then of Adams

THE MEN

William Bligh: Captain of His Majesty's Armed Vessel BOUNTY
Fletcher Christian: Acting second in command of BOUNTY and leader of the mutiny on BOUNTY April 28th, 1789
Thursday October Christian: Older son of Mauatua and Fletcher
Charles Christian: Younger son of Mauatua and Fletcher, nick-named Hoppa because of his club foot
John Adams: Able-bodied seaman
William Brown: One of BOUNTY's gardeners and previously had been a ship's officer
Isaac Martin: Able-bodied seaman
William McCoy: Able-bodied seaman
John Mills: Gunner's mate
Matthew Quintal: Able-bodied seaman
John Williams: Able-bodied seaman
Edward Young: Acting midshipman
Hitihiti: A noble from Bora Bora
Manarii: Tahitian
Niau: Tahitian and a younger cousin of Tararo
Oha: From Tubuai
Tamatoa: Chief of the Western half of Tubuai
Taaroa (Taaroaatohoa): Chief of the North-Eastern district on Tubuai
Tararo: A noble from Raiatea, related to Mauatua
Tamahere: Mauatua's son by her dead Tahitian ex-husband
Teimua: Tahitian
Tinarau: Chief of the South-Eastern district of Tubuai
Titahiti: (Taaroamiva): From Tubuai, younger brother of Chief Taaroa

CHAPTER 1

October 26th, 1788: Matavai Bay, Tahiti

Mauatua kicked through the lacy edge of the lagoon, drowning the clatter of the shells that wriggled and danced in the last of the ocean's strength. Her son irritated her. His palm was in hers, and he yanked and jerked her left arm as he pranced in deeper water. Tamahere was tall for a six-year old and as straight-backed as his mother. Of course he was. She had done her duty. She'd been disgusted to know warriors fought over who was going to father her children, all because they coveted sons who would grow even loftier than her enviable height. Some had brawled with fists and some had even cast priestly spells.

Was it fair that one of the few ways for a woman to be valued on Tahiti was to be tall and then to produce taller sons?

She stamped both feet, showering herself and her son with gobbets of warm salt water but then pulled him tight to her until he promised not to retaliate. He'd want the game to go on and on. She was unsettled and wanted her mind free to collect and consider again her options for escape from Tahiti. If there were any.

Across the black-sanded beach she saw friends and neighbours sitting or sleeping in the shade of wispy *toa* trees and under the clattering fronds of banana and coconut palms. A man no older than she was, perhaps 25 sun cycles, simpered as two fawning women oiled and decorated his long hair with shells and feathers and flowers. That was another thing that made her ache to get away from the island. Why couldn't she have long hair?

She knew the answer by heart. Men. Men decided everything about a woman's life on Tahiti, especially the men of her clan. Well, his oiled hair would still have nits and he'd still crunch them between his teeth, just as she did. No wonder other islands called Tahitians 'nit-eaters'.

She angrily ruffled her right hand through her hair, shorn earlier with bamboo shards by her girlfriends. These were friends who had shared the shock of menstruation and then disbelief at the pain of tattooing, yet this morning they ignored her protests and cut her hair, insisting they were doing her a favour.

Really?

Just because some nagging old uncles complained about its length?

She hadn't spoken to her girlfriends since, but she turned over her right shoulder to see how far behind they were lagging. She couldn't do without them for long.

Tamahere's hand tightened in hers and when she looked his left arm pointed across the lagoon. At first she saw nothing unusual. She hadn't looked far enough away. When she raised her eyes towards the shark-tooth peaks of the nearby island of Mo'orea she thought flocks of white birds were wheeling over the sea.

Then the sun pierced the clouds, throwing a single blade of brightness directly on to the vision, as though the gods wanted no confusion. It was no flock of birds. Her chest tightened with disbelief and she quickly crossed her fingers in a screen before her face to lessen any harm in case this were dreadful magic.

She waited for her short sharp breaths of fear to subside and then dared brief, pecking peeks through gaps she made. What she saw caused her no injury and so she opened her fingers to look fully. It was the white gods returned, in one of their great canoes that travelled with no outriggers but many sails, bringing *popa'a*, men with pale skins covered in strange cloth.

They also brought her the chance of escape. She smiled in jubilation. Her mind raced with images of a different life and she pulled Tamahere close to her again, hoping this would stop his questions and whimpers.

The great canoe spat a white cloud toward her and thunder rolled on into the soaring diadem of mountain peaks behind Matavai Bay. As the boom bounced and echoed, villagers ran to the shore and stopped, uncertain of what the noises and signs might mean. Then the priests arrived, high-headed in helmets of feathers. They prostrated themselves on the sand, respectfully baring their shoulders but whether in fear or celebration she couldn't tell. She calmed Tamahere's panic at the unfamiliar commotion by picking him up and holding him high on her back, so his head was as tall as hers and then she moved back into the shadows.

Mauatua already felt disconnected from the island.

She was the only one who didn't dab her head in and out of the coarse sand until the scented oil made the black grains into a crust on everyone's forehead, confusing the differences in class and dress and privilege otherwise so carefully observed.

And then there was such madness that she laughed. Every man, woman or child who could swim that far, or who could cram into a canoe, raced one another across the water. More decorously, cloaked priests stood aggressively with long, carved staves on the high platforms of double-hulled canoes that flew enormous writhing streamers of gorgeous feathers that flashed in the slightest breeze. Their drummers beat precise rhythms that reverberated about the lagoon and land as loudly as the thunder from the gods' canoe had done.

The air shook with the drumming and she felt the beat of the deepest-voiced drums pound through her skin and in to her core. Once, the sensation would have frightened her. Instead, she stood straighter and more certain. This time, each shuddering thud competed with her heartbeat to make her blood run faster with thoughts of flight.

A few of her girlfriends joined her as the foreign canoe grew bigger and bigger. She was certain they knew what she was thinking and so swallowed her smiles.

Her thoughts were none of their business, not for the moment.

The vessel found the break through the frothed rope of salt-sea that marked the reef. It stopped pitching and rolling and then sailed serenely across the lagoon to Pare, a good long walk to her left.

She left Tamahere with her girlfriends, his other mothers, and stalked away, furiously pulling at her hair. Her head looked like half a broken coconut, just when she should look her best,

She had been thought too young to share the treasures white men brought on earlier visits, yet she had looked and listened with great care. She'd not forgotten their round things called wheels that made it faster to go places and easier to carry harvests. Or the sharp, shiny fingers joined together that cut tapa cloth far more cleanly and for longer than bamboo, or the bright tools that did not chip like the heavy polished stones she had to use.

Once she specially envied the long hair of the carved idol of a woman who guided an earlier *popa'a* canoe. She had climbed out onto the pointed branch high above its prow to admire it.

On normal days she held her breath and listened carefully when a breeze agitated leaves, because those rustles and hisses were voices, messages from the gods and spirits who lived in every part of this land. But now the *popa'a* were back she heeded only the small insistent voices from the most secret part of her head.

If white men really did come to Tahiti from another island called Peretane, if there really were other worlds, why couldn't she visit them? Her relative Mai had sailed to Peretane on an earlier . . . ship? Was that the word they used or was it a boat? There was a way to remember but for the moment she had forgotten?

He said women's lives were different in those other worlds. He said they were free to eat what they wanted and to have as many children as they wished. Wouldn't that be nice she thought, wishing there were safe ways to shout about such freedoms for women?

During the night she remembered the phrase, that 'boats were carried on ships', so the word was ship.

When she woke she found the ship had headed eastwards inside the reef and was anchoring in Matavai Bay, where she lived. The stink of it overpowered Matavai's sweet morning air but finally assured her the sight was not a wanton trick of gods and spirits. These wooden ships were always drenched with an awful stench that was multiplied by Tahiti's sun.

There was the black pitch used to plug holes in the decks and the pungent tar that darkened and waterproofed the lines strung from their masts. Sometimes there were animals and their waste on deck, too, but always there were unwashed men and nauseating cooking smells and stale water that slopped in the wooden hull, mixing all those and adding more unpleasantness of its own.

Ma'ohi priests had taught her these visitors were like Tahitians under their coverings, except they were inexplicably pink and with body and pubic hair, uncut foreskins and bad teeth. Even so, it was widely believed these stinking strangers were gods. There was no other explanation for what they said and did, and for what they had on their great ships.

As she considered what all this might mean to her plan, the sun moved higher from its bed. Her skin glowed in the brightening light that also made the tiny tattoos of stars and flowers on her hands seem sharper and darker. She'd already bathed in the stream and scented her hair and skin with *tiare*-scented oil, using more than usual of the heady perfume Englishmen said reminded them of gardenia. She hoped it would deflect what she'd encounter on board.

There were no surprises when she clambered up the side steps of the ship. Two peoples parched for novelty and variety crowded and clamoured as they competed for what the other offered. The ship's company guzzled whatever food was brought on board, stuffing it into their mouths with both hands, but still talking. They noisily mashed the best honeyed bananas in their eager mouths, heedless of portions drooling out, like lazy, vomiting infants. While *fe'i* bananas from the mountains and mealy baked plantains were gummed into pastes, their filthy fingers pulled at roasted pork, small fish and whole baked chickens. Some men had already dribbled another good feed onto their beards and clothes, yet they still snatched at cooked sweet potatoes and taro puddings baked in banana leaf. She laughed quietly behind her hands to see so many slurping the sweet water from coconuts, two, three or even four, one after the other.

By tomorrow their guts would be water, too.

The more she looked, the more confusion she felt. These gods said their voyage took many moon-cycles, so why didn't they bring food with them? Surely gods might conjure fish from the water and pluck coconuts from the air? Why didn't they wash before eating or dip their cooked meat and vegetables into sea water, like humans did? When she saw the way these supposed gods ate she found it difficult not to think about animals. Perhaps they weren't gods at all . . . She wondered which would be better for her plans, gods or men?

She didn't dare stand to watch the melee on deck. Her height made her too noticeable and loitering in one place would be read as sexual availability. She wanted no part of that.

On every side of her women of all ages were eagerly satisfying the willingness of visitors to pay for their bodies. *Titoi. Reporepo. S*he heard sex-starved men whisper and cajole with these words and then saw half-naked women clasped against the sailors' disarranged sea-going slops, and in full view of others. It had to be so, for while priests were watching no woman would go below decks, so others were walking above their heads.

That was forbidden.

The women's ideal reward was something of metal or a garment of the cloth said to be made from the hair of animals. Anything new or different would do but Mauatua knew these rewards were immediately handed to the husband or brother or father who had encouraged the coupling.

Typical.

It was as well the ship was now anchored, for Tahitians far outnumbered the ship's company, what she thought could only be 40 or so pink men. The trails and ladders of vines that worked the many sails were like spiders' webs stuck with brown bodies and the open deck was as tightly packed as bananas on a stalk.

She side-shouldered her way slowly through the crowd, assaulted by the screaming shrieks and laughter of conquest, choking sometime on the acrid reek of a white man's hairy pink body channelled with sweat from the sun and from their shameless gorging and rutting.

Sometimes she had to force her way and twice retched as her passing released a greater smell of old sweat and ancient dirt from a *popa'a* chest or shoulder. But she said nothing so she could hear everything, not even when she slipped on the mess of discarded skins and bones and the semen from men whose excitement couldn't wait. If she listened she would hear more of what she wanted to know. Her grandmothers, her *tupuna vahine*, had taught her that, that if you ask too many questions people might not tell you what you most want to know.

Was the man Tahitians called Tute captain of this ship too? None of the men she saw in an officer's blue coat looked anywhere near his great height. It had been 11 sun cycles since he was last in Tahiti, and that was his fourth visit. She quickly reckoned his first must be 22 or more cycles past because she was at least six then, maybe more. He'd brought men to watch the Morning Star pass in front of the Sun and that's when she began to store their words in her head. The mouths and tongues of *popa'a* had different sounds in them, so she struggled to say them the right way too, not the lazy Tahitian way.

Tahitian men didn't know it, but by now she knew much of the speech of these visitors, gods or not. The way to say the captain's name was Cook not Tute and Peretane was really Britain. More than 20 years ago she worried her tongue and mouth until she could say 'Cook from Britain'.

Every time a British ship came to Tahiti she learned new words and remembered them and every day she rehearsed words from Britain in her head. She wished these pink-white gods took as much trouble with her language. If she was asked her name she said Omauatua, just as her cousin Mai, the one who had sailed to Britain with Cook, would answer Omai, but the pink men never understood so still said Omai, or spoke of Otaheite instead of Taheite.

She turned to look back at Matavai Bay from the ship. She had long recognised the folly of challenging the men of her clan about the laws and customs of Tahiti. Her horrible short hair was proof of that. Instead, she'd chosen to defeat them, all Tahitian men, with knowledge they did not have. She'd use her British words to persuade a British officer to take her away from Tahiti.

She'd spotted one or two officers who seemed about her age but hadn't made a decision. She turned back to inspect them more closely, hoping they would, at least, be cleaner. Holding a scented wrist to her nose she bullied her way through the chaos on deck. As she did she silently shaped her lips around the name of the ship that would be her saviour.

'BOUNTY... BOUNTY...'

We found Teura in 1980 in Papeete Flower Market. She was much younger than Mauatua but my expedition to Pitcairn Island agreed she was the epitome of their modern image of 18th century Tahitian women.

CHAPTER 2

Fletcher Christian's body shuddered with a single enormous breath of relief. The anchors were down, the anchor buoys were in place, his duty was done. BOUNTY and he were both safely in Tahiti after ten months of misery, danger and the immolating isolation only long-distance sailors can know. His lungs sucked in the air once again and expelled it in gasps as though unloading poison.

His mind raced with images it also wanted to jettison. Of endless dishes of tough salt meat insufficiently desalinated and then boiled in slimy brine, of the dull thudding as men dumbly thumped ship's biscuits onto mess tables to shake out infestations of grubs.

He recovered scarring memories of the weeks BOUNTY challenged the very worst of Cape Horn in the southern winter - and lost. Furious seas towered over the ship. Ferocious winds threw jagged ice and sleet that cut into men's clothing and faces and hands and that changed direction as maliciously as mad dogs worrying at sheep. It shouldn't have been so, wouldn't have been if the Admiralty in London hadn't so stupidly delayed their sailing orders.

He shook his head free of the painful images. Other captains might have chosen a new route. But not this captain, not William Bligh. His orders were to get to Tahiti by rounding Cape Horn and so he fought with every personal and naval resource to do so, keeping fires burning continuously below decks, even giving up his own cabin so men had warm, dry clothing, bedding and somewhere secure to sleep.

The task was never possible.

When Bligh admitted defeat, he took little comfort that the entire company cheered him and then cheered him again. Their relief was ill-placed, for crossing the South Atlantic to the Dutch settlement of Simon's Bay, on the bottom tip of Africa, meant sailing into the wind at that time of the year, and the galley stove pumped smoke through the living quarters day and night.

Yet, with Bligh's constant administering of soups made from dried vegetables and compulsory dancing every day, BOUNTY hadn't lost a single man from ill-health. In Simon's Bay Fletcher discovered ships that had lost men to scurvy on a direct run from Rotterdam.

He ran a hand over his chest and rib cage for reassurance and then felt his hips and buttocks. He was still well muscled and had his strength but he wasn't carrying enough fat to burn and light his way up a flight of steps.

His eyes squeezed shut and streamed with water, imprisoning their dark brown pupils against the tropic light. It wasn't tears, although he wouldn't have resisted them. After so many months of seeing only the browns of the ship and the limited blues and greens of the sky and sea, his eyes were embattled by the variety of colour before him. When he could open them, he turned away from the extraordinary scenes on deck.

He reached for a roasted chicken leg from a bag of woven palm leaves that was passing.

'Woof woof, Mr Christian.' He turned to the able seaman beside him.

'Woof?'

'That's dog that is. Dirty savages.'

The insulting stance was what he expected from a sailor like Quintal, rumbustious, illiterate and Cornish. But he couldn't be seen to support the attitude, not as second in command of the ship. He bit into the thigh, his first roasted fresh meat since they had left Africa almost four months ago. Quintal shrugged and turned away.

The fatty flesh was vaguely game-like but with an unsettling after-taste, slightly bitter. As soon as Quintal was out of sight, Fletcher tossed it over the heads of the crowd and into the lagoon. He turned to look more carefully at Tahiti but Quintal was back tugging at his sleeve.

'Here's what it's all about, Sir. Breadfruit, Mr Christian.'

He shook Quintal's hand from his jacket. 'So this is it,' he said softly, his eyes widening with interest as he picked up one. Breadfruit were why he found himself on the opposite side of the world from home. BOUNTY was contracted to take breadfruit plants to the West Indies, so the English owners of sugar plantations no longer had to rely on American revolutionaries for flour and bacon as food for their slaves.

The breadfruit was something like the size of a man's head but oval and with a flattened top and bottom. The skin was a bright, clean green sometimes clouding into yellow. It looked rather like a raw, plucked chicken and had flecks of black where once feathers might have stood and felt rough in his hands.

A Tahitian urged a cooked segment onto him. Its skin was now scorched grey and black, perhaps cooked over an open fire or in embers.

The revealed flesh was a rich creamy colour but when he put it to his nose there was nothing of yeast or of the starchy sweetness an English man expected from bread.

He pulled at the flesh and tasted it. Bland and sweet, yes, and with a comforting satiny texture. It felt in his mouth like floury potato mashed with plenty of farmhouse butter and fresh cream and grated cheese. It would be easy to eat prodigious quantities.

But why was it called breadfruit when there was nothing of bread to be enjoyed? Of course. He remembered Captain Bligh telling him it wasn't supposed to taste like bread but to act like bread, a food that could support life, daily bread that required little daily toil and would cost the plantation owners nothing once the trees were producing.

He pushed his way to the rail, gorging more of the breadfruit. There he dropped the remains overboard, more immediately intent on feeding the hunger of his excited eyes.

Below him on the lagoon, more than 100 canoes of all sizes butted for a place on BOUNTY's hull, each of them piled with offerings of flowers and food, much of it still living. The easy muddle was amusing, an entertainment compared to supposedly civilised ports, where only crooks, pimps, gypsies, usurers and whores jostled to come aboard.

The scene wasn't totally new to him. He'd studied the drawings and watercolours by earlier visitors in books Bligh carried in his quarters.

To his left he recognised the protective arm of a low, narrow point that Captain Cook had called Point Venus. From here, the black-sanded beach spread away to his right in a gentle encompassing curve of a mile or so.

Behind the sand was a dappled plain where banana and coconut palms and generous spreading trees erupted over luscious undergrowth jewelled with fruits and flowers.

Ahead sharp-edged flames of black-green peaks leapt into the sky, most so sheer men could never have set foot on them.

The sun stung his hands and face and made him uncomfortable under his blue officer's jacket, but its light was crystalline. Colours seemed to burst and fragment into unsuspected tones. Browns became reds and greens. Greens gave up purples, blue and yellow.

He had to shade his eyes and turn away.

He'd expected half-naked women to come on board, bare breasted and forward. This was the legend. Instead, the women before him wore an underskirt almost to their ankles and over that a shift of some creamy-white material, often tied around the waist.

Some men wore what looked like the togas of Ancient Greece, but most wore almost nothing, a cloth of the same white stuff tied between their legs and high around their waist.

Both sexes seemed to have perfect teeth: something not a single man could claim on BOUNTY. Many of the eager faces he saw were as noble and finely boned as classical statues and some Tahitians were as pale as some Englishmen, except for the extraordinary configurations of tattoo that covered so much of their hard bodies. It seemed the paler they were, the taller they were, too, much taller than he was and thus over 6 feet.

They must be the higher class of Tahitian he had read about.

He touched himself, recognising he was excited by more than the crush of golden bodies swarming over BOUNTY's decks, by more than the public couplings he saw or heard at every turn.

He had been appointed to command the land camp for the breadfruit plants the ship hoped to collect in Tahiti.

He felt his heart flutter and his head tremble with incredulity. Nothing he'd seen in India with the Navy or when he'd previously sailed to and from the Caribbean prepared him for the luscious landscape that challenged him across the satin-watered lagoon of Matavai Bay. And he was going to live there for longer than any Englishman ever had.

His chest swelled and he smiled broadly, but he wanted to keep his excitement to himself. He hid his upturned mouth by pulling his chin into his collar.

'So, Mr Christian. What do you make of it?' Fletcher started, blushing as he covered himself with his hands before turning. It was Captain Bligh, who then continued 'Your home for the next three or four months, eh?'

Fletcher paused, willing his mind into sharp concentration. Even simple conversation with Captain Bligh could become difficult and demeaning. He'd learned never to answer at once, not until each of Bligh's words was analysed for hidden challenge or insult.

There was a long pause before he felt certain he would not damn himself. 'Does it really have to be so long, Sir?'

'Aye. The winds will be against us until March next year, maybe even into April.'

'Mightn't we go with the current winds, via Cape Horn, Sir?'

'Not what my orders say, Mr Christian. They say we must sail westwards and return via the Torres Straits, and that we will do.'

Fletcher flapped the fronts of his jacket to cool himself and make some time. What he'd suggested was exactly what might needle Bligh. Yet it was true. They could leave months earlier if they rounded the Horn from the Pacific.

As Captain Bligh had not reacted, he mooted the idea again, but the man irascibly pursed his lips, choosing not to contradict or insult his second in command.

The two men turned back to the landscape and Fletcher wondered if the life he now expected to lead ashore would be anything like that of a Cumbrian landowner and farmer.

As a younger son, he'd anticipated growing old somewhere around Moorland Close, the family farm close to the market town of Cockermouth. Then, just as he was about to go up to Peterhouse in Cambridge, his widowed mother was bankrupted by his older brothers' profligacy and had to sell up.

There was no shame in his choosing the Navy at 17, for in the Senior Service men were promoted according to ability rather than for family or fortune, the way it was in the Army.

Now, after only seven years at sea, he was second in command of BOUNTY and on a mission for King George to Tahiti, Tahiti in the far-flung, fabled South Seas. It was an excellent recovery from misfortune, and who knew where the experience might lead?

He broke the silence both men had shared, deliberately opening a subject that would allow him to praise Bligh. The man had been an important mentor to him, and always appreciated reminders of this.

'Those letters begging to serve with you certainly led to great things, Sir. Even if it did take two years,' he said to Bligh.

'Two years, it was as long as that? You spent that time in London, did you not?' Fletcher nodded. 'And that was a hardship, Mr Christian? I'm led to believe you were forever Your Gracing and Royal Highnessing and racing in carriages from one fine gathering of women with feathers in their hair to another.'

Fletcher noted the thread of envy in Bligh's voice but even so expanded on the implied criticism. 'London life answered my natural curiosity.

'There was nothing in Cumbria like hearing Herr Mozart's new music in Norfolk House. Do you know *Eine Kleine Nachtmusik,* Captain Bligh?'

'You need not enumerate your superior social position and experiences, Mr Christian. It might be thought you were looking to display some advantage over your captain.'

'That would never be the case,' Fletcher said, bowing with a courtly sweep of his arm, certain now he could control where the exchange would lead. 'It is you who has given me all my advantages, you who refined my navigation when we sailed together, to and from the Caribbean.'

Bligh accepted Fletcher's compliment with a brief twist of his pursed lips and then reminded him that Fletcher had got that job by writing he wanted to be able to do the best part of every job on a ship, and by saying there was no knowing when an officer might be called upon to replace a crew man and to do his job just as well.

'The wider world will one day know it, Captain Bligh. My success will be your success.'

'Success? Don't be too cocky, Mr Christian. There remain plenty of mistakes for you to make.'

'And you will be kind enough to point them out, Sir?'

'Duty, duty, don't y'see . . .It's my duty.'

Fletcher inclined his head as Bligh left. Bligh could be a sharp-tongued bastard but his single objective was to follow orders to the letter, with his ship in good shape and as few dead men as possible. No sailor should fault him for that.

Privately, he called him Foul-Weather Bligh and it was a privilege to see him at work if ever the ship was in danger. It was only when a ship wasn't at risk that Bligh became unpredictable and, he'd have to say to a court-martial, a bully.

He turned back to the celebrating throng on deck, content as ever to watch rather than participate. Some of these women were as pale as the risen cream he ladled from settled milk in the farm's dairy, some were even taller than he was. It would be a struggle to resist them.

And then reality hit, blowing him in the chest as sharply as any bare-fisted prize-fighter might.

He staggered slightly and clapped his hands over his mouth as he fought to stop a groan of misery escaping.

He must resist. If not there was only shame and disgust to come.

There is no known portrait of Fletcher Christian. This sketch was created by combining the most common Christian family features from a number of contemporary oil portraits of his uncles and first cousins. It was created by John Luce Lockett (www.lucelockett.co.uk) for cartoonist Adrian Teal (adrian@tealcartoons.co.uk) to illustrate the latter's English-degree dissertation on the portrayal of Fletcher Christian.

CHAPTER 3

Fletcher watched and learned as Bligh took his time with Teina and his wife Itia, the regent chiefs of Matavai District, flattering them with gifts of cloth and red feathers, with red glass beads and with axe heads, all bribes from King George of Great Britain. The feathers were the most persuasive, for in Tahiti red feathers denoted the most high majesty and sacredness.

'They don't seem interested in giving anything in return,' he observed to Bligh as once more they were rowed back to BOUNTY with nothing to show for their king's largesse.

'Not yet, they don't. They are frightened we might ask them to give too much of something they value. But watch what happens when I mention the king is interested in breadfruit plants. It'll be like giving King George chests of gold and suggesting he gives acorns in return. They'll think we and the king are quite mad.

'Let them think what they like. Once I've delivered breadfruit to Jamaica, it will no longer matter if those damned Americans overcharge for their wheat-flour and bacon and vegetables. The slaves in the Caribbean will eat breadfruit instead. His Majesty will be well pleased with me.'

Fletcher dared not wink back at the oarsmen behind Bligh. The entire ship was amused at the way Bligh continuously claimed the breadfruit expedition relied exclusively on his skills. Behind his back they laughed harder when they considered what would happen to him if it failed.

Two weeks later Fletcher was confronted with a low forest of 600 breadfruit shoots, lined up in pots behind the beach on Point Venus.

'Breadfruit grow like bananas,' Nelson the botanist told him. 'Sport no seeds but reproduce by running shoots. We could have thousands if we wanted. Any time of the year.'

'And sail away next week?'

'Aye, we could. But who would want that, Mr Christian?'

He disagreed with Williams about the general joy at their extended stay in Tahiti. Tahiti was properly legendary and what was said about the pleasures of its climate and women and food seemed true. Yet he was constantly home-sick, for his mother and for his sister Mary particularly.

Sense would prevail, as it usually did. He would endure Tahiti and then be back in Britain one day. There his adventures in the South Seas would make him the toast of Society in a way no-one else on BOUNTY could imagine. No, not even Captain Bligh.

He directed his energy and strength into helping build a long thatched accommodation hut between the sands of Matavai and the fresh-water stream that intersected Point Venus. He enjoyed the quick discovery by BOUNTY's carpenters that he was as practical and capable as they were and eagerly displayed quite how much stronger he was than any of them.

Word swiftly spread among the locals and there were always some who quietly sat in shadow for hours to watch him work in the sun with the saw and chisel, the axe, a hammer and nails - the metal tools Tahitians thought must have godly origins.

He accepted his audience's offer to thatch the roof but upset them when he laughed at the low picket-like fence they voluntarily made around the camp. Did some crew member yearn for hollyhocks and daisies?

The Tahitians sulked at his ridicule. Their fence wasn't to keep domestic animals inside but to keep out Tahiti's free-running pigs and dogs. He had to bribe them with nails and feathers to complete it.

'Every Tahitian house, *fare* they call them, has a fence around it,' Bligh bridled, chiding him for the dispute.

'How could I know that?' asked Fletcher defending himself. 'I've never walked even a few steps from Point Venus.'

This squabble apart, he thought of his camp as a happy little patch of Britain, albeit with a Tahitian fence around it. As its appointed lord and master, he staged a small ceremony to mark the breadfruit camp's completion. Two able seamen hoisted a Union Jack and then the camp toasted it with rum. Thereafter the flag was flown daily.

Four able seamen served him as guards and general servants in the camp and these were regularly rotated. David Nelson, the ship's botanist, and his assistant, William Brown, were stationed there permanently. So was William Peckover, who had nothing to do with the breadfruit project but was in charge of all official trading with BOUNTY.

His fourth fixed companion was Peter Heywood, just 16 and a Manxman. Fletcher appreciated this appointment. The Christians had lived on the Isle of Man since the 14th century and his mother, brother Edward and sister Mary moved there after Moorland Close was lost.

He had continued Peter's education at sea, teaching him classic languages and mathematics.

Fletcher rapidly rediscovered his childhood thrill of seeing plants respond to his care, and slowly relaxed. When Captain Bligh was not ashore he wore fewer clothes, and then no shoes.

He knew shipmates and Tahitians alike expected him to take lovers and to bond to a special male friend, a *taio*. He never woke with another beside him and treated every Tahitian, man or woman, as special. There were one or two women he judged superior but he didn't want to risk rejection.

It vexed him to overhear Tahitians agreeing he must feel himself too sacred to be touched by human beings. They stopped speculating after a few weeks, accepting him as overlord of the breadfruit camp but not quite like other men. He settled into the life he preferred of public friendships, immune he hoped, from private disappointment.

Mauatua was attracted to Fletcher Christian for all the differences that separated him from other men. She knew ordinary men would be no use. She hid high in tall trees or walked alone on the beach so she could practise saying his name out loud. It wasn't hard, even though some sounds weren't in Tahitian words. Others stumbled to call him Titreano, almost swallowing the last vowel, as though tired by the previous ones. She knew how to make the 'k' of Christian explode at the back of her tongue, and to hiss through her teeth to say 'sss'.

She waited patiently, always out of his direct sight, until she saw Fletcher's breadfruit pots were inside the fence, his little house arranged and he stood wondering, she thought, how he might spend the months before BOUNTY sailed again. She paddled silently along the stream and stood in its shallow water behind him, to look carefully once more.

His hair was long and rested its thick weight on broad muscle-roped shoulders. It looked black, like all Tahitians' hair, but she'd seen it catch the light. Then it was a dark brown, darker than the very best soil for growing vegetables, and sometimes it flashed red. He couldn't have nits, because he wore no oil on it, so when it was not tied back at his neck, it floated when there was wind. She liked the way he sometimes caught it with one hand and held it away from his face, so his enormous brown eyes were untroubled.

He was not as tall as she was, but would have been if his knees didn't stand out. Her girlfriends giggled he must have testicles the size of coconuts. She'd laughed with them, but wouldn't care if such a thing were true. She had seen that men who were not quite perfect, who had a defect others noticed, could be more sympathetic, especially to women. Sometimes, these men went the other way, were defensive and aggressive, but she had watched Fletcher long enough. He was not like that.

Of all the officers of the ship he seemed the most likely to understand her mission to leave.

'Hello, Mr Christian, *ia orana,* good morning,' she said.

'And good morning to you, Mauatua. *Ia orana.*'

She tipped her head down with sudden shyness when he turned to her. The warmth of his voice greeted her like a friend, yet she had never once seen him look at her or whisper about her.

'You know my name?'

'For a long time,' he said. 'Why are you the only one who can say my name properly?'

As she dared look at him fully, he gathered his hair away from his eyes. A sharp impulse darted through her heart and into her nipples, leaving them tingling.

'I like to do things others cannot, Mr Christian,' she said, directly into his compelling eyes.

At once, she felt no boundaries between the two of them. She leaned forward until their noses touched in *ho'i,* mingling the intimacy of their breaths for the first time.

And then, confident of her choice but overwhelmed by her welcome, she smiled and walked back the way she had come.

She knew Fletcher was not a god. He was a man, a man as tall and muscular as any Tahitian nobleman even if a bit browner of skin than ideal. He had skills and knowledge not one of her country men could match but would he share them with her?

Was he the longed-for ally, the man who would help her escape? It was too soon to know or to ask. Anyway, there was plenty of time before BOUNTY sailed.

Over the next days she enticed Fletcher many times to the shade of coconut palms and they sat with their backs to Matavai's waters and BOUNTY. Slowly, stumbling with the vocabulary of English words she had treasured over two decades, and he struggling with the Tahitian he had learned on board from men who had been to Tahiti before, Mauatua made Fletcher tell of his ancestors. He detailed his long line of Christian grandfathers, gentry as First Deemsters on the Isle of Man since at least

1342, and also as great landowners, farmers and miners in Cumbria. He drew maps in the sandy ground and told her the names of the lands the family owned. On every score, she judged him perfect.

A man who could recite 14 grandfathers in a direct line and on the same lands would be welcome in any family. In Britain too, she imagined.

She told him of her many forefathers, of her equivalent *ra'atira* rank and of their lands on this and other islands. He was more interested in establishing her age. He admitted to 24 and they agreed she was four if not five years older. She looked anxiously for signs this would lessen his interest, but found none.

She wanted to keep their conversations amusing, a constant entertainment, and got mad at him when he wanted to talk like a farmer, to know how this plant grew, when the season for that was, how often sows would litter. She worried he might learn to like Tahiti too much, so much he'd want to live with her here. That wasn't the plan at all. Yet he'd be suspicious if she resisted his curiosity too much.

Keeping their bantering chatter on points of correct interest to her was as difficult as trying to walk a straight line after drinking too much *kava*.

She didn't mind when he asked about tattoos. As Matavai's men and women passed before them she showed him the marks that defined a man or woman's rank and clan or district.

Some were just decorative, like the tiny flowers and stars on her hands and feet, and like the solid black backsides of men.

'Can you guess what that means?' She pointed at the even, jagged pattern on the thighs and biceps of a fisherman who carried a spear over his shoulder that flamed with the bright colours of reef fish.

'They look like – are they shark teeth?'

'They are!'

The lines of teeth were a talisman against danger from the sea, she said, and turtles meant that too.

A gecko design he liked signified hope for long life and endurance and pleaded for good luck. She had geckos over her loins.

'Look, I'll show you,' she said and lifted her skirts over her naked buttocks to show him. She slyly watched his eyes. They flicked to look at her hairless cleft and lingered longer than for mere curiosity, so nothing wrong with him in that way. But he didn't put a finger or palm on her tattoos. No other man had resisted tracing the whirling images.

She'd hoped lifting her skirt might have stimulated his sexual interest. It was about time, after all.

Instead he pointed at her face and laughed mockingly.

'Why do all you women have the same flat nose, with no bridge?'

She didn't think the question deserved the scorn she heard in his voice. She was humiliated but checked any sharp answer. Noses gave her an opportunity to tell him what she thought about Tahiti.

'Men,' she said, laying a finger across the length of her nose. 'Because men want it that way. Our noses are stroked into that shape from the day we are born.'

'But, that must be dangerous?'

'Push too hard and no holes grow for the breath. But that's Tahitian men for you. Whatever they want, goes.'

She wanted sympathy, instead he was smiling.

'You are laughing. That's rude!' She punched his shoulder.

'What happens when a man breaks his nose and looks like that?'

'We laugh at him. Tell him that with a flat nose he shouldn't have *ure* down there. You know, his . . . what's the word for that?' She leaned to touch him between his legs and he jerked forward to protect himself.

'That's cruel, to laugh at a man for something like that.'

'You are silly, Fletcher. We laugh at everyone who is different. We laugh at your legs.' She knew she was wrong to say that. His smile crumbled and his head jerked back. While his face was still angry he poked a finger at her head and put his face so close to hers she felt the heat of his anger.

'Well, we laugh at your pointed heads. Why do you think they are so beautiful?'

She couldn't answer. Didn't know how to calm or divert him. Every baby had their soft-boned head wrapped so it made a cone, tapering back from the face and it stayed that shape the rest of their lives.

She didn't know why and couldn't think what to say. She laughed but turned her face from his so he didn't suspect mockery.

'I know. Teach me to make the marks that say my name?' she asked. Men rarely refused if you asked them to show off one of their skills.

It was while she laboured to copy her name in the sand that she decided writing and reading might be the greatest of the many gifts that pink men brought to her.

CHAPTER 4

Fletcher didn't like it at all. He tortured himself with the phrase as he paced inside the breadfruit camp's fence. He didn't like how much he thought about Mauatua. He didn't like how she filled his mind, whether he was eating, or watering breadfruit plants or listening to Bligh yet again telling him nothing was more important than the breadfruit plants.

Yet, he allowed there was good reason for him to be so occupied. More than one, actually. The worst was that he was becoming besotted. Exactly what he had promised he would never do again.

How had Mauatua done this?

He thought of himself as tall at 5' 10' and Mauatua was taller. Yet even with that height and her flattened nose and supreme confidence he never saw a sign of masculinity in her and never felt dominated by her. Every movement she made was poised, elegant, and feminine. She used the tapered fingers of her long slim hands for emphasis as would any aristocratic Englishwoman.

Her natural, ivory-gold skin was more alluring than the artificial whiteness of Society faces. The tiny tattoos on her hands might have been the freckles of an English country girl, but she was no bumpkin.

Her radiant confidence wasn't the certainty that ignorance gave the ill-educated. Hers came from an inner security of purpose that made her a natural leader, that attracted what he supposed should be called followers.

Was he weak enough to be a follower? He'd always hoped he was the leader. That's certainly how it seemed aboard BOUNTY, where men came to him rather than Bligh for comfort or reason and encouragement.

Soon, he felt, there would be a challenge between them and then he might know for certain which of them was really dominant.

Until then he couldn't resist her company, like it or not.

He decided to demonstrate superiority by doing something about her nits. Whatever Mauatua said or did one hand was constantly searching and scratching in her hair and then she'd crunch the harvest between her teeth. Any thought of intimacy was at once beguiling and horrid. He even resisted putting their heads together to whisper. He didn't want nits and was grateful her hair was short enough not to fall on to his.

They had dozed in the mid-afternoon shade of hibiscus bushes after he'd talked to her for hours about the rest of the world he had seen. He propped himself on one arm, careful his elbow didn't slip on the woven coconut frond mat and force him on to her.

'How would you like to be the most special woman on Tahiti?' he asked, hoping she didn't detect his uncertain bravado.

She kept her eyes closed and whispered that her rank was not high enough to be so special. He teased her, trying to make her guess what he meant. When he thought she was intrigued and comfortable enough, he offered to make her the only woman on Tahiti without nits. It was a dangerous, intimate thing to suggest to a woman he barely knew and yet his very boldness seemed to delight her.

'How would you do that?' she asked, already standing to follow him.

He splashed hot water into a big tin bowl outside the camp's thatched hut and watched her kneel to use BOUNTY'S yellow soap to lather her uneven, rag-tag hair into a thick cream of bubbles. When he poured fresh water over her she laughed constantly and then jumped up and down like a child when she discovered her hair was so clean it squeaked, shouting that never happened with the leaves she normally used.

When she was calm he mixed vinegar from the ship with fresh water. She had to dunk her head deep into the bowl and then swish it about to ensure every strand was covered but when she asked him to help, he refused her.

'You'll have to be able to do it yourself when I'm not here,' he said and wondered why she immediately became distant and silent.

He thought no more of her strange behaviour when her low easy laugh again became unstoppable as she searched in vain for nits. She lifted her hair with spread fingers to dry it in the sun. When it settled, thick and black, he told her it reflected sunshine as brightly as the polished buttons on his jacket.

She tipped her hair forward but it was too short for her to see the shine for herself, so he ran inside and brought back a small looking glass.

Fletcher was as delighted as she was that she no longer had nits. But her sparkling eyes were hooded, alerting him to something he should have assumed. She was grateful and wanted to show it the way she thought he would expect.

When she leaned forward and stroked his thigh he couldn't help jerking away. His old fear erupted, swelling and paralysing his throat into a mute column of anguish. He gasped for breath and his cheeks burst into flame.

He pushed her hand back with a forearm and held it away, fighting to be gentle when his brain screamed for swift action and for him to flee. When she nudged his arm, thinking it a game, his stomach heaved and he felt the ghastly stinging of his scalp begin.

He leaned forward to *ho'i*, desperate not to be too brief. His eye lids crushed together and he breathed faster knowing even this subterfuge couldn't hide the distress in his eyes.

Stumbling as he stood up, he wiped a forearm over his brow and hoped the smile he conjured would tell her he was not insulted by her move. She deserved to know that much.

'*Araua'e,* Mauatua. See you soon.'

'See you too, Fletcher.'

He despised the confusion in her eyes. He'd seen it in so many faces and had become resigned to watching it descend to horror and disgust. But not with her, he pleaded to all his senses. If he could get away very quickly they might both survive the awkwardness. If he kept to the shadows, she'd see nothing else.

'Very soon, Mauatua.'

He turned swiftly and strode through banana and coconut trees into the camp's thatched building and closed the door behind him. Peter Heywood was waiting for him with a written order from the ship.

'The breadfruit camp is BOUNTY on dry land, Mr Christian,' Bligh had written. 'You must be on duty or on call at all times and never more than half a mile from the camp.'

Fletcher's fury cancelled the effect of Mauatua's advance. He became clear headed but was angered beyond bearing. He tore the order to pieces and then ranted at Heywood.

'Mauatua offers a relationship beyond my expectations, but I don't have the balls to accept it. And now Bligh makes me a prisoner in what is supposed to be Paradise. It's as well I am so content with my own company. I can see that's all I'll ever have.'

He stamped, shouted and drank for some hours, until his anger was diluted. His eyes were blooded, his hair and his clothes slicked to his body with sweat and he still punched at anything he thought could take it.

His camp mates ignored his implied dismissal of their companionship and as a man drank with him, agreeing he deserved compensation for

Bligh's harshness. All they could think of was to share their daily adventures with him.

He enjoyed hearing about what he could not experience and soon specially looked forward to hearing from Peter Heywood who was new to sex of any kind and forever returning with stories of outrage.

'Fletcher, I swear she wasn't more than eight or nine. She said not to fear 'cos she'd already had eight different men.'

'All this in sign language?'

'Most. Even her friend wasn't more than 12. I mean, they had, you know, no hair down there.' Fletcher lifted his eyebrows.

'They showed me, without asking.' Peter blushed.

'None of these women have hair 'down there'. They all shave it with sharpened shells or pull it out.'

'They want to look like children forever? That's weird.'

'No. It's lice protection. It's what the locals do. Anyway, you've never seen Haymarket in London, have you? I don't know about eight, but there are plenty of ten and 12 year-olds pushing their fannies into your face. Encouraged by their Ma and Pa.'

'The men are hairless there, too, Fletcher. And this bathing in a stream every day? That's not natural. Can't be.'

'It is to Ma'ohi, Peter.'

CHAPTER 5

Fletcher revelled in being alone in the shadowless early hours of the day. When the sun sat fat with promise on the horizon everything on land was sharp-edged and saturated with colour before it was smothered by shimmering heat.

His ears could now tune to the South Pacific battering into foam on the reef and without looking he'd know how high the rollers hoisted themselves each morning. He recognised bird calls Cumbria and London would never hear and recalled a game he and his brothers had played in the fields and woods of Moorland Close. So he mimicked some of the birds and made bets with himself on how close they would hop before realising he was neither threatening nor flirting.

Whenever he paused one deep breath brought invigorating salt-air, compost-rich earth and such burgeoning of tropical foliage that every part of him pricked with the pleasure of being alive.

Only early fishermen ever saw him checking the lines of breadfruit pots. He did this every morning, taking personal responsibility for losses, whatever the cause. Freed from the relentless rhythm of BOUNTY's bells, no-one else was awake in the breadfruit camp. They'd quickly learned that if everything made of metal was locked away they didn't need night watchmen.

Yet he resisted any idea he had been entrapped by Tahiti. He thought constantly of London. He often dreamed he was in its theatres applauding a new opera or praising some nobleman's saucy mistress in a play. He would wake still hearing music and thinking he was amongst swishing silks and satins as couples danced past midnight under candle-heavy chandeliers.

Sometimes he tasted again the refined dishes once laid before him on porcelain from China, and he remembered exact conversations on the *canapés* and *fauteuils* of the grand *enfilades* of mansions and palaces on Piccadilly and in St James's.

How could someone like Mauatua fit into that life?

'Something from my mother.' Tamahere handed him a newly woven eye-shade. He looked up to see Mauatua waving from the beach and nodded back knowing she'd not see this as an invitation to join him. She might not belong in London, but she was a woman with perfect manners.

She'd never mentioned his flight from her and with perfect understanding she was always close by, yet never intruded.

He gave Tamahere a pot with a weak breadfruit and asked him to carry it to the end of the line. Other strugglers had been collected there.

From the corner of his eye he saw Mauatua still waving. Why so energetic, he wondered.

'Mr Christian. A moment if you please.'

It was Bligh. Mauatua had been warning him. But why was he here? Bligh never came ashore this early.

Bligh stood imperiously, already sweating in his heavy uniform and hat. John Smith, his personal servant, hovered a few steps behind. Midshipman Ned Young was beside him.

Fletcher at once suspected Bligh had a devious purpose and that he would be the target. Making time to compose himself, he took the pot from Tamahere, removed the eye shade and gave it back and then went to Bligh and saluted. Bligh pointed to a spot some feet closer.

Fletcher tensed his lips, stepped forward and saluted again. His suspicions were correct. Bligh was determined to goad him into saying or doing something for which he would be punished.

Perhaps he had already done it?

He accepted that getting on with Bligh was a constant game. Bligh commanded by scathing reduction rather than flattering or encouraging those he outranked but sometimes the man made new rules, even invented new games.

'Explain,' said Bligh, flinging his white, womanly hand towards Tamahere.

'Sir?' was all Fletcher dared say.

'This theft.'

'Theft, Sir?' Repeating Bligh's word was the only challenge he risked until he knew what was on his captain's mind.

'That black child was stealing one of those pots. They are the property of His Majesty. As his representative, such theft is theft from me.'

'Sir, the boy is not stealing. He is helping me.'

'My orders were for *you* to tend the breadfruit, Mr Christian, not some thieving native child.'

Tamahere understood the insult and kicked Bligh solidly in the shin. Mauatua rushed to collect her son, stopping only to glare at Bligh. Bligh feigned ignorance of the kick and of Mauatua's look.

Fletcher defended the boy again.

'Sir, the pot the boy was carrying has a suspect shoot. He was carrying it to others like that. They'll be checked when the gardeners return. Sir.'

He crossed his fingers the gardeners would stay sleeping until this affair had ended.

'Pah! You know as well as I do that anything left lying around disappears. Allowing these people to take the king's property is condoning theft, Mr Christian.'

Fletcher stepped forward, his voice low. 'This is unreasonable, Captain Bligh. That child . . .'

'What? Your native whore's bastard?'

'Sir, such insult is unwarranted.'

Bligh further closed the gap between them. 'So, now you are questioning my right to an opinion?'

Fletcher would have struck any other man by now. He was closer to hitting a superior officer than he'd ever been. He appealed to Bligh as a naval officer.

'Sir, I am second in command on BOUNTY. You made me so. That position comes with authority to act independently of you. Particularly here in the breadfruit camp.' Fletcher lowered his voice further, to a hoarse whisper. 'It also commands respect, Sir.'

'Not from me,' Bligh shouted, checking Smith and Young were listening. He continued loudly. 'I see living on this island has softened you even further, Mr Christian. You, with your Latin and Greek and fancy relations in high London places. I can't think why I ever wanted you on this voyage.'

'Because we are friends,' Fletcher offered. 'I've had your children on my knees, William.'

Bligh turned away, his eyebrows raised with exaggerated enquiry.

'William? William?' He yelled at Young. 'Are you William?'

'Ned, Captain Bligh.'

'You are John, are you not, Smith?'

'Sir.'

Bligh searched melodramatically amongst the Tahitians who were gathering, attracted by the shouting.

'I find no William here, Mr Christian. Where is this William? And why did you dare speak to another while I was speaking to you? That is further injury to me. No?' Bligh clapped a hand to his forehead.

'Oh, Surely, surely you were not so familiar as to call your captain by his Christian name? That would be insult *and* injury. Well?'

Fletcher ached to respond with the insult and derision Bligh deserved. He spoke quietly, struggling to keep the challenge manly and between only his captain and himself.

'This is unbearable. Sir.' Bligh sniffed contempt and looked away. Fletcher returned to the Navy as justification for his stand.

'You may say what you like to me, Captain Bligh. For reasons known only to yourself you have argued with me and insulted me ever since we were in South Africa. I am used to being the butt of your black tongue. But kindly do so in private. I am an officer in the King's Navy.'

'Arrest that child!' Bligh barked.

Fletcher strode to protect Mauatua and Tamahere. The standoff with Bligh was broken by the noise of an approaching crowd. Bligh's expression sweetened when he recognised the young noble Tararo, who strutted ahead of his court.

Tararo was the ideal of a youthful upper-class *ari'i* man, pale-skinned, tall, handsome, muscular and proud. Lesser Tahitians bobbed their heads lower than his and uncovered their shoulders in a show of respect.

Bligh broke Fletcher's eye contact with the young lord by moving between them.

Then he bowed to Tararo, doffing his hat with a wide sweep.

Tararo ignored him. 'I heard shouting, Fletcher. Is all well?'

'He might play at being in charge here, your lordship,' said Bligh, side stepping to keep Fletcher out of view, 'but he is merely a *teuteu*, my servant, and really rather low. A noble such as you need not be troubled.'

Tararo shrugged and continued on, raising an eyebrow at his cousin Mauatua.

Fletcher knew Bligh would not resist one more wound. He stared ahead until it came.

'Mr Christian, I suggest you keep yourself better covered. You are starting to look like a nigger. We have Mr Young here for that.'

Bligh fixed him with a venomous eye and then turned to stare at Mauatua, a triumphant smile on his lips. So that was it, Bligh wanted to humiliate him, but to do it in front of Mauatua.

He exchanged a quick look with Ned Young. Ned held back a few steps. He too was targeted by Bligh, who mocked him because of his black West Indian blood. Ned shrugged his shoulders and spread his palms. Fletcher acknowledged their mutual understanding with quickly pursed lips. They knew protest would be pointless. Bligh justified every vile thing he said or did by insisting it was in pursuit of his duty.

Once Bligh left, Fletcher clamped his hands tightly over his face, his head bowed. Did Mauatua understand all of what had been said?

Bligh's point had been to diminish him to her, as well as to question his ability to manage the camp. Both were to ensure neither forgot who was captain of BOUNTY. It was child-like but now it was he who felt like an abandoned infant.

He was desperate for compassion, yet if she came to him his rawest secret would be exposed. The prickling scalp had begun and he felt the rest of his body trembling on the very edge of collapse.

She came, silent at first and then whispering, honouring his choice not to be touched or to touch back, a soothing sister rather than a mothering woman. 'What can I do, Fletcher? Can I do something?'

He broke his cheerless pact to protect himself from pity. There would be no shame in turning to her.

He dropped his hands from his head, keeping his face averted, and gave in to his body's evil surrender from decency.

She would first think he was hot, very hot. He lifted his chin and forced himself to face her. He was humiliated but not offended when she bit her lip and clamped her hand over Tamahere's mouth before her son could voice any fright.

He stood in sunlight but knew he looked as though he was under torrents of rain. Sweat ran from his scalp so freely it scorched his eyes and he blinked constantly. Streams dripped from his shirt's sodden folds and into his trousers or onto the ground. He flinched and stepped back when Mauatua held his shoulders but this time she fought to hold him firm.

'There's nothing, nothing anyone can do about . . .' he said, weak with hopelessness.

'Has Bligh put a curse on you?'

'No, nothing like that. But . . .He drives me into states where this happens. It only began . . .They call it Hiperhydrosis . . .'

Saying the word rekindled the horror of becoming a social outcast because of his sudden episodes of excessive perspiration. And his hands. They were always wet, always cold.

It started three years ago and he had retreated into melancholy solitude, resigned to remain single, literally out of touch of the sort of woman he might acceptably marry.

Being at sea, out of Society, made this self-sentence marginally easier. There, only Bligh mentioned or noticed his hands. Only Captain William Bligh felt obliged to suggest he should carry a handkerchief so his hands didn't soil everything they touched.

He feared his wretched state might unthread his relationship with Mauatua before he had dared name it. He had lived only with men for more than a year, withholding all thought of intimacy and love, and now didn't know how to react to what this woman offered. He was too old for mothering. Too frightened for love. But he needed something, from someone. And who was most likely to sympathise without tawdry emotion?

He felt Tamahere put his arms around one of his legs and hold him tight, ignoring the sweat dribbling on to him. Mauatua lifted a corner of her shift. She wiped his forehead and then dabbed his inflamed eyes. His resolve collapsed at these expressions of care. He stretched out his arms and turned up his palms. She ignored them. Seeing she had no idea of how his palms were relevant, he resisted when she pulled his arms around her, but it was too late for any more self-imposed denial.

He took her in his arms for the first time and his hands clasped her back. It took seconds for the clammy wetness of his palms to soak through her thin tapa cloth. He had no more secrets from her. In spite of his discomfort, he hardened against her.

'Thank God for you, Mauatua. Thank God,' he said into her neck.

CHAPTER 6

'Did it stop?' Her girlfriends were agog for details.

'It did, except . . .'

'For what? What?' Teehuteatuaonoa was thrilled to discover a new complaint. Called Tee by most, she always had at least two of the latest aches, pains, sniffles or fevers.

'Except, well, except for his hands. He said they were always wet and cold. That's why . . .'

'He never touched you,' chorused the group, relieved at last to know.

Poor man, poor man, she added to herself. It had been horrible. Not just the realisation of what his hands were like but knowing they would always be like this, even when the sweating of his scalp and body stopped.

She thought constantly about Fletcher's hands and how he must loathe being a victim of his body's weakness. Imagine having to think of your hands before touching anything, before touching anyone.

Could she ever forget his hands?

Tee interrupted. 'Did you give him anything for that head rain? Put something on his scalp?'

She hadn't attempted any of the Ma'ohi remedies she and Tee knew as *tahu'a ra'au*. Being medical specialists was one of the few important roles open to women on Tahiti, but she'd thought her therapeutic secrets of plants and fruits, of insects and of the organs of certain birds and fish couldn't possibly work on a white man. 'You must have done something. I know, you pulled out his *kokoro* and make him feel better in your *pahua!*' The women collapsed with high giggling, Mauatua, too. Teasing didn't stop when childhood passed. 'We are not lovers,' she insisted. 'We gave him a coconut. To put back the water he lost.'

Tee changed the subject. 'I think Fletcher must be *mahu*.'

She thought the women would expire from laughing.

'No one has seen it, have they?' Tee asked. They slapped one another and made rude signs with their fingers and hands.

'May be he likes to put his stick into other men's mouths. Or into . . .'

They pointed to where these other indecencies might occur and laughed even harder.

'Maybe, maybe it's the other way around?'

Tee toppled onto her side, her fatness shuddering with mirth. She heaved herself up to add, 'Maybe, maybe he does it to that Bligh. That's another one who doesn't want his banana peeled by *vahine.*'

This caused hysteria. The women fell upon one another simulating what might be happening between the two men. '*Mahu Mahu! Mahu!*' they screamed at one another, their fingers connecting to each other's mouths and jerking backsides.

'No,' shouted Mauatua, suddenly angry. She kicked at the women on the ground. For the first time in her life she didn't want to joke like this.

'He is as hard with a woman as he should be.'

'Is he as big as Ned Young?'

'That is all you need to know.'

Now he trusted her, Fletcher told her most things. He believed Bligh wanted him to stay in the breadfruit camp so there was no danger of him writing a competing book. She knew he'd obey and that would help her cause. Confining Fletcher to the camp meant she had easy and constant access to him. She could beguile him until he too thought she should sail away with him.

So, to entertain Fletcher she brought to the breadfruit camp by night all that Bligh searched for by day. As soon as night fell and she knew Bligh was back on board, she would call to waiting men and women who would come running through the trees with lit flares.

Every night there was a different type of entertainment. Sometimes there were archery or javelin competitions, or wrestling or boxing. Fletcher told her the choruses of men who sang falsetto sounded like the castrati of Italian opera and she nodded as though she knew what that meant. Once she brought penis and testicle manipulators to exhibit their many gross abilities, knowing Bligh's indignation could not stop them here, as it had done elsewhere.

She joined the hip shimmying dances where the most modest women exposed their genitals, even pulling their intimate lips apart. Like them she covered herself the moment the insistent drums stopped.

Fletcher never reacted to say she should or shouldn't dance like that. Never told her he didn't want other men to see her like that. Still, as long as he wasn't interested in other women . . .

By day, she encouraged Fletcher to play Ma'ohi sports on the same level ground she danced upon at night. He posted lookouts against Bligh's appearance and then he and his breadfruit-camp colleagues learned the games of young Tahitian men. Fletcher learned fast and competed so well that soon many young women and some men came to watch him.

He joined teams competing to score points by aiming a ball between posts at either end of an agreed space. In one game Fletcher learned to hit the ball with a long stick. In another he mastered the skills of kicking a bigger ball to get it past the opposing team without using his hands.

Mauatua handed them drinking coconuts as Fletcher and Peter flattened themselves in shade, gasping for breath.

'What do you think of that for fun?' Fletcher asked Peter, between gulping his chest full of air.

'Why don't we have games like this back home?' Peter countered.

'I just can't see Englishmen racing around after large spherical objects,' Fletcher answered, after some thought.

She had no doubt Fletcher had a better body and as much strength as the finest of Tahitian *ra'atira* or *ari'i*.

She saw him revel in the vicious boxing and the abandoned style of wrestling Tahitians enjoyed. She celebrated as much as he did when he won throwing javelins or shooting arrows. She couldn't help him with those but she could teach Fletcher to swim.

The sea disguised the shame of his wet hands and so disrobed him of shame. His land-locked reticence dissolved and he bloomed in the water, allowing every muscle of his body to welcome her touch. He touched and held her as freely. They danced in the water as she twisted his arm to correct a stroke or held down the leg which beat faster than the other.

When they teased and cavorted under water he didn't resist or complain when she touched his penis, not even when she was deliberate. But he was always too exhilarated by his new skill to react sexually. He swam until he was breathless and incapable of anything but floating.

So much for that she thought, wondering if she should bother to give him such pleasure when she got little in return.

Whenever Bligh was well inland or indisposed they would canoe or stroke to the open sea on the other side of the reef to see if he could master the astonishing skills of sliding on the waves.

'I've done it, I've done it,' he yelled as he splashed his way up the beach and into the breadfruit camp. She followed him laughing helplessly at his boyish pleasure.

'Did you see me, Peter? I stood up on this board and rode on top of the waves for yards and yards, all the way to the reef, like a sea god, like a merman, like a . . .

'Like a Tahitian,' Mauatua said, so proud she would have allowed him any intimacy he could conceive. But it seemed the only physical prowess that mattered was his, that his was the only body to be pleasured.

Even with so much competing and swimming she couldn't keep Fletcher from noticing darker sides to Tahiti. His skin crawled when he heard the ominous hoots of conch shells and then saw every Tahitian cower until those priestly howls were dumb again. She never answered when he asked about the conches or about the curious constructions and unsettling smells that drifted across the lagoon from the sacred royal place on the headland opposite.

She wouldn't explain the constant wars between clans and islands that meant even the happiest day was clouded by the constant need for vigilance against sudden aggression from sea or land that could end the life of a son or lover, brother or father.

Eventually he stopped asking about such things, telling her he had no need to know the darker secrets of Ma'ohi life on Tahiti.

'What use would they be to me on the high seas, or back in England?' he asked, appearing to dismiss her culture.

The wound she felt when Fletcher said such things sharpened the pain of doubting she would share his life with him, not even in Matavai Bay. At first she'd let him talk for hours about the secrets of the worlds she had never seen, and could easily make him tell her about America.

'Say the word again,' she would coax, as she fed him dollops of wobbly young jelly coconut or rubbed oil into a new strain in his muscles. He would pretend not to understand but eventually he would say it playfully, rolling his tongue to begin and holding the last sound as long as his breath could manage.

'Rrrrrrevolutionnnnnnnn' he said. 'Rrrrrrrrrrrrrrrrrrrrrrev – ooooo – lutionnnnnnnnnnnnnn.' She only ever repeated it in her head, thrilled at the images it conjured of freedom, of having new land to shape the way you wanted it, of being mistress of your future and the creator of a new world for your children.

So far, she had only hinted at leaving Tahiti with him, but if he was as clever as she thought . . .

CHAPTER 7

Mauatua called into his room in the breadfruit camp. 'The boat is still waiting, Fletcher.'

'I've told them. I am not going. Bligh can eat his bloody Christmas dinner without me.'

Bligh had come personally to invite him. Fletcher had erupted with sweat the moment he saw him and Bligh had joked it was a curious time of the year for rain. If a Tahitian had said such a thing it would be a joke and they would all laugh together. Bligh was cruel. His laughter was joy at the injury he had caused.

She stopped Peter when he ran up from the beach.

'The longer you wait the more fretful Fletcher gets. For the friendship you have, please leave him . . . and I ask it too.' She held Peter by his thin shoulders until she could see he agreed. He ran back to the beach calling that he'd give the old bastard an excuse from Fletcher he'd have to accept.

Fletcher wouldn't tell her much about Christmas or about the times he spent it with his family. He agreed they might have sung the songs that floated over the lagoon but his repeated thought was how lucky he was his mother couldn't see how Bligh had reduced him.

'He promised her I'd be safe with him,' he muttered. 'He promised. And now look at me.'

She pulled him by his reluctant hands and led him to lie on a low soft bed of tapa cloth she had prepared in his quarters. He had stopped sweating a few hours ago but looked exhausted. Perhaps that was why he finally agreed to being massaged. It was her special treat, to repay him for her nit-free hair, but she also banked on learning more of his secrets.

She filled one of her palms with fragrant coconut oil, *monoi*, profoundly scented with Tahitian sandalwood and *tiare Tahiti*. Fletcher said *tiare* was like gardenia, his favourite scent back home. As she smoothed the oil generously over the length of her arm its opulent fumes wound a cocoon of intimacy around the two of them.

'But you were friends once?' she asked as she knelt.

'I'm very nervous about this. Do I really have to be naked?'

'Tell me about you and Bligh,' Mauatua coaxed, knowing physical contact out of water was difficult for him. She'd assured him Tahitian massage didn't use hands and that encouraged him. Still nervous, he told her he met Bligh on the Isle of Man, where Bligh's father-in-law was Collector of Customs and made people pay to unload their ships.

'Money for King George,' he explained.

She took off her top, oiled her upper body and arms and began by sliding her slicked right arm back and forth and around his right arm, lifting it high to continue the movement until his hand was almost in her hairless armpit, and her right breast hung close to his lips.

He was already getting hard and insisted on turning over.

She pressed lightly against his side and then moved deliberately up and down, up and across. When his back was glossed with her oil she bore down harder, from each buttock across the corded muscles of his back to the stone-like mounds of his opposite shoulder.

Fletcher had no words to describe his feelings. The rhythm of her scented weight, naked and warm, was mesmerising, leaving each part she touched alive and effervescing. An awareness of the difference between their bodies grew, of the big-boned, hairier, harder feel of his, the smooth, finer-boned, cushioned feel of her flesh. He had never imagined such intense physical contact. His experiences with women had been quick ejaculations for the sake of a bet, or curiosity or, as he thought, weakness. That was only sex. There had been no exploration, no sense of discovery or sensuality.

She slipped off her tapa cloth skirt and her hairless pubic mound slid against the small of his back, smooth and child like. But was she aroused? Was she wet for him, or was that the *monoi*? He didn't have the experience to tell. But he did know about nipples. Hers felt harder now, but that could be the contrast between them and her body skin. She oiled her arm again, turned it sideways, and slid this over his buttocks and then between them.

He'd heard about men who obtained pleasure from this unseen part of the body and wondered about it. He hollowed his back, pushed his buttocks higher so she might massage deeper, closer. It was acceptable with a woman, surely?

He withheld his breath as her arm and elbow created greater intensity. He moved his hips against her and spread his knees apart. He was shamed and thrilled but already so far beyond his expectations he no longer recognised boundaries.

Her arm ground the coarse hairs against the softness of his opening, exciting sensations he could barely admit. She concentrated the rougher texture and weight of her sharp elbow on the very root of his cock, behind the testicles. They, once hanging low for the heat of the late afternoon, now pressed tight against his shaft. Sometimes she teased them too.

He floated in the bliss created by her snaking arms and body. It was three years since he'd touched a woman sexually. His hunger to catch up on those lonely days was urgent and he dismissed any fear it might complicate his attraction to her. His face and neck and chest reddened. His breath became shorter, shallower. He reached for his right nipple and pushed hard against her. She yanked his hand away from his chest.

'This is a massage Fletcher. You do nothing.'

He flopped flat onto his stomach again, panting, embarrassed, but on a path he could not abandon. His voice broke several times as he found his place again.

'When I left the Navy, I wanted to sail with Bligh. He is famous for being a great navigator, taught by Cook himself.'

'I remember Cook. I liked him.'

'Everyone liked him, even though he was a far tougher captain than Bligh. He was always having men flogged and no-one complained. Bligh's problem is he doesn't flog enough. When he does it's unfair, for something trivial, and it's resented by the whole ship.'

He turned to sit up and then struggled to say out loud what he had always kept inside. 'I knew Bligh was a difficult man. I just wanted to be as great a navigator as him. And Cook. I thought I could get around him.'

'Lie on your back,' she said. 'And put that thing away,' she added when she saw the erection he was hiding between his thighs.

'What do you expect?'

'You were telling me a story.'

He felt the slim muscle of her forearm on his feet and then on his legs. Why hadn't he known feet could be so sensual?

She shook him off when he reached out to put his hand on her hair. and nodded at him to continue.

He told her he had to wait two years to sail with Bligh to and from the Caribbean. That was how he learned what made the best sort of leader, by watching what he thought were Bligh's mistakes.

'There has to be mutual respect, even when a captain is using the harshest discipline.'

'Flogging, you mean?' she asked.

'That's only Naval ships. No-one on a merchant ship would stand for flogging or for the Navy's food. It's a far worse punishment at sea to be ignored by your shipmates for some crime or mistake.' He fell silent and lay back again. She massaged oil into the top of his thighs, her forearms lightly brushing his testicles, again and again.

Planes of pleasure ebbed to and from his erection. He continued with difficulty. 'Even so, a bad captain was sometimes made to pay. I'm going to tell you something only Bligh knows. You promise to tell no-one?'

She took his hard penis in her hand. 'By this, I do.'

His body jerked as her hand enclosed him. He forced her hand away and took a few calming breaths.

'My brother Charles, he's a doctor, he led a mutiny against the captain of a merchant ship. MIDDLESEX she was called.'

'Mutiny?'

'When the company takes the ship from a captain.'

'Auee! That must have been a bad captain.'

'Mean with rations and a bully too.'

'What happened to, to Charles?'

'I don't know. BOUNTY sailed the morning after I saw him. But he won't be hanged. He was on a merchantman, not one of the king's ships.' He saw she was puzzled. 'Hanged. They put a rope around your neck and pull you up from the deck to dangle from the yardarm. You choke very slowly. Your tongue swells. It goes blue and then black and flops out like a slimy jelly. Then your trousers are soiled and wet. Hideous. I have seen it.'

'Disgusting. We only hang up dead bodies. Dry 'em out in the wind.'

She moved upwards, first using her arms and then her body across his abdomen. Talk about hangings had softened him. Her passing nipples brushed his erection into steel as she began and finished every rhythmic sweep. She slowly increased her speed and weight.

He bit his lip hard and tasted blood.

She pulled away, leaving his abdomen and chest hot and tingling. She used just one finger tip to rub oil around his areolas, as dark as any Tahitian's. She didn't touch his nipples until her teasing hardened them. Then she pinched his right nipple between her finger tips.

His back arched. He squeezed his eyes tight.

'Don't, don't do that,' he whispered with urgency.

She leaned close to his ear. She copied his hot whisper. 'And you men think you are in control of us. Hah!'

Next, she massaged the swells of his chest and shoulder muscles, sometimes digging deep with her fingertips, sometimes teasing and tickling from his nipples to his shoulders and then up his neck. Sometimes her abdomen and her mound connected with his cock. He writhed, tipped his head back in an ecstasy for which he had no comparison.

'So Bligh was different on those ships?' she asked.

'Stop, stop for a minute,' he begged. 'Stop if you really want to hear.' He ran his hands lightly over his chest and shoulders, disbelieving they had been the source of such gratification. His hands fluttered up and down his body, over his cock, over and under his balls.

He wanted to feel further behind them, perhaps even to touch his... He couldn't and went back to his nipples and then his throat. How could a body be brought to such rapture just by the touch of another? He held himself, edging, uncertain if he was expected, or even allowed to ejaculate.

He opened his eyes and concentrated on her cleft. If she turned just a little more, the remaining light would strike her there and he could tell how wet she was. She gripped both his hands and held them tightly by his side, pressing with as much weight as she could. Her domination made his cock throb harder, weep profusely.

If she would just lean and bite on his nipples . . .

She stepped back, faceless against the light of the setting sun.

'I'm waiting,' she said, quite tonelessly. Fletcher forced his hands off his body. He swallowed several times before he felt able to go on. His breathing was fast and shallow.

'Bligh, well, he can't help insulting men with his tongue. He never understands any hurt he causes. Anyway we were never more than a few weeks from a port and so I made a joke of it when he was rude to me. It didn't mean he couldn't hurt me. I just never let him see it. I think he took that for friendship.'

'Was it?'

'He was more of a father figure. I was four when my father died.'

'Just like Tamahere,' she said. Before he could ask her if she thought this had some significance, she cuffed his cock with the side of her hand. 'You know, our men have this bit cut along the top, so it's not tight.'

His dark-pigmented foreskin opened to a rivulet of viscous fluid. She flicked the topknot of twisted skin. A shining gobbet hit his chest. He put a forefinger into it and then into his mouth, sucking at the saltiness, teasing her with his eyes, but pleading, too. She turned away.

'And they bathe once or twice a day. They can *titoi,* pull it back easily and wash there.'

'What are you saying?'

'There is a smell.'

'It's a man smell.'

'It's a dirty smell. That white stuff, *taioro,* creamy like inside sprouting coconuts. It goes hard and bad. Same as the cheese stuff you tried to make me eat. Auee! And that hair down there. You'll soon have nits.'

'Not if it's your head down there.'

Mauatua blushed and turned her face away, shielding it with her hand. He made to get up.

'Now I am embarrassed,' he said.

'Then I am sorry. I'll make you feel better.'

The flame started behind his balls. It curled over them and ignited a fine, feathery fuse that licked up the inside of his cock. He held his breath. There was a moment of profound stillness. He clasped his hand over hers on his cock, using his strength to stop her jerky stroking. The flame continued to catch, piercing, blazing and consuming, from the very base of his cock to the tip. A fiery sword with a million needle-sharp blades thrust up between his legs and commanded release.

She reached and roughly rolled one nipple hard, and then harder. Their hands rubbed his cock just twice more. He took a hard quick intake of breath. His free hand cupped her heat. Their wetness combined. He turned his hand to make a fist. She contracted strongly and slowly on his knuckles and then ground down on them and whimpered like a kitten.

Fletcher's body gave in. His darkest part, the part neither of them had touched, contracted and pulsed, thrusting sensation from his cock's root between his legs to his scorching tip. The full length of his cock was sharing his climax for the first time.

She put an oiled finger on his hole. She forced her finger deep and twisted it up against the nut. She saw his *ure* spit ten times, first over his shoulder, then on to his neck and then less fiercely into his navel. He kicked and twisted, shook, gulped, gasped, sometimes screamed as each boiling contraction brought another part of his body to climax. Even his feet arched to spasm in union with his hole and his cock.

'Now,' she said, wiping her finger on his abdomen, 'you *have* to wash, Fletcher.'

He was unused to that idea. He still panted, incredulous his body had the capacity for such sensation. She pulled him up from the tapa bed, but it was too soon. His knees buckled. When his chest brushed her, there were still shocks, places that could not be touched.

She laughed softly and easily. He hoped it was the laugh of a gratified woman. Still naked, they ran into the moonlit salt-sea of the lagoon and swam. Christmas carols from the ship pranced over the water, smothering from other ears the joyous celebrations of their closer relationship.

Mauatua was still awake when the sun revisited Tahiti, wondering why she hadn't let Fletcher inside her. It wasn't the thought of his hands. Everything was wet in the water. He had tried but without any real insistence, and didn't complain when she resisted. Perhaps he was more used to refusal than most? Not one of her girlfriends would have said no.

It was as though she and Fletcher were waiting for something special to happen before they made love properly.

CHAPTER 8

The plans she once said only quietly in her head now fizzed through her thoughts. She was determined not to behave like a silly girl, chasing who or what ever took her fancy. She had to know for sure and so for a few tense days more she considered every point to be certain she was right, until she had no doubt.

BOUNTY would be the ship that sailed her away. Fletcher Christian was the man who would allow her to be the woman she wanted to be.

Exhilarated by her bravery and by the thrill of her unknown future she went to Fletcher in his camp, bringing him a pineapple. He smelled its sweet-sour richness before she was beside him and spun to see it with his arms flung wide with astonishment. It was a treasured new fruit, she said, brought to Tahiti by a ship that came from South America.

He pressed his nose to the sharp golden web of its skin again and again as he told her only the richest of the rich could grow pineapples in England and then needed special hot pits and glass houses. Her eyes ignited with anticipation of his delight with her plan.

She watched impatiently as he trimmed the rough skin and deep-set eyes off a thick slice and refused when he offered her the first dribbling chunk. While he was eating with his eyes closed ecstatically she said what she had been rehearsing.

'Fletcher, I would like to go to Britain, like my cousin Mai. Will you take me on BOUNTY?'

He splattered her with half chewed pineapple, laughing and apologising at the same time as he picked pieces off her and rubbed at the juices on his chin with his forearm.

'Mai was a man.' he exclaimed. 'Bligh would never have a woman on board, not with so many men. What a crazy thing to ask.'

In those few dismissive words he had shackled her to Tahiti forever and made her feel small and stupid. She held her face in a smile and shrugged to signal she understood. She turned away to let away the silent, juddering breath that took her future with it.

'It doesn't matter,' she said over her shoulder, 'I knew you'd say that. That Bligh! Enjoy the pineapple.'

That Bligh! How stupid could she be? She'd seen his cruelty and his strictness yet she hadn't considered him in her plans. Too much thought of

Fletcher, of Britain, of escape and of silly things like long hair and freedom to eat pig meat. And men. Men were her problem and now men blocked her solution. Of course a single woman couldn't be on a ship with 40 pink men and their smelly, pining *ure* for so long.

But what would Fletcher have said if he were captain instead of Bligh? Well, enough of that, enough wasting time thinking about what was past and what was impossible. She'd have to start all over again, but she had no thought of abandoning Fletcher. He had much more to teach her, for them to share as a permanent mark of his time on Tahiti.

It wasn't going to be a baby. They decided that easily. Yet she wanted something lasting out of their relationship and Fletcher did, too, although he preferred to call it a friendship. She'd forced him to admit he feared full sex would bring regret, saying it would be more difficult for them both when he left. So what could they share, something permanent they would both treasure more than, say, black pearls? Her solution was very Ma'ohi and perhaps too exotic for him. But what else was there?

'You know, Fletcher, if you were tattooed, like a Tahitian man.'

'But I'm not a Tahitian man,' he laughed, tickling her feet.

'Listen.' She pulled her feet from him and Fletcher changed to an expression of comical concern. 'Be serious.' she said, putting a finger over his lips. His bantering could go on forever. 'It is something we could do together and then never forget.'

She waited for a clever response but he was listening intently. She told him how the pain of complete buttock and loin tattooing was more than crossing a threshold into adulthood. If she was beside him it would brand an eternal bond between them, something deep, precious and invulnerable.

'Your tattoo would be burned into the eye of my mind forever. And, every time you see it the eye in your mind will see me.'

She arranged for priests from Matavai district's biggest marae to agree the most suitable patterns and talismans and then they chose the tattoo specialist who most respected the resonance of these images. As the sun went down on the first day of 1789, she brought the chosen *tahu'a ta'tau*, the experienced elder who would pound and dye the designs onto Fletcher.

Fletcher refused to drink rum or *kava*, the peppery local narcotic drink. He wanted the full Tahitian experience of being pricked in to adulthood. It was half way through his expected time on Tahiti and he was determined 1789 would be a special year. He would learn to partner Bligh rather than humour him. For that he would need to find new sources of truth and strength. As well as the souvenir Mauatua wanted him to have, the tattoo would be a tangible totem, a marker of his determination to be a bigger and better man.

To keep his secret from Bligh, each session was late at night. The soft glow of tallow candles added a European sense of sanctity to each episode.

He adjusted slowly to the pattern of pain. It was not constant injury but short bursts of violence when the greasy soot from *tutu'i*, the candle-nut that lit Tahitian houses, was hammered into his skin. He didn't cry out. But the *tahu'a* lost his temper when Fletcher twice tensed his buttocks in anticipation of pain.

Mauatua told him to hold his breath during the tapping and then to breathe deeply while the tool was dipped again into the dark dye. With this rhythm his mind and body slipped into a new state. The constant, even episodes of the hammer on the combs of needle-sharp teeth became a mantra, reinforcing a sense of other worldliness.

There was another build-up of pain, too, different from the piercing wounds. The serrated piercers also bruised the skin. Tiny pricks of individual injury fused and then spread. First his buttocks and then more and more of his body floated in a warm sea of pain, a sea with no apparent shores. It was like smoking hemp in India except this was happening naturally. He was in this world, yet there was an unearthly separation of mind and body.

Soaring the way he thought an angel must, he understood why tattooing on this scale was a rite of passage. He transcended time and place, welcoming the continuation of pain because the pain led to unfailing ecstasy, where he glimpsed what was normally hidden. Tattooing on this scale opened portals through which you never returned.

He had no doubt his tattoo would be defence against anything Bligh could throw at him.

It was many weeks before his buttocks were tattooed solid black. Saw-toothed, dotted, trefoil and wavy arches claimed their place above them, on his loins. When the fresh pain subsided each night, he was left with a cushion of heat. Next day, the heat remained as a badge of achievement that swelled his pride. Mauatua's constant care with *temanu* oil ensured the thousands of wounds healed cleanly, without lumps or scars. His hips were well covered for Bligh's visits.

'But he knows you are being tattooed?' she asked, massaging the healing oil into his newest patch of swollen skin.

'Yes, but not where. Not for sure.'

'Let him land a small fish. Then he will not look for the big one.'

'Meaning?'

'Have a smaller tattoo, something other men have. Look as though you are trying to hide it.' Fletcher laughed out loud at the devious audacity of the idea. 'You are very naughty.'

'We like *ha'avare*, to tell stories that mislead. Sometimes, there's nothing else to do on Tahiti.'

They stood inside the fence of the breadfruit camp and she rubbed oil into his left breast until she knew Bligh was close.

'Keep rubbing it,' she advised as she left, pretending not to see Bligh.

The golden-dark oil's peculiar odour called up colliding images from Fletcher's past. First the acridity of the roasted spices in India's *kari* sauces came and then the rich sweetness of Caribbean brown sugar overlaid that, distracting him as he waited for the comment Bligh would be unable to withhold.

'Are you having a heart attack, Mr Christian?'

'No, Captain Bligh. Why do you ask, Sir?'

'You are rubbing your chest, and looking distinctly distant. Are you in some sort of pain?'

'I am, Sir.'

Bligh pulled back Fletcher's shirt. 'So. Another who thinks he should be wearing the king's Garter star. That's an order of chivalry, not a tawdry scribble to decorate sea-going scum.'

Bligh yanked Fletcher's shirt front back into place with enough force to pull him off balance. 'I except you from that, of course, Mr Christian.'

Bligh walked around him, sniffing and snuffling like a pig rootling in a farmyard's midden.

'I expected something more for all the fuss. But, it's piss and wind from you as usual, Mr Christian. And still you need a round-heeled doxie to soothe it.'

Fletcher conjured an image of the bigger, blacker Tahitian tattoo on his buttocks and loins. The dancing patterns of inked amulets pledged protection and fortitude. Bligh would never have endured the tattooing. The certainty of his superiority kept Fletcher calm.

'As you say, Captain Bligh.'

Bligh's face flickered with insecurity. Fletcher kept smiling until he saw self-doubt root deep in Bligh's eyes. Bligh was not used to men agreeing when he sought to lessen them. This was the start of his better, more mature relationship with Bligh.

Bligh dropped his eyes, pretending to have discovered something under his shoe. 'Very well, Mr Christian. Carry on.' He stamped away, calling his servant and midshipman.

Mauatua brought Fletcher a long looking-glass she had asked Peter to bring from the ship. 'It's so you have it in your head. Our people have to peer into dark pools and rivers to see their tattoos.'

He was solid black from beneath the inward curve of his buttocks to a line above his coccyx that crossed both buttocks. The effect of a clinging undergarment tapered around both hips to points above where there was once pubic hair. She shaved that off before tattooing began and he'd kept it like this, enjoying the coolness and continuous heightened awareness.

'Makes me look bigger,' he'd boasted.

'Even bigger, you mean.' He'd smiled and swaggered ever since.

She oiled his tattoos with sandalwood *monoi*. The black designs in the reflection became deeper, shinier. As he twisted this way and that, his thick-muscled buttocks seemed more alive, echoing the sensuality she encouraged in him. He flexed his biceps and tensed the cushions of muscle on his abdomen.

'Behold. *Ecce homo*,' he said.

'*Toa*, warrior,' she whispered, '*Toa*.'

The afternoon was hot and still and Mauatua sat on mats on the border of the beach, helping Tee find new ways to wear flowers in the long hair she was permitted to grow. She told Tee she thought his tattoo had made Fletcher more confident, somehow more of a man.

'One way to know that,' Tee giggled.

'Don't you worry. He's over all that thing about his hands. No girl is safe if he gets her into water, fresh or salty.'

'He the one for you?' Tee asked. She couldn't answer easily, even to her best friend. After a long silence she risked saying something she had never said out loud, that talking with Fletcher had convinced her the wrongs she felt about Tahitian men were justified.

Tee slapped her cheeks between her palms.

'You think men will ever let you do what you want?' Her chins shimmied home as she waited for an answer.

'I don't expect to do whatever I want,' Mauatua said. 'It's just, well, I don't want to do *only* what men tell me.'

'You are a dreamer, girl. You don't get happy that way.'

'You don't get happy doing nothing. If you don't like something, you have to say: 'What am I going to do about it?'

Tee waved a finger in Mauatua's face. 'You're going to have a bad life, girl. A bad life. Forget that Titreano. Good to meet him. Better to get rid of him. Bye bye!'

Tee shuffled closer on her buttocks. 'You know who likes you?'

Mauatua didn't want the conversation to turn to other men. She turned her head from Tee, but that didn't stop her.

'That Tararo, that's who. I know you like them younger, like Titreano.'

'Tararo's a cousin. And he's from Raiatea. All that religion!'

'Hush. We are all the servants of the spirits and gods.'

'So men say. Have you been on to a marae, ever seen the ceremonies?'

'I hope the spirits in these trees aren't listening to us.' Tee looked heavenwards. She allowed her fat back slowly to fall and spread onto the beach. 'He's very tasty, that Tararo. Big man everywhere, Mauatua. Make nice tall boys with you. Get you some more rank, too.'

'*Mamoo, vahine.* Be quiet. You are very bad. I am listening no more.'

Mauatua threw down the flowers. She kicked away through the sand, her arms folded tightly, high across her breasts. Much of what Tee said rang true. There was no way she could change Tahiti, not even Matavai. She leaned against a coconut palm, crossing her legs. She lifted her folded arms and thumped them back into her chest again and again.

Fletcher Christian. They had spoken again and again of a better way to live. Where men and women were equal, and of how revolutionary blood in America had bought freedom for personal convictions. But she was a single woman. There were no other fighters for her cause in Matavai Bay. Nothing would ever change.

For a while Fletcher made her dreams seem possible. But they weren't.

It was just as well he was going.

CHAPTER 9

Fletcher circled the 1st of March 1789 in the daily journal he kept. 'Decision made', he wrote and then underlined the two words. That was the date Bligh had agreed they should begin preparations for the voyage home, again honing both ship and company into a single safe and competent unit. That gave him about a month before they sailed and this finally sharpened his resolve about Mauatua.

Every day a man from BOUNTY or a Tahitian woman wept before him at the prospects ahead of parting. He bolstered himself with the certainty it was his duty to be stronger than the men. How could a ship's company possibly obey an officer who was as tearful and emotional over a woman as they were?

His decision was to see less of her and slowly to repair back to the solitude he better understood. It would be kinder to her too. Mauatua and he should be together but would never be together. That was that. By being a manly example he'd be helping BOUNTY's company, leading by example, and incidentally ensuring the men would more quickly blend into the single-headed, many-bodied being that would make the ship safe.

As ever, happiness would come from doing his duty.

Thoughts of duty also turned to Bligh's management of the ship and he shared his views with Ned Young as they strolled the sooty curve of Matavai Bay.

Ned agreed Bligh should have kept BOUNTY sailing while they waited for the trade winds that would send them westwards, even if only around the closer islands. Bligh could have done a huge amount of surveying and mapping and these would enhance his reputation.

'He's been seduced,' Ned said.

'Haven't we all?'

'No, I meant, seduced by his book. No other English captain has spent so long ashore in Tahiti. I don't think he's thought about the consequences. I dread to think how undisciplined the men will be after we sail.'

Fletcher agreed with Ned, rehearsing why BOUNTY was the first British naval ship to sail without a single press-ganged hand even though their destination was kept secret until after they sailed. Every man of the company that sailed was ripe for adventure.

'You know what I think is the most dangerous thing, Ned? It's not their girls but the attachments, their *taio* and the way they are welcomed into their families. Most of them have never had a family before.'

'My God, that's true, Fletcher. Bligh is almost the only man aboard with a wife and children. No-one else on board has much reason to go home.' They walked faster and exchanged not a single word more.

'Cats, Mr Christian,' Bligh ordered. 'Cats, as many as you can, as soon as you can. Send them aboard with your sentinels. We must conquer the insects and damned cockroaches.'

Fletcher was also made responsible for settling the 600 potted breadfruit plants into the greenhouse, BOUNTY's biggest and best quarters. Built by extending forward what was usually the captain's stateroom and command centre spanning the complete rear of the lower deck, the floating conservatory was the only space on that deck with windows for light and air.

As well as five large leaded windows across the stern there were three smaller ones making what looked like half a leaded lamp in quarter galleries on both the port and starboard side. New gratings had been cut into the deck above, directing even more air and light for the prospective cargo. Attached to the outer bulkheads and in a new false deck were timbers with holes cut into them to take the potted plants individually.

Bligh also made him responsible for the efficient working of the expensive lead-lined, water-recycling system of irrigation and for the coal-fired stove that would heat the floating garden if needed. And then more was added to his duties.

'Mr Christian, we have no idea how many breadfruit will survive the voyage to Jamaica. We must tip the odds in our favour. Find more space, Mr Christian. Collect more specimens.'

Fletcher began by co-opting the chicken-coop space behind the ship's wheel and in a few days reported that BOUNTY now carried over 1000 breadfruit plants, as well as tropical citrus and fruit trees. Then he encouraged 23 pigs and 17 goats into pens on the fore deck.

He worked incessantly and alone, with only the interaction needed to complete his orders. Yet his mind was overwhelmed by Mauatua and the dismal certainty he could never find a woman like that back home.

Equally he was certain living in Tahiti wasn't an option. He was too English, too civilised, wasn't he?

He withdrew from most social interaction aboard and spoke to Bligh only when it was his duty to do so and then when men complained to him about Bligh's orders for each man to get rid of every curio and souvenir that would not fit into their single personal sea-chest.

'Sir, those souvenirs are their profit from the voyage. Just as you rightly expect to make a purser's profit from the galley.'

Bligh's eyes closed and he pushed his lips forward as though he'd discovered a cockroach in his mouth. Fletcher was obliged to continue, for he knew men were listening through the door.

'They've nothing but their miserable wages. And they're only paid those if they make it back home.'

'See it is done without exception, Mr Christian,' Bligh thundered and then turned his back, his eyes still snapped shut.

When he could bear their separation no longer, Fletcher quietly left the ship and found Mauatua singing to herself, echoing the rhythms as she beat out tapa cloth with the long squared *e'e* of wood. Tapa was usually made in groups of women and he guessed she too was trying to hide from the truth of their separation. He called on the confidence his tattoo gave him, and so spoke first.

'We have to say goodbye, Mauatua. The ship could sail anytime now.'

As she put down the tapa beater and uncurled from the ground he marvelled at her height again, at the imperious stature her long straight back gave her.

'I'd rather you didn't.' Her low voice trembled.

'Didn't what? Say goodbye yet? I have to . . . we do.'

'I know you are going. But if you don't say goodbye, I can pretend I'll see you again.' She wiped the corners of her eyes. He felt his scalp prickle and prayed the sweating would stay away.

He turned his back.

'We'll both be alone in worlds where we don't want to be.'

She stood quietly behind him, the way she did when she first spoke to him in the breadfruit camp.

'Do you think you'll come back, Fletcher?'

'Bligh did. Cook did.'

She walked around Fletcher and took his hands in hers. His scalp relaxed, soothed by her ease at doing something he thought no woman would do again.

'I am going to pray,' she whispered. 'To all of our gods and to yours.'

'I am too. Even though I don't know a single god I can trust.' He lifted her fingers to his lips. She slid her hands out of his and onto his buttocks.

'Your tattoo will give you the strength to do whatever you must.'

He wanted to weep and hold her forever. Who else had such faith in him and asked so little in return? She wanted what was best for him, even though it was the worst for her. If there was a god of any sort, he or she had played a vicious trick on them both.

'Nothing is impossible, Fletcher,' she said with little conviction. She put her head close to his, so she saw only his eyes.

'Except the things I want.'

He pulled the hair from his face. 'And what I want.'

With that awful understanding so invincibly threading them together, he forced himself from her arms and walked away. It was wrong of them both to dangle hope and then to cut the thread it spun on. He turned once to wave but she had gone. And then she called him through the trees.

'Fletcher. One thing. A small thing.' She pulled Tamahere behind her. Her son's face shone with expectancy.

'Will you change names with Tamahere?'

He couldn't think why not and so he became Tamahere and the boy became Fletcher Christian. They could never truly exchange positions and possessions, as a Tahitian would expect, but Fletcher thought of something to say that might give the switch lasting significance.

'Now young Fletcher, you must look after Mauatua as well as I would.'

It rained constantly for the next two weeks. The incessant, battering downpour tormented him, imprisoning him. On deck it was hot and drenching. Below decks it was hot and humid. Everywhere was clammy and that brought out more of the ship's stink. Throat-catching mould grew relentlessly on the ship's timbers and bedding.

It took every drop of his courage and stamina to ensure his duty was not ambushed by feelings for Mauatua or by conflict with Bligh and the company. It helped that she honoured their agreement and didn't once join those who wept and keened on the shoreline or in canoes.

At 5pm on April 4th 1789, he agreed with Bligh that the right wind blew. He acted as bow lookout as BOUNTY made for the reef under clear skies, harried by hundreds of canoes and swimmers. He knew the loud wailing, chanting and drumming from the morbid fleet hid the desperate thuds of sharp stones beaten into scalps until blood flowed.

Unable at last to resist an emotive gesture, he begged a garland of flowers from a canoe and, just as BOUNTY sailed through the reef, threw the *he'i* into the lagoon.

She'd promised that if a garland floated back to Matavai's sands the giver would return.

His tears made it more like throwing flowers onto her grave.

CHAPTER 10

Fletcher was in charge of the shore parties on April 23rd when BOUNTY anchored at the small atoll of Nomuka to take on more fresh water. He was riled that Bligh stood in a boat with oars shipped, a few yards from the narrow sands. Why is he suggesting to the world I need supervising, Fletcher worried. Then he dismissed it as one of Bligh's simplistic games, jostling for status when what he and the watering parties needed was more men on land.

He chided himself for being petty. What if Bligh was being especially vigilant rather than personally spiteful? Yes, that must be it. Poisonous imagining was what Bligh did, not he. He pulled his thoughts back to the present. He needed every one of his senses for the job at a hand.

Nomuka was not welcoming. He continuously ran back and forth between the beach and through the bush to the fresh-water pool to ensure the small gang-casks were properly filled and then carried safely to the boats. The water parties were secure only if vigilance and suspicion of every sound or sudden movement protected them from belligerence.

When a group of Nomukans did attack, his speedy, clear orders and brave, direct fisticuffs defeated them. Even so, some casks had to be abandoned.

He was last to leave the scrubby path, scuttling crablike with an eye on both the undergrowth and the beach, acting as a final bastion of protection for the water party and the casks.

Bligh bellowed across the thin border of sand. 'Mr Christian, you are a cowardly rascal, afraid of Natives while you are armed.'

'The arms are no use when your orders prevent them from being used,' Fletcher shouted back to Bligh.

'No, Sir!' Bligh yelled back. 'You are a coward in face of danger.'

He was last into the boat. He sat with his back to Bligh and shrugged dismissively when he caught careful, silent looks of sympathy. He didn't blame men for looking away immediately. His eyes must smoulder with the dark fire of injury he felt. An abyss had opened before him.

He could cope with any indignity of duty Bligh threw at him. That was Bligh's way. But to be publically insulted for following Bligh's order not to use arms against Nomukans? Bligh's attitude must be personal, wanting to wound him as Fletcher Christian rather than as an officer. And this from a man he had adored. A man who had agreed to nurture him, to shape him for great future command.

One word pounded in his mind. Betrayal. The injustice of it was inflammatory. Waking or sleeping, and there was precious little of that, the word kept up a constant hammering. He spent most time alone, feigning illness so he did not have to accept Bligh's invitations to dine.

He felt shrunken, no longer one of the tallest and fittest men on the ship. His dark face was blackened with anger and disbelief. He turned to his tattoo for the stoic bravery it demonstrated and pledged. He sucked strength and resolve from the imagery, just as Mauatua said he would.

Even that couldn't prevail and Bligh's accusation thumped incessantly in his head.

And hadn't he dismissed him as only a low servant to Tararo on Tahiti?

Days later Bligh called the ship's company to assemble at short notice. He announced that a snap audit proved his personal store of coconuts had been raided. Fletcher felt relieved that so little was on Bligh's mind. He stepped forward.

'I confess, Sir, to taking one last night. It was very hot and I was thirsty. It was but one. I will replace it, Captain Bligh.'

'No, Mr Christian. You have stolen more than one. You have stolen many more. You are, plainly said, a common thief.'

A servant, then a coward and now a thief? Name calling over a single coconut was totally against acceptable social and naval conduct. Bligh was clearly determined to reduce him not just as an officer but as a man, too. But why? That was sadly easy to answer.

Bligh fed his brittle sense of superiority by insulting and demeaning others and he had been unsettled by Fletcher's new confidence. He must have seen it as a challenge and feared Fletcher might no longer be seen as the junior officer by the ship's company.

Each letter of each of Bligh's insults shattered into a thousand pricks of pain. As they spread Fletcher felt them battering his brain. Boring through his skull. The sweating began.

Even Bligh said nothing when, first insulted in public and then by his body's inability to keep that shame within, Fletcher fled below decks.

Later in the day Fletcher was impelled to settle the chattering voices in his head, even knowing he looked unhinged, his hair badly dishevelled and his eyes reddened from the sweating.

He knocked at Bligh's cabin door and walked in without waiting for permission. Bligh stood, blustering about good manners.

'Manners, Captain Bligh? Manners? From you that is rich.'

Bligh folded his arms defiantly across his chest. 'You have a point you wish to raise with me, Mr Christian?'

'Indeed, Sir, I do.'

'And that might be?'

'You would learn that, Captain Bligh, if you had the manners not to interrupt me!' Fletcher's anger rose further. He had to speak up quickly or Bligh would manipulate the situation to his disadvantage.

'How can you speak of manners, Captain Bligh, when you treat me worse than a dog? In the last week you have called me a coward for no reason and now a thief, and both times in front of a company from whom we expect respect. It is insufferable, Captain Bligh. I demand an apology. In front of the ship's company.'

'I will not apologise, Mr Christian. Both occasions were justified.'

'And if your judgement was wrong?'

'Wrong! Wrong, Mr Christian? I am captain of this ship. My judgement is what I wish it to be.'

Fletcher twisted the cloth in his hands until it was as hard as steel. He changed tactics. 'Many would think our status on BOUNTY is equal. We are both lieutenants. You are but an *acting* Captain.'

'You are an *acting* lieutenant and I can change that any time I like.'

'It would be spiteful. The company would not like it. We should present a single face to them, with no more personal insults. That would be good for them, and for the ship.'

Bligh turned his back and then twisted his neck over his shoulder.

'Am I to understand, Mr Christian, that you think you might captain this ship better than I?' His voice was thin and wheedling.

Fletcher saw the trap. The least suggestion there was any truth in Bligh's question would be mutinous.

'No, Captain Bligh. That is not what I think or what I meant.'

'Oh, I just wondered. It rather runs in the family, does it not?'

Bligh spun to face Fletcher, his face a contorted mixture of malice and the expectancy of victory. Fletcher answered quickly. The sentences had been rehearsed in his mind.

'Sir, the mutiny of my brother Charles is irrelevant. I have always done my duty. I have never questioned you or defied you, not before the company or in private. I am sorry for whatever I have done that has upset you, but these attacks must stop. They are not deserved. It is not good for the ship's discipline. We have dangerous waters ahead.'

'None as dangerous as those you are in currently, Mr Christian. It seems to me you are indeed saying you would run the ship better...'

'That is not an option I have, Captain Bligh.'

If the exchange continued Bligh would trap him into saying something mutinous. Mutiny. What would that solve? Fletcher saluted and stamped out and up the companion way ahead of him and on to deck.

The chattering in his head stopped but one voice persisted. It told him to leave the ship. That would be the honourable thing to do. Without tension between two opposing officers, there was a chance the company would blend into one again. He would sacrifice his position so they would be safe. At least they knew what to expect from Bligh.

It was only he who did not.

He shared out the souvenirs he had collected, except for a very few Mauatua gave him. He stuffed his daily journal and personal papers into the galley fire and dumped his officer's hats and jackets at Ned's feet.

He would become a nobody, so low no-one would care enough to insult him. His life and lot in future might be theft and refusal of authority, but then every insult would be deserved. He would find dignity in poverty and anonymity, forget any ambition of regaining the position and fortune his brothers had squandered. There was no ambition left in him except for refuge from unearned abuse.

Later that night he bargained nails from the Purcell the carpenter. He constructed a raft as far from Bligh's cabin as he could get, so the noise of his hammer didn't alert him. He stole biscuits and cooked meat from the galley and wrapped them into a pack with some of his coconuts and bananas. There were enough islands about. He would reach one in a matter of a few days.

At first, his plan to escape unnoticed was impossible because a great, bright moon hung in a cloudless night sky. There was a volcano erupting on the nearby island of Tofua and men constantly came on deck to wonder at the red lava flows. Shortly after midnight, deserted decks made it safer to leave and he pulled his raft to the midship railing.

Men suddenly ran at him. He panicked and kicked the raft overboard and then scrambled after it down the ship's side ladder. The men had no interest in him. They were running to see sharks. Only Ned Young understood. 'No, Fletcher! How would we cope without you?'

'You will have to. I can bear Bligh's abuse and insults no longer.'

'I understand, we all do, the whole ship feels for you but for God's sake Fletcher there must be another way.'

'God? If there was a God situations like this would never have arisen.' Even now he recognised it was the second time he had said such a thing. Once to Mauatua and now about Bligh. Confused and disappointed, Fletcher climbed a few rungs so his head was above the deck line.

Ned crouched. 'For me then, for my sake only. Please, Fletcher, I'll say nothing. No-one else saw the raft.'

Fletcher looked away to avoid Ned's foul breath and saw the raft already out of reach. He couldn't swim to it, not with so many sharks.

His tongue separated from the rest of his consciousness. It parroted Bligh's words over and over again, but he had no control over it. It was someone else complaining to Ned, someone else churning the words around his mouth and onto his tongue and out through his lips.

He became the chatterer that usually tormented his brain.

Ned attempted to divert him. 'Come on, Fletcher, you can still get some sleep before your watch.' Ned gave him his hand and pulled him back onto the ship. Fletcher's mind plunged back into deepest introspection. How dare Bligh call him a thief and a coward?

Then a greater hurt came into his mind but this one did not reach his tongue. Bligh had tried to trap him into mutiny. Did the man really think him so mentally feeble? Brothers couldn't both be driven to the sea's greatest crime. Bligh would never catch him that way.

He couldn't sleep. He abandoned himself to vicious swirling thoughts and images. A single new idea emerged. It calmed him into the sort of ecstasy he felt during tattooing. The idea of deserting BOUNTY faded.

From a confused hell of rant and babble, from the pain of words of insult and injury, a triumphant solution presented itself. If he were in the right, why should it be he who left the ship?

He heard Bligh's malevolent wheedling again, asking his poisoned question: '*Am I to understand, Mr Christian, that you think you might captain this ship better than I?*'

At last he knew how to respond. It would be justice, not mutiny that drove him. And it wasn't his idea. Bligh had put the idea into his mind.

He went back on deck. The moonlight sparkling on the dark water, the angry glow of Tofua's molten lava, the great bright moon itself, he saw all these extraordinary natural phenomena as affirmations of the determined new man he was. His fingers flickered over his tattoos, tracing the rhythms of the soot.

He lifted his face to bathe in the moonlight and when Ned again found him he assured Ned wordlessly that all was at last well.

He caught a little sleep and when he woke his mind raced, churning the old insults again. Servant, thief, coward . . . mutiny. His sweating was as bad as he could remember. He tied one of his bigger handkerchiefs around his forehead, hoping to keep his eyes clear.

Suddenly he heard Mauatua's voice, telling him the question he should ask when faced with a problem: 'What am I going to do about it?'

Her answer, her solution, was to act, to act to put all that was troubling behind her.

That's what he would do. There could be no blame. *He* hadn't put the thought into his mind.

And hadn't Ned said the whole ship understood?

CHAPTER 11

April 28th, 1789: off Tofua, South Pacific

'Hell. Hell! I've been in Hell with that man for weeks, *weeks* of living Hell! Bastard! Bastard!' Fletcher Christian leaned over the stern rail, wildly waving his cutlass.

He pulled constantly at his neck, releasing his sodden hair. His shirt was transparent with sweat and clung to his torso. His eyes blazed with pain, irritated beyond relief by sweat pouring debris from his scalp into them. Even wearing his flat-crowned lieutenant's hat hadn't helped. He had no care for any of this, and stabbed his sword into the air.

'Well, that's over! *Over* Captain Bligh! Who's in Hell now?'

His heart pounded with pleasure to see Bligh stand awkwardly in BOUNTY'S launch only a few yards from the ship's stern, still in his striped nightshirt, his hair awry. He relished knowing the bouncing launch was designed to carry just 13 men including six oarsmen. With Bligh and 18 other men, their trunks, most of Bligh's papers, navigating equipment, water and food, there were just a few inches freeboard. He didn't care. Bligh was lucky to have a boat at all.

It had been a joy to point out that the jolly boat was worm-ridden and unseaworthy due to Bligh's own neglect in Tahiti. It was droll and proper that the seaworthy cutter was too small to take Bligh and his cronies. He'd said it into Bligh's face. If Bligh had kept all BOUNTY's boats ship-shape his party might have sailed in two rather than one.

Fletcher wasn't going to be left with only the rotten-planked jolly boat. No Sir. Not likely, Captain Bligh.

Peter tugged at him. 'There's still time, Fletcher.'

'Time for what! More of his bullying and insults?' His head dropped. He felt tears close and welcomed the relief they would bring.

'He has treated me like a dog, the company like Turks. Called me his servant, and a coward, and a thief.'

'I know Fletcher, we all know. But mutiny?'

'It should have been murder.' He leaped back to the rail. 'That's right, Bligh. Sail away now you bastard until you are out of my sight. Forever!'

Bligh silently defied him. Fletcher shouted again.

'Damn you for what you have done to this ship. Damn you for what you did to me, day after day. You have threatened and bullied me and these men enough, Captain Bligh! Set those sails and disappear.' Bligh raised a fist.

Fletcher had not finished. 'If you do not, I will turn the guns onto you and by God I will take away your dignity and your life as absolutely as you have mine.'

At the threat of a gun, Bligh's temper burst. 'Think you can frighten me, Christian? I'll sail this boat to England, you'll see. You, all of you, will swing from the highest yardarms in the British Navy. You'll be first, Christian. You ungrateful son of a tailless Manx whore.'

Ned Young ran to BOUNTY'S stern. 'Captain Bligh. I think it better if you didn't . . .'

'Don't bother yourself on my behalf, you nigger blackguard.' Bligh roared across the water. 'You make a pretty pair, you and your sweat-sodden dog of a...'

'*Mamoo! Mamoo*, Bligh! One more word and you are dead.'

Fletcher strode to a swivel gun mounted on the gunwale and aimed it at Bligh. His fury fired up others. They threw breadfruit pots at Bligh and the launch. As its reluctant company struggled to protect itself the over-laden boat rocked and took in water. Bligh lost his balance and fell heavily.

Fletcher smirked as Bligh at last ordered the sails to be raised on the launch's two masts.

By the time the launch was under way, he heard BOUNTY's mood of anger and insult become shouts of happiness.

'The ship is yours, Mr Christian,' Ned Young said.

Fletcher wiped a sodden sleeve over the stubble of his chin, blinking repeatedly to clear his eyes. He looked along the deck and saw groups of men guarded by muskets or swords. So, not everyone wanted to be part of what he seemed to have done.

'Not quite mine, Ned. Not quite.'

He sank into a reverie, finding himself close to slipping into sleep.

'The men will need orders,' Ned prompted. Fletcher started at the voice. He shook his head sprinkling the deck with sweat from the ends of his hair. He hesitated, and then squared his shoulders.

'Orders, yes . . . orders. I'm ordering now. Rum. Yes, rum all round.'

'Aye, aye, Sir. See to that Peter.' Peter saluted and ran off.

Fletcher mumbled to himself. 'I'll show him how a man runs a ship. The bastard, the bastard.'

He allowed Young to hold him tightly by the shoulders for a long time. He dismissed any idea it might be unmanly because the physical pressure of Ned's hands helped his mind to relax. He swept an arm across his face and then trembled violently for some minutes. When this stopped his sight seemed clearer. There was new clarity in his mind, too.

He shook himself from Ned and marched to the stern. Bligh's sails could still be seen. He took a quick, frightened breath, and turned.

'Did I? Did I really?' he asked. 'Was there blood, Ned?'

'Not a drop.'

'No-one shot?'

'Not a single shot fired.'

'Thank God for that.' He turned back to watch the last tip of Bligh's sail dip beneath the Pacific. 'Who tried to stop me? Any of the officers?'

'Not one. I believe they thought you had grounds.'

'I thought I was strong enough to resist him,' Fletcher said, regretfully.

'It no longer matters, Fletcher. Bligh has gone. BOUNTY is yours. We need orders.' Fletcher looked at the chicken coop behind the wheel, already cleared of breadfruit pots. He looked forward, past the knots of prisoners to the animal pens.

'If we are to survive in the Pacific and no longer eat like jailed villains, we'll need more pigs. Yes, and the cow and bull Cook left in Tahiti.'

At the first mention of Tahiti, the blind fiddler Byrne perked up and played a jagged version of a Tahitian melody. Fletcher was assured when the sailors began to dance. Some had learned the thigh-shaking answer to women's hip shimmying. Some jigged alone, others danced the hornpipe in couples or groups.

The company's shouts of 'Tahiti' and 'Huzzah for Tahiti' became more and more urgent. Good, very good. Under his command BOUNTY would be a happy ship as well as orderly. He smiled.

'Aye,' he said clapping Ned on the back. 'Tahiti it must be.'

Later, he wished he hadn't agreed so quickly.

Returning there would mean facing Mauatua. He'd look weak when she had thought to make him strong.

Seeing Mauatua again was the last thing he wanted.

CHAPTER 12

He couldn't believe he had turned Bligh overboard. He remembered little but scarlet-clouded rage. Yet here he was, settled into Bligh's small dark cabin. He felt threatened by the shelf-lined bulkheads, some still stuffed to overflowing with books, ephemera and navigational aids he had apparently refused Bligh to take.

Ned knocked and held out a shot of rum. He waved it away.

'Why didn't I just lock him up in here, Ned? Take him back to Britain as a prisoner and put him into the hands of the Navy.'

'It was suggested.'

'I *couldn't* listen. I was taken over.' His search for certainties continued to worm its way out and into the airless cabin. 'It was a sort of madness, Ned. A way of escaping the Hell he'd made for me.'

He stood and waved his arms aimlessly.

'And now I've created a new Hell, for you, for everyone aboard.'

Ned ignored this, instead urging him to tell the ship's company what to do next. 'Have you never imagined how you would run the ship?'

Fletcher answered morosely. 'Doesn't every man who is second in command think about that, Ned?'

Once Ned left, Fletcher struggled to identify his feelings. Isolation? Yes, but of a depth none of his self-imposed segregation ever approached. And fear, too, fear of the future. Was he really expected to run the ship? Could he do that? Where would they go?

What would happen when the mutiny was discovered?

He searched for answers yet could see nothing certain ahead but blankness, and that came with mounting fear.

He went for hot water from the galley, avoiding every eye, and then carefully shaved. The diversion calmed him. He took time to dry and then comb and tie back his hair. What could he do to colour and shape the future, his future, BOUNTY's future and of all those aboard? As he reached for a clean shirt he was startled to hear snatches of conversations he'd shared in the privileged dining rooms and salons of London.

Once again he heard himself conversing with elderly diplomats who had once been criminals in the American Revolution, and with young aristocrats escaping what they feared in France.

Josiah Wedgewood, celebrated for his inventive potteries, spoke forcefully of his determination to ban slavery in every part of the world. So did William Wilberforce, a young MP and evangelical Christian.

Many of the rich and advantaged families that entertained him in their grand houses owed their fabulous fortunes to slavery but the new thinking of these two men had persuaded him against it.

He trembled again, with excitement this time. Was it possible? Could he become the sort of social pioneer he talked about so much in London?

He recognised he was at that future-defining point American revolutionaries told him about, the singular moment a man could ask: Why not? Why not me?

With clear thinking and determination, his unforgiveable mutiny could stand for more than a quarrel between two men. He'd follow his family's centuries-old heritage of public duty and service, but in a new way.

Cousin John's friendly societies and model farms and pioneering steam engines in coalmines would be nothing compared to what he'd do. He'd start immediately by asking the men to confirm him as captain. If his new world was going to be fair, that had to mean democracy from the very start. For every man, even the simplest sailor.

Once his ideas of social advance were put into practice in the South Seas the mutiny would not be his epitaph. Instead, he would be remembered for the revolutionary society he created next.

He finished dressing in stockings and white breeches, resolute and proud of what he would achieve. He buckled his shoes and slipped on a pristine full-skirted blue and white lieutenant's undress frock coat. His sweating stopped before he stepped back on deck. He stood by the ship's wheel and spoke confidently.

'You all know that without discipline neither king nor God can make this ship safe at sea.'

Adams, a cheeky Londoner, stepped forward, emboldened by rum. 'But half the officers has been tipped overboard by your good self, Sir.'

Quintal, the raw-boned Cornishman, added his piece. 'And the other half's still snivelling about it.' He laughed raucously and aimed a kick at one of the men he guarded with a musket.

Fletcher leapt forward and twisted the musket away. He needed only one arm to hold it squarely at Quintal's eyes, which were barely at his shoulder height.

'There'll be none of that on my ship.'

Confident of the men's attention, he continued. 'Some of the ship's best men are no longer aboard, and some of the officers left behind are not the best liked.' He waited until the guffaws of agreement died.

'But, liking a man has nothing to do with sailing a ship. From now on, the best men will do the most important jobs, whoever they might be. But only if you agree. These decisions will be yours.

'We will vote on who is best suited to be in which post.'

Quintal stood forward again. 'We don't know nothing about this . . . voting, is it? Them's your decision. You be Cap'n now.'

'I have made enough decisions for one day,' Fletcher said with great certainty. He spoke louder to overcome the ripple of riposte and amusement.

'We are in the middle of the South Pacific, in a ship that must now be sailed by some who have never been sailors.' Many faces changed.

He saw this point at least was understood. How often had he heard them cursing about orders given by himself or Mr Young or Captain Bligh? Who hasn't thought himself better than the officers, he asked. He ignored the surly grunts of recognition and repeated that they were at last being asked for their voice.

There was plenty of shuffling. Sun-dried brows wrinkled further. The older crewmen looked appalled and only a few of the younger men seemed interested. Still, no one said a thing in response.

'This is new to me, too,' said Ned Young, stepping forward to stand by him. 'But think. What you are being offered, what I am being offered, is a say in our safety and survival.'

'That ain't the way of the King's Navy!' Quintal shouted.

'No,' Adams agreed. 'That's what you bleeding officers is for, mate!'

'But this is hardly the king's ship anymore,' Ned interrupted.

Fletcher thanked Ned with a quick look. He continued calmly and slowly, saying that, if he appointed any of the men being guarded, Quintal would be first to complain. Yet if he gave a responsible position to an able-seaman like Adams, others would complain the ship was not being sailed properly.

'Do you think any of you would ever see Tahiti? Do you think you'd get within a sniff of your girls?'

Reduction of the argument to personal pleasure was more convincing than his appeal to the common good.

'We'll start then. Let's agree who will be captain of this ship.'

Once the company voted for him as captain, Fletcher's past musings on how he would run a ship became fact and action. He shared every major decision and it was quickly agreed they would first call at an island called Tubuai. Tubuai sounded an ideal hideaway. Europeans had discovered the island 350 miles southwest of Tahiti, but not landed on it.

Fletcher soon complimented himself on all BOUNTY became. He'd discovered Muspratt was a tailor before he joined BOUNTY and so men were organised under his leadership to sew jackets from canvas.

These were simply cut, but not simple. Each was edged with blue fabric from Fletcher's uniforms and fastened with bright brass or mother-of-pearl buttons salvaged from jackets left by the men turned off with Bligh or cut from spares in the slops room.

His mood of self-blame swiftly changed to pride. Under his command, BOUNTY became the first British naval ship to work by agreement rather than challenge or orders, and then became first to have all its company in uniform. No-one would accuse him of running a discontented ship however he had come to command her.

His accurate navigation brought them to Tubuai precisely when he predicted, on May 24th. The island had a lagoon encircled by a reef and a fringe of coconut palms, but he was astonished to see the island's central mountains were like the age-softened peaks of Cumbria's Lake District. Their pastel colours, pale greens and yellows and purples, were the colours he saw every day he rode his pony out of Moorland Close and cross country to school in Cockermouth.

Ned interrupted, asking if Bligh had given Fletcher tips about first contacts in the South Pacific.

'Not really. Except that every island is different. What is acceptable on one can be *tapu* on another, forbidden.'

CHAPTER 13

'It's this ship that'll be our death,' Quintal said, walking past on watch duty. 'It'll come from the sea if the Navy spots our masts.'

'BOUNTY is our escape, Quintal. In the meantime it is also a village of men and tools to call on, somewhere safe to live on while we get established on Tubuai.'

'Aye, well, I see your point, Mr Christian. It'd not be the way I'd do it.'

'I'll put scuttling the ship to the vote if you'd like, Quintal.'

'Aye, that you would, that you would. But sometimes, it's the minority that's right, Mr Christian, the minority.'

Quintal turned and shambled untidily away. Fletcher called after him, reminding him his hair should be in a pigtail when on duty. Quintal retorted he wasn't aware he was still in the King's Navy. Fletcher slammed his hand hard onto the ship's rail.

'Navy or not, damn you! If we are to survive we must have rules and you will obey them. Put your hair up in the next five minutes or you will be clapped in irons. Is that clear? Is it?'

Quintal sullenly put down his musket. McCoy offered to help and the two muttered as he folded Quintal's hair into a queue.

The next time Quintal passed both men smiled as Fletcher said, 'Very smart today, Quintal. Well done.'

Fletcher guided BOUNTY slowly around the island but by late afternoon slanting light and scudding clouds made it difficult to see the danger from shoals and shallows and he'd still found no obvious entrance through the reef.

'We'll heave to here, Ned, and try again tomorrow.'

Early next morning Fletcher called a meeting in what had been Bligh's dining space. There was every likelihood of danger and conflict. He wanted to be certain everyone was prepared to face this.

'So, Mr Stewart, are you willing to command the cutter? It'll be best, I think, for identifying any break in the reef.'

'Aye, Mr Christian. I am. I will.'

George Stewart sat across the table, bottle shouldered and inhibited socially by a thick accent from his native Orkneys. He was a strict disciplinarian and a Bligh loyalist and thus not widely liked. Yet BOUNTY's men had voted for him as second in command. They'd seen him moved up to acting master's mate when Bligh promoted Fletcher to acting lieutenant and now the men had put him into Fletcher's shoes a second time. They ignored the man's personal traits and voted for the greater likelihood of Stewart keeping them safe.

Voting aboard was working just as he imagined it would.

When Stewart found a way into the lagoon, it was so narrow there would be little room for mistake. Fletcher signalled he should stay there in the cutter and guide BOUNTY through. With every man on BOUNTY focussed on this task, it was only by chance

Fletcher looked to the shore and saw canoes being launched. He yelled at Stewart to get back on board, but there was no time.

He prayed his sweating wouldn't erupt as he assessed the Tubuaian canoes, each 30 to 40 feet long he reckoned, each powered by 20 fiercely dressed warriors whose powerful bodies sped the canoes through the calm lagoon waters. What might be these swift paddlers' intentions?

On an uncontacted island, he had no way of knowing. He couldn't panic, yet he'd never been in a situation like this. None of them had, and that explained the sudden hush that fell over BOUNTY.

The silence confirmed his first thoughts, that there was only menace in the canoes' dull red hulls and their high prows of fantastic animal heads glittering with fish scales and shells.

His fears increased as the canoes came closer to Stewart's boat. All the warriors wore a thick sort of armour, seemingly of tapa cloth, white or painted the red of their canoes and wound around their bodies again and again. The skins of the attackers were stained a bilious yellow and every man wore a helmet like a conical beehive, some covered with white cloth and crowned with black feathers. Others flaunted pearl shells or a coronet of wild duck wings.

He turned away from the lagoon, unable to bear the sight and the threat it signalled. Was he going to lose men so soon, perhaps even lose the ship? The foes of his childhood adventures were imaginary but here . . .

When the leading canoes mobbed the cutter and its six sailors his stomach contracted and he jerked forward in pain, feeling emasculated. The boat's men tried to beat the Tubuaians off with their oars but they bounced off their attackers' helmets.

Fletcher punched blows into the air, helplessly willing their force to vanquish the attackers.

Some Tubuaians boarded the cutter but at such close quarters their exceptionally long spears were useless. Stewart's men grasped their oars close to the blade and held the warriors at bay by batting at them.

When Stewart eventually fired a pistol, it didn't work.

He yelled at Stewart to fire the second and again he bent almost double with alarm when this pistol also misfired. Yet somehow it managed to wound a Tubuaian.

Fletcher straightened with relief as the warriors tumbled back into their canoes and raced back to the beach.

'It wasn't just the size of them and their armour,' Stewart explained, as the frightened men were pulled back on board. 'It was the smell of rancid oil and stale sweat and that they were so close, right on top of us.'

'I would have shitted myself,' Ned said.

'I did,' Stewart admitted. 'And I'm not the only one.'

Fletcher vanished into the gloom of his cabin and shook. Every part of his body trembled as he grasped for the first time the dread weight of the responsibility he had for so many men's lives.

It made no difference if men were flogged to death by Bligh or murdered by a savage. A dead man was a dead man, and for all his venom no-one aboard BOUNTY had ever died because of Bligh. Yet by wanting to settle on an uncontacted island he was exposing the ship's company, mutineer and non-mutineer, to the passions of Ma'ohi men who might kill to keep what had always been theirs alone.

His mind turned to Mauatua, for what she might tell him to do. But what could she have advised differently? He hadn't started it.

Late that night he met with the men chosen as officers and a vote confirmed none was deterred from exploring Tubuai as a future home. In fact, most of the company aboard seemed excited by the earlier clash, sensing a chance of real South Seas adventure as relief from the boredom of sea life.

He agreed extra sentries should be on duty overnight, and next morning BOUNTY finally edged her way into the lagoon. It was not encouraging. The white-sanded beach was jammed with natives and BOUNTY was soon crowded by canoes.

The noise was constant, not only wailings of human voices but drum beats and the dreadful blares of conch shell trumpets.

Fletcher and Peter discovered the local tongue was similar to Tahitian, but could persuade no-one to come on board.

It was three days before Fletcher cajoled one old man to climb out of one of the barrage of canoes. He laughed whenever the Tubuaian started back in horror if he was eyed by a dog or goat or pig and then the man admitted Tubuai had no mammals other than rats.

His greater discovery was that the man's major intent was to count the number of men on board. He plied him with gifts and walked him willy-nilly around the deck to disorient him and then helped him overboard.

Another tense day of constant confrontation from the water passed and then he warily watched a double canoe approach the ship, richly caparisoned with garlands of flowers and bright ornaments of pearl shell.

The cargo on the platform lashed over the two hulls was eighteen young women, bare breasted and with hair in ringlets that hung past their waists. He ordered every sailor quickly into their uniform jackets and doubled the guard in every direction.

As soon as the women were on board, the guards on the leeward of BOUNTY urgently reported fifty canoes were sailing as one towards the ship. Their combined crews must have been over 1000 men and the rapid move to attack was encouraged by drums and conch trumpets. Fletcher ordered muskets fired into the air, and their sharp challenge persuaded the war party to retreat.

The women aboard BOUNTY seemed satisfied once they'd been given gifts. The men who followed them aboard were more troublesome.

One reached under the broken glass of the compass and stole the card with the cardinal points marked on it. Fletcher got the card back but it was torn in the struggle. His superior strength sent the thief hurtling over the side after some well aimed stripes from a rope end. The other Tubuaians quickly followed but when they were in their canoes, every warrior on the lagoon then took out and brandished weapons they had been hiding.

'Sir, look.'

A native in a canoe was cutting the line to a buoy that marked an anchor. He killed the offender with a single shot.

By now, the ship's company was fed up with the uninvited belligerence. He swiftly mustered enough agreement and then a single cannon was primed with grape shot, three tiers of small iron balls held between iron discs and connected with a central pin.

He watched impassively as the balls burst out of the rope-bound canvas bag that contained them and then scattered, like the pellets of a shot gun, but much deadlier. Many Tubuaians in canoes were killed, more were wounded. He hoped this chaos and fear would put the island in no doubt about the courage and superiority of the men on his ship.

He ordered the boat launched and chased the last canoes back to the beach, personally shooting muskets or pistols at any defiance.

The place was named Bloody Bay and, still convinced by the mellow promise of the island's central mountains, he ordered the anchors up and sailed for Tahiti. It was May 31st.

During the voyage back to Tahiti Fletcher spoke directly to every man on board. He promised them instant death if they told a single Tahitian BOUNTY would return to Tubuai.

CHAPTER 14

Mauatua's mind tumbled with confusion when BOUNTY once more dropped anchor in Matavai Bay.

'Can I talk with Fletcher? Is he still on board? Tell him it is me, Mauatua,' she yelled up from her canoe.

Hers was one of many calls from a muddle of canoes with surprised *taio* and lovers and friends. All were ignored. At different times she thought she saw Peter and Brown and Williams but when they caught her eye they quickly went below.

She waited on the lagoon for most of the first day and into the night and was among the last who paddled back. Was the ship's return a gift from the gods, a second chance for her? She wanted to protect herself from more of the misery she lived after BOUNTY had sailed. She tried to keep her mind neutral but even her son knew she thought only of Fletcher Christian and no-one had seen him.

'If something has happened to him,' Tamahere said, 'it's just as well we changed names. Now I am Fletcher I can take you away in the ship,' he promised. 'We can go somewhere nice, just us. We might go to Peretane.'

As the sun rose she took him to watch BOUNTY from the shaded edge of the beach. She'd prepared a small picnic of bananas and cooked puddings but neither could eat without nausea, she through fear, her son from over-excitement.

She began to weave a garland of ferns and flowers but even Tamahere knew better sense than that, saying nothing was sadder than a *he'i* with no one to wear it. The spirits loved such invitations to wreak tragedy. He took the unfinished tribute from her and buried it. Late that night Fletcher Christian, the real one, had still not stepped onto the beach.

She left her son sleeping as soon as light again began to seep into the sky and swam to the ship. There were armed guards on deck but they were tired and disinterested after their long dark hours without sleep or company. She was recognised and, as no other Tahitian could be seen, was allowed to board and told to go to Bligh's cabin.

She pulled what water she could from her hair and her shift and although desperate for an answer had to force her feet down each steep step of the companionway.

What awful thing would Bligh have to tell her about Fletcher?

Across the small lobby the door of Bligh's cabin was half open. She paused to beg the gods to forgive her for allowing other men to walk above her head and then lifted her eyes. Even in the collision of stinking miasmas she knew the sleeping man did not smell like Bligh.

Then, when he moved, the night-lamp over the companionway lit the highest curves of Fletcher's tattoo.

She blew onto his scalp. Fletcher woke and turned to bury his face. He brushed away the insistent irritation of her breath. Again and again he flicked, slapped and brushed it away. Again and again she blew, patient but impatient.

He sat up to batter what he must have thought was a fly. She jumped back, bruised.

'I had to know.'

'Why we are back?'

'If *you* were back.'

She expected him to smile. Her eyes, now well adjusted, showed he was distressed. 'This is not where you used to sleep.'

'Bligh is not the captain anymore.'

'Dead?'

'No idea.'

As she started her next question, Fletcher held up his hand.

'I've done something terrible. You remember what I told you? The secret about brother Charles?'

He reached out to touch her. Her skin was damp enough for her not to notice his difference.

She struggled to remember the word. '*'orurera'a?* Mutiny?'

'Yes, me too. Bligh is overboard, in a sailboat. God knows what will happen to him. Or to me.'

'Nothing will happen to you if you live with us. Not if you honour our gods and spirits.' Fletcher put his hands under his head. No retribution for sins if you simply change your gods? Attractive, but not likely.

Although his mutiny meant Tahiti was forbidden as a refuge for Fletcher, she quickly understood he wanted to take Tahiti with him. She stood beside him as he skilfully lied to Teina and Itia that BOUNTY had caught up with Captain Cook.

The untruth didn't matter to her, not when bending the truth was so much a part of life in Tahiti. Anyway, hadn't Bligh lied, too, deliberately withholding news of Cook's much earlier death in Hawaii?

Fletcher deftly convinced the regents that Bligh was helping Cook establish a new South Seas settlement and Cook had asked for help from his friends on Tahiti. Believing this, Teina and Itia gave Fletcher all he wanted. Soon Mauatua was busy in the greenhouse helping to plant up a steady supply of young trees from Matavai district. BOUNTY became Tahiti afloat. Bananas in their many guises stood in pots where breadfruit once ruled. Citrus trees, too, hibiscus and fragrant Tahitian sandalwood and gardenia.

Her rank meant she even cajoled six prized pineapples from a high-blooded relative's guarded garden.

She watched from the red-splashed shade of hibiscus bushes as Fletcher used his strength single-handedly to push off another boat on its way back to BOUNTY, wallowing only just afloat with a cargo of more plants and livestock. As the oars first cut into the water he stretched. He was hot and filthy from handling nervous piglets. He saw no threat when he glanced about and so unslung his musket, pulled off his shirt and ran into the lagoon waters. He swam out into the lagoon and then using only his arms swam underwater until his fingers touched the sand rising to the shore. She waited in the ripples at the edge of the water with a green coconut cut ready for drinking. A scarlet hibiscus nodded in the nut's drinking hole. Beside her Tamahere watched with head cocked and one eye closed against the sun.

She put the flower behind Fletcher's ear and guided him off the baking beach and into the cool fringe. He had been honest about the mutiny and about his fear of her reaction and she knew Fletcher was sailing soon but he refused to tell her anything more.

She longed for escape from Tahiti, but not at any price and it was time to discover what might happen to her now Fletcher really was captain. A dream come true? Possibly not when she saw he kept the ship as a prison for everyone else aboard. And it was a ship only of men.

Their intimacy was quickly recovered but his secrecy about where he planned to settle made her wonder what else Fletcher might be lying about.

'Do you want me to come with you, Fletcher?'

'I do. You *are* coming, aren't you?' She avoided Fletcher's anxious look and countered his question. If she didn't know where they were going, she wouldn't know who she was. In Tahiti she knew, because she understood what must be done each day, who must be fed, who must be honoured. Fletcher assured her she would have to honour only him.

'How I would live, in England?'

'It can't be England, for reasons you know.'

'But you said I would be an English lady.'

'No. I said an English officer's lady. His only one.' She thought his answers unsatisfactory.

'Well, soon then. Soon I will tell you...' She reached for the hibiscus and tried to put it back behind his ear. They tumbled like frisky puppies as the flower was comically pushed and pulled until Tamahere was included in the knot of bodies.

'I am watching you, Titreano,' he said from their twist. 'So you don't take my mother away in your she-ship. I know she wants to go . . .'

'You'd come too, silly,' Mauatua said.

Suddenly Tararo hurried past on the path behind them as fast as his rank would permit, surrounded by servants and followed by chattering others. Tamahere jumped to his feet.

'Look something's happening. Let's go.' Tamahere dragged at her until she was on her feet. Fletcher reached for his musket and then followed.

As they strode inland through Matavai Fletcher would discover areas he'd never seen because of Bligh's restraints. It would be testing for him.

Within minutes his eyes narrowed as he struggled to absorb new smells and sounds and sights, but she hurried him as fast as she could past *fare*, through fruit groves and swampy taro plots, across streams and through low ferns and palms. He insisted on stopping at a small area paved with flat stones that stood in a dark, over-shadowed clearing. At one end bigger stones stood upright on a low platform.

'What is that?' he demanded.

'*Tupuna marae*. A family marae. A place of worship. Every family and kin group has their own.'

They followed until Tararo turned off the main pathway to another dark marae. Behind it was a low hut with slow fires burning outside each corner. A woman constantly threw small pieces of scented wood and oil into the smoulders, making incense of the smoke. Mauatua stopped some way back and explained to Fletcher before he drew attention by asking questions too loudly.

'A birthing hut, for a baby with high ranking blood,' she confided.

'How do you know that?

'The *maire* fern fronds that cover it. Very fragrant, like the scented smoke they join the baby direct to his noble ancestors.'

She held him back from his intent of questioning Tararo, who now stood close to the hut, arms folded. He was listening keenly to the anguish of birth, but she didn't think Fletcher knew that.

Then there was second of silence followed by a single dull thud.

Her eyes never left Fletcher as a man came out of the hut and handed Tararo a bundle wrapped in tapa cloth. He opened it. There was a mess of blood and matter and splinters at one end. Fletcher looked to her for explanation, his face drained and his chest heaving in short bursts as though he might vomit.

She answered quickly. 'The mother is a lower rank than Tararo. Children with blood that crosses ranks are not allowed to live.'

She stopped him confronting Tararo, but she couldn't prevent his loud outburst. 'He's just walking away. Without a thought for his dead baby or for its mother.'

The Tahitians around him laughed, as she knew they would, hurting him with their mockery and derision.

'It must have been a girl,' Tamahere said, reaching up so he could whisper loudly into Fletcher's ear.

'We nearly always kill them.'

CHAPTER 15

'That baby's been murdered. You don't care?' Fletcher took a cue from the laughter and kept his voice down, but his horror was undiminished.

His chest and throat blazed with blood and its heat swept over his face to prickle deep into his scalp.

Mauatua shrugged at him. 'If babies have not taken their first breath or opened their eyes, they have not joined us.'

'Nonsense,' he shouted. 'And the people who do it, Tararo, the mother, the man who . . . They'll go to Hell when they die and will be punished horribly. Don't they care? Do you?' Her nonchalant attitude and his response to what she said confused him. His hands trembled and he stopped her seeing this by grabbing her wrists roughly, demanding a direct answer rather than an evasive Tahitian one.

'Care about what? Why? If I honour the gods and the spirits during my life, I'll have another good life when I join them after I die.' He relaxed his grip a little and shook his head from side to side. It was supposed to clear his mind, but didn't, and he felt the bubbling of sweat appear again.

'You believe there's no punishment in the afterlife, no price to pay for sins committed in this one?'

'Why should there be?' she laughed. 'Punishment for sin comes in this life. But only if you are caught or someone is angry enough to want revenge.'

She slipped her arms out of his hands and walked away from him, pretending, he thought, more hurt than was warranted. Yet there was more than a woman's silly games here.

She must be planning to say something else.

Before he could deflect her expected words, his head jerked up.

His breath stopped. He saw no visions and heard no dread voices of doom, yet he knew with awful clarity he was experiencing a moment of Biblical import.

Mauatua had revealed the simple secret of Tahitian life to him.

Tahitians had no dread of death because there would be no reckoning of the life they had lived. That was the reason for their constant joy and apparent contentment. He came back to the present, breathing again but blinking hard. Could life be as simple as that, so free of the hideous burdens that Christian believers bore so stoically and proudly?

Tahitians must laugh and sing so freely because they knew nothing of the bludgeoning fear of death that so brutalised so many back home.

They believed the opposite of what sustained England's awful industry of priests and ministers.

He wasn't the most religious of men. Yet no man who sailed dared dismiss the dogma of Heaven and Hell, especially when there was no proof either way. What Mauatua believed was very appealing. He could expiate his conscience and cheapen the price of any further sin just by worshipping Tahitian gods rather than the Christian trilogy. He certainly had sin enough to forget, but . . . Surely it couldn't be so easy?

Except, changing what you believed had fuelled the bloody Protestant-Catholic confrontation for centuries.

What if neither of those was right and only Tahitians had the Truth?

He walked away from the crowd that had stayed on to idle and gossip. She had pushed him to the very edge of certainty. He clasped his hands to make their trembling less obvious and then Tamahere pulled at his arm.

He followed but with so much focus on his inner struggle about bludgeoned babies and religion he was barely aware which way he was being tugged.

Suddenly he was bumped and knocked to the ground. It was jogging priests carrying between them the body of a young man with a deep head wound. The swinging corpse, still warm, had hit him. Other priests fought to stop a distraught woman touching the dead youth.

Tamahere clapped his hands. 'If she touches him they have to get another body. You can't have a sacrifice if there's a woman's mark it.' Tamahere hugged his arms tightly to his chest. 'You are seeing all the good things.'

Fletcher stood slowly, barely trusting himself to speak or think.

'Sacrifices?' he asked, brushing himself off without meeting her eyes. He was calm now, perhaps too calm but before Mauatua could answer, Tamahere cheered. The woman had almost touched her son's body.

'This is the Tahiti Bligh didn't let you see,' Mauatua said coldly. 'So you couldn't write a book about us, too.'

'Is it true? What Tamahere said about girl babies?'

Her instinct was to ignore him. She needed time to compose what she would say. This was the moment she had both hoped for and dreaded. She asked her gods to help her, to ensure that what she was about to tell him would tie Fletcher to her forever, finally making him understand her need to flee Tahiti and thus become the resolute ally she wanted him to be.

If not, it would ruin all chance of escape with him.

She walked on quickly to compose herself and then waited until he caught up to her. She spoke without looking at him. She didn't want to see disbelief or contempt in his eyes.

'Here is one of the many things you don't know about Tahiti. Most girls are not allowed to join us unless they are what are most valued. Long size counts, pale skin colour does if they are *ari'i* or *ra'atira*. The skin must be unblemished and all the limbs perfect. No cripples, none who have humped backs or twisted hands or curled feet, none with split lips or swollen heads. Those who are not acceptable do not join us. Of course all this is also true of boy babies.'

She pressed her hand over Fletcher's mouth, afraid of what she might hear and waited for his lips to still.

When she was certain of his silence she continued. 'The perfect girls who live then enslave their mothers. Until they leave home girls eat only food that has been gathered and cooked by their mothers. Then they become victims themselves, of their own daughters. Sons are always more welcome but when sons like Tamahere are grown, they might be ripped from their mothers or wives by priests and sacrificed.'

'I-I never knew, I'm sorry . . .'

Her revelations besieged him. He held his hands to his head, as though trying to push back the beads of sweat she saw dribbling between his fingers. She gave him no comfort but walked on knowing she could vent some of her anger by having to shout back at him.

'Sorry is not enough, Fletcher. Women know *only* sorrow. Mothers, daughters, lovers or wives - Tahiti means nothing to them but sorrow.'

'And men?' He'd raced to catch up.

'Men know *nothing* of sorrow,' she snapped. 'Nothing, except when they are sorry they are not heaping sorrow on to our heads.'

'Why didn't you tell me this?' he demanded. She didn't like the accusing way he spoke or his indignant expression, as though she had been holding back something he expected to be his due.

She couldn't help mocking him. '*Aueeee*, Fletcher Christian! Have I hurt your feelings? Has a woman dared upset a man?'

She blocked his path, standing with her feet apart and her hands on her hips. 'Why didn't I tell you such things, Fletcher Christian?'

She shook a finger at him. 'Because you said you didn't need to know Tahiti's secrets.'

'Then why tell me now?'

'Because now you will be living amongst us, Fletcher Christian.'

She didn't help him when he turned and spewed out all that had been in his stomach. Anyway, she comforted herself, vomiting was shorter and sharper than a sweating attack.

Shouts alerted her that the desperate mother had succeeded. She'd broken through the priests and scratched her son's body. The priests dropped his corpse and kicked her until she too seemed lifeless. Then both were abandoned, one dead, one barely alive and smeared with her dead son's blood.

'Would you want such a life for me? Or for your sons?'

'Yet, you still can't tell me if you want to come with me,' he said, gasping for fresh air. He was still bent with a hand across his diaphragm, heaving to dribble out the last sourness.

She spat her answer. 'If I go and there are Ma'ohi men there, nothing will be different. When people say they are escaping they can't help taking who they are with them. I don't want to find more of it there.'

Fletcher straightened, looked at her icily and spoke with no expression in his voice as he wiped his mouth. 'If that is so, why do you talk so much of escape? How are you going to be different and leave everything behind you, or be different when you are in that new place?'

He grabbed her again.

'You'd better have an answer. Because if not, you'd better forget coming with me.'

She swung her head away, nauseated by the vomit still on his breath. Her instinct was to fight, to punish him for pushing her and saying such words into her face, but she swallowed his angry words and hers. She understood he wasn't threatening to abandon her but setting out the only way she could truly abandon Tahiti.

If she wanted to escape, she would have to leave everything of her old life. If she did not, it was no escape.

Fletcher Christian was a very clever man to force her to see that. Simply sailing with him might not be enough.

Next day she found Fletcher in Bligh's old cabin. He held a handkerchief in each hand and constantly wiped his sweating brow as he turned page after page of book after book. She'd been watching him for what seemed like half a day and although she knew he expected contrition her patience was nearing its end.

'Why are you still searching your tattoos on cloth? What are you looking for, Fletcher?'

'Perhaps the island I've chosen is too close to Tahiti.'

He ran his hands through his dank hair and waved his hands helplessly over the charts. She saw he was frightened, still angry. He thumped his fist onto the table again and again, thundering that he must sail soon and yet couldn't go anywhere until his men had women. His voice dropped and he muttered hoarsely.

'You do understand, don't you Mauatua? Every day I wait here I am in more danger. The king will send ships. They'll be hunting me down.'

She slapped her hand on the cabin bulkhead, as frustrated as he was.

'Don't blame me. How can I bring women to BOUNTY when you won't say where you are going?'

'I can't say. No-one must know. The king's ships would follow us.' He swept books and charts onto the floor. She stepped closer to him, not caring she stood on them and matched his anger.

'Tell me, Fletcher. Tell me and then I'll bring women to sail with you.'

She saw her words were bouncing back at her. She put her mouth to his ear. 'Plenty *vahine* would sail with you to Britain.'

'You want me to hang?'

She was annoyed when Fletcher got that serious. Well, she could be serious too. She told him her girlfriends didn't want to come because then their friends and families wouldn't see them with their *faufa'a*, their metal nails and other special *popa'a* presents.

'That's a silly reason,' Fletcher murmured.

Mauatua shrugged her shoulders. 'Only a man thinks like that.'

Fletcher walked aft and into the ship's greenhouse and then pushed open a leaded window. Alone, uncertain, he doubted a future existed for him at all.

He couldn't rely on Mauatua sailing with him yet he knew he needed her wisdom and skills. Why should she sail? They weren't married. Barely even lovers.

Anyway, he hadn't seen her for days, not since their silly arguments about the past and about what silly girls thought about their silly presents.

A fresh salt breeze stirred the leaves of the potted forest. He focussed his eyes past the reef and the island of Mo'orea to the open sea and sighed for the promise it offered but that he was unlikely to accept.

So far there had been no trouble aboard and no-one had revealed Tubuai as BOUNTY's probable destination. But a ship manned by men kept constantly under guard was not the freedom he sought or likely to attract women aboard.

It was now the third week of June and he had been back in Tahiti over two of those. Once, BOUNTY made Matavai jump with excitement and happy fulfilment. Now she wallowed beneath his feet as an ominous stinking prison. He found it harder to keep discipline in sight of Matavai Bay than it was at sea. He started at every unexpected noise, day or night, fearing he would be mutinied against by men who had seen how easy it could be if there was general support.

Social revolution needed more than his personal resolve and men kept aboard by force. He needed men who wanted change as much as he did, men who could be convinced to follow him willingly.

That was clear but he had no idea how to solve the women problem.

The experience of Tubuai wasn't an encouragement. His ambition of a socially advanced community on a South Pacific island seemed so simple after the mutiny but was already unlikely.

An unfamiliar noise startled him. He spun, pistol in hand, but there was no threat. It was Mauatua and Tamahere.

'We are coming, Fletcher. As I promised, I have nothing of Tahiti to bring. Nothing of the past. Just these, these good things that everyone needs everywhere.' One by one she showed what she had reduced her life to so she could sail away with him. Most were to do with cooking.

Her *penu* was a mortar of dark basalt used for pounding purees of breadfruit or sweet potato, of banana or plantain, on flat surfaces of polished wood or stone. Also hung about her were an adze-like tool of hard wood for splitting coconuts and breadfruit, some large calabashes for holding fresh water, some knife-like blades of bamboo and an *umete* or large shallow, serving dish. Her *'ana* was a small stool with a large pointed shell attached for scraping out the flesh of coconuts and she carried a curved headrest on legs for sleeping that had been painstakingly carved from a single piece of *temanu* wood. Several long, squared and scored batons were her tools for beating out tapa cloth.

'And what's that woven bag over your shoulder?'

'My medicine bag'.

It was held by a cord of twisted hibiscus bark but made of finely woven coconut-palm leaf. She opened it to show her store of healing oils, berries, seeds, nuts and leaves.

'And those tubes around your neck?'

'Scented oils, *monoi,* the ones you like so much. Sandalwood and . . .' She unplugged one of the short sealed bamboo lengths and wafted it under his nose.

'This one is Tahitian gardenia, the one you said was your favourite.'

Behind her Tamahere struggled to drag a tall, bound pile of tapa cloth of different thicknesses and textures, such as any single woman collected.

'These are all I need to live,' she said.

The simplicity of her possessions encouraged Fletcher to believe once more that a comfortable life in the South Seas was an easily achievable goal. Once cooking, eating and sleeping could be solved everything else was a bonus.

Then suspicion erupted. What ordeals from the past was she keeping hidden from him, in her head? What if her hatred of Tahitian men was simply transferred to him and to whatever he did that didn't please her?

In an instant he determined to put all such worry aside. He would have to trust her. There would be no home for him in the South Pacific unless he could rely on the self-interest of Mauatua and other women.

Even if Mauatua never became something more than an intimate friend he was doomed without her.

On the other hand, he believed that with her beside him any ambition was capable of achievement. He was a stranger in her world, but when he added the advantages of his world they would create something never before seen on earth.

Only one concern lingered to trouble his thoughts. Surely her son Tamahere was something from the past that she should have left behind.

Mauatua's decision persuaded others. Tee joined and then seven more women came aboard. Eight men volunteered, followed by a gang of ten loutish adolescents, newly tattooed and keen to thrust themselves against whatever challenges this new world could bring. She pleaded once more.

'What can I tell them, Fletcher?'

'Nothing, Mauatua. It is a secret. On pain of death.'

Fletcher would never know, but his determined secret excited her. Voyages with no certain outcome were in her blood. That was how the first Ma'ohi landed on Tahiti. Sailing away on BOUNTY was the same. Not knowing was part of the adventure, actually *was* the adventure. And she seemed to have more of that need boiling in her blood than others.

As BOUNTY once again bucked against the long, slow Pacific swell, she stood on deck and released every one of her buried invectives against the island and its men. There was no care that those who heard her cursing and swearing were astonished a woman of her rank knew such language. She pulled up her skirts, turned and wiggled her bare, tattooed buttocks at the island in an irrevocable insult, the *tipou*.

Tararo and his handsome younger cousin Niau had come aboard at the last moment and the older noble was now first to congratulate her.

'Just as well curses by women don't come true. What would happen to us, eh *tane?*' She watched impassively as Tararo turned to the other men, grabbed his testicles and screwed up his face as though in great pain. Other men danced around him, aping his noise and movements.

She hoped the women watching knew that if there was a joke it was on the comical men.

CHAPTER 16

For the next three days and nights Mauatua believed the gods and spirits of Tahiti were wreaking revenge for her *tipou*. Mountains of water hurled over the decks of BOUNTY, throwing spume high into the close-reefed sails. However the ship reared, rolled or pitched on wave crests, however hard it flopped to flounder in the deep troughs between them, there was always more rage to come.

She'd never imaged such fury from the sea and the blood blanched from her face until she was as pale as white men. But she was determined never to be enslaved by Tahiti's gods or their spite again. Whenever it was possible to move safely she buried her fears beneath a veil of concern, for seasickness struck almost everyone aboard, and she alone seemed capable of tending them.

The storm flushed out Hitihiti, a young *ari'i* from Bora Bora, and his retinue of youths. They had stowed away because they heard the ship carried too many men and feared being refused if they applied properly. She added them to her self-sorry patients.

The ship's Ark of terrified animals on the exposed Main Deck needed as much attention. With 300 pigs penned on board, those already fallen were trampled by the others, doubling their terrified screaming, a horrible, high counter point to the bellowing of the outraged bull who refused all her blandishments to make him lie down. The cow had safely buckled but bellowed ceaselessly. However she struggled to pen them more tightly, the goats skated and scattered and bleated. Dozens of hysterical hens flapped and squawked at her and roosters leapt at her with vicious spurs whirling.

There was little she could do above or below decks without help but anyone not seasick was under orders from Fletcher to help sail the ship.

These conditions would change, but when? Swallowing the fear in her throat, she pinched and slapped her face until she felt it coloured with blood again. Then she dragged herself along a rain-sodden safety line.

'How much longer, Fletcher?' she begged, as he and Mills struggled with the tiller against the sea's fury.

'We'll sight Tubuai tomorrow morning,' he shouted and then saw Tamahere racing along the safety line after his mother.

'Get that little bastard back below decks!' he yelled, waving his arms in exasperation as he left the tiller.

'He only wants to be a sailor like you,' she retorted, just as angrily.

'It's too dangerous up here.' BOUNTY corkscrewed. The rudder jerked the tiller savagely, throwing Mills to the deck.

'If that had been your son he would have been hurled over the side.'

Mauatua shrugged. Perhaps Tamahere might have held on tighter, but she didn't dare say so. So she waited silently, blinking rain from her eyes and holding her son to her. She could see there were fewer black clouds and the wind seemed to be gusting less.

She kept pointing until Fletcher reluctantly left the tiller again and fixed her and the boy with a raised finger. 'Don't let him move.'

He took a light line from the binnacle behind them and awkwardly tied it around Tamahere's waist, irately wishing the boy wore clothing. He crabbed across the deck and hitched the other end to the closer of the port-side four-pounder cannons.

Tamahere ran as soon as Fletcher's hands left him. She watched proudly as her son precisely judged the pitch and rolling of BOUNTY and navigated the length of the deck without collision. It made her laugh to see her son bravely shout and jump and wave his arms at the ship's menagerie. But the enraged bull spun and reared towards him, his flaming eyes flaring open and his mouth foaming. Fletcher jerked the rope harshly and yanked the boy off his feet. As he pulled him back, the ship's snub bow pitched violently back from a boiling chasm of ocean. The lunging beast's huge rear quarters twisted violently on the slurry of excreta and sea water and his enormous bulk thundered on to the deck where Tamahere had stood.

Fletcher grabbed the struggling boy by one arm and swiftly hacked him free with his knife.

'Down. Now. Stay there!' He slapped Tamahere hard on the bare buttocks to hurry him below decks.

'Don't hit my son!' she screamed, running forward and grabbing Fletcher's punishing hand. He twisted and reversed her grip cruelly.

'He will be hit whenever he deserves it. I am *not* going to live totally your way. Some things have to be *our* way, *my* way. Like England.'

It was the first time she'd felt threatened by him. She was scared by his anger but she couldn't let him get away with this. The wrinkled twists of skin either side of his grasp were white and burning and she was losing the feeling in her hand. She had to protest, but to a fuming man in these sailing conditions a slight barb might seem like a spear thrust, and then what would he do to her?

Her challenging glare stayed on his hand around her wrist until she felt his eyes were there, too. Although shaking with cold and uncertainty she spoke as normally as she could. 'So! We must have things from *your* past, must we? That's allowed, is it?'

Fletcher's grip loosened. She had pricked his arrogant certainty but couldn't afford to show any regret for this. She tossed her head, only just suppressing a cough of derision.

'In that case, so must I bring my past.'

She wrenched her arm free and stood back, rubbing circulation into her wrist. She dared one more jibe, a stab with the same poison as his words.

'Some things must be *my* way too, Fletcher Christian. And that means Tamahere and what *I* think best for him.'

She ran after her son, desperate to feel his arms at her neck but wondering if she might ever feel Fletcher's there again.

When Fletcher was relieved at the tiller he came directly to his cabin with a thundering face. Mauatua twisted away from him, holding Tamahere out of his reach as he shouted at them.

'I'm not going to apologise. That boy could have been killed!'

She couldn't resist his strength when he pulled at her shoulders to confront Tamahere. 'We'll never get that bull up. He's probably dead of a heart attack.'

Tamahere buried his head in her breasts but Fletcher took it between his hands, slowly pulling the boy away and holding him until she and her son showed less fear. His voice softened but she heard such steely determination that dread choked her throat again. She furrowed her brow and narrowed her eyes, focussed on defence if he threatened to beat either of them again.

'Two things you must both understand,' he said, following her nervy, darting eyes. 'No-one must come between me and the safety of this ship. It is, until better days, our home. I do not wish it to be anyone's coffin.'

'There is something else. Something else I will protect with my life.' She flinched when he bent closer. 'Nothing and no-one must come between *us*, Mauatua. Nothing and no-one.'

The significance of his pledge darted directly to her heart and heated it with pleasure. With a man like this, even half the freedoms she wanted would be enough.

When he leaned further forward to *ho'i*, his wet hair and clothes mingled with the sweetness of his breath to create a unique intimacy. She knew she would never find another man like Fletcher Christian and to keep him there would be costs to her.

For months he had lived her life on Tahiti. And now she must live his until they found a home of their own. It was fair that if Tamahere hindered or endangered that . . .

Fletcher pulled her out of his cabin and through the doors of the lobby where Bligh had dined and on into the open space of the Forward Lower Deck that was the mess and sleeping quarters for most on board.

There was no sweetness of air there. Instead, trapped by the battened hatch, it was thick with the stench of vomit and the spilled urine and excrement of the seasick who lay in hammocks or on the deck. Holding her under one arm he bellowed so he could be heard over the ocean beating at BOUNTY's hull.

'These are my priorities. None of you should ever forget them. First, Mauatua. Then this ship. And only then your life or mine. In that order.' When he was certain he was understood he turned and left.

Tee had been renamed Jenny by Mills. She heaved herself onto the floor beside Mauatua in Fletcher's cabin.

'So, *vahine*. That make you, Mrs Christian?'

'I don't know – yes I do. I'm not. He's never asked. We don't even, well, you know . . . And he hasn't given me an English name. Like you are called Jenny.'

She felt foolish and blushed like a child. Jenny pursed her lips. She dropped her head into her chins, the way she did when she made decisions.

'Don't you dare,' Mauatua said, with little conviction.

Fletcher woke her, nuzzling her with his beard the way she liked.

'Isabella,' he whispered. 'Isabella.'

She sat up, trying to clear her head. 'What, what is that word?'

'A name I would like to give you. Isabella. You like it?'

She did. She could say it, but *Itavera* is how Ma'ohi would struggle to say it. Only English men and women would call her Isabella. That made it very special and she forgave Tee for forcing Fletcher. Even so, giving and taking names was a serious thing. She couldn't simply say thank you. What if there was another Isabella living?

Fletcher was embarrassed, slurring his answer. 'Yes, Isabella Curwen. I expected to marry her. A cousin some years younger than me.'

She folded her arms and pulled away from him.

'Did she have land?'

She saw him preparing to dissemble so she said nothing until he felt obliged to fill the accusing silence with the truth.

Marrying Isabella Curwen would have put him right up with the riches and position of his first-cousin John, the head of the Christian family. Isabella would have brought a mansion at Workington with her. Plus coal mines and farms. Even Belle Isle, a round house on an island in Lake Windemere that was named after her. But she was too young, a school girl. So he sailed with the Navy to India. When he got back she'd eloped with cousin John. She was still only 17. John was in his 30s.

'That when you wrote those letters to Bligh?' she asked. When Fletcher eventually spoke, she might not have been there.

'I can see myself in the big houses, with the hounds and the horses and carriages. I can. But now I think I need a different sort of woman from Isabella.'

'Different from *that* Isabella, you mean!'

The ship's bell rang for a watch change before he could answer. He shook his head, disassociating himself from her accusation and left without another word.

Why his confusion and mumbling she wondered? Did he see her as a second Isabella Curwen? Was he expecting her to give him back what he'd lost? What if he still loved that first Isabella?

The storm faded and the ship settled but she was awake and unlikely to sleep. She had finally escaped Tahiti thanks to Fletcher Christian. But what was her future with him? In spite of his public declaration she would be foolish to rely on a man whose mind seemed shaped only by loss and anguish, by his lost father, his lost love, his lost home, lost financial and social position and now a lost career.

Oh yes, and the sweating he thought lost him all chance of normal relationships with women.

She decided he could call her Isabella only in private, until she was certain the first was forgotten. But could Mrs Christian ever be more than a name, would she ever be a true wife to him?

Her lips puffed with a short breath of dismissal and a more beguiling question occurred, one that brought with it a twisting smile.

Now she had left Tahiti its so-called gods and spirits should have nothing to do with her future.

Her future was more a matter of what she could get Fletcher Christian to do for her. The smile remained as she at last fell asleep.

Cousin Isabella Curwen, who married John Christian, Fletcher's first cousin and head of the Christian family. Here she is seen with Belle Isle, her round house on a private island on Lake Windemere. Fletcher called Mauatua Isabella at one time, reflecting the fact he had wanted to marry his heiress cousin himself but was thwarted when she eloped at 17.

CHAPTER 17

'Plenty to eat, eh *vahine*? Lots of pig meat.' Mauatua and the recovering Ma'ohi women stood on deck assessing the dead animals. Overnight the carcass of the bull slid forward to squeeze the pigs tighter together. Pillowed and cushioned by one another the pigs survived what the bull could not. In the end only four pigs died and one goat.

She had developed a taste for spit-roasted pork. Tahiti's pit ovens sealed in the steam of cooking and rarely produced totally crisp skin. Pigs roasted before an open fire could be burned on the outside but still raw in the middle. Pork spit-roasted in front of BOUNTY'S great metal oven was constantly turned by a sort of magic. The heat from the fire somehow drove wheels and these turned the meat constantly so few juices escaped, the skin was crisp and the meat cooked through. Best of all, the ship was flooded with fragrance.

'I heard that.' Tararo joined the women with Hitihiti. 'No, no pork for women, it's not allowed.' He turned to Hitihiti for peer support, who agreed, saying *pua'a* was just for men, to make them strong lovers.

Mauatua feigned ignorance. 'That's not something I've experienced, have you, Jenny?'

'News to me, too. Most buggers would need to eat a whole one, and that'd mean they'd just go to sleep.'

'What? Even sooner than usual?' joked one of the women.

Tararo shouted over the laughter that his women never ate pork, that it had always been forbidden.

'Except when you wanted something,' Mauatua countered loudly.

'Then I bet you sneaked pork home. Just the way you did for your favourite dog.'

The women howled with laughter at the insight she dared to air. Tararo and Hitihiti straightened their shoulders and looked out to the horizon.

She waited for the women's laughter to finish and then challenged the two nobles.

'Now, you listen good to what I say. I am on this ship because no man is ever going to treat me like a dog again.' The men snickered at each other and turned away.

'Don't do that when I am talking to you.' Her threatening tone stopped the men. They turned with bored resignation in their eyes.

'Talk as much as you like, Mauatua,' Tararo said. 'Women do not eat pork, not when I am around, not when Hitihiti is around. It has been like this for generations.'

She eyed them carefully. 'I see. Not as long as you are around. Is that right? There's an easy answer to that.' She turned her head and winked at the women. 'Don't be around!'

The women crowded behind her offering physical if not vocal support but the nobles hustled forward, raising their arms and jostling the women with their elbows. Other Ma'ohi men joined them and the jeering mob herded the women onto the ship's rail. Just as slaps and punches were imminent two shots whistled past their ears.

Fletcher gave the smoking pistols to Ned. Ned cocked two more and handed those to Fletcher. Tararo opened his mouth to speak but Fletcher pointed a pistol directly at him.

'I want to hear the women's version first.' He flicked his head for Mauatua to speak. She told him it was a small thing, that the nobles had made an understandable error.

Tararo was aggressive. 'We do not make errors.'

'That was one.' Fletcher countered, the aim of his pistol unwavering.

'Now, Mauatua, you were saying.'

He listened carefully as she explained the nobles made what she diplomatically called the understandable mistake of insisting that, because women were forbidden to eat pork on their home islands, it should not be allowed on BOUNTY.

'Women not eat pork on this ship? That's nonsense.' Fletcher shoved the pistols into Ned's hands. 'This has to be settled. But we'll do it agreement, not by confrontation like this.'

He made his proposal very clear. Mauatua and Tararo would each speak for five minutes. After another five minutes to talk among themselves, each Ma'ohi man and woman would stand behind the person they supported, for or against women eating pork. Mauatua protested there were over 20 Ma'ohi men but only nine women.

'Then you will have to speak particularly well.'

Tararo spoke first, saying it was wrong that guests in the South Pacific questioned the customs of those who belonged there.

He strutted and struck challenging poses, as though calling men to war, careful not to insult BOUNTY or Fletcher Christian, but insisting the old ways should be honoured. He ended classically, striding away and standing still for some time. Then he relaxed and turned back, released from the spell of his words.

When she was a child Mauatua had listened from the surrounding bushes and trees as her father and grandfather, both revered orators, spoke during marae ceremonies. She knew the spoken rhythms that were most persuasive, the changes of pitch and pace that demanded attention, how to use pauses to create tension. She had always thought she would be as good as men but had never had the opportunity.

Cursing Tahiti's men had encouraged her.

When Tararo finished she walked to a central point on the deck. She looked out over the sea and tossed and nodded her head as though arguing with herself. And then she thundered, rising to greater heights of passion and injury than she had reached when sailing from Tahiti.

Once more she outlined the iniquities of women's position in Tahiti and the lack of respect they endured.

'Not one warrior would fight if a woman had not endured the pain and indignities of his birth. Thus, not a single Ma'ohi warrior, not one Ma'ohi worker, not one Ma'ohi noble landowner should withhold a single pleasure from a single woman, from any women. And certainly not from a woman who has carried his children in her body, bled and hurt to bring them into this world and then fed them from her body.

A woman should have more, not less, of the pleasures of the sea and the land.'

The Ma'ohi men grumbled at her affront to tradition but she dismissed them with a sweep of her arm.

'The world is not ordered the way men bully us into believing.

'Without women's pain there would be no men. That is the way this world is ordered.'

Many of the Ma'ohi men and women giggled, some laughed outright. She expected that. All were startled to see a woman speak with the passion and skills of a man. When the men's outrage had subsided and there was no more muttering from them she spun and pointed a discomforting finger

'I know you men's response to this. You are saying: This is not the way decreed by the Gods.

'Is it? Is it really? Have Gods ever spoken directly to women to tell them pork is forbidden? Do Gods invite women onto a marae to put into our ears what you say are their holy judgments? They do not. Because women go to a marae only when they are born, in the hours they are still learning to breathe. There they are given their sacred family name, by men. After that all they know of the marae is what men tell them. What *men* tell them, not what Gods tell them.

'No woman will ignore laws meant to honour or protect her or her children. But why should she respect laws that demean and devalue and dominate her, laws imposed not by Gods but by men?

'Why should women dance and sing for men around the fires of a roasting pig, dance with its smell in our nostrils and then have to please men between our legs with pig on their breath and fat on their chins? Yet not eat it?

'We will eat pork. And tuna and turtle and shark and everything else men say is forbidden to us. We will eat these foods. Not because we wish to defy these noble *ari'i*. But because we believe the Gods made we women equal to men. If there are Gods.

'Until the time these Gods speak directly to forbid us, until that time I will eat pork and other women will, too.

'Those who agree will stand behind me.'

Hitihiti at once pushed all the Ma'ohi men and women to stand behind Tararo. Jenny berated the women and dragged them away, but Fletcher stopped her, saying the choice must be free. Mauatua whispered to Jenny.

'Dogs. Use the dogs.'

'It is a simple choice, my sisters' Jenny said, emboldened and speaking louder than she had ever done. 'Do you wish to be treated like dogs, grateful for the leftovers men throw you? Or do you wish to be women?

'And, you my noble brothers. Where is the warrior in treating women like animals? Where is the *mana*, the authority and wisdom, so proudly inherited from your fathers and grandfathers?'

'They did the same. It is the way.' Tararo was sulking already.

'That is not an argument. That is fear of change,' said Jenny defiantly.

She paced back and forth but kept her eyes continuously on the nobles.

What did their grandfathers, their *tupuna tane* know of ships like BOUNTY, of men like Fletcher Christian, she demanded? If they had known them, might they not have taught a man is only superior when he respects women, that it was not noble for men to treat women as only a canoe to ride when the tide pleased them?'

Then Hitihiti surprised everyone on deck. He came forward and spoke thoughtfully, walking in slow circles.

'I left Bora Bora because I wanted to hear new things, to see new things,' he said. 'I am again with new sorts of men and again on a sailing ship from Peretane. And now I hear of a new way of deciding. Where we nobles no longer alone bear the burden of wrong decisions. This is interesting to me. So was Jenny's argument that our grandfathers knew nothing about ships like this or about *popa'a* men.

'I regret, Tararo, I no longer think it's important to forbid women to eat pork. I do not say you or we are wrong. I say we are in this unfortunate position because of the mistaken decisions of others who came before us.'

Hitihiti stood behind Mauatua and his acolytes followed him, so the number of men was equal on both sides. She acknowledged his speech and his support with the smallest nod of her head. A few of the young men from Tahiti joined her too, bragging suggestively about how they expected to be repaid by the women.

Sensing possible defeat Tararo puffed his chest with bluster.

'Where I come from it is *ari'i* that make such decisions. Others follow. Mr Christian is *ari'i* of this ship. If he says women should . . .'

'What he says is there will be a vote,' Fletcher interrupted.

Bored by now, one of the younger men behind Tararo put his hands up like paws, stuck out his tongue and panted. Others followed or mimed feeding pork into their mouths. The sharper youths barked. When Tararo laughed at the yapping boys, the women looked to Mauatua who lifted an eye brow. They scurried to stand behind her, giving her a clear majority.

'It was good for the nobles to see other women as determined as you. They were surprised by that.' Fletcher clasped her to him.

'So were some of the women,' she said.

She felt him stroking her hair with the back of his hand. It covered her ears now. She shook her head so she could feel her hair's new weight settling back. 'Very nice,' he said. 'It suits you – will you grow it even longer? I'd like that, very much.'

Mauatua trembled under his touch. For the first time she was certain, absolutely, in every part of her body. Fletcher Christian would allow her to be the woman she dreamed.

She laughed at herself. Imagine loving a man, following a man, because he liked her to have long hair.

CHAPTER 18

Mauatua wanted the ship thoroughly scrubbed before they broached Tubuai's reef, declaring no island would offer hospitality if BOUNTY contaminated their lagoon with torrents of animal waste. It hadn't occurred to Fletcher and he stood by awkwardly while the ship did Mauatua's bidding. The animals and their pens were sluiced, the decks scoured. Every hatch was opened along the deck, every sky light and window unlatched in the green house. She was encouraged to see the stiffest of the ship's company relax, enjoying the sense of domesticity buoyed by having nine women aboard.

At the same time she oversaw a big dinner for noon and was proud of the respect and co-operation she now enjoyed from men who once thought the galley their exclusive preserve. She and Jenny baked yams and sweet potatoes and plantains in the closed oven, and produced *po'e*, traditional recipes of pounded banana or vegetable and coconut, in a fraction of the time they took in an earth oven. There was still plenty of wine from Tenerife in the hold, and Fletcher brought up flagons for the mess tables, pleased to have a task.

She couldn't persuade the company to eat together. The Ma'ohi ate on deck, sitting cross-legged and apart from one another, not just sex apart from sex, but separate enough so the constant batting away of insects with their individual fly swats did not disturb a neighbour. She joined them as they dipped each mouthful into fresh sea water from coconut halves or bowls and mugs taken from the galley.

Then most slept where they had eaten. One deck below, the sated English sailors sang after their meal until most were also asleep.

Only Fletcher and the few lookouts were alert and armed.

BOUNTY dropped anchor just inside the reef in the middle of the afternoon. 'How do they speak here?' Mauatua asked him.

'A bit like Tahiti. Better ask Peter. He took notes.'

'Let me welcome them, Fletcher. Tararo and Hitihiti should be beside me. It is a matter of kinship and blood. These people must at least know of Taputapuatea, the most sacred marae on Raiatea. Even if not, they will know of our common ancestors. They will respect our kin lines.'

'And what will I do? I am the captain, you might remember.' She ignored the testy sharpness in his voice.

'You should remember, we are of this world,' she said, pointing to Tararo and Hitihiti. 'But we will make you seem a God. I'll only be your messenger, your mouth in this world.'

'Can you do that, as a woman I mean?' he asked, increasingly huffy at the way she was dominating the day. 'Will they respect you?'

'Bloodlines are powerful,' she assured him. 'No man dares argue against them. My kin lines are not as splendid as Tararo and Hitihiti. They are *ari'i*. I am only *ra'atira*. I may not wear red feathers.'

'Thus, we should stand before you, not behind you,' Tararo claimed.

'Yes, you could, my lord, but can you speak in the tongue of Tubuai?'

'Can you?'

She held up her arms in apparent supplication. 'By the grace and wisdom, by the all-pervading love . . . *and* the notebook of Peter – I can!'

Fletcher was hurt and obsessed by Mauatua's sudden authority yet could find no reason to resist it. Her oration in defence of eating pork had given her too much confidence. Now she was dictating the way his ship connected with Tubuai.

If this showed the true woman, what did it mean for him?

He traced the arches of his tattoo through his clothes but none told him that he should challenge her.

Sudden drums signalled the departure of the flotilla from the beach. Fletcher ordered the Europeans on board into their uniform jackets. Mauatua conferred with Tararo and Hitihiti.

'That is not a threat beat,' she announced. 'Not in any of our islands, anyway. Now, everyone must do as I say. Jenny, bring up those parcels of cooked pork. All of them.'

What parcels of pork? Whose ship was this? What happened to voting? His new view of Mauatua soured further. She saw his displeasure.

Yes, she agreed brusquely, perhaps she should have explained her plan. What was more important, she demanded, to keep the ship safe or to waste time talking?

'I know how deceitful Ma'ohi can be,' she explained. 'We must accept nothing at face value.

'When I say so, fire a musket or pistol, and first get everyone to line the rails, all round the ship, very even. Anything ceremonious will show we respect them.' He agreed this would look very impressive but peevishly added he should have thought of it.

Mauatua ignored his disguised rebuke and took a few red feathers from Traro and Hitihiti and put them on to his hat.

'Now, you must stand very still, with your arms folded. After you fire the musket nothing must appear to affect you until you are asked to speak.'

Mauatua, Fletcher and the nobles stood together at the midship rail. All round BOUNTY men stood to attention in their uniform jackets, evenly spaced from one another. The fleet was half way across the lagoon, which shimmered with the afternoon heat and reflected the long thin banners flown from every canoe.

'Remember,' she said, 'do only what I say. They will slow down soon.' When they did she turned to him and shouted. 'Fire!'

The single shot paralysed the Tubuaians. Men fell, expecting they were hit. Some canoes tried to turn back but collided with others. When the Tubuaians saw no blood spilled, they continued approaching BOUNTY.

'The nearest four men, stand very close to each cannon,' Mauatua ordered. Their quick movements ensured the flotilla focussed on these men and the cannons. She stepped in front of Fletcher and cried the traditional Ma'ohi greeting, pitching her voice high so it carried further.

'*Haere, haere mai. Haere, haere mai, haere mai.*'

Her voice held the last word every time, letting it fade slowly, so the sounds swooped and fell through the tropical air like courting birds. She welcomed the flotilla again and again. It would not be considered a proper greeting in Tahiti, wasn't the full formal salutation Tubuai's priests and nobles would expect, but Mauatua gambled on being direct rather making a mistake in formalities.

When the canoes came close enough to see the faces in them, she trembled her out-stretched hands, a traditional feature of Tahitian greeting she hoped would be understood by the Tubuaians. She heard no other sounds from BOUNTY and no acknowledgement or welcome had come from the Tubuaians.

She warned Fletcher. 'They might think they can take the ship. They could have fire hidden, and dip spears into it.' Fletcher dropped his arms.

'That would be a disaster.'

'Keep your arms folded,' she snapped.

She pitched her voice even higher.

'*Haere mai ta'ma'a*' she called. '*Haere mai ta'ma'a*'. BOUNTY's company recognised this as the most important welcome of all, an invitation to eat.

She signalled for the parcels of warm and cold roasted pork wrapped in banana leaf to be lowered over the side on lengths of twine. The leading double canoes approached. There was sniffing, touching. She called, again and again.

'*Haere mai ta'ma'a! Haere mai ta'ma'a!*'

'What's their problem?' Fletcher asked. She reminded him there were no pigs on the island and no Tubuaian had eaten pork flesh on board. These people had no way to make the connection.

Fletcher lifted his hat to her.

The canoe with the biggest and most ornate platform came close to BOUNTY. A tall young man pushed two priests ahead of him. One of them took a parcel of pork. After much smelling and touching the bravest of the priests tore off some meat and put it into his mouth. His eyes widened and he trembled his head in disbelief. He pushed more and more of the flesh and the crisp skin into his mouth and began to laugh, so that fat and saliva dribbled down his chin.

Mauatua told Fletcher it was alright for him to laugh too, and soon most of BOUNTY was laughing at the priest's slobbering enjoyment. Quickly all those on the platform tore open parcels and were soon eating and laughing in equal disbelief. They called to other canoes that then hustled to take more of the dangling packages. Hundreds of men dropped weapons and fought instead to be among the first to eat this new food.

When she saw the highest levels of amazement reached, she called a different greeting.

''*Ahani, 'ahani, paha ho'i 'Ahani*! Listen to that I wish to say.'

BOUNTY and the Tubuaians fell silent but few Tubuaians stopped eating. She dropped her pitch and spoke formally and then she introduced the ship and herself and the nobles in the more accepted Ma'ohi way.

'Now, you speak, Fletcher,' she commanded. 'Speak slowly in English. Tell them what you want. I will translate.'

CHAPTER 19

'I am Christian. I am paramount chief of this floating *motu*, this island that carries all that is needed for life.' She translated in long cadences and with great ceremony, so Fletcher slowed and deepened his voice. He didn't always continue immediately when she finished, but stood still and silent, enjoying his unchallenged dominance.

'I bring you messages and gifts from King George, *ari'i nui* of Great Britain. His kingdom is many times the size of your land, tenfold and then a hundred times more of that tenfold. He lives where the sun and the moon go when they are not in the world of the Ma'ohi.'

Fletcher pointed at the cannons. 'All King George's great canoes have such mouths, mouths that can keep the peace, or make war.' The Tubuaians reacted for the first time and an angry chatter swelled and subsided.

Mauatua whispered to Fletcher it was time to present the Tubuaians with their first live young pig. To demonstrate profound respect for Tubuai's nobles, Tararo and Hitihiti had been chosen to lower the piglet. She told him what to say next, but Fletcher found it more difficult to speak her words than his own.

'We have more *pua'a*. These red-feathered nobles of the Ma'ohi people of other islands join King George in bringing pigs to *all* the people of Tubuai. In future days your families will always eat the fragrant meat you now taste for the first time.'

Once they finished poking and prodding the tiny suckling pig, and were weary of trying to make comical squeals the way it did, a priest on the first canoe called a response to their visitors.

'We beg for the honour and privilege of giving King George of Britain gifts from our land. We are very poor. But we understand the honour of your presence and the value of your gifts. Ask and it shall be given.'

Fletcher was excited by the prospect of success. He spoke in Tahitian, confusing his audience.

'His Majesty wants nothing for himself. He asked us only to find the best Ma'ohi people and then to live with them.'

Mauatua slapped a hand over his mouth. 'English, only English.'

Behind him, BOUNTY's men were as outraged by her as he was. But she was smiling. There was no malice in what she did. Fletcher apologised, happy to be corrected, and spoke in English again, saying they would share the land and water of Tubuai, that they would share the mouths that kill, the *pua'a*, the tools that do not break, cloth made from the hair of animals, liquid that burned to make clear light.

The tall young man on the platform of the biggest canoe stepped forward. Fletcher tried to follow her long conversation with him, punctuated with excesses of compliment, apology and promise and then did as she asked and let down the last package of pork directly into his hands.

'We've done it,' she announced. 'There is no paramount chief on the island, but three separate chiefs. This one is Tamatoa, chief of half the island. The other two have much less land. He invites us to his district and to find a place to live, "so we can grow old together and so our children and their children's children can share the gifts and bounty of King George of Britain" blah blah and so on.'

She wanted Fletcher to acknowledge this. He thought quickly and then clicked his heels and saluted her. He repeated both directly to Tamatoa. Tamatoa's reaction was to laugh, to laugh at this thing he had never seen before. He turned to his retinue and copied the salute and more merriment followed.

'Are they mocking me?'

'Have you learned nothing, Fletcher? Ma'ohi do not like to lose face by not understanding. We laugh because it gives us time to understand.'

When the Tubuaians returned to shore Mauatua collapsed to sit on the deck, her head against the coiled lines that hung from the pegs along the rail. Fletcher stood over her, his face shining with pride.

'That was brilliant Mauatua. We couldn't have done this without you.'

Tararo pushed Hitihiti forward to speak. 'This is very dangerous, Fletcher. You are our friend and so we must tell you.'

'What? We shouldn't trust the Tubuaians?'

'No, Mauatua. She should not have the honour to speak for us.'

'But she is bloody marvellous!' Fletcher sat and put an arm around her but she tossed it off. Hitihiti spoke as though she wasn't there.

'That is why it's dangerous, Fletcher. This is why there are laws about women. If there were no rules, we men would be nothing. Women would tell us everything to do. It is not the proper way.'

'You are afraid of strong women?' Fletcher asked.

'Of course not. Well, yes . . . But, we are protected from them. By many ancient laws.'

'But there are many *ari'i* women who speak out,' he said.

'They would not act as Mauatua. She is telling you what to do.'

'That is because she knows my mind better than I do. She explains my mind to me when I don't understand what it wants me to do.'

He recognised he had picked up the Ma'ohi custom of laughing when embarrassed or in doubt.

'Anyway, I like it. But, you have made me think. It's my mother's fault I suppose. All my life, anyway since I was four and my father died, the greatest influence in my life was a woman. My older brothers were away most of the time. Authority was in her hands. My mother was the person who taught me . . .'

'I am not your mother, Fletcher.' She strode to the companionway, halting before she went down. 'What can be wrong with women talking or acting? What if they are better? What if they know more?'

Tararo dismissed her with a flourish of hands. He reminded Hitihiti there were only nine women on board and they both had higher rank than any of them.

'True,' said Hitihiti. 'But one of them is Mauatua.'

She sat alone amongst the trees and humidity of the greenhouse, taking comfort from the rich aromas of the damp earth and animal compost of the pots. For some hours that afternoon she had been the woman she imagined, a woman doing something because she was better than a man.

As good, anyway.

So, why was she sitting alone, feeling like a naughty child?

'*Auee, vahine.*' Jenny shouted from the doorway. 'There you are. That was some show.' Mauatua barely acknowledged her.

'Leave me alone, eh girl? My head is not well.'

They sat together for a whole minute. She was collecting her thoughts and imagining Jenny's. Eventually, she wanted to share her mind.

'I don't know why I was allowed to do all that.'

'Allowed?'

'I'm not the only one who could have spoken. Fletcher speaks good Tahitian. Some of the others could have done it too, Peter . . .'

'He's hardly old enough to have hairs on his *hua*.'

They laughed together. She felt their bonds warming and tightening.

'You know that for sure, do you, girl?' True or false, the idea of tall, big-breasted, broad-hipped Jenny having the new-dropped testicles of the thin, white youth in her hands was enough to start them both laughing until they couldn't see for tears.

'Go on, tell me,' Jenny said. Mauatua found it easier after the laughter. 'It's Fletcher. I'm not sure why he let me do it.'

'Did you forget already? Fletcher said you had to come first.'

'I know, I know. But this was different. Coming first mustn't mean being a mother to him, or taking his place as a leader. I don't want him as a son, or for him to be dependent on me. I want him to be the leader, or my equal partner. . .'

'Too many wants, *vahine*?'

Once Jenny left Mauatua's mind quickly dismissed her introspection. Instead it was tangled by the practical tasks to be faced on Tubuai. Her relationship with Fletcher was secondary to finding somewhere safe to live. She didn't think Fletcher understood what was before him.

Did he even know how Ma'ohi built their houses?

Well into the night Mauatua woke with a start. Of all the extraordinary events of the day, one had invaded her dreams, demanding the attention she had not given it when awake.

What did Fletcher call it? A vote? Voting?

Fletcher stretched with his hands under his head. For the first time the night guards' duty was to stop boarders rather than escapers. BOUNTY was secure and the men said they were looking forward to life on Tubuai. He dared to believe his vision of somewhere safe to live might be possible.

As long as Mauatua was there. But would she be, and as what?

He didn't see her as somehow taking the place of his mother, he was certain of that. She was more like a brother or sister. Maybe that was all she wanted, and that was *her* problem. She had taken control of the first meeting with Tubuaians so effortlessly.

What else might she do to achieve what she wanted? Might she want to take his place? Might she not want him at all?

It was bewildering to think about these personal problems when there was a colony to set up. Ned pointed that out. It would be the first British colony in the South Pacific as far as he knew. No man had done what he would lead the others to do tomorrow, and one day all those talkers in

London would admire him. The success of the settlement had to take precedence over all other thought.

Mauatua wouldn't be going anywhere. She'd still be around when he was ready to clarify what they were to one another.

Fletcher's dreams were of childhood games, of the make-believe worlds he created around his family home, fantasy worlds played out on the red-brick battlements and towers at Moorland Close or on the ramparts of Cockermouth Castle. There, every boy had both a mother and a father and was happy just to build hideouts for himself and pens for his pets.

Next morning he kept Tamatoa waiting on the beach for several hours before landing. The intense sun of the southern summer was now abating but that day's heat was piercing. Mauatua wanted Fletcher to wear a shirt and an eye shade. He reminded her she was not his mother and wore his naval jacket and hat, with breeches and buckled shoes.

'There will be a lifetime to dress like natives,' he added.

He saw only tropical serenity. A sparkling lagoon dotted with tiny palm-topped islets, sand so white he could barely look at it, an island that seemed a benign combination of familiar and dream like, and on-lookers that included women whose sexual intent was startling and clear.

Chief Tamatoa presented him with many lengths of fine tapa cloth and then led him west along to the sands to Tonohae, his sacred family marae. Tararo and Hitihiti were invited onto its paving of flag stones but Fletcher forbad them until Mauatua was included. More gifts were exchanged, red feathers, axes, chisels and sparkling glass beads. And then Tamatoa exchanged names with Fletcher.

'That makes us safe,' Mauatua whispered to him.

Tamatoa introduced Tinarau and Taaroa, the chiefs of the lesser two districts of Tubuai and then relatives of the three chiefs gave more tapa and so many baskets of fresh and baked fish and breadfruit, plantains, coconuts and yams Fletcher could barely been seen where he sat.

'Bounty everywhere I look,' he joked.

CHAPTER 20

Mauatua rejoiced in being on land again, having sand and soil beneath her feet and following old, worn pathways. She luxuriated in the flowers she could smell and wear. There were fruits to pick and bite into and breezes that came to her sweet with blossom and dried grasses. She breathed deeply, pleasured by the absence of salt and tar and bilge. When the land had profoundly nurtured her, she spoke to Tubuaian women. Later, she told Fletcher what they said.

When he was first here Fletcher had convinced Tubuai he was a god of great power because so many died. It wasn't the grapeshot. Most of the island came to see BOUNTY and so there were hundreds, maybe thousands camped behind the beach, watching. There it was swampy and damp and some evil disease gripped them and then killed them, so they thought Fletcher had also shot infecting spells from the cannon.

She believed Chief Tamatoa was only being helpful as protection against Fletcher using such powers against him but agreed with Fletcher that this could be skewed to their benefit.

For two unrewarding days she followed Fletcher as he searched to identify a site for a settlement in Tamatoa's western half of the island. The chieftain became irritable at the time it was taking and Fletcher's hands sweated prodigiously. When Tamatoa stubbornly anchored himself in a spot he thought suitable, Fletcher's scalp and face erupted. The sight frightened Tamatoa.

'Is he going to change?' he asked her. 'Will the god become something evil and punish Tubuai again?'

'It's very likely,' she said sternly. 'He must be humoured.'

The parties sat in separate groups, silent and dispirited. Tararo and Hitihiti found the prospect of searching for a home distasteful and anyway suspected Tamatoa of being interested only in his own status. BOUNTY'S men were useless. Not one of the sailors had an idea or showed emotion other than fear for his own safety.

No wonder Fletcher's mind was so splintered.

Her first thought was to take the sodden cloths from his hands. He tried to strike her away but she ignored the rebuff and wiped his face. She whispered into his ear, reminding him of what he had done, of how few choices he had. Then she split one of his cloths into strips, joined them together in a single length and tied this around his forehead to interrupt the sweat pouring from his scalp.

She warned Tamatoa gravely.

'If he does not find what he wants, he will fade from this world and all will be lost. We must call on the spirits of the land to guide him.'

Tamatoa worried too loudly if his gifts would follow when Fletcher faded away. 'I expect so,' she said severely.

She stood the men in a large circle in a glade and pushed Fletcher to its centre, explaining that his reluctance was awe for the status and powers of other gods he might meet.

'There must be space between you so gods and spirits might pass freely to speak to him. Now, repeat my chant and don't stop until I tell you.

Haere mai, atua. Haere mai, vaite aitai. Come on. Repeat it, say it. Welcome Gods, welcome Guardian Spirits. Use English if you like.' She went through the circle of reluctant, chanting men to Fletcher.

'What the hell will this achieve?' he snarled. She made Fletcher take off his jacket and threw it to one side.

'I know why you haven't found a site,' she said, quietly echoing his anger. 'It's you. You haven't explained exactly what you are looking for. I'm not sure you know.'

Fletcher was immediately defensive. 'But you know, do you? You know what I want, as usual?' His aggression only made him look more wretched but she couldn't give in. She was fighting for her future too.

'Yes. I do.'

She stared Fletcher out as his jaws worked with an unspoken rebuke and then leaned closer.

'Three things. We can't be too far inland or our escape to the sea could be cut off. We need to see the open sea but without BOUNTY being seen by other ships, and we need to have our own water. That about it?'

Fletcher lifted an arm and she flinched. But he put the arm around her shoulders. 'Thank God for you, Mauatua. Thank God.'

Her head bowed as she walked out of the circle, as though not daring to look at higher beings.

'You can stop chanting. The spirit guides have spoken.'

BOUNTY's company lounged where they liked on deck, enjoying the stillness of the ship on Tubuai's lagoon.

'I want to explain why it is taking time,' Fletcher announced.

'Englishmen build a fortress wherever they colonise. I've seen them. In India. In Africa and in the West Indies. We will do the same.'

'Jesus, do we need that much protection from the natives?' He understood Quintal's question. From BOUNTY's deck it seemed impossible such a beautiful island could be a threat. He explained their fortress wasn't just to keep them safe from the locals.

'We must be able to protect ourselves from the King's Navy, too. That's obvious but eventually other ships will come here too. Americans, French, Spanish, who knows? They'll want it for themselves if we've prospered well.'

'So much for a quiet life in the South Seas,' Quintal said. He spat into the sea and everyone else on deck expressed surprise or fear at the sudden fragility of their possible future. Fletcher had to shout to continue.

'So – so we'll build a fortress with a moat. It will be an Englishman's castle, defended with English cannons, yes, and flying the Jack. But it must have its own water.

'That's what is taking the time, finding that water.'

'What will you call it, this fortress, Mr Christian?' Quintal called, ever anxious to settle matters quickly.

'I won't call it anything. That's up to you.'

Someone suggested Billy Bligh Memorial Fort and soon everyone was shouting. Adams swore he didn't want to remember that bastard and suggested Christian's Castle.

'There's one of those already,' Fletcher said, thinking of his playground at Moorland Close. Most wanted to name the fort for the king and shouted out their ideas. 'Georgie Porgie Castle?' 'Fort Roly Poly?' 'George's Madhouse.' 'Oh aye – or Castle Hanover.'

Fletcher doubted anything sensible was going to emerge.

'Look, he's King George, right? So, how about Fort George?'

The name was loudly cheered. 'Then he'll know you didn't mutiny against him, Mr Christian,' Adams added. Quintal wanted more certainty and demanded to know how they'd build it.

'Earth,' Fletcher answered with clear determination.

'We will dig a wide, deep moat. Then, we'll pack the earth from that to make our defences.'

'Not in this bleeding sun we won't, will we boys?' McCoy shouted.

'Of course we won't be working under the midday sun!'

Fletcher repeated himself several times. When he had their attention again he added that there were enough mad dogs on this ship. They'd work in shifts, early in the morning and late in the afternoon until night fall.

'It's the equivalent of winter here,' he reminded them. 'The days won't be as long so it won't seem so much of a task.'

He explained as much of his vision as he had calculated. A moat twice as wide as the walls would be high, and as deep as they would be high. The damp subsoil earth would be packed hard into wooden frames to make walls of impenetrable sun-baked mud.

'And where will this fortress be, Mr Christian?' Quintal asked.

'You'll know as soon as I do.'

Mauatua couldn't conceive what Fletcher meant by a 'fortress with a moat'. A wall men could walk on and a ditch of water around it? What did these look like? She'd have to trust him because whatever he built would be her home too. He'd want to be as safe as she would, surely?

For all her confusion, she saw his plan invigorated BOUNTY'S Englishmen and there was a grin on every face. All she heard was talk of being kings of their own castle.

She pulled Fletcher from the search party as it again set off westwards to explore more of Tamatoa's half of the island.

'Too many eyes to see the signs in that party,' she said. 'And not enough of them are Ma'ohi.' He didn't resist when she turned him east and Stewart rather liked being left in command.

They crossed two small rivers but their banks were already inhabited. What if that was true of all Tubuai's water sources? Fletcher's enthusiasm waned and he wanted to back track and join the main party but she pushed him on ahead of her. It was very hot and she was half-blinded by the glare from the white sand, something she'd never seen on Tahiti. Wherever possible she kept to the shade of the scrub and the feathery-leaved *toa* trees that grew down to the beach's edge.

A sudden different sound stopped her. Had her foot had been held infinitesimally longer? She touched a little of the earth to her tongue. It was damp but there was no salt. She looked to the central peaks, where all the island's rivers rose and then ran to the plains.

Rivers didn't always run overground.

Fletcher had stripped and dived into the lagoon and so she said nothing to him. She traced a faint line of moistness inland. Less than 100 paces from the shore she discovered a spring of fresh water.

The reef opening was now well to her left, but would be easy to monitor. There were plenty of small islets in the lagoon to hide the hull and masts of BOUNTY. There was no sign of a surface stream that could be blocked or poisoned by an enemy.

When BOUNTY's shore party arrived they were ecstatic.

'Gentlemen,' Fletcher proclaimed, 'we have found a home. Three cheers for Fort George.'

Everyone who had a head covering flung it high into the air. They celebrated the rollicking good times they would have in Fort George, but failed to notice how few Tubuaians shared their carousing. Mauatua kept her tongue. It was good to see such life in Fletcher's eyes, for him to be so manly and determined and honoured by the others.

When they were alone on BOUNTY she told him why Tamatoa and his men had left so quickly.

'Seems that is not Tamatoa's land. We are in Chief Taaroa's province.'

'So the name change with Tamatoa?'

'No use now'. But she couldn't tell him if this would cause a problem.

BOUNTY'S draft was too deep for her safely to reach the lagoon opposite the Fort George site. Fletcher ordered water stores to be discarded and the bilges pumped. Once she was riding higher, he waited until the sun was over head and then ordered the company to kedge the ship through the treacherous lagoon waters while there were no shadows to hide rocks or sudden shoals that risked shivering her timbers.

When BOUNTY was securely moored he ordered Stewart to put half the boars and sows onto one of the islets and the goats and some fowl on to another, saying they would be easier to tend there. He thought the cow would be happier close to the fort and ordered the rest of the stock freed on the island, so the Tubuaians might learn how to husband them.

The placid cow was last to be landed and by that time Fletcher and Stewart were weak with laughter.

200 pigs and goats had rushed inland with such astonishing speed many collided and knocked each other unconscious.

The two men were besieged by insulted priests and infuriated men and irate women. Tubuaians had no fences because they'd never had large animals on the island. The pigs and goats had uprooted, eaten or attempted to eat everything they encountered, including gardens and the thatched roofs of Tubuaian houses, which reached to the ground.

Fletcher's pledge of gifts beyond imagination did nothing to assuage the anger. The belligerent crowd backed them to the beach and then into the lagoon. He drew his pistols and ordered Stewart to do the same. When they were knee high in water he shot his pistols into the air.

The pre-arranged signal was quickly answered by a single cannon shot from BOUNTY. It whistled over their heads and when it fell to earth rodents spewed into the air.

The fleeing Tubuaians tripped and fell onto hordes of equally terrified rats, whose squeals blended into a single high whine.

The sun fell swiftly from the sky and in less than a minute battalions of buzzing, biting insects invaded. Fletcher slapped and scratched his skin and on his scalp and under his clothes. He and Stewart squashed and squeezed them on one another, but it was one-sided warfare. In minutes he burned with venomous bites and was nauseated by a dank, sharp smell he'd not recognised during the day.

'What's that stink, Stewart?' Fletcher asked, stepping back and sinking lower into the lagoon as defence from the biting insects.

'I'm sorry to say, Sir, I believe it to be rats' piss.' Stewart disappeared under water, too. 'And shit,' he added when their heads next concurred above the water.

'The land must be soaked in it.'

'Infested with the brutes, I'd say.'

They kept their heads bobbing and their bodies under water until they were rescued and rowed back to BOUNTY.

Back on board Mauatua told Fletcher dogs kept rats down in Matavai. The storm of night insects explained why locals painted themselves and lit smoky fires inside and outside their houses.

'Welcome to Paradise, Mr Christian,' Quintal sneered, as Mauatua rubbed herb-infused oil into the furious bumps all over Fletcher's body.

Everybody in earshot laughed but Fletcher saw something darker in many eyes. None had suspected Tubuai would be anything but the blissful ease of Tahiti.

As he tried to sleep Fletcher realised this was another mistake he'd made. He, too, had expected to find a new Tahiti.

CHAPTER 21

Fletcher woke unburdened by regret for mistakes. He had no doubts his vision would be achieved. He had a work force of 45 men on shore and nine women willing to cook and to keep BOUNTY ship shape. The hot, hard work meant the men demanded a full meal at night as well as at noon. He also doubled the men's ration of wine. Mauatua told him none of the women felt demeaned by the domesticity of their tasks. They specially liked cooking in the pit ovens on shore because that was traditionally done by men, just as BOUNTY'S galley had once been a man's preserve.

The ease with which he solved problems and the clarity of his plans for the fort meant every man and woman knew what was expected of them and did it willingly. Some excavated the moat, some carted buckets of soil or rammed it hard between wooden forms. Deep reservoirs were dug and slowly filled with water from the spring.

An early task was digging deep long-drop lavatories either side of the planned drawbridge towers, not just for the easement of the workers but so that in future their evil contents could be drawn up and dropped as a deterrent to attack. In the meantime, tall makeshift lookouts were built.

'Get BOUNTY'S swivel guns onto each one. And there must be sentinels night and day,' he ordered.

He put himself everywhere the work was harder, the soil rockier, the bucket heavier. He led by example, bare to the waist, his head wrapped in a turban of tapa cloth. Men competed to keep up with him and generally his rule was never questioned. And rule it had to be, sometimes through committee agreements, often independent and instantaneous.

'Clap that man in leg irons,' he ordered without hesitation when he discovered Quintal had been absent on shore without leave. He kept his pistol to Quintal's head until the key had been turned on both legs.

It became a habit on board to swap stories about Tubuai after the evening meal, especially about the problems of getting girls for sex. Fletcher and Mauatua always sat in on these evening yarns, expecting the rum inside the men might encourage them to say what they really thought. James Morrison, the boatswain's mate, was the best story-teller. Even when he repeated a story a third or fourth time he mesmerised listeners.

'Y'know,' Morrison yarned before lights-out at 8 pm, 'they've only got a couple of low doors in those haystack houses of theirs. At night they burn a smoky fire at every one of 'em to keep out them pesky mosquitoes. Don't know why they bother. You spend all your time swatting, never a moment the buggers ain't diving and buzzing or biting or sucking. And when you lie down, well then, mates, well then, it's fleas and lice that join the battle for your blood. I don't mind saying, I sometimes forgot what I was there for!'

Fletcher joined in as the lower deck's ribaldry drowned Morrison's words. Morrison let the ribbing die down. 'Well. That's not the end of it.

'When I eventually went to sleep with my girl, rats ran over us in droves. I tell you, at some time in the night, I brushed her hand away, wanting some sleep.

'It wasn't her hand, mates, not her hand at all.'

From BOUNTY's deck Mauatua could see the fortress walls were up to her head height on all four sides. Fletcher said they would have to be twice that height to be really safe. She stopped him as he hurried past. She was confused about how everyone was expected to live inside something just 40 strides long and wide.

'The fort is only a fall back,' he explained. 'We'll sleep there for a start and retreat there in case of attack and then gradually expand. We'll all have our own houses and gardens outside the fort.'

'And what about the rats, Fletcher?'

Every morning she shuddered as she heard the task force's first job. They chased the hordes of infuriated rodents that had fallen into the empty moat but couldn't scrabble up its deliberately sheer sides.

The laughing men battered the rats to death with their shovels and picks and then hurled the bloody pulps far into the undergrowth.

Fletcher saw no solution until the moat was filled with sea water.

'Pity they're not edible,' he mused.

'One day they might have to be,' Mauatua worried into the wind.

Later that morning Quintal burst into Fletcher's cabin 'It's Adams. Tinarau's got him.'

'Ask Mr Young to arm 10 volunteers.' The ship's company saw the pursuit of women through the island's jungle pathways as a dangerous and enjoyable break from their relentless work load.

The outcome was often sexual victory but these adventures were now being met with undeserved belligerence.

Fletcher marched south to rescue Adams. When he called to Tinarau the chief fled, so there was no chance to negotiate peace terms. This angered Fletcher more. He posted guards and then entered the house and raided Tinarau's precious ancestor fetishes, hideous heathen idols decorated with the hair and teeth and fingernails of the grandfathers buried beneath them.

'Now, burn it,' he ordered. 'Right to the ground.'

'He'll never forgive you,' Mauatua warned him when he showed her what he had taken. 'He'll do anything to get his ancestor idols back.'

'I'll be ready,' Fletcher said.

A month later Fletcher saw Tinarau marching along the beach to Fort George with conch shells hooting, drums beating and a procession carrying mammoth baskets of food.

'You're happy to stand here with me, Stewart?'

'I am, Sir.' Fletcher stood at the sea-facing entrance to the fort with arms folded, his face set, appearing unwelcoming yet carefully alive to every sound and movement around him.

Tinarau wore a towering ceremonial costume of tapa and painted coconut fibre covered with pearl shells and strings of scintillating pearls. Some were black and iridescent with green or purple or blue. A few were an unearthly pale gold. A phalanx of gaudily dressed priests formed either side of their chief and then Tinarau gave a sign to the priest with the highest headgear.

'Titreano, Titreano *ari'i*. We greet and praise you. May you flourish and be beloved by the gods of the heaven and the land and the sea. May you live a life of peace. May your gardens bring you joy. May your fishing fill your belly.'

Fletcher sighed loudly and turned his eyes to the skies, but the priest was not deflected from intoning.

'Oro bless you in every task you commence and Oro bless every endeavour you complete. These are the greetings of the High Chief, Tinarau, *ari'i* and loved of all Gods . . .'

'Just tell me what you want, Tinarau,' Fletcher interrupted as casually as he could manage. 'We're a bit busy here.'

When there was no immediate response, he turned away and engaged Stewart in conversation. The snub confused the chief and his priests and many anxious voices were raised in protest.

'You are correct, my dear friend, Titreano,' said Chief Tinarau ingratiatingly. 'There is no need for such formality between friends.'

Fletcher didn't respond and so Tinarau came closer. 'I wish to make an agreement with you.'

'That would be good,' Fletcher said, and then walked into the fort. Tinarau followed close enough to speak in a conversational voice.

'Titreano, I come to make peace with you. Look how much I like you. See, I bring you many gifts.' He beckoned forward dozens of men carrying heavy baskets of fruit and vegetables and fish.

Fletcher appeared to assess the amount of tribute but said nothing. He and Stewart moved deeper into the fort. Tinarau and his attendants had no choice. They followed, Tinarau rehearsing the number of gifts he had brought and asking for his ancestor idols in return. Fletcher finally engaged with the chief.

'I will give them back to you, Tinarau. But first let me tell you what I want. I want none of these gifts. They have no value between friends.' He strode towards the farthest wall of the fort until all of Tinarau's tail of followers was inside the ramparts and then he spoke defiantly.

'First, Chief Tinarau, you must lift all restrictions on women going with my men, in their own houses or on BOUNTY. Do you agree?' Tinarau was encouraged by the priests to agree.

'Next, you must return every piece of clothing stolen from my men. Every piece must be delivered back here. Tomorrow. Do you agree?' The priests said Tinarau could.

'And I want you to kill any man or woman who ill-treats or lies or even attempts to trick or to steal from my men. I mean any of my men, including the Ma'ohi who sail with me.'

There was a longer pause before Tinarau was given permission to agree. He clapped his hands. 'Now we have agreed we must drink *kava*, Titreano. I have brought the roots, brought the bowls. I knew we would be friends. Ah – but my ancestors?'

'I will exchange them for the clothes of my men, tomorrow.' Tinarau looked hopefully at the huts built inside the fortress.

'Don't waste your time, Tinarau. They are on the ship.'

Tinarau's servants hurried to lay tapa cloth on the ground and then brought out sun-dried kava root, large carved bowls and heavy pounders of volcanic rock. Tinarau pounded the root with water to make a muddy looking liquid.

'Don't like the stuff,' said Fletcher, refusing the prized first serving. Tinarau struggled to remain polite and offered it to Stewart. He turned it down, too. Tinarau was furious but too proud to turn and ask for more advice from his priests.

'Titreano, *ari'i,* we make an agreement and now you insult me. You do not drink the kava made just for you. Why do you want to hurt me so?'

'I ask you the same, Tinarau,' Fletcher said, raising his voice over the increasing clamour of discomfort in the fort. 'Why have you come here to attack me?' Tinarau spun for guidance only to see his priests fleeing, hands defending their heads.

'You should leave while you can,' Fletcher warned, showing Tinarau BOUNTY's marksmen standing on the walls.

'This is Tinarau,' he shouted to them and pointed repeatedly at the chief so there could be no mistake.

'How did you know, Titreano?'

One of BOUNTY's cannons whistled grapeshot over their heads. Tinarau didn't wait for Fletcher's answer. He joined the retreat, clumsy in his costume, ordering those still in the fort to gather up all the gift baskets they could.

Fletcher grabbed the nearest Tubuaian. 'Tell Tinarau my god knows everything and tells me everything. I knew he hoped to fuddle me with kava and then kill me. Next time, I will kill him. I will put him into one of BOUNTY'S cannon and light it myself. He will fly to his gods faster than any man has.' He shoved the Tubuaian on his way and followed that with a sharp kick.

Later in the day he explained to Mauatua how he discovered Tinarau's trick. 'One of our Tahitian boys saw his men putting weapons into the food baskets and ran ahead to tell me.'

'They could have attacked you any time.'

'But I had the marksmen on the wall before Tinarau arrived. And I sent the boy on to the ship with the order to fire a cannon at the first sound of any gunfire in the fort.'

'I heard no shots.'

'I'd also said if anyone was seen running away from the fort, they should send them on their way with something to remember. Four pounds of grape shot certainly did that.'

He meant to tell Mauatua about the horse of Troy but fell asleep.

Whenever she could, Mauatua discreetly left her tasks and talked with Tubuaians. None would speak to Fletcher they way they spoke with her. In a few days she was able to tell Fletcher his assessment of the island was simplistic. He thought Taaroa and his family were flattered by having the ship and Fort George in their territory. That Tamatoa to the west was over any sulk about losing the Europeans to a lesser chief and that Tinarau to the south was now calm. But her advice was that it was the priests he had to fear and not the three chiefs.

'The priests don't want you here now they have seen you white men are not gods. While you are here, they think you should bow down to them.'

'That will be the day.' He fiddled with the papers on the folding ledge that served as his desk, struggling to appear calm and thoughtful. 'So, the priests are more powerful than the chiefs?'

'There are many priests but only three chiefs.'

'But if we are not gods, what frightens them?'

'They think you will use guns to become superior, and then priests will have no authority.' He sighed heavily and held his head in his hands, muttering he couldn't understand why the priests couldn't accept him and his simple plans.

She clamped her hands over his. 'It is a very good and very simple thing you want. But you take no account of what other people want.'

He pulled his hands from under hers and turned his head away, his chin lifted defiantly. Her mouth dried for fear of how she was hurting him, but she had to continue.

'Many Tubuaians don't want us here. And what about the men who didn't mutiny? They don't want to be here either.'

She couldn't tell what he was thinking.

He didn't seem angry, so she risked saying the painful thing she most wanted to get out of her head and into his.

'I don't think you will live here, Fletcher. Or see your fort finished.'

He swirled and raised his fist, his voice hissing. 'How dare you? How dare you say that?'

Mauatua held his furious challenge, well able to stand eye to eye. She grabbed his arm and shoved it down to his side, her eyes fiery with challenge. She continued before the words forming on his lips could escape and harm her.

'There's more you should know, Fletcher. I have been discovering what others on the ship want.'

'You are making this up,' he said dismissively, but she saw fear hovering in his eyes.

'These are not my ideas, Fletcher. They are what others have told me or I have heard them saying.'

She waited until she felt he believed this. He reached into his Indian chest for a camphor-scented handkerchief and put it to his nose. When he was composed, Mauatua repeated what she had been hearing.

'First, the people of Tubuai are scared because the priests have convinced them your ditch will be a mass grave for them. Thus, there are as many plans to destroy you as there are men on the island. And women.'

'Moat, the word is moat not ditch.'

She slapped him on the arm. 'You are very bad to care about little things like that. This is your life I am telling you about. And mine.'

He rubbed the sting from her slap and looked contrite but that's not what she wanted. He had to be bold, assertive, to be a leader. She spoke deliberately, to be certain he understood.

'Those friendly Tubuaians who sometimes help build the fort, the ones you treat like brothers, they have been plotting with some of the Tahitian boys to kill you white men and bury *you* in the moat. Then they'll divide all the animals and everything else on BOUNTY as compensation for the losses caused by your pigs.'

'Don't mention pigs again. Please.'

'There are men scheming on board, too, Fletcher. That Morrison, he's been working out his chances of survival if he stole one of BOUNTY'S boats and sailed it back to Tahiti. Others have been offering bribes for a place in it.'

Fletcher hung his head as the woes she told him fell heavier and heavier onto his shoulders. 'Is that it? Is that the lot?'

He closed his eyes and leaned back on the outer bulkhead. From time to time he shook or nodded his head. Mauatua's instincts told her when it was right to add her own thoughts.

'Perhaps you are fooling yourself, Fletcher. You know, this is not the games of your boyhood you tell me about, where everyone else always magically wanted what you wanted.'

She watched anxiously as each one of her words fall between them like the steady, destructive beats of a chopping axe. Fletcher was silent for so long she thought she had severed their bonds.

'Is that what you think?' he asked in a thin whisper. 'That I am simply a child, playing games, having adventures with castles in the air?'

'No.' Her answer hung long enough for him to absorb and believe it.

'I think your dream of a safe place to live is very possible. If the British Navy wasn't coming after you, it might have been on Tahiti. But your dream will never come true anywhere unless you are welcomed there.'

A loud cry of pain from Fletcher cramped her torso. She bit the tip of her tongue and sucked in her breath, holding it still and painful in her chest while she waited to see how badly she had injured him. He stood and moved slowly to her, so slowly she convinced herself she would be beaten. His brown eyes blazed with dismissal of all she had said.

Without thinking she threw her arm across her face. Fletched quickly grabbed it and they struggled until he pushed it behind her.

Only then did she see that the sparks of fiery temper in his eyes were actually of delight and gratitude.

'Where do I start? Which problem is the biggest?' he said, accepting all she had said to him.

'The biggest problem is the one we haven't spoken about. And should not speak about on board.' He moved swiftly to the cabin door and opened it. There was no-one listening. He locked it. 'It's safe if you keep your voice down.'

'You are surrounded by men waiting for you to show weakness. At the first sign, just one sign, one of them will strike. Then the others will.'

'But that could be anytime, anywhere.'

'Then you must be strong and vigilant *all* the time. I know you can do that, if that's what you still want.'

They stood with their eyes locked, unflinching, for many minutes.

'I do want that and I can do it with you. Thank God for you. Isabella, Mauatua, Mrs Christian. Thank God for you.'

'Remember, I want somewhere safe and new to live, too,' she said. 'Like you, I can't go home. We both have to find a new home. It's just that, well, it might not be Fort George.' Then she spoke quickly, focusing on the future.

'We are learning. Who else has done what we are trying? The ancestors who came to Tahiti must have made mistakes, they had to learn. I don't know your god, Fletcher, and I don't believe in mine. But sometimes there seems to be a helping hand, a guide. Don't you think so?'

He dismissed her question. 'All this effort to build the fort - so some *thing* could teach us we shouldn't be here. That's unthinkable.'

'We *must* think it, Fletcher. It wouldn't be weak and wouldn't be easy.' She repeated advice she had learned from her grandmothers and grandfathers.

They told her it can be braver, wiser, to recognise defeat and move on, that this could be braver than being staunch and inflexible. Staying, they said, might be *ha'amehameha,* the cowardly way, cowardly because you were not facing the truth and the demands it makes.

'We can't be cowards. We are too young.'

His bowed head dropped hot tears onto the cabin floor

'*Toa,* Fletcher. *Toa.* Warrior, remember?'

When he lifted his head he still had tears in his eyes but he told her they were not lamenting the loss of his dream.

He was weeping with elation, because she had said 'we' before he had found the courage.

CHAPTER 22

Fletcher considered all Mauatua revealed and by the end of the next morning put it to the back of his mind. He must have misunderstood what she said. Anyway, how much of what Mauatua said had been coloured by her fear of returning to Tahiti? Women had different doubts from men, and more of them. Didn't they?

His greatest memory from last night was not the threat of the moat as a mass grave, not even her using 'we'. She had said they were young and could make mistakes. He agreed. But there was one he wouldn't make. He wouldn't abandon the fort. The fortress would solve all their problems.

Fletcher rammed soil into the wooden frame of the first of the tooth-like crenellations on one of the towers that would suspend a drawbridge over the moat. Mauatua's warning about the priests seemed unfounded.

Every day he saw the fort grow he expected them to realise how superior his forces were and give in. They'd be friends one day. Then he would make a home here, a home that would keep him as happy as it kept Mauatua and gradually it would become a model for modern thinking elsewhere. He would lead a revolution in living without constant confrontation, not even between men and women.

The first step was to finish building Fort George.

He paused to stretch his muscles in the sun and to wipe his forehead. He forced himself to take these short breaks. Every time he did he drew encouragement from the sounds of effort and endeavour around him. This time he was arrested by silence. No one was working in the fort and a low grumbling was getting louder. He dropped his heavy tool and spun to look. Every man had put down his equipment or must have thought it better to do so. Quintal stood at the base of the wall.

'A word, Mr Christian,' he shouted, squinting into the sun. 'Will you come down?' More and more men joined him, most of the Europeans and all of the Ma'ohi men and boys. Fletcher felt safer where he was.

'No, no need, I can hear you'. He couldn't see any of the women and they were supposed to be cooking in the pit oven. 'Where are the women?' he demanded.

'We have sent them away, to dig up cockles.'

'All of them? But they won't be safe.' He began to slide down the sloping inner wall that reinforced the fortification. Quintal shouted he should stay where he was. 'There's no problem, Mr Christian. Burkett and Millward are with them – and Peter's there to keep an eye on those two.'

'All the women?' Fletcher queried nervously. 'Mauatua, too?'

'We are *very* hungry.' The nasty laughs that followed put him more sharply on guard.

William McCoy spoke up 'It's the women we want to talk about. There ain't enough of 'em.'

Quintal agreed. 'We've been talking and we've been voting, like you showed us, Mr Christian We're not working until we've got a wife. Every last one of us.'

McCoy and Quintal had boarded BOUNTY together. Both were tough, stocky men in their mid 20s and scarred with knife wounds all over their bodies. Both had been quick to support his mutiny against Bligh. With neither intelligence nor learning they acted or reacted according to base instinct. Now they were threatening him and he'd have to take them seriously. He hoped being conversational would keep everyone calm.

'But that's a big job, to have a wife for every man. From where? Going to Tahiti would take weeks.'

'Forget about Tahiti!' McCoy shouted belligerently.

'Aye,' Quintal agreed. 'We done enough waiting. We want the girls we've got, the ones we brought with us.'

Fletcher was horrified to hear the mob bray its support, nauseated by what these men must be imagining. Their plans would include Mauatua.

'No, no, no. This cannot be, must not.' The panic in his voice made him sound weak. He recomposed his approach as he climbed slowly back to the top of the wall.

'Look,' he said, his arms outspread, attempting to be placatory. 'Look, this is a bit sudden. There must be another way. We'll talk it through.'

'Aye, Mr Christian. You are very good at talking and you usually get your way. This time it is our way that must count and we've voted already. We're not working for you any more, not until every man's got a woman. Shared or not.'

Fletcher heard only a raucous chorus of agreement, rooted in genuine anger and dissatisfaction. He was lost if so many of BOUNTY'S mildest men supported Quintal and McCoy.

'So, you'd force them, all of the women. Is that it?' He was unable to keep fear for Mauatua out of his mind or anger out of his voice and paced back and forth on the rampart as a device to disguise its tremor.

'You'd make them sex slaves? Just slaves – is that all? With not one of you ever again repaying them with the slightest kindness?'

'Oh there'd be payback alright, Mr Christian,' Quintal taunted. 'Give us the girls and we'll pay you back by finishing your fort.'

The crowd responded with cheers and whistles and loud clapping. Quintal played to them, egging them on with sweeping arm gestures. When they stopped both men stood with their arms tightly folded, Fletcher in fear, Quintal in swaggering triumph.

'I think that's a deal, don't you, Sir?'

Fletcher waited as long as he dared, blessing his long years of not reacting immediately to Bligh so he could respond calmly and blandly.

'I think this is too serious to decide here. Perhaps the women will agree? Who knows? I will ask them when you release them.'

'And we'll tell you what their answer should be!' McCoy shouted. He lifted his left hand, made a circle of his thumb and forefinger and jerked his right index finger in and out. The taunt was contagious. Man after man held their obscene gestures as high as they could to Fletcher.

One young Tahitian humped another's high firm buttocks, his hands linked over the other's prick and balls. Others joined in until there was a long obscene hip-jerking line. Fletcher feared there was enough rebellion and sexual charge in the air for it to degenerate into violence. He pointed his pistols directly into the mob and called on every ounce of authority.

'Stop! Stop!'

When they saw his cocked pistols the men broke up, some more reluctantly than others. 'You have made your point. I am obliged to take it seriously. You might not like where you are, or why you are here.

'But remember one thing, if you please. You are safe, alive and in good health. Wanting women so much proves this. And why are you alive and safe? Because I have protected you. Not one of you has come to harm. Isn't that true?'

The appeal was simple enough for the ringleaders to understand. 'Aye Mr Christian, that's true,' Quintal agreed.

'But what is your point?' McCoy asked.

'Give me some time. Give me, let *us* take three days. All of us. As you suggest, there'll be no work on the fort, but we must still mount guard here day and night. Otherwise everyone sleeps on BOUNTY. Three days. By then we will have a solution. I give you my word.'

McCoy turned to the crowd. 'Three days, is that fair, ship mates?' There was a willing chorus of acceptance.

'Now, I want those women brought back here,' Fletcher said.

'Never been away, Mr Christian. All them women is on the ship. Just in case, like.'

That night Fletcher was baffled by how quickly things had changed. He refused his evening grog and ate no supper. Suddenly there was loud banging from somewhere below his cabin. It was followed by muffled sounds, attempts to stifle laughter. Or was it anger? He grabbed his pistols, telling Mauatua to stay and to lock the door after him.

He sped down the companionway into the hold and turned to where a candle-lamp exposed the miscreants. He expected it to be a fight over sole possession of a boy.

Sometimes the sexual tension of the lower deck burst its poison into petty jealousies of friendship, physical handling where none was invited or necessary. For some that was not enough.

No longer restrained by naval law, which punished homosexual acts with death, some of the company had turned to the smooth-skinned Tahitian youths. Their possession raised tempers higher than competition for any of the women.

Instead of confronting sexual assault, he found McCoy had forced open the scuttle to the spirit room in the hold.

'This is mutiny!' Fletcher thundered.

'You'd know,' Quintal said.

'By God, Quintal, one more word of mockery from you today and I will shoot you.'

He leapt forward and pushed his pistol hard into Quintal's chest. Quintal responded with a belligerent, mocking smile, forcing his ribs tighter into the pistol's nuzzle. Fletcher stood his ground.

'Not an inch more. I will shoot. I have nothing left to lose. But you would be dead and I would still be alive.'

Ned Young was officer of the watch and rushed from the upper deck to investigate the disturbance. He forced himself between the antagonists.

Fletcher put the pistol into his belt, grabbed the lamp and lifted it to inspect the sullen faces of the men, seven of them.

'Mutiny deserves finer fellows than this. And deserves a finer reason than fuddling your minds.'

'There won't be much else to do these three days,' Quintal sneered.

'There was supposed to be clear-headed discussion.'

'I said nothing about clear-headed, Mr Christian,' said Quintal with a mock bow of exaggerated courtesy.

Fletcher was threatened by Quintal's unrelenting cockiness and feared the words he felt burning on his lips could descend to puerile scrapping and then to uncontrollable violence.

'Very well. Mr Young, kindly note in your watch log I have doubled the grog ration for all hands from midday tomorrow. For three days only. See this hatch is repaired at once.'

'It's started,' he told Mauatua, as he locked them into his cabin.

'But it's not finished, Fletcher. It must be you who finishes it. It cannot be men like that who finish this.'

Next day a miserable harrying wind pried its way into every corner of the ship. Wherever she was on BOUNTY Mauatua felt the wind or heard it moaning somewhere close.

She wrapped herself in a coarse blanket from Fletcher's cabin and spent her time watching after Tamahere or tending to the daily toll of patients with dysentery or diarrhoea, whom she and Jenny treated in a makeshift ward on deck, so the filth and smell was easier to cope with and clean.

By night fall she'd gathered the general mood was for returning to Tahiti, if only as a welcome break from the labour and loneliness of Tubuai. In her distress she then sought out the mutineers, who had spent most of the day huddled in a separate group. Most of them were dead set against Tahiti, but did she want such men as allies?

'Mates, going to Tahiti even for just a few days might be all that's needed to get us discovered and arrested.' Quintal said to whoever would listen. The awful balance against the mutineers' concern not to be discovered was the hope amongst loyalists they *might* be discovered.

The only certainty she felt was that the more there was to eat, the more the men sat and talked over food, the more likely it was that they'd reach some equitable compromise.

She supervised a larger than usual supper, starting with what was left of a generous stew of fresh pork from dinner time. It was well flavoured with the parts that took longest to become tender, with trotters and cheeks, the tail and the ears. She added plenty of salted pork, now made more acceptable by Fletcher's insistence by soaking for two days in changes of water. When it was Bligh's ship salt meat was hardly soaked at all, and often cooked in the same briny liquid.

Mauatua's two big meals did generate a greater feeling of companionship and comfort aboard BOUNTY. But not for her. She told Fletcher that she was more frightened of Tahiti than she was of Tubuai.

Her concerns confused Fletcher's thinking. The notion grew he might have to forget her.

She wasn't his wife, so abandoning her somewhere was a possibility. Yet every time that thought broke into his mind, he pushed it back.

Tubuai proved the South Pacific was not a paradise and that his understanding of it was flawed. Without Mauatua there would be no survival, no chance of creating the brave, safe, new world he imagined.

On the third day he called a meeting on deck at eight bells, noon. He wore no hat or jacket and like able seamen, wore no shoes. His hair was loose and his shirt had been worn many times. He wasn't sweating, but leaden bags under his eyes told the heavy toll taken by the past months. He leaned back on the port cannon closest to the main companionway, so those in Mauatua's open-air infirmary could see and hear him.

'Gentlemen, you are right. I will take you back to Tahiti. You will have as much time there as you wish.'

Mauatua was aghast. Tahiti! Tahiti was a death sentence for her after her *tipou*. Where was this love he so recently professed? She pressed herself behind the mainmast, wanting no-one to read her distressed face. Everywhere else the immediate cry was 'Grog! Grog! Bring on that grog!'

'There is one condition,' Fletcher called over the noise.

'Just the one?' Quintal scoffed 'Hush boys. Hush. Mr Christian is now going to tell us the bad news.'

Mauatua slumped to the deck, feeling weak and crushed as more and more images of her probable fate on Tahiti crowded her mind. But she had to know Fletcher's conditions and forced herself to listen.

'Not so bad, Quintal,' he said. 'And I'm not telling you anything. I'm asking. There's something you must vote on. Because of what I have done,

I am forever a man alone. I have no family. No career, no home or country. No honour. No future. When I have taken you to Tahiti...'

Fletcher choked. He lifted a palm to cover his eyes and then pressed them with his handkerchief. When he began again, his voice was calmer and stronger.

'When I have taken you to Tahiti, I ask you...'

Mauatua silently urged him to continue what he had started yet dreaded discovering he had already forgotten his pride in her saying 'we'? What if his 'one condition' proved he was selfish, prepared to abandon her?

Determined no-one would see she cared what Fletcher said, Mauatua got to her feet, composed her face and straightened her back.

It was hard not to run and stand by him but she might end up looking foolish if she did. The tumblings of her mind wanted to hate him but she couldn't help feeling pity. He looked so lonely and vulnerable, like a disgraced youth forced to say out loud all he was most ashamed to admit. But at least he wasn't sweating.

He stood away from the cannon, set his face and squared his shoulders.

'I ask you to give me BOUNTY, to tie the foresail and leave me to run before the wind.

'I have done such an act that I cannot stay at Otaheite and I will never live where I may be carried home to be a disgrace to my family.'

She was still numbed by Fletcher's announcement he'd sail back to Tahiti. And now he wanted to sail on alone.

How could she be abandoned just like that, without a word?

She ran to confront him. She looked deep into his dark eyes and immediately found there what she wanted. They wordlessly begged her with the last tatters of his fragile pride.

Of course he wouldn't leave her in Tahiti if she wanted to sail with him. He leaned forward to whisper, saying he hadn't wanted to use a single word of persuasion.

They held each other close, so close it was like wanting to wear the other's skin.

CHAPTER 23

'I'm resigned to sailing where the wind takes me,' Fletcher continued, still holding Mauatua. 'Somewhere, anywhere. . . but it will be to oblivion. Then one day, if it pleases God, you will forget me and what I have brought you to.'

It took less than a minute for every man aboard to agree to Fletcher's request. Only the Ma'ohi women hadn't voted, still uncertain of such freedoms. She asked Fletcher if he wanted them to vote, but he said this time it was not important. Even if they disagreed with the men they were certain to be outvoted.

Fletcher ordered the grog ration served. He was supervising the daytime addition of water and lime juice to the high-proof Navy issue rum when Matthew Quintal suddenly stepped forward and stood with his hands on his hips, clearly about to make another of his abrasive pronouncements. Mauatua's heart sank. Why was Matt Quintal always so aggressive?

'Mr Christian,' Quintal said, loudly enough for everyone to hear. 'We might not always agree. But you've been a fine and good captain since you kicked Bligh off this ship. Like you said, you've looked after us.' There was a ripple of agreement. Quintal rode it like the proudest politician.

'I'll not let you sail off alone,' Quintal announced. 'I'd be proud to sail on BOUNTY with you.'

Mauatua dug her fingernails into Fletcher's arm. Was this the sort of man they wanted on board? She dared not look at Fletcher or give the slightest hint Quintal was unwelcome.

She knew a lot about the men on BOUNTY and had heard all their stories as they gossiped and yarned in the breadfruit camp. More came to her ears as she tended sick men on the deck with Jenny, as though they thought Tahitian women didn't understand English. Just as she had kept English words for so long in her mind, Mauatua stored away what she had learned about each man.

Nothing in her memory gave her confidence about Quintal.

Quintal was the first man Bligh flogged for insolence and mutinous behaviour and was first to join Fletcher against Bligh. He was a born trouble maker and a bit too free with his hands, even when fevered with dysentery. The boldness of Fletcher's plan, if it could be called a plan, should have daunted men like Quintal. Yet he had opted for a future with no goals, no boundaries except to wander the South Seas, forever hoping to avoid retribution.

When William McCoy ventured he would sail wherever his mate went, Mauatua hid her face in Fletcher's arm. These were not the sort of men Fletcher would choose, surely. But, could he, could *they* refuse?

She heard another man step forward and turned to see it was Jenny's new lover Isaac Martin. Martin was as tall as Fletcher and another victim of Bligh's contradictory orders. He took 24 lashes for striking a thief while he wrestled back stolen goods. Martin vacillated during the mutiny, first refusing to support Fletcher and then agreeing. She looked to find Jenny, raising her eyebrows to ask if this meant she would sail with them.

'I think so,' Jenny called. 'But, well, soon, I'll give you an answer soon.' Mauatua remembered how frustrated Fletcher was when she had said the same thing. 'Soon better be very soon, Jenny.'

Fletcher next took the proffered hand of Brown, the assistant gardener of the breadfruit camp.

She judged him a gentle man, much more the person they should have on board. It was encouraging to see Fletcher smile.

'Am I right, Mr Brown, you were a career naval officer before choosing to be a botanist?'

'As far as acting lieutenant. I was actually a second in command, too.'

'You are doubly welcome,' Fletcher said. Mauatua unwrapped her arm from Fletcher's and went to Jenny.

'This is better, he'll be a good friend for Fletcher,' she confided. 'They know the same books and talk about worlds I don't understand. They are equals, I think.' Then she laughed, remembering Brown once refused to join the daily dancing on board BOUNTY.

'He get a flogging?' Jenny asked.

'Something worse for *popa'a*. His daily grog ration stopped.' The two women laughed so loudly Fletcher bellowed to quieten them. When he turned back another volunteer faced him.

'Mr Mills. You want to join this . . . this improbably mad adventure?'

She was frightened of Mills. He was a bully, the self-deluding sort who excused sadistic taunting or physical abuse as 'only having a bit of a laugh'. John Mills, gunner's mate, was a Scot from Aberdeen and went below with Fletcher to arrest Bligh. At 40 Mills was one of the oldest men aboard and one of the few as tall as Fletcher Christian.

She despaired. How did Fletcher feel when only men like Mills and Quintal and McCoy wanted to join him? Except, if mutiny was as bad as he said, what right did he have to expect the best men to follow him?

John Adams came forward next. He'd stood beside Fletcher from the earliest moments of the mutiny. In Tahiti he took up island life easily and more fulsomely than any of the company. He was first to be tattooed and first to have a permanent Tahitian mistress and a *taio*. She thought he'd suit South Seas life better than any of the others.

Fletcher then accepted the offer of Williams, another active mutineer. Black haired, slender and tattooed, he was as short as Quintal, Adams and McCoy. Williams received six lashes in False Bay, South Africa, when Bligh found fault with the way he heaved the lead, by which the ship knew how much water was beneath her hull. Fletcher suddenly had a company of seven. And her.

She looked carefully at his face and knew it was not saying what he wanted to say. She fled back to him and led him to the ship's rails..

'I expected no support, no company. I didn't even dare include you,' he admitted. There was a sharp wind gusting, which whipped up the waves of the lagoon and insulated their words from other ears. He was suddenly angry.

'How ridiculous, how immature and child-like I must have seemed. Wanting to sail away alone. As stupid as thinking I could abandon BOUNTY on a raft, before the . . . that morning. I shouldn't do it. I shouldn't make decisions while I am under stress. I think badly and go for the big gesture. I behave like the boy I was at Moorland Close. But then my, my, well, fantasies – my fantasies affected no one else.'

She spoke softly to him, attempting to turn his mind from the past to the future. 'You are a very good leader of men. I think it is only yourself and your emotions you cannot always manage.'

'What a child I am,' he repeated, still punishing himself. 'The reality of sailing alone into the South Pacific only came clear when you stood beside me.' He turned to her and she saw the child in him pleading for comfort.

'Is there anything positive out of this?' he appealed.

There was truth in what she was going to tell him, but there were hidden barbs and she didn't want to start a sweating attack, so she spoke carefully. 'I think one thing is very positive. Now you will sail only with men who are genuinely content to wander the seas with you. There will be no men on this ship for your eyes to miss, no one to fear when you sleep.'

And then Ned Young tapped Fletcher on the shoulder to volunteer, the eighth man to do so.

Born in St Kitts in the West Indies, he readily agreed he was the worst looking man in the ship, with features that could be frightening when first met. His lilting, vowel-caressing Caribbean accent was made more indistinct by a mouth of teeth that were entirely rotten or well on their way, the result he explained of being brought up on a sugar island. Men went to great lengths not to be downwind of his breath and not to sit opposite him when he ate.

'You'll be wanting at least one other officer, Mr Christian,' Ned said.

Ned's mother, or grandmother, was a Negress. He'd never been quite clear about that, but he wanted to get away from the Navy and the endless taunts of 'nigger'. He was well educated and seemed as well connected, a proper companion for Fletcher.

'No. No you can't, Ned,' Fletcher protested. 'What's the future in that for you?' Ned smiled, keeping his lips closed. He lifted an eyebrow, querying why Fletcher didn't know.

'Was he a mutineer?' Jenny asked.

'No,' Mauatua explained quietly. 'But he has been a good friend to Fletcher ever since.'

Ned then answered Fletcher's question proudly.

'The future for me? Something better than the prospect of being strung from a yardarm on the other side of the world. I wasn't a mutineer but I did nothing to stop you. Bligh is bound to have it in for me.'

Then Ned added something she knew she'd remember for the rest of her life.

'We will never leave you, Mr Christian, go where you will.'

CHAPTER 24

Yet again Mauatua believed the long Pacific swell resented BOUNTY riding on its breast. Cross currents of wind whipped waves into barriers rather than lifting the ship to fly.

This time she wasn't allowed to sympathise with sea sickness. BOUNTY had to return to Tahiti looking plump, well cared for and content. The seasick were permitted to work slowly, but work they must.

Fletcher was determined BOUNTY would reap maximum profit from the great number she carried from Tubuai. Once he sailed from Tahiti there would be precious little man power to keep her fully ship shape. Now he was master of a ship's company of over 50. Two more bloody confrontations had left countless Tubuaians dead or wounded and Fletcher Christian's most supportive allies on the island had begged to sail with him to escape retribution for that friendship.

Norman, once the carpenter's mate, was tasked with making good the ship's two remaining boats. Teams were appointed to help him and to chop, split and store wood for the constantly lit galley stove.

The upper deck's planks had shrunk under Tubuai's sun because they had not been doused and scrubbed every day. Fletcher ordered regular scrubbing and the caulking between each plank was replaced to make BOUNTY watertight once more.

Mauatua was grateful for any occupation because she became more and more terrified as Tahiti came closer. She didn't want to lie, not even to herself, but there were big questions about her future. The biggest was the oldest. Fletcher clearly loved her, but was it as a sister or as a woman? If he loved her like a brother might, should they be doing the things they did, even if their sexual play brought them closer? She knew brothers and sisters who played like that. But they were still called brother and sister.

What was the name for her after she and Fletcher satisfied each other?

For five trying days and nights the South Pacific offered BOUNTY no respite and there was little less inside Matavai Bay's lagoon. As the anchored ship pitched and rolled Mauatua watched the palms on shore bend and sway and the locals scurry with bent backs and with hands over their eyes to protect them from the swirls of dried grasses and leaves. She knew what they would be thinking, how each household hurried to check their thatch and their animals. She always ran to pick flowers for her ears or to make wreaths for her hair, in case the wind tore them away and then there would be no more for weeks.

The wind whipped salt into her hair and into her nostrils and she tasted it on her lips. Her heart beat too fast, too hard, hammering in her chest. How many would remember she was on board? The hammering would be all over her body once her *tipou* insult to the island was known.

Above Matavai lead-dark cushions of cloud hung like glowering brows over the peaks and from them winds swept messages she interpreted as contempt. What chance had she here when even mountains didn't want anything to do with her?

Jenny had agreed to sail with Martin and was one of the first to go ashore. Mauatua begged her to send some of their friends onto the ship, other *ra'atira* women. They deserved better than to sail away only with *manahune* girls, the ones who came most easily onto a ship. It wasn't just that these working-class girls were darker skinned. They had been brought up differently, weren't as careful with their tapa making or how they danced or spoke.

'Perhaps we need them more than we think,' Jenny said before leaving. 'We aren't always the ones to get our hands dirty, are we *vahine?*'

Fletcher was uneasy that the great waves and constant harrowing winds made it dangerous to load a small boat with departing men and their possessions as it tossed and bucked against BOUNTY. He ordered the ship's cutter, the only boat Norman had made seaworthy enough, to spend as little time against the heaving bulk of BOUNTY as possible. He assisted where he could, wanting to keep the best possible relationship with the men he was leaving behind on Tahiti, whether loyalists or mutineers.

The boat went back and forth by manpower or sail all day. Each time, barely half loaded, it carried just a few men and all they possessed for life on shore for an indeterminate time. Because the crew of the boat rested after each trip, each return trip took as long as two hours and yet he could persuade no-one to go ashore in native canoes, even though the Ma'ohi were better sailors in these waters. That was frustrating. Fletcher wanted the 'deserters' as he privately called them off as soon as possible. There were almost twice as many, 16 to his nine.

He'd sent Hitihiti and his youths to deliver Tinarau's household gods to Tu and his parents, Teina and Itia. They were ecstatic. Canoe loads of food and animals and tapa cloth were sent in return, hour after hour. Fletcher didn't want the tapa, but Mauatua reminded him that refusal would be insulting. Gifts of agriculture were never considered enough on Tahiti. Produce from Nature had always to be accompanied with something handmade, tapa or a carving, pearl earrings or other jewellery or carved fishhooks, ideally from human bone.

Each return trip of the ship's boat also brought Tahitian men and women, because Fletcher had said to spread the word there was a party on board. Jenny sent women onto BOUNTY with arms that barely met for their enormous harvests of flowers and ferns, palm leaves and sennit thread. They sat on deck, singing and weaving *hei,* neck garlands, and head wreaths, *hei upo'o.*

Tamahere was more excited than anyone to be back in Tahiti. He ran into the middle of their circle, took an armful of the blossom and threw it high in the air and then did it again. The shower of fragrance and colour was intoxicating.

None of the women was annoyed. They laughed at the pleasure he had given them and made him a special *hei* of the finest *maire* fern and the most fragrant white and cream flowers and then tied it around his neck.

Peter Heywood was the last of BOUNTY's men to leave.

'Fletcher will miss you,' Mauatua said as she sheltered with him behind the mainmast from as much of the winds as they could.

Peter couldn't hide brimming tears when she reminded him he was family to Fletcher, like a young brother. She urged him not to go without spending time with Fletcher.

Fletcher had been watching. 'Is he alright?' he asked Mauatua.

'Not really,' she said. 'Are you?'

'It's going to be difficult,' he acknowledged. Peter heard Fletcher's deep voice and unashamed of his tears turned and clasped him tightly.

'Give my love to the island,' Fletcher said gruffly.

'Which one?' Peter asked. He tried to laugh and so did Fletcher.

'The Isle of Man. And your family there.'

Peter agreed he would see Fletcher's mother in Douglas and also promised on oath never to excuse his mutiny. Fletcher entreated Peter to speak fearlessly of the cruelties he'd seen with his eyes, heard with his ears. But explain, he insisted, never excuse. Mutiny was wrong, whatever the reason.

'Can you believe it, Peter? Two mutineers in one family. I can't imagine what our mother will think. Or brother Humphrey, he's a soldier on the Barbary Coast. And Edward, you remember him, he's a lawyer, like John, the oldest one.'

Fletcher dropped his arms and stood back a step. He shook his head ruefully. 'Sorry, Peter, I haven't thought of them for months, but I know you'll see them one day, God willing.

'But look at us, grown men but both snivelling like girls. Ah, and speaking of girls – my sister, Mary. Tell her I'll name my daughter, my first daughter after her. Promise?'

A loud hail from the boat interrupted them. Fletcher embraced Peter one more time. Then he turned his back so he did not see him leaving.

Now all those staying on Tahiti had left the ship, he ordered Quintal and Adams to unlock the promised store of arms and ammunition and to land them.

The wind had turned on itself, carrying Fletcher's voice to her. A daughter called Mary?

Self doubt hit her like a breaking roller and washed away her confidence in the future. He'd said nothing about daughters. Or sons. If he had plans for a family it was clearly not with her. She saw what she would become . . . A lonely woman tramping the seas because, because what? Because she wasn't prepared to live like other Tahitian women?

Well, so be it.

No Ma'ohi man wanted her as she was and she didn't want one of them the way they were. There was only Fletcher.

If even he didn't want her, her life would continue as it had been, an arid separation of wish from fulfilment.

CHAPTER 25

September 23rd, 1789: Matavai Bay, Tahiti

Later in the day Mauatua noticed a surprising number of canoes on the wind-harried beach, each with huddles of people about them. Some were the white men who had left BOUNTY and she supposed she would want to look back at the ship, too. This ship had been those men's home for almost two years, mother and father, brother, wife and sister to men who had few or none of these. Uncomfortable familiarity was as hard to leave behind as true friends or real family.

Behind her the deck was crowded with flower-decked Ma'ohi. Some had been there most of the day, lounging, drinking, laughing.

At quiet times, nose flutes fluttered and by now there was also enthusiastic singing and sporadic dancing to drums and clapping. Sunset was about half an hour away and Fletcher ordered candle lanterns hung about BOUNTY'S deck.

Mauatua imagined how magical the ship then looked from the shore. She'd seen her only once like this, the time Bligh had celebrated Christmas. The lanterns and their reflections danced with the ship and the water.

When she was a girl she thought spirits looked like this, shimmery streaks of light, forever swooping and flashing as they watched and discussed humans.

But phew! If only those tallow candles didn't stink so much.

Tamahere pulled her to sit on the deck to shelter from the wind and to play cat's cradle. She had taught him all the patterns she knew but he wanted to be quicker, slicker. Sometimes he practised all day. Fletcher had been astonished to find them playing the game, saying it was something boys and girls played in England, too.

She jumped when Jenny suddenly crouched beside her to whisper. She'd just climbed aboard but her eyes were firmly fixed landwards.

A flotilla of canoes was being launched and its purpose was not to party. Each canoe was paddled by Tahitians, and in each one an armed BOUNTY man stood. That was why they had waited on the beach, for the arms they had been promised. She pushed Tamahere into Jenny's arms and ran down to Fletcher's cabin. He burst back up the companionway, unsheathing his cutlass.

'*Mamoo! Mamoo!* Silence,' he yelled at the noisy revellers.

Tamahere escaped from Jenny and ran from one end of the deck to the other. '*Mamoo. Titreano* says *mamoo.*'

Fletcher was grateful for the tense silence the boy's shouts created. He grabbed Mauatua by the hand and ran to the bow of the ship. Ned Young and Brown followed.

Fletcher handed his cutlass to Ned and extended a telescope.

'The men who didn't want to sail with me, the same bastards I returned safely to Tahiti and then armed . . . Those same treacherous bastards have decided to take BOUNTY from me.'

'From us,' Mauatua interjected firmly, looking to Ned and Brown.

'Yes, from us,' all three men agreed at once. Fletcher drew a long single breath. By the time it returned he had a plan.

'We'll have to go.' He looked up into the rigging. 'I think the wind's settling in. If it does we've got a chance.'

'But we've got the guns, the cannons,' Young protested.

'Nine men can't man cannons and sail a ship.'

Brown woke from the deep trance fear had produced.

'The bastards,' he roared.

'We are all BOUNTY bastards,' Fletcher barked back at him. 'But there are far more BOUNTY bastards out there than there are on board. And they've got the arms I let them have for their own safety!'

Fletcher snatched his cutlass back from Ned.

'No more betrayals. First Bligh, now them. No more. We are sailing, Mr Young. Is that clear? Get some bloody canvas set. Now!'

BOUNTY was anchored close to the reef. That might be their saving. The attackers had some distance to come, on treacherous waves and into erratic winds. He hacked at the anchor lines with his cutlass until the ship was free and at once felt BOUNTY begin to swing. If she caught the right wind they might escape without shots being fired. He turned to see if the sails were yet helping. As he swung around he lifted his arm.

His cutlass struck Tamahere, slicing him from right hip to left shoulder.

Tamahere was too shocked to cry out. It was not a deep wound, just a shallow cut at a very acute angle, made with only the tip of the blade. Little flesh was pierced but there was blood, plenty of blood. The white and cream petals of Tamahere's *hei* sucked at it and blushed.

Fletcher and Tamahere stood dumb with outrage at one another. Mauatua grabbed the boy from Fletcher's reach.

'You nearly killed him. Are you mad?' She stabbed at him with a tight fist, hitting him again and again on his windpipe.

'Get him off the bloody ship,' Fletcher yelled, swiping them both away. He hurried aft, coughing away the bruising pain in his throat, smearing his bloodied hands on his breeches as he kept his eyes on the sails.

'Mr Christian, I need help here!' Adams shouted, supporting a very drunk Tararo and Niau. He was trying to get them below deck but they were resisting with surprising vigour.

'We'll need fellows like this,' Adams called.

'By God, and we will.' Fletcher added his strength, holding his cutlass as a bar between two fists to help force the two men to the top of the main companion way. They tumbled down it, landing heavily on the lower deck, but were drunk enough to feel little pain. Fletcher ordered Adams to lock them up and close the hatchway. No-one was to come back on deck.

'Some of them girls down there already asked if we was leaving.'

'Tell them, tell them we are moving up to Pare. Just a little sail. Keep whoever is down there, down there.'

The first shots fired from the lagoon added to the tormenting threat of the flotilla's thundering drums. Double canoes over burdened with Ma'ohi had joined the single canoes. Fletcher was enraged by the cracks of their muskets and Mauatua could barely keep up with his maddened strides. She dragged and then carried Tamahere with her.

They had to fight through pandemonium to reach the ship's wheel at the rear of the deck. Drunk or sober, howling Tahitian men, women and children ran to dive overboard or argued about it. Those too drunk to know or care made dangerous obstacles in the candlelight and food and drink were scattered perilously underfoot. Fletcher tripped and took them down. Tamahere's blood now covered all three of them.

'He's a menace. Get him off this blasted ship!' he ordered. She ignored him. He shouldn't be blaming her son for the mess he was in.

She tried to interfere when she saw Adams and Quintal pushing women down the rear companionway but could do little with Tamahere so heavy in her arms, still whimpering and bleeding. One woman slithered out and dived overboard without looking. Another whom she recognised as her friend Teio held her infant girl, only a few months old, whose frightened wailing stabbed through all other sounds. Quintal tried to yank the baby away. Teio's resistance was heroic and Quintal managed only to force away one of her protective arms. He pushed it up her back.

BOUNTY'S hull thrashed into opposing waves as it strained to obey its sudden urgent orders. Mauatua stumbled, losing Tamahere and falling into Quintal. His cruel grip on Teio was broken. Adams evilly took advantage this, spun the disoriented woman and forced her down the steps. She tripped and dropped the infant who fell onto the press of women already on the companionway. Quintal and Adams pushed on her back. As she fell the resisting women had no choice but to tumble into a heap with her and the baby on the lower deck.

Mauatua found Tamahere again but another lurch of the ship over balanced him. He slipped on trampled bananas and tumbled into Fletcher, who was shooting towards the flotilla.

The shot went wild and whistled past her ear.

Tamahere slammed his eyes shut, pushed hands over his ears and held his head tight to his chest. She recovered from the shock of the missed shot and reached out for him. Fletcher pulled her away. His hand trembled as he pointed back at Tahiti, now sooty and intimidating in flickering, cloud-masked moonlight.

'He'll be safer there. He's been a bloody pain in the arse every day for the last months. And now look, he's snivelling because he's wounded and bleeding and you were nearly shot dead because of him. I almost murdered you because of him and we haven't even sailed.'

She was incredulous. The only comfort she truly trusted was that of her son. She grabbed him and held him tightly as she attempted to focus her mind. Fletcher took her by the shoulders.

'You told me. You told me yourself. Boys have many mothers on Tahiti. He doesn't need you.'

She was disgusted he would say such things but before she could respond Fletcher leaned closer to her.

'But I do. I need you.'

He repeated the words again and again. She searched for the truth in his eyes, their dark brown irises quickened by the candles' golden flickers. What did he need her for?

She broke free and ran with Tamahere to the ship's side. Renewed gun fire from the lagoon had stopped the free-fall flight of Ma'ohi from the ship. Frightened men and women cowered behind the protective stanchions, hesitant to go, fearful of staying. Fletcher brutally handed Ma'ohi aside to follow her. One of the men he pushed slipped and then fell into the sea. His cries were copied and exaggerated by the crowd. He had no time for Ma'ohi histrionics.

'*Mamoo*,' he shouted. 'Or I will shoot you.'

She fought him to jump with her son. In their struggles his hand caught Tamahere's neck garland. It broke. The distraction allowed him to pull her further back onto the deck. She wrestled to free herself but he held her until she relented.

He released one wrist and pushed the crushed *hei* into her palm.

She saw only empty bravado in him. He was doing what he thought looked right, not what he really wanted to do. He hadn't asked for BOUNTY so they could be together, but only for his selfish need to escape punishment. How could she believe Fletcher wanted her?

The uncertainties before her unleashed every one of her buried inner conflicts, illuminated everything she had never wanted to think or say. Racing tears liquefied Tamahere's drying blood on her cheeks. She spat as she spoke, still fighting for the freedom of her other wrist. She screeched. There was no other way to get it out.

'Why are you stopping me? You want a Mary daughter but who will be her mother? Not me, I bet.'

'It's not true. It's not true. You are wrong.'

'You have to say that!' She heard herself screaming, frightening Tamahere in her arms.

Fletcher's face shocked her. It had settled into what seemed to be resignation, a readiness to bid goodbye. She looked at him from the edges of her flooded eyes. He was searching deep into her. She didn't want to succumb but once more she felt his eyes on her heart.

'I am telling you the truth,' he continued, his voice even and determined. 'I can't do this without you. If you don't come with me, if you jump I will jump. But I won't be following you. I'll swim away until I sink and then need no one.'

'Go on then. Jump!' Tamahere screamed into his face, pummelling his chest. He pushed the boy's head away from them and kept his palm over the struggling boy's face. He spoke in a low, persuasive voice.

'I would jump. I would.' He looked over the melee on the deck and out into the darkness ahead. 'That is the truth.'

A flash of memory evoked the moments only weeks ago when they seemed to think and plan as one. Now she doubted him. He was certainly warming her heart again, but she might be reacting to his outer charisma, the ploys she suspected he used to win any personal confrontation whatever the cost in truth or his dignity. Yet if his feelings were genuine. . . *Aueee*! Would a Tahitian woman ever read a *popa'a* man?

'Yes, it is, it is really the truth,' he said again. Then he faltered. 'I do need you, but that is not *all* the truth.'

He glanced away and up into the sails. They remained confused, flapping uselessly as the wind still gusted unreliably. He took his hand from Tamahere's snivelling face and looked forward to see Martin was keeping good watch and then to the stern to see Brown was attentive at the wheel. Most of the canoes were now distracted by swimmers, their paddlers anxious to avoid crashing into one another rather than determined to reach BOUNTY.

He left her to urge more and more party goers into the sea, yelling back that a living human shield would be as effective as dead men and women in the canoes. As people jumped they cleared more deck space.

She felt exposed, isolated and wanting to be among what she understood and knew, whatever the risk to her. It would take only seconds to leap from the ship but Fletcher sped back and took in his arms. He leaned his head close, ignoring her protests as he spoke.

'Here is my *whole* truth, Mauatua. We spoke about it before. If we are to have a life together, there should be nothing from our pasts. Nothing.'

Her mind locked in confusion.

Fletcher continued before she could speak.

'I'm right, aren't I? Boys do have many mothers on Tahiti. And fathers. Don't they?'

It was just she feared, Fletcher wanted her only as strut for his weaknesses. Yet wouldn't allow her Tamahere. Didn't he understand the bond between a mother and her son? He of all people.

She searched for another touchstone, a truth that would instead promise her a partnership with him.

In a voice she felt might not be her own she asked a question no woman would have dared on Tahiti.

'Would you make me kill my babies? Like men do here . . .'

Fletcher's mouth was forming what she knew must be his final words when she heard a sail snap. Another flapped and then sighed as wind properly filled its belly at last.

'We've got it, by God, we've got it! We are away.'

Fletcher broke into exultant laughter. He released her, clapped his hands and danced a few steps.

She didn't run to jump overboard with Tamahere. Not yet. She wanted to hear Fletcher's answer.

He stood away from her, his arms outspread in invitation.

'Why would I kill your babies?' he asked. 'They would be our babies, *our* babies.' He held her face and kissed her forehead.

There was nothing of the past she needed, not with the future he promised. She had weaknesses. If he could support her in those, she could support him in the extraordinary adventure before them.

The straining canvas that forced the ship onwards sang of a new future truly together and of making a new sort of world.

Mauatua pressed her nose to Tamahere's nose, whispered to him and then, praying to the land she so loved, she walked to the edge of the deck and threw him as far as she could from the heaving side of BOUNTY.

'*A rohi,*' she called. 'Have courage. '*A rohi, rohi.*'

She watched only long enough to see Tamahere bob to the lagoon's boiling surface and then be scooped into a canoe.

Her lips shivered. She tightened them until her sobs had been swallowed. She flung back her head.

'Yes, a boy does have many mothers on Tahiti.'

Fletcher smiled at her, with pride she hoped. He must have been waiting for her to abandon Tamahere, to prove she was committed as he.

'Any one of them is better for him than a woman like me,' she said loudly, to be certain.

BOUNTY moved faster. The drumming faded and the canoes fell back, defeated by human jetsam and BOUNTY'S sail power.

Watching the fluorescent skein of the reef ravel and unravel beside BOUNTY'S quickening course, she became increasingly alive to the prospects before her of the hunt for a home.

This was what Ma'ohi had done for generations, as far back as the gods. Yet none had done what she was about to do with Fletcher.

'Anyway,' Mauatua said, as adventurers always comforted one another. 'We might come back soon, eh Fletcher?'

'Or, we might not.'

Fletcher kissed her cheek, that funny wet thing *popa'a* liked. She turned and offered her lips. As the reef was breached, she opened her mouth and kissed him like a *popa'a* woman for the first time.

She looked back at Tahiti just once.

The clouds had lifted and Orohena, most thrusting and dominating of its peaks, now shimmered in lucid air and vivid moonlight but she had no interest in what such portents might warn.

If Tahiti had gods they could say nothing she wanted to hear. There would be other gods in her new life, gods that respected women.

She turned away and did not look back again.

CHAPTER 26

BOUNTY skated with delight beneath her feet. The Pacific no longer confronted the hull but sported with it. The bow wave hissed beguiling songs, and the sound of the water racing beneath the hull was sweet and comforting to Mauatua's ears. She supposed even the wind sighed with pleasure in the welcoming sails.

During the day the deck had soaked warmth from the sun. Now the oaken planks returned it and released the tensions in her muscles.

She joined Fletcher and his eight sailor-followers by the wheel as a group for the first time. He gave his initial orders aboard BOUNTY as a truly free man.

'I think most reefs and islands are marked on the charts but who can be sure? We'll set temporary watches tonight. Include me. Four to eight am, and then work around that. Anything else, gentlemen?'

When he glanced up discreetly to seek the comfort of the constant Southern Cross she saw every other man follow his look.

Around it, the bowl of night sky was as star-punctured as light through the finest tapa cloth.

'We'll sort out everything in the morning. Watches, women, where we might be going. In the meantime head west and then south towards the atoll of Tetiaroa.

'Come on Mauatua. I'll need help to face what's waiting down below.'

Fletcher didn't need her help to comfort the unwilling passengers aboard BOUNTY, not with his gift of charm. She stayed in the shadows as he spoke to every man and woman sober enough to listen, and each thought they were his greatest concern.

Those most anxious were touched, held, stroked. He gave assurance BOUNTY would pause at Tetiaroa atoll in the morning so they could return to Tahiti. For now he invited them to relax, eat and drink. There was plenty of food, all the roasted pigs and fish and vegetables from Teina and Itia. And rum for those who could face more of it.

She watched Fletcher's muscles as they slipped back and forth beneath the skin of his bared arms. His square hands, each with an opulent mound of muscle beneath the thumb, spread like an opening flowers and gave pleasure to all they touched. His neck broadened perfectly into shoulders straight enough to judge the horizon. It was easy for her to picture the curving muscles of his tattooed buttocks and the thick cords of his thighs or the cushions of his calf muscles responding each time he leaned or kneeled or squatted on the deck.

Something new had grown in her head and heart. Now it flickered throughout her body and she could ignore it no longer. *Navenave*, that's what it was, real sexual desire for Fletcher. She no longer wanted games.

She wanted Fletcher Christian as a lover.

There was nothing of that in the past.

'You're too late, *vahine*,' Jenny had crowed. 'You never do it with friends. Takes the excitement away. Better look somewhere else. He'll be doing that, too.'

Did married couples really have to choose between being friends and having sex? It couldn't be true. The longer she spent with Fletcher, the more she knew him, the more she was excited sexually by him. Both had now passed through weighty portals of no return, battled to make a new place where their focus could be only one another

She was ready for him as a man.

Fletcher locked the cabin door.

'We've done it,' he said.

'Done what?' Mauatua pressed her body against his and fondled his dark brown hair, still longer than hers. She tipped her head back, so she missed nothing of the liveliness of his penetrating eyes, of his lips that swelled as though stung by a poisoned leaf.

They usually separated when she felt him fully erect. This time she stayed close, moving her hips slightly, giving enough friction to make it easier and more exciting for him to release the lubricants he produced so fulsomely. She would match him tonight.

She leaned to his ear and nibbled and blew into it, until he squirmed, wanting it to stop but never able to refuse offered pleasure. Then she undid his belt.

'I know you don't like to be in charge all the time,' she teased.

Fletcher laughed low in his throat. 'It's good to give in. Not to be, well, not to be *quite* so much of a man.'

He stood naked on the pile of his clothes. Mauatua leaned forward to kiss him with an open mouth, and her hands cupped his testicles.

Limb after limb, muscle after muscle of his body involuntarily stretched, the way a languid, sun-sodden cat might do before settling to sleep. All he had to do was be complacent and she would do the rest. He laughed softly again.

'This is not one of those times.'

He lifted her from her feet and lowered her face-down onto the thick carpet of tapa on the floor of the cabin. And then he slowly undressed her and worshipped her. His tongue was hard and determined as it flickered, exploring each smooth shape of the track of her long neck and endless spine, her entire body writhing around the single point of scorching vibration etched by his tongue tip until she begged him to stop.

Fletcher continued licking and nibbling, biting and teasing. He turned her over and lifted her legs to his shoulders and then excited every inch down both legs, until, starting behind her knees he licked around her thighs and towards her cleft, each sweep longer and longer, one leg after the other. When his tongue finally reached the top of her thighs she opened her eyes to watch. His tongue circled and teased her, closer, further away, pressing hard and then fluttering lighter than a butterfly, sometimes wet, sometimes dry, sometimes fast sometimes agonizingly slow.

'Do it, do it, touch me,' she urged. Her voice was shameless, thick and urgent. He pushed out his tongue as far as it would stretch and plunged it into her, his upper lip and teeth niggling at her *tane iti*, her erect little man. Her cry was unearthly.

Now wetter and smoother, his tongue flicked her nipples and up and down her neck. Her heat was on his breath. He hesitated and their eyes locked. In this instant of stillness, she believed completely in their future. He plunged his tongue into her again. Then his tongue was in her mouth and they were sharing her scents and tastes. Their entire world was concentrated on the twist of their mouths and what was in them.

Fletcher positioned himself, feeling just with his hot, wet tip, now so engorged it cleared his foreskin. When they had drunk enough of each other's mouth, Mauatua stretched and widened her legs. Fletcher thrust his buttocks once and swiftly entered her for the first time. Neither gave quarter as their athletic bodies fought to give and to exact most pleasure. She felt they were abandoned, as wild as the animals he had shown her in books, quite unfettered by shame or convention or human weakness. Yet instinctively they understood they were also reaching the highest level of being human, of loving and being loved.

When they simultaneously knew their bodies' demands had only one further plateau to breast, she was on all fours and held his hand on the pivot of her ecstasy. Fletcher pulled out and flipped her onto her back. He fell lumpen onto her entire body length. She panicked, pushing her hands against his chest. Fletcher contracted the fist-sized muscles of his torso. He straightened his arms on either side of her and then went up onto his toes, hovering over her like a wraith begging sanctuary.

His sweat-sheened biceps and thighs trembled as he lowered himself so only their taut nipples touched. He dipped his head so his nose touched her nose and then he settled his lips on hers as lightly as petals fall onto water. United only by shadowy kisses from both their worlds he entered her again. It was ethereal after the roughhouse of the last hour. Here in exquisite serenity, her world became only the bliss of the slow shunting heat of his cock inside her. From flared nostrils and through barely touching lips, their breaths danced, swirled invisibly between them into whorls as significant as the most sacred *ta'tau*.

Fletcher's strength kept their aching bodies apart. He moved faster and faster inside her. She lifted her hips, creating a suspended cocoon of heat and sensation between them that intensified with every thrust, hurtling her to undreamed of heights with the certainty there would be a pinnacle from which she must then blindly leap. Together they abandoned their last shreds of self and simultaneously crashed into a scintillating abyss of light.

It took a long time to compose their shuddering bodies, hoarse throats and racing hearts. Now she believed what Jenny told her, that men from the other side of the world took time to make love because they were not pre-heated by watching lascivious dancing. They were not already straining for release when they came to a woman. And the longer a man took with a woman . . . Now she knew why she never really cared for fucking. It had always been quick and brutal, one-sided.

At last, she knew what a woman could feel, should be.

'Now I am Mrs Christian,' she crowed, circling her fingers around his nipples. She saw his face cloud and so tapped her forehead swiftly.

'In here, anyway.'

CHAPTER 27

Fletcher barred her way when she stepped onto the deck early the next day, insisting events must settle without their interference. All over the deck she saw small groups argue, push and pull, sometimes in anger, sometimes because they lost their footing as the ship loitered in the rolling swell off Tetiaroa atoll. As the seven mutineers without wives decided which woman or women to take with them, BOUNTY'S deck, already packed with discomforted pigs, goats and chickens, was a noisy and noisome marketplace.

Fletcher refused to sail closer to Tetiaroa because he had no idea how friendly the atoll might be. She insisted he must, because she knew most women aboard wanted to leave but couldn't swim that far. Surely he asked, even women who think they don't want to come now, might get used to it?

He shouldn't have said that. Why should they? She would make sure none of the women was compelled against her will.

'Come on, boys,' she shouted, interfering as she knew she must, 'be fair. These are big decisions for anyone. You made yours by free will. These women must be allowed to decide for themselves too.'

'We don't want some of them to decide.' Quintal shouted back. He roughly pushed a particularly fat woman to the side of the deck. 'We've decided for her. She's too fat.' He grabbed the wrist of another. 'And she's too old.'

Mauatua grabbed Quintal's hand from the old woman and put a protective arm around her.

'Then have some respect, Quintal. She is not an animal in a market. This is a woman who has brought up sons as old as you. She is a grandmother. She is part of a family group. She came aboard for a party, not to be treated like leftovers after you've eaten.'

By now the woman had seen canoes paddling out from Tetiaroa. She struggled until Mauatua was forced to let her go. She ran to the side and dived into the water. Taking advantage of the surprise, the fat woman followed. A few more dived after them.

None waited for rescue but swam vigorously towards the canoes, helping one another, ensuring each was safe.

'That was disgusting, Quintal,' Mauatua said. 'We must all be equals on board this ship. We must treat people the way we want to be treated. It is pointless voting if. . .'

'Aye, well you know my views on that. Voting is for the rich of this world, not for poor sailors.'

She turned to Fletcher, who shook his head in disbelief. His disapproval of Quintal was tacit approval of what she was saying and doing, interfering though it clearly was.

'If you don't like the way this ship is run,' she challenged Quintal, 'you can jump and swim, too.'

'He might like to jump with a few of these, then,' Adams yelled. He herded up the men and women who had been locked below decks.

Tararo and Niau stood blearily behind them, woolly tongued and not really understanding the situation. Four other Ma'ohi men accompanied them, quite as fuddled and standing very close so body contact gave them confidence. She recognised two of them as Tubuaians. One was Taaroamiva, younger brother of Chief Taaroa. He had already changed his name to Titahiti, so she was confident he was looking for a new life.

She hated men who were drunk or suffering the after effects. She spoke curtly to them. Yes, we are at sea she told them. Yes, we are looking for a new home. No, we are not going back to Tahiti. She pointed to Tetiaroa as their last chance of escape. Fletcher came to her elbow.

'We will need men like these.'

'But not under compulsion. That would be as bad for us as for them.'

These six Ma'ohi men had tasted adventure in Tubuai and were happy for more. They agreed to sail on BOUNTY but asked her for something to eat and then to go back to sleeping.

'You will want women. There are plenty to choose from.'

Tararo squinted into the sunlight, shrugged and then quickly walked around the groups of women, still shading his eyes. When he returned he told her there were none he would refuse. Niau ran his eyes over Tararo's physique proudly, saying, 'And none who would refuse him.'

The four others strolled around the women and told her they too would not fight for or against any of the women. She could see the prospect of co-habiting with Ma'ohi men seemed more interesting to the women than the white men did. She understood this. It was the stale, sweaty smell of so many white men.

The ship needed women confident enough to improve the habits of the men, rather than to allow themselves to become as unwashed.

There were now 15 women together with nine white and six Ma'ohi men who wanted to continue on the ship, so there was one woman for each of the men. Should she encourage the other Ma'ohi men to stay, or hope they would desert? Fletcher was nervous, wanting to sail on, far beyond the reach of Tahiti's big sailing canoes and out of the way of ships from Europe. She wouldn't agree until she was certain every woman was happy.

'My sisters, *vahine*. I am sorry you find yourself in the middle of the ocean when you did not decide this. The men who left BOUNTY came back to fight us. They might have thrown flames and burned the ship or sunk it some other way. By sailing so quickly, Fletcher saved our lives.' The women dipped their heads and shoulders towards Fletcher.

'This means we sailed away earlier than expected. There will be no turning back to Tahiti. Instead we will sail until we find a new home. There men will not rule, you will be asked your opinion and will be allowed to say it without punishment. Listen to these examples.' She beckoned the women closer.

'You will not be forbidden to eat certain foods. You will not have to follow *tapu* rules about who can touch what and when, usually to the advantage only of men. You will not feed daughters only with food gathered with your own hands. And you will not have to kill your babies.'

Her hand slid up the back of her neck and she tilted her head back, slowly lifting her hair so it flowed between her fingers in shining streams, each profoundly blacker than any tattoo.

'And I will have long hair, because that is what *I* want.'

The women laughed and slapped one another but she recognised it was more likely to be disbelief at her boldness rather than excitement at a new future. She noticed from their accents some of the women were not from Tahiti. She was honest, telling them she could not promise a paradise, but she could promise independence and respect Ma'ohi women would never have on Tahiti – or on Huahine or Raiatea.

She turned again to Fletcher.

'Is this not so, Mr Christian?' He nodded without speaking.

Mauatua looked more deeply into the group of expectant faces. None of the Ma'ohi women was as tall as she was, some were darker skinned, all were younger, some prettier.

Fletcher quietly said that curiosity is what he most wanted to find. If a woman had curiosity in her makeup, she would make a good companion and she too looked for that in their eyes.

Fletcher surprised her by speaking up to tell them BOUNTY's women would be remembered as the first of their kind. They would create a new race of children, half Ma'ohi and half European, a new breed with the best of both worlds.

'Or the worst,' said a miserable woman, whose constant tearful sniffling caused deep thought in the other women. She ran to the side of the ship and saw the canoes were much closer and that they were big enough to carry more than the women already in the sea.

'Not me,' she shouted and jumped overboard.

The undecided Ma'ohi men were shocked to hear what had been said about the status of women in this new life. Several stood with their hands unconsciously over their testicles. Mauatua knew what that meant. They would not be coming, yet wouldn't be seen jumping overboard like frightened women.

Quintal grabbed one of the remaining women, little more than a girl and with her chest still quite flat. He crushed her into his arms and smothered her face with kisses.

'You'll do though, my beauty. You'll be Matt's *vahine* won't you? Here, cop a feel of what I've got for ye my beauty.' He rubbed his cock against her thighs through his trousers and became increasingly excited by her writhing against it. The girl harangued him in a high, harsh voice.

'You stinky! I rather do it with a billy goat. They not so smelly. Ugh!'

'Dear me,' Quintal said, trying to kiss her. 'A bit of a scold is you? I likes those high spirits. I do.'

The girl managed to push him away and then slapped his erection hard with the back of her hand. Matt had to laugh as much as the other men did, but his truer feelings of outrage showed on his face.

The girl had not finished. She turned to an equally young friend and then in her natural low voice said, 'I like no hairy arse and no stinky armpits and no rotten mouth. Ugh!'

The image she so sharply promoted persuaded her friend. They ran to each other and then jumped with linked hands.

'Pity,' Mauatua said to Fletcher. 'That's just the sort of spirit we could do with on this ship.'

He agreed, women would need great spirit to cope with his shipmates.

Quintal pulled another woman to him, with the same sexualised blandishments. Brown yanked him away.

'Bugger off,' Quintal said, struggling to keep the woman from Brown's hands. 'No mate, you bugger off. You're a bloody pox on us all,' Brown yelled, spitting his anger directly into Quintal's face.

'We're already down to 12 *vahine*. Keep going this way and buggery will be all you get.'

Quintal loosed the woman and brought up his fists. McCoy stood between the men. 'He's right, Matt. Lose any more and we got real trouble.'

Matt Quintal counted sullenly, pulling down his fingers and thumbs to keep a tally. 'We've got 12 of them and there are 15 of us, including the black fellers. Don't work.'

'Might be your fault, Matt.' Quintal again shaped up to punch Brown. The other white men bunched around him. He dropped his fists and forced a laugh. 'Just joking, boys,' he said, apparently hoping the ploy that worked for Mills would work for him.

The less excitable mutineers ignored all this and quietly spoke to the remaining women. Young was assessing each woman slowly, but even so, Mauatua thought, for everything except her mind and what practical skills she might bring.

Still he was taking it seriously and treating them with respect.

Only Adams looked genuinely interested in what each woman had to say. In spite of his cruelty last night, his early adoption of the Tahitian way of life and his excellent Tahitian meant he was the only one who looked like a home maker.

'Wait. Hold on now,' McCoy said. 'If six of the 15 men are those black bastards, that's solved. They can share. They like that.'

She fiercely corrected McCoy. 'No,' she shouted back. 'That's what you'd like to think. Those men will share only if it is their free will. And the women have to agree, too.'

Fletcher could contain himself no longer. 'Listen, shipmates. Tubuai proved we will only be safe if we find an uninhabited island. If this is so, these women could be the only ones you will see for all the rest of your life. Do you understand that? The only ones for the rest of your life.'

This resonated deeply with everyone deck including the women, who began looking more carefully at the only men they might see for the rest of their lives.

The 12 women left on board all seemed willing to sail, although one or two wailed about the household tools they wished they had with them. Mauatua took them to see the *popa'a* tools in the galley below, all of which made a woman's life easier. There were also Tahitian tools left by women who didn't make it back onto BOUNTY last night. She would share these out, for she understood such utensils expressed an important part of Ma'ohi women.

They must serve the same sort of purpose as men's testicles, she said, the way they were always fiddling to check if they were still there.

Before Fletcher had given sailing orders, she was back, with six elderly women discovered hiding in the greenhouse. They were too frightened to come on deck the night before and had slept in the hold cabins. They were disoriented and alarmed and she saw their continuous whining moans irritated Fletcher.

'Now what?' he demanded.

'Do we need them, should I try to persuade them?' The general attitude of the other mutineers on deck answered that. They were dismissive, insulting and laughing. The group of Ma'ohi men on deck, who might once have been persuaded to sail on, joined the clamour, demanding they too be put off the ship.

'Too late,' he snapped at them. Unwilling to accept that, they crowded him, demanding to be taken back to Tahiti. Mauatua silenced them. The men would simply have to accept they had made a bad decision she told them. She pulled Fletcher aside.

'It would be better to put them somewhere safe, the men *and* the women, I mean,' Fletcher pursed his lips and dropped his head, only just managing to hold in his frustration and anger. She reminded him he was now a man with no timetable. They had as many days to idle or waste as there were, and no obligation to spend time this or that better way. They would lose nothing by being kind and surely he did not want unwilling passengers who might mutiny?

'We'll take them to Mo'orea,' he relented. 'That's the closest to Tahiti I'll go.' He piloted BOUNTY to Mo'orea's west coast, the one furthest from Tahiti. As soon as the men and the elderly women had been rescued by canoes he set BOUNTY off sharply.

His ship's company was now nine European men, six Ma'ohi men and 12 Ma'ohi women plus Teio's baby girl.

'Mr Brown, Mr Young. This afternoon you must begin to teach our new shipmates how to sail this ship.'

He set a course to the Marquesas Islands to the north east, at last daring to feel truly liberated. What his fellow mariners wanted from him is what he wanted for himself. He pulled Mauatua to him and they watched as the sails filled and BOUNTY turned in the new direction.

'Last night, well, for me that was the start of our voyage.' She returned his kiss, lightly brushing his lips.

'Think of it as an early birthday present, Mr Christian,' she murmured into his ear. He pulled away, startled.

'Birthday? What's the date?'

'Not today, tomorrow. September 25th. Ned told me you will be 25.'

'I will be,' Fletcher said thoughtfully. 'I'll be 25.'

'It's a sign,' Mauatua said. 'A very good omen, a marker.'

'Except for last night the last 25 years ended rather horridly. Let's hope the next are somewhat less exciting.'

He walked Mauatua to the bow.

Ahead of BOUNTY they saw only blue skies and blue water.

CHAPTER 28

Mauatua quickly convinced Fletcher the reef-ringed islands of the Marquesas were a dangerous choice, for although seeming far flung, men and women from these islands travelled easily to and from Tahiti. Some gossip here, repeated there, became a tale known everywhere. Suddenly, there would be Royal Navy ships firing at them. There was no disappointment when Fletcher turned BOUNTY westward and headed to search for a home in the vast, largely unexplored waters of the South Pacific.

He zig-zagged the ship, averaging about 200 miles each leg, searching in latitudes that promised the easy climate of Tahiti. He was certain she was well enough crewed and was safe for the moment. But for how many months? Even with her copper-sheathed hull to protect her from shipworm, BOUNTY's timbers had limited life without a ship's carpenter or men with specialty maintenance skills on board.

Day after day after day Mauatua saw nothing but sea, sea and then more sea. All that changed was the rhythm of its waves and the colour reflected into it from the sky. It wasn't long before the ship's mood of adventure dissolved and she sensed the women had joined her in the mental state that ships require and that has little to do with life on land.

The sounding of the ship's bell and of standing watch became their measures of time rather than the passage of the sun or the positions of stars. She watched vigilantly and soon told Fletcher that every one of the women was content and playing her part.

The person least affected by being at sea was Teio's baby girl now called Sally but which quickly became Sully on her mother's tongue. She had 11 other mothers who as easily fed her with breadfruit pap or held her. Whoever was off watch when Teio was on duty looked after Sully without a second thought.

Adams was the most likely of the men to comfort, watch or hold the child. He told Mauatua why.

He had been brought up in a workhouse orphanage.

It hurt that he had never had the haven of mother's arms, not even a father's lesser embrace.

When he stood in for Sully's mother he was giving what he had never been given, and in return found a serenity that made him the happiest and quietest of men. 'It feels like closing a circle,' he confided.

BOUNTY was built needing only 15 hands to man and to sail her safely. With 27 adults on board, there was no reason for Fletcher or Mauatua to stand watch.

While Fletcher captained the ship, Mauatua busied herself with issues of general welfare and with food in particular. One woman and one man from each watch were detailed as extra help in the galley. One helped Mauatua with food for the company, the other for the animals on board.

She ensured there was always good food available whenever men and women came off watch, even at 4 in the morning. Spending so much time in the galley meant she saw who was eating well and who was not, knowing that when food brought sailors too much or too little comfort, it signalled a saddened expectation, or frustration or hurt.

Her womanly insights were shared with Fletcher and between them they ensured every man and woman aboard was valued and knew it.

Together they insisted on the Royal Navy's routine of clothes being washed every week and this became a yardstick of discipline and respect on board. Hammocks were aired every day it was possible. The decks too were washed and scrubbed daily, exercise as useful as Bligh's dancing. Nits were attacked too, whenever enough water could be spared for washing and rinsing.

Slowly she discovered the intoxication of long-distance sailing. It took time to appreciate that when she talked or cooked, slept or made love, BOUNTY was always moving onwards. However familiar the sea's horizons they were constantly different and every second, every minute, every hour, every day brought her inescapably closer to her new home.

The first place Fletcher dared anchor was an island Tararo called Rarotonga. Inside Rarotonga's reef, Mauatua and Tararo recited the history of the ship and their own genealogies and then listened to those of the priests and chiefs who greeted them.

Once these age-old courtesies showed neither was a threat to the other Rarotongans flocked out in hundreds of canoes bringing pork and chicken, fish and coconuts, bananas, breadfruit and taro and sweet potatoes and each gift came with tapa cloth or something else wrought by hand. None asked anything in return but Fletcher gave generously from the ship's red feathers and glass beads, axe heads and chisels.

Mauatua proudly showed groups of women over the ship. They owned pigs and goats, chickens and dogs, so the ship's cats were the only animals that intrigued them. They were more astonished at everything below decks, at the touch and shine and cut of metal knives, of cooking pots, at glass and china, canvas and cotton, and at the galley's great stove.

What impressed the women most were the streams of fresh water that kept the plants alive in the greenhouse. There was no question in any woman's mind about what they were seeing and they told her so. This ship of pink-skinned men was something unheard of, a floating island with its own freshwater streams. She let them believe what they wanted. While they thought they might be in the presence of the beloved of gods and goddesses they were less likely to steal.

Even so, one novelty aboard was loudly envied. No Rarotongan dreamed such a fruit as oranges existed in the world. So, healthy, fruit-bearing trees were given to the island, together with instructions for their best care.

'This is the first European ship to find Rarotonga,' Fletcher boasted. 'The orange trees will forever be proof BOUNTY was here.'

They continued westwards and next explored the Friendly Islands but stopped only at Tongatabu, less than a hundred miles from Tofua, close to the site of the mutiny. There was more trading and more gifts and BOUNTY was increasingly well provisioned, in direct proportion to the degree of frustration growing aboard. No matter the blandishments and promises of the island, Fletcher ordered the ship to sail on, for here there were memories of Captain Cook.

Where would the Navy search but on islands already known?

Yet on this early November morning Fletcher steered BOUNTY neither west nor east, north nor south. He had stopped their search for a home. His ship lurched unevenly, drifting in slow broad circles wherever winds and currents and a disinterested helmsman took her.

Fletcher was sweltering over books in his cabin but Mauatua pestered him until she eventually extracted the reason from him. He listlessly admitted he had no more ideas of where to search.

On their furthest horizon were the most southerly Fijian islands of Lau. Bligh's books told him they had every allurement but also marauding cannibals. Ahead he knew only of more islands with the same reputation and then of vast seas to the Indies and whatever the continent of Australia might offer. The Indies were the Spice Islands, and swarmed with European ships. Australia was so far away and unknown, and there were awful stories of its aboriginal inhabitants.

When BOUNTY was not sailing forward there was little exchange of air on the lower deck. Fletcher was sweating badly again, not just from the heat but because of his anxiety about not fulfilling his promises to find a home. Not knowing what to say or do to comfort Fletcher, she turned to leave him to his sullen reading.

She was blocked by Tararo, his arms and legs spread between the sides and top of the door, his contorted face increasing the effect of a malevolent golden spider. The five other Ma'ohi men crowded behind him and beyond them was a small group of white men and Ma'ohi women. Some, whose faces she couldn't see, stood on the companion way.

'It is enough, Titreano.'

'What is enough, Tararo?' she demanded to know.

'This sailing with nowhere to go!' Tararo's anger was intense. He leaned further forward into the cabin, a threat of violence implicit.

Fletcher breathed slowly before he answered.

'If you bothered to read the stars we might know where to go, Tararo.' She knew the stillness in his voice meant he was close to the edge of anger. 'Don't stars show you where the islands are?' Fletcher asked in a tight voice, almost too quiet to hear.

Tararo tossed his head. 'They do. But every time we find an island you say no. There is only one thing to do now. And yes we all agree. You must take us back to Tahiti.'

'Tahiti?'

Fletcher's head fell onto his books.

'God save me.'

Tararo pushed past Mauatua into the cabin.

The cat in Fletcher's lap arched her back and hissed. Fletcher tipped her to the floor and jumped from his chair to stand against the outer bulkhead, pressing himself as far as possible from Tararo. The cat flattened herself on the floor and scuttled out between Tararo's legs. Fletcher swayed. Mauatua supported him.

'What? What's the matter?' she asked as discreetly as she could.

'Get them away,' he whispered. 'It's, it's so hot and I . . .'

He turned closer to her ear. 'Suddenly I can't stand the smell of them, any of them. I feel sick.'

The Ma'ohi men had lately let their body hairs grow. With so little water spared for washing, decayed sweat on these became a competitive sign of masculinity, of equivalence or superiority to the mutineers. Fletcher was the only man on board keeping himself free of body hair. No wonder he was overwhelmed by Tararo's invasion. So was she.

'Go, go you must all go,' she said, waving up a book to sweep the choking muskiness out of the cabin. There was little to replace it but more of the same. She pleaded silently for Fletcher to say something.

Instead, he reached for one of his cloths from the camphorwood-lined mahogany chest. He took several inhalations of reviving scent and then whispered, as though frightened by what must be said.

'No, not Tahiti. That is impossible.'

When protests began he held up his hand and waited until there was silence. 'I have found our home. It's just I didn't know how to tell you' he admitted. Only Mauatua saw him crossing the fingers of his other hand..

Quintal pushed through the melee and into the cabin, making the heat and stench worse. 'Better bloody well tell us where!'

'First, I'll tell you about *what*, rather than where, if you will allow me.'

He stared Tararo and Quintal down, demanding silently that all attention was on him. When the jostling crowd behind them was listening expectantly he held up a book.

He pointed at the cover, showing the important parts of its long title: Hawkesworth's *Account of the Voyages . . . in the Southern Hemisphere.*

'Everything about it is in here.'

The crowd couldn't contain its excitement. Mauatua jostled him, too.

'Read it, read it to us.'

The reaction was so singularly enthusiastic she thought Fletcher was back in control, but she felt him sway against her again.

'It's too hot and crowded here,' she said decisively. 'Let's go on deck. Tell the others, we'll meet at the end of the afternoon watch.'

When they were alone again, she lost her temper. 'You know how anxious they are. How *could* you keep this to yourself?'

He sat heavily again and his head stayed bowed. 'You will understand, when I . . . I need some time alone.'

He turned to her and she saw reproach. What had she done wrong? Fletcher continued before she could protest.

'Don't you think I want a solution as much as everyone else?' he demanded. 'Tararo and Quintal aren't the only buggers tired of searching for a home.'

Alone at last, Fletcher smartened himself up as much as he could, refreshed his senses with a little gardenia *monoi,* and then sat to read the description of Pitcairn's Island once more.

Was there something he had missed?

Captain Philip Carteret supposedly discovered it on July 2nd 1767 and named the island after the young midshipman who first spotted it. Was it exactly what everyone dreamed of? What had Carteret not known, not seen? Fletcher feared raising false hopes, and that is why he had not told Mauatua. No hope was better than hope that would be dashed.

He came up from his cabin almost as soon as the afternoon eight bells were struck. A brilliant sky bled warmth and ease into all on deck. There was an air of contentment, as though the company knew and agreed with what he was about to tell them. The sea-soft breezes swirled the *monoi* about his head reminding him of the incense that shrouded priests and for a happy instant he felt he was some Old Testament prophet, about to read from a revealed tablet.

He said no words of introduction but stood where he was easily seen and heard and then slowly read the description of Pitcairn's Island, pausing after each distinct fact, so each could be absorbed.

'We continued our course westward till the evening of Thursday, the 2nd of July, when we discovered land to the northward of us. Upon approaching it the next day, it appeared like a great rock rising out of the sea.

'It was not more than five miles in circumference, and seemed to be uninhabited.

'It was, however, covered with trees, and we saw a small stream of fresh water running down one side of it. . .

'I would have landed upon it, but the surf, which at this season broke upon it with great violence, rendered it impossible.'

Then he read faster.

'It lies in lat. 20 2' south; long. 133 21' west. It is so high that we saw it at the distance of more than fifteen leagues . . . and it having been discovered by a young gentleman, son to Major Pitcairn of the marines, we called it PITCAIRN's ISLAND.'

When he looked up most faces wore a grin.

'By God, you've done it, Mr Christian.' 'Uninhabited?' 'Aye, that's the one for us!' 'Mate, I like the sound of that.' 'Too good to be true – you sure this ain't a fairy story?' 'If it's that easy to see, we'll be able to see anyone coming our way in plenty of time.'

Mauatua brought the group to their senses, clearly still angry Fletcher hadn't talked to her about the island.

'Yes, Fletcher,' she shouted to him through the excitement. 'But where is this island, this Pitcairn's?'

'Where? That's the slight problem, well, perhaps a big problem.'

He saw jaws tighten and grins become knowing looks of resignation. Young and Brown exchanged shocked glances when he was reading, so they certainly knew what was coming.

'I'm afraid Pitcairn is, well, it's almost back where we began, on the other side of the Pacific, about 1300 miles south east of Tahiti.'

He expected the groans of disappointment. When he discovered the island in Hawkesworth's volume he had pounded the page with such force a man's face would have been pulped, demanding to know why the book had not told him weeks earlier. But there had been so many books to read, so many maps.

The women were all talking at the same time. Mauatua waved to catch Jenny's attention.

'The old people, didn't they speak of an island down that way? You remember anything, Jenny?'

'Yes, yes I do,' Jenny called back. '*Hitihiti au reva reva,* I think that's how it was known. Good place for making tools. No-one goes there now.'

For once, Quintal was enthusiastic. 'Anyway, one good thing, it sounds like a bloody great fortress already. No more digging moats, eh boys? We'll use the Lord's moat, the bloody sea!'

The general laughter was a relief all round.

'Yeah, but we do have to land on the bastard. Sounds bloody dangerous. But we'll do it. Be worth it, won't it boys?' He caught Mauatua's disapproving eye. He smirked. 'And girls, of course.'

'We still bloody well have to get there,' McCoy said miserably.

'Aye, we do, and that's the real problem.' The clamour slowly drained away until only BOUNTY's straining lines and timbers broke the silence. Fletcher dug into his deepest reserves before he dared explain what a voyage to Pitcairn really meant. The winds were against them, so Pitcairn was many weeks away.

He corrected himself to protect against future grievance. Pitcairn was almost certainly several months away at this time of year.

'It means sailing far south, into the south-east trade winds rather than with them. We'll have to sail much further east than Pitcairn lies and then sweep up with the same winds from the south east. It will get very cold and very rough. But as we get closer that will improve.'

He paused. There was no reaction. 'We should arrive there at the best time, the middle of the Season of Abundance. It might be as late as January, mid-summer down here.'

Still there was silence. Had he said something wrong? He smiled as fulsomely as he could summon but no-one reacted. It was as though he had given, and then taken all hope from them.

He knew most expected somewhere only days away, perhaps a week or two, and through calm, warm waters. Surely no-one would still vote for Tararo's alternative, they couldn't vote to sail back to Matavai Bay, could they? The ridicule they would endure would be unbearable. Tahiti's priests and chiefs would swank, saying their defeated return showed how powerful the Tahitian Gods were and that white men should go away from Tahiti and never come back. Mauatua wouldn't even catch his eye.

'I think it's fair we don't vote right now but have time to think about it. What do you say, tomorrow morning? Grog time?'

Tararo stood and turned to the crowd, laughing loudly, as though already victorious. 'No need to wait until tomorrow to get my vote, Mr Titreano. Your island might not be Tahiti, but at least we will be closer to Tahiti than we are now. I tell you, that makes Pitcairn a perfect choice.'

Tararo bent his knees and shook his thighs at an astonishing rate, the way men matched the trembling hips of dancing women. Then he struck challenge poses, grimacing and rolling his eyes.

Fletcher saw Tararo's unexpected thought sweep all his unhappy shipmates' considerations to one side.

Then Ned Young stood. It was a while before he could be heard. 'I said once before I would follow you wherever you go, Mr Christian. You have chosen Pitcairn and I support that. You will have my vote tomorrow.'

'Why wait until tomorrow to vote, Titreano?' Tararo asked fiercely, still tightening his muscles into poses and grimacing and prancing as though preparing to go to war. He towered over the few men and women who were standing. His determination was infectious, even among the white men who would commonly ignore his opinions. His feral stink was sweetened with fresh sweat that further burnished the sheen of his body. It was disturbing, wilful posturing that demanded recognition of his belief in the superiority of his rank and sex. Few eyes resisted.

'If we are going to vote at all . . .'

Tararo made a high leap and landed feet apart, his hands firmly on his buttocks. 'I reckon it's right here, right now!' he shouted, lewdly fathering each word with a sharp forward hip thrust.

He puffed his cheeks, let the air explode out and then took several stamping steps, signalling there was no argument left to hear.

Fletcher looked for guidance to Mauatua.

She shrugged, mouthing 'Why not?'

'Well, if you all think so. . .'

'Pitcairn,' Tararo said, immediately spinning back and putting up his hand. It took seconds for everyone else to agree.

Fletcher was astonished. Perhaps he had under estimated the appeal of Pitcairn's proximity to Tahiti? Had he thought about that at all? Probably not, considering how relieved he was to have found Pitcairn.

Mauatua was the only one who hadn't voted. When her arm went up he smiled with gentle resignation.

'Well, it seems we are all agreed. Pitcairn's Island.'

The Ma'ohi women stood as one and began clapping and swaying. Quickly they adopted the same rhythm and each woman instinctively added her voice to create the unique, haunting harmonies of Tahiti. First it was only celebratory sounds. Then, someone made up a few lines that rhymed and these were repeated and interwoven with new words, tossed back and forth between them into intricate melody. But the words sang only of Tahiti. Feet shuffled, hips shook, eyes sparkled, hands twisted and butterflied in the air.

The Ma'ohi men joined in and then the European men stamped and cavorted too. Only Fletcher and Mauatua stood apart.

'Are they dancing on our graves?' he asked her.

CHAPTER 29

Fletcher asked everyone to agree his estimate their voyage to Pitcairn might take more than two months. That way they could jointly make decisions about rations, about the sensible use of wood and coal and water. Mauatua marvelled at how easy it was to create harmony among such disparate men and women. All you had to do was connect them with decisions. Everybody's mind was set to the brutal truth of the voyage ahead and, true to the spirit of a happy and well-run ship, any complaints or trepidation about the conditions or the rations were now kept secret.

Her priority was to make the ship's fresh provisions last as long as possible. The generosity of the islands meant hands of bananas in various degrees of ripeness hung all over the ship, inside and out. Taro and sweet potato and breadfruit were stacked in baskets. Coconuts were stored in wide-based piles.

It was impossible to escape food and food became the overweening subject of interest, more than was usual at sea, according to Fletcher.

She harnessed the entire ship's company into telling her when they suspected a hand of bananas or basket of sweet potatoes might be passing its best. She would then incorporate these into the earliest meal she could, before they became good enough only for the animals.

There was competition among men to work with her in the galley. There was no sense this was only women's work, for Ma'ohi men had always cooked the foods forbidden to women and the white men joked that although kitchens were traditionally a woman's place the most celebrated chefs were men.

Many of the happiest times on board came when something new was created. The Navy's weekly boiled duff was conventionally made with flour and the fatty scum from cooking salted meats plus a handful of musty currants and raisins. She experimented to make this stodgy dough lighter with more generous amounts of the sourdough yeast Fletcher showed her how to make from flour and water. She made the dough sweeter with fresh rain water and with rendered pork fat rather than with grease from boiled meats. She added chunks of fully ripened banana soaked together with the dried fruit in undiluted Navy rum. Sometimes she even cooked the dough in a flat pan, like a lumpy pancake, the white men said.

The fragrance and the explosive flavours in the mouth of pudding or pancake were a huge success, reminding the white men they were in the fabled South Seas, even though the seascape looked as dreary as the English Channel.

When she deep-fried breadfruit fingers the white men said they tasted as close to hot bread as they could remember. The Ma'ohi simply thought them the best thing they had ever eaten. They had never had utensils in which to fry.

Po'e, the soft savoury puddings Tahitians baked in banana leaves in earth ovens, became a great favourite in the new ways Mauatua helped dream up based on adding ship's flour to pounded fruit or vegetables and grated coconut.

This baked into what Fletcher called a cake even though it was served hot with roasted meals. Soon squares of it were being carried about as cold snacks. Each watch strove to make an original version from her recipe:

> *Grate enough sweet potato or mash enough ripe bananas and then you add grated coconut until you can see plenty and then you add flour until you can just taste it. Salt as much as you like. Then you bake it as deep as one or two finger joints in something in the galley oven until done. No need to wrap in banana leaf.*

She knew white men couldn't master the glottal stop, so invited them to name her new dish and thus Ma'ohi *po'e* became BOUNTY's *pilhi*. She recognised the word as a first tangible icon of their new life ahead.

'My God,' Fletcher agreed. 'You're right. Our new society might as well have a new language too. Pilhi – it's the first Pitcairn dish and the first Pitcairn word too.'

One night he confided that BOUNTY was not built to sail against such raging winds or onto such high, thudding waves for such a long time.

She wished he hadn't and listened fearfully as BOUNTY strained, complained, creaked, groaned and sometimes, when stranded fleetingly on the peak of a wave, would shudder, determining, she would think, whether to fight on or give in.

She believed the ship would always choose to go on, even though Fletcher often doubted it. As well as the enormous strain on the ship, which meant leaks and weaknesses began to show, there was an equal toll on the company.

It became common for her to treat bruises and gashes from falls. Heads spun from slips to the deck. Backs and neck muscles were strained or torn. Moods dropped and stayed dull.

Few slept well, even with rum in their blood.

As she expected, the menstrual cycles of the women on board had coincided but if 12 menstruating women all stopped work the ship couldn't possible sail safely. They agreed amongst themselves only the most painfully affected would take time off, and just for a day or so. This was new for them and for Ma'ohi men, who expected menstruating women to hide away so they didn't foul or curse them and their possessions.

'We are blessed with these women,' Fletcher said when Mauatua explained what the women had decided, thinking of the ship and common good rather than themselves. 'I'm not even sure which . . .'

'This is a good thing,' Mauatua interrupted. 'We don't want men to know. On Tahiti we would be made to hide away, like rats. What is best,' she enthused 'is this is not because men forced us.

'It has been *our* decision.'

While Fletcher was so well disposed, she asked him if the women might have a special place on board. Her idea was voted on and soon half the false deck of the greenhouse had been taken up, from the aft end that had the windows and fresh air.

Tapa cloth was laid thickly on the deck and suddenly BOUNTY boasted a tropical glade as verdant and fresh as any on Tahiti.

On one unique calm day she begged Fletcher to allow the women to gather together and he changed standing orders so they might.

They sat in the clearing soothed by the luscious scents and foliage of the greenhouse, exchanging food and thoughts, braiding and scenting hair, massaging one another with precious oils.

A low tentative voice brought to them a thought held silently behind Ma'ohi's women's eyes for unknown generations.

'Surely,' the voice said, 'our monthly blood is something potent, a sign of life? Surely it is something joyful, which should be celebrated?

'Why should we hide away because of the very thing that most makes us women? We are not *tapu* or sick. We are women.'

There was a long silence. And then another spoke.

'This must be why men tell us to go away, because it is something more potent than that sticky stuff they have.'

The 12 women blasted the plants about them with laughter. Their mirth turned into a hand-clapping song and then dancing.

Mauatua left the greenhouse, seeking the comfort only of the ship's rail. When salt spray leaked in to sting her eyes she opened them wider, welcoming its sharp reminder she was voyaging towards a new world.

She was not alone.

She was not the only woman with revolution in her heart.

CHAPTER 30

Mauatua constantly worried about how they would start afresh on an uninhabited island. If Pitcairn's shoreline was great cliffs, there would be no gentle river beds of cool fresh water for bathing. With no shallow water inside a reef, how could they do their daily business there and allow the tide to float it away? How would they live the first few days, under what shade and shelter?

She and Jenny managed to get practical agreements from Fletcher. These were not things that required a meeting or voting. As she and Jenny thought of tasks and projects, he wrote them down and then put them into an order of importance.

There were certain things he wanted done his way.

To show her he drew the layout of an English village. A great common square, perhaps with water, and each man's house around that, with home gardens and animals there and other bigger gardens outside the village. Just the way it had always been in England.

There might be a gathering place. BOUNTY's bell would have pride of place there to summon meetings.

Wasn't this something from the past, something he should not be thinking about for their new sort of life? She kept her tongue and searched the ship for what suited Fletcher's plans.

With so many mouths they'd need to cook in earth ovens from the first day, but what if Pitcairn didn't have the right sort of stones? Cooking pots must be the first items taken ashore.

Gradually others on the ship began to think about possible problems and probable solutions.

'It's encouraging, Fletcher,' she said. 'It means their minds are making a better picture of Pitcairn and how to make that picture real. Each will be planning what you call a paradise.'

'I hope not,' Fletcher said glancing up from copying a list. 'I think Pitcairn will be a very fragile paradise for quite some time.'

Tension built notably as the seventh week of sailing eastwards began, still without seeing a speck of land. By New Year's Day 1790 anger and regret infected the ship. She made Fletcher take his maps onto the deck to show where BOUNTY was and how far they still had to sail.

By now Tararo was increasingly moody. As the other men and women on board became more comfortable with democratic, shared workloads Tararo more and more missed the differences his rank once accorded him.

Fletcher tried to include him by asking Tararo for advice, wondering if he saw signs that would help find Pitcairn. The noble dismissed his conciliatory approaches. He said such an island was too small to make signs anyone could read from so far away. When Fletcher asked if perhaps the stars had something to say, Tararo grunted and walked away from him.

Ten days into the New Year, Fletcher announced they would see Pitcairn Island within 24 hours.

'Do the stars tell you anything now, Tararo?' Fletcher tried again.

'Yes, yes, they do,' he answered curtly.

Tararo pointed to the sky between their north westerly passage and north. His arm was tense and trembled. Each tendon and vein stood thick and angry and his finger shook.

'Those ones, those stars do! Do you know what they tell me? Do you?' It was the loudest Fletcher had heard Tararo speak for weeks. It was difficult not to be frightened.

Tararo strode to stand toe to toe with Fletcher. 'No, of course you don't know. You know nothing of my world.' He pointed again.

'Those stars, Titreano, they tell me Tahiti is there. Further away than Pitcairn, but closer than it has been for many months. Very much closer, Titreano.'

Tararo relaxed with a single, deep breath of satisfaction. He smiled disdainfully down his nose, sniggered over his shoulder at the other Ma'ohi men and then joined them, laughing softly.

He mocked Fletcher all that next pregnant day.

He pretended to see a bird or land, raising expectations and then dashing them with another cruel laugh.

'You see,' Tararo kept saying. No island out there – except Tahiti. Keep sailing Titreano. We'll soon be home. Tahiti's that way.'

'This is unbearable,' Mauatua scorned, regretting anyone should see her lose control. She was shocked not to find Pitcairn when Fletcher had so confidently predicted it. She was distressed by Tararo's mockery and confused because now others were baying for Fletcher to abandon the search for Pitcairn and to sail for Tahiti. She held Fletcher beside Brown at the wheel. Everyone not on duty waited with them or crowded vantage points.

By the time the sun dropped below the eastern horizon not the slightest sign of land had been seen. Fletcher and BOUNTY had sailed them to the exact spot. Pitcairn was not there.

She led him into the calm atmosphere of the greenhouse clearing. He didn't resist. She thought he might not have resisted anything.

'Think, Fletcher. What can you do? Should we stay here and what, sail in bigger circles tomorrow? It must be here, mustn't it?'

He sat as still as stone, his skin sallow beneath his sea-burnished face. She rubbed *monoi* into his temples and slowly his shoulders dropped and relaxed. 'Fletcher, don't just sit. Talk to me, tell me your thoughts, please Fletcher? We can't have sailed all this way for nothing.'

Fletcher's head came up but he kept his eyes closed, enjoying her attentions for a long time before he spoke.

'That's exactly what could have happened. The island could be a joke, a fantasy to make Carteret's voyage more interesting. It could be a lie that he's got away with it for more than twenty years.'

'There are plenty on board who would welcome that lie.'

'Because they want to go back to Tahiti,' he agreed, dull with despondency.

'That's true. But the women have been away from Tahiti long enough. They see what life was really like for them. Life would be worse if they went back.'

'You think the women will support me, at least long enough to look properly – or for somewhere else?'

'I do. But I can't think you have all the time in the world, Fletcher.'

He jumped to his feet and she toppled backwards. He grabbed and saved her from falling into pots of breadfruit trees.

'Time, time – of course, of course! That must be it.'

Fletcher bent his thumb and chewed on the joint, mumbling as he did.

'Time, that is the answer, of course, of course it is. And you . . .' He picked her up and spun her around. 'You are a goddess. Pitcairn Island does exist but not where the map says.'

He darted around the lower deck, telling everybody he met to get up onto the main deck.

She'd never seen him so excited. She followed him, picking up what he knocked over, explaining to those who had not heard him properly.

He came back on deck carrying a small polished box.

'Pah! More white man magic. More time wasting,' Tararo said. 'We should be sailing for Tahiti.' Mauatua and Jenny exchanged worried glances. Fletcher was smiling benignly at Tararo and that confused them.

'As you say, Tararo. And that is exactly what we will do.'

Fletcher allowed the mixed cries of anguish and joy to take their full measure before his lifted chin showed there was more to be said.

'You have my word. We will go back to Tahiti. But, only if what is in this box does not find Pitcairn for us.'

He ran his hand over the case. It was small and sat neatly on his palm. It was mahogany buffed to a rich tobacco brown and bound with brass straps, like a miniature military chest.

At first, what he revealed looked like any gentleman's silver pocket watch, but was perhaps larger than usual. When Mauatua looked closer she realised it was somehow more elegant than the few pocket watches she had seen. There were not two hands but one, an exceptionally graceful tapered hand that swept around the dial in what Fletcher said was sixty seconds.

None of this made sense to her and she understood why the constant sweep of the hand spooked so many of the Ma'ohi. They started back but then their innate fascination with novelty made it irresistible. Like Mauatua, they knew he did something to this object every day, but nothing else of it. Once everyone was still, Fletcher explained.

'Carteret didn't have one of these, a chronometer. BOUNTY is one of the first ships to sail with one, a new type of time piece that keeps perfect time anywhere in the world. Those dials at the bottom, one for hours and one for minutes, they tell me the time in London.'

'Does it tell you when it's time to go to Tahiti?' Tararo laughed raucously. He was hissed and told to be quiet.

'No, Tararo. It does many things but not that. You and your people navigate by stars but you do not make maps to show other people where you have been. We do, we make charts and maps and sometimes put them into books with words that tell you more about what has been seen.

'With our sextants we look at the sun to tell us how far North or South we are. We make several readings and put them together also to tell us how far East or West we are from England.

'There was always one problem.'

'Just the one?' This time the interjection came from Quintal. The crowd jostled him, impatient to hear the rest of Fletcher's story.

'Yes, just the one, and it's a serious problem. There was no exact way of knowing how far east or west you were. Many a ship sails safely and carefully around the world but arrives back in England – or Spain or France - in bad weather and runs aground and is lost on rocks they thought were many miles to their east or west.

'This chronometer can tell us exactly how far we are east or west because we can compare the sun at midday with the time in London, there on the bottom dial, and that tells us where we are, exactly.

'Carteret's readings were wrong. He didn't really know where he was because he had no way of accurate time keeping. Give me five more days and I will find Pitcairn. Do I have five more days?'

Mauatua put her hand up immediately and so did the Ma'ohi women. The mutineers agreed. Tararo scowled under a heavy furrowed brow, so no other Ma'ohi man voted in favour. Fletcher was disheartened.

'The island is out there. Pitcairn is there. If we can find it.'

'There's no '*if*' Fletcher,' Ned insisted.

'I won't sleep until I find it.'

'We might have a better chance if you do sleep, Fletcher.'

For three more days BOUNTY tossed on the featureless South Pacific. Fletcher seemed to be on deck all the time, keeping the chronometer beside him.

Knowing Carteret's latitude marking was likely to be correct, he sailed the ship in swooping curves either side of this, hoping he had correctly guessed in which direction Carteret might most have been wrong.

By sun and moonlight men and women watched impatiently, some even sitting straddled on the bowsprit.

On January 15th, Mauatua was working despondently in the galley when she heard the call that land had been sighted.

She ran up on to deck.

The sun was setting but there on the horizon was a dot, barely a smudge, but clearly it was Carteret's 'great rock rising from the sea'.

The sun set too swiftly, cruelly taking away the sight. The sea was calm, and, with no roar of surf to give notice of rocks or reefs or shoals, Fletcher dared not sail too close. But there was a wind that keened high above them and that skidded clouds across the moon's light, teasing with brief glimpses of Pitcairn.

Ecstatically happy, Fletcher called the ship's company together.

'Gentlemen, *vahine*. I have done what I promised

'I have brought you to Pitcairn. But I have delivered you somewhere better than just a place of safety.

'Almost none of these maps show Pitcairn Island. Those that do, show it almost 300 miles east of where we are.'

He crushed the maps together and held them fiercely, his fists trembling. Then he exploded them high into the night air.

'That means that after eight months and after almost 8000 miles of sailing - we are invisible!'

CHAPTER 31

Mauatua expected to find him glowing with satisfaction next morning. Instead, she found Fletcher exhausted, as rumpled, limp and pale as a drowned animal. He was naked, except for a scented cloth over his nose. It was already hot and humid. The smell of cooking food from the galley wallowed in the air and the rotten smell of bilge water mushroomed strongly up into the ship. If she jammed back the door to let more air in, it also let in more of the stench.

'I feel slightly dead,' Fletcher sighed. 'Now we are here, I feel I've done what I had to do. What do I do next?'

She sat beside him for an hour, fanning the thick air as he dozed. Fletcher was not the only one with a feeling of anti-climax. As a ship's company each man and woman aboard knew what they should do and what to expect from others. Now few knew what to think.

They were no longer sailors and explorers but were not yet settlers.

She shuddered more than once as BOUNTY circled the island. The view from the deck changed little. Pitcairn was a nature-hewn fortress that staunchly guarded itself yet looked like a flimsy piece of soiled tapa cloth that had been thrown to the ground, ragged, rugged and crumpled. The constant corrugations of scarred and wounded red-ochre cliffs seemed to be bleeding wounds, as if the sea were sucking at the boulders and soil that disappeared into it so abruptly.

Yet behind and above this ceaseless struggle a still, brooding silence hung. Perhaps there was good reason Pitcairn was uninhabited? When she shared these thoughts with the other women, she discovered they were as fearful. Pitcairn was forbidding, its cliffs and impenetrable green mantle were threats rather than promises of security and comfort. And why so silent? Where were the birds?

She climbed to the mainmast's lookout platform and watched for many hours but she saw no sign of animals. The only birds were occasional sea birds. Whatever the secrets beneath the island's overgrowth, she could see no easy, flat and clear site for a settlement. They would have to fight for somewhere to settle.

So far, there was every disturbing sign something would fight back.

Or someone.

There were upright stones, marae stones, just behind the edges of some cliffs. Whoever erected those intended to live on the island, must have lived there some time. But were they still living there?

The island's covering of trees looked thick enough to keep a secret of domestic smoke. Gashes of tumbling orange-red earth showed the land was constantly moving. These scars were too steep to be manmade or gardens. Could they be erosion by wind and rains Mauatua later asked Jenny. They might be disturbance from underground eruptions she suggested. Tararo pushed in, saying it could be both.

'The gods who do such damage recognise no exclusive rights.'

Whatever the truth, Pitcairn's hushed mantle slithered down the cliffs, stole across the waves and suffocated BOUNTY. The entire ship was uneasy. No-one ran and no-one shouted. It was the first silent island anyone on board had experienced. She turned her face away when a rare gull or a white tropic bird's red-spear tail floated above the spume. They could be malicious harbingers from the protective veil of gods and spirits every island should have. Pitcairn's dumb facade might herald tranquil serenity but it could just as well be hovering evil.

Fletcher put together a search party. He included Brown the gardener and chose McCoy rather than an officer like Ned Young because he was more likely to be handy in a confrontation. Three of the Ma'ohi men also went with him. Tararo was asked but refused. Only Mauatua protested at her exclusion.

'I want to know the medicines, the herbs, if there are trees for making tapa?'

Fletcher interrupted her sharply. 'Discovering them will make no difference. They're here or they are not. Knowing either way will not change our minds about settling here. We have to know only if Pitcairn is uninhabited, that it is safe. We'll take food for two days and nights. Mauatua, I'll trust you to see to that. I'm also trusting we will need none of it, that Pitcairn will be abundant.' Fletcher laughed and was hurt to see not at a single other face cheered by his thought.

'And if it is inhabited, what then?' Tararo asked defiantly, his lip curled.

'Then I will keep my promise. I will take you to Tahiti.'

'No need for that. It *will* be abundant.' Mauatua didn't want thoughts of Tahiti to edge out Pitcairn.

'But abundant with what?' Tararo mocked. 'Remember how calm, how pleasant Titreano thought Tubuai looked?'

Her shipmates who had been there loudly recalled the hordes of rats and the infuriating mosquitoes, the battalions of biting insects and the stinking, yellow-dyed warriors forever threatening to kill them. For those who knew nothing of Tubuai, these stories forged greater determination to face no more challenges but instead to sail on gratefully to Tahiti.

Teio held Sully tighter to her suckling breast. 'Whatever Tahiti is like, at least we know what is expected of us there,' she complained. 'Perhaps that's the best any of us should expect.'

Mauatua rounded on her. 'No. That is giving in just because someone speaks louder and longer. That's wrong. On this island, that one there, on Pitcairn, you – all of us – will raise those expectations. We will live a new sort of life.'

Tararo interrupted her, dancing about her with whooping cries of derision. She shouted back into his face. 'It will be what we do as women on that island that will be remembered, Tararo. Never forget that we know the powers you men think you have.'

He laughed scornfully but stopped his dance. She stood eye to eye with him. 'You do not know what women can do'

Teio called. 'What I want is an easy life, not the same war between men and women on a different island.' Mauatua lost her temper.

'Ha! The comfort of discomfort. That is how you empower men,' she taunted. 'When a woman accepts whatever is given to her. When you know you are miserable but do nothing about changing it. That is how you become comfortable with discomfort.'

Teio melted into the Ma'ohi women, their soft voices and whispers sharing thoughts Mauatua could only guess. She had surprised herself. Her head raced with sharp words and clear thoughts that had been murmurs before. Now, with the island before her, they were demanding to be heard. Women would be different on Pitcairn, so men would have to be too. She showed her face only to Pitcairn. There was where she would prove what women could be.

Fletcher came up quietly to stand beside her. 'Without you I'd have no chance there,' he said. 'Pitcairn will need a strong woman.'

'Like you had at Moorland Close?'

They were both still smiling as the cutter with Fletcher and five heavily armed men hoisted a sail and sailed for their first footfall on Pitcairn.

'About your ideas, Mauatua.'

She turned from watching Fletcher's boat bounce towards Pitcairn. Jenny held Teio's arm tightly, trying to drag her away, but Teio was determined to have her question answered.

'We hear your ideas every day, but I want to know where you get such ideas. Who told you such things? Who tells you they are right? I need to know your answers if I am to believe you.'

Mauatua persuaded Jenny to free Teio. Jenny shrugged her shoulders, threw up her hands and turned to leave.

'No, Jenny, stay. You hear the same questions, I think. Stay, so you learn the same answers.'

Most women moved closer, some held back. She hadn't been telling the truth when she told Fletcher all the women supported him. There was constant, silent fear in some hearts. Sailing away on a white man's ship had been an enormous step. Some thought they had strayed too far, that they had already tempted fate and the gods more than they should. Like Teio, the only life many saw on Pitcairn was the one they knew on Tahiti.

'What tells me I am right is here.' Mauatua pointed between her eyes. 'Deep in the darkness we know but never see.' She beckoned the women toward her and let them settle on the deck. She remained standing.

'Don't you remember how it was when we were children? There were no differences between boys and girls. We roamed free and played free and no-one dared chastise us. Girls could be boys, boys could be girls.

'When sex became interesting, we were told to go away, groups of us. We pretended for weeks on end to be grown up. We built huts and cooked badly and made love even if we were not ripe enough to have babies. We made babies of wrapped up green coconuts and pretended to suckle them from what were not yet breasts. Some boys did the same and some girls, like me, played games with sticks for spears and bows and arrows.

'Of course, there were roles each of us played more easily. But, we didn't play to exclude one another, did we? We wanted to make one bigger, happier life.' The women had not uttered a syllable. She saw smiles skittering on some lips and imagined the happy pictures that had generated them. It was time to cut deeper into their memories.

'But this was cruel. It showed us a life that was never to last, never ever to be enjoyed again. For when the time came for boys to have their foreskins slit and girls started to bleed, when it was time for tattooing . . .'

She stopped. The women were already uncomfortable, remembering what they hoped was forgotten because of the pain it caused them.

'*Aueeee!* I remember now, I cried at night so many times,' Teio said. 'Not because I did not want to be a woman and not because I did not want to go with a man, as you will know.'

The other women slapped their chests and laughed.

'It was well known I was a friendly girl but these boys we had played with could no longer be my friends. Everything that had once given me pleasure was denied me, except for sex. Was this new way to my advantage, my happiness?'

The women agreed with Teio, none of it was to her advantage or to theirs when their turn came. But their voices were muted, as needles of buried pain emerged to prick their skins and minds.

'After that happy time everything was for them, the men, so you were where they wanted, when they wanted, for what they wanted.'

'And only for as long as they wanted,' Mauatua agreed. She bunched a hand to her chest then flung it at arm's length and opened it.

'Just like that you could be discarded, no longer a wife, only a mother, if that had been allowed.'

She dare not guess at the number of babies these women had conceived but had not been allowed to welcome to this world. A dark mood grabbed the women and savagely shook them in its cruel mouth. It was bitter truth but she told them men thought it did not matter, believing women never grieved for these lost children. 'But, you do, don't you', she asked, 'every day of your lives, just as I do'.

'What must life be like for those who had lost six or even eight babies? It is worse,' she insisted, 'for our sisters who can't have children they want because they have been damaged forever by deep massage or poisonous herbs or pointed grasses poked blindly into them.

'You all fell in with this all of you. Without questions. But me, I thought too much. I thought, surely women should have all their babies if they wished. I believed a woman should be honoured if she grows men's essence into a new life.'

'These are white men's ideas, Mauatua,' Teio interrupted, irritated by what was being said so publicly. 'That's where you got them.'

'And why not?' she countered, fighting to keep her voice calm. 'Have our men invented the wheel? This would make life easier even for them, for bringing bananas from the mountain or taking tribute. But no, we carry everything on our backs in Tahiti. Have our men invented ovens that stand above the ground? Or built ships like this? Or baked clay to make pots to cook in? Or discovered how to write and read? What sort of gods do we worship on Tahiti if those gods do not want such things even for men?'

The women couldn't argue with those facts and knowing she was nearing the time they would stop listening, she summed up.

She told them what Fletcher said was the most important difference between England and Tahiti. He did not say it was always right or that it was never cruel or unkind.

In England women were largely protected by laws and men to safeguard their fortunes and their womanhood. On Tahiti women are protected by laws passed only to bolster men's idea of their manhood.

At last the women reacted strongly. They talked loudly, interrupting one another but she saw that her last point had struck home.

'*Vahine*,' she shouted holding out her arms for quiet. 'What does it matter what England does or Rarotonga or, what's that big new country, America? You have seen for yourself on this ship.

'When women eat pork, men do not sicken and die. No god struck when we mingled with men while we were bleeding. Did men rot, did their *ure* wither and drop off just for standing beside us? Did meat turn bad and fish poison us or water turn to fire and fire into ashes?'

She was angered by the meekness of the women. She clapped her hands once as loudly as she could.

'Answer me, sisters!' They clapped back, but in a shared, dancing rhythm. Some smiled and swayed on their buttocks, nodding their heads. A few sang and twirled their wrists. None seemed to disagree.

And then a new thought inflamed her, the thought that encapsulated all she was saying.

'Fletcher and I agree. Our past as Tahitian women must be remembered, but as our teacher and not our master.

'Once we each put our feet on that island the past must be our teacher. Never again our master.'

Teio still doubted. 'Who says this is so, who is telling us all this is possible? That is what I asked you.'

'You,' Mauatua said quietly. She put her long tapering forefinger between her eyebrows again. '*Vahine*. It is not necessary to be taught by another and certainly not by a man. New ideas do not have to come from another's mind. They can come from you.

'Listen to the voice behind your eyes that you have never heeded, the voice that comes furthest, from far beyond the beating of your heart or the breath of your chest.

'That is who tells you what is possible, that is the voice that gives you new ideas, gives you permission. The voice that is you.'

Mauatua paused to gather every woman's eyes to her.

She stabbed her forefinger between her own eyes repeatedly, marking a rhythm under her words.

'It is you who knows the deepest truths, you who gives permission for you to have new ideas.'

The faces she could not read were those of the few men, Ma'ohi and white, who were standing in the shadows.

CHAPTER 32

Fletcher and his party were expected to be away for two days. She leaned over the rail, begging the mute island to give her a sign he was safe. Tararo stood close to her but spoke looking out across the foam-flashing rollers to Pitcairn.

'You tell good stories, Mauatua. That island will have women with spirit. It is easier to tame spirit than generate it. We will benefit.'

'We? You mean you men?'

'I mean us. That is a Pacific island. We belong here in ways your *popa'a* will never understand. Fletcher will not be happy on this island. You will need another man and I am the noblest. We share the blood of many splendid ancestors. It is we who should become Pitcairn's chiefs.'

'Why are you saying this, is it because Fletcher is not here?' She tried to make a joke but the lump of fear on her tongue made her sound serious.

'That helps. Why should we share our plans? I am telling you, Fletcher does not belong on such an island. I do. You do. I am a very patient man.'

'You will need to be.' Tararo did not mind her snub. He turned her shoulders so they faced one another and then took a step back.

'When we look at each other, we see ourselves. Tall, golden, handsome. We will have beautiful children and with blood twice as noble. I would allow you to keep them. We will need many to ensure our line.'

'There will be no line.'

Mauatua fled. She locked herself in Fletcher's cabin and held a shirt of his to her nose until her fear dissolved.

For two days the ship's cutter was still where she'd seen it dragged up over the long spew of rocks on the western side of the island. Not a single column of smoke or gunshot showed her Fletcher was alive. Surely an island only a mile by a mile and a half shouldn't take so long to explore?

She calculated that if Fletcher and Brown were dead, only Ned Young could sail them to somewhere else. But Tararo boomed constantly he knew how to sail to Tahiti from here and pointed to the stars again and again.

Ned posted armed guards overnight, to ensure Tararo did not take matters in to his own hands.

Wind and currents drove BOUNTY to the eastern end of the island during the second night. By the time they had tacked back west again it was late on the third morning. At last she saw the sails of the cutter heading back to BOUNTY.

She grabbed the telescope from Ned's hands. Steadying her elbows on the rail she fought to get the boat into her sight but the small round image of the cutter constantly jerked out of her vision. It took gut-wrenching minutes before she could count six living men in the boat.

Six men never smiled as broadly as those she welcomed back on to BOUNTY's deck.

'Paradise,' Fletcher said quietly. 'Paradise. Tell them Mr Brown.'

'Whatever you want to know,' Brown said, proud to be the bringer of such good news, 'the answer is good. It is not inhabited but it once was and there are still gardens and orchards. There is water, plenty of it, in springs and pools. We won't need many of the plants we have carried.'

He spread out the branches and leaves and young plants he carried back as evidence.

'Look. Three types of banana, and a plaintain for cooking. Sweet potatoes, taro – not very much breadfruit . . . certainly *aute* for tapa making. And look, look at this.' Brown turned to a bundle of banana leaves tied with strips of coconut frond. It had moved several times, frightening some. He unknotted it and revealed an enormous lobster.

'That's the food of kings,' Brown said, with considerable awe.

'So many you can almost walk on them,' Fletcher added proudly. 'We will not starve on this island, even if we do have to eat lobster every day. We have found paradise, an invisible paradise.'

'Mosquitoes? Rats?' Quintal and McCoy asked together.

'Very few, considering this is midsummer, and we saw no rats. Just land crabs, but you can hear them coming and they don't smell.'

'It's been worth every second of the voyage.' Fletcher stood proud and silent. Then she made the whole ship laugh when she said there was one thing she wanted more than anything else.

'I want my bare toes digging into earth once again and then wriggling in fresh water.' All BOUNTY cheered her simple thought.

The mutineers put Fletcher on their shoulders and ran him around the deck, again and again, as much to the consternation of the penned pigs and goats and chickens as to the Ma'ohi men and women.

'It sounds very good for our future,' Tararo whispered into her ear.

'There is no 'our' future,' she said. When she next raised her right arm to salute Fletcher's jogging procession, Tararo moved close and cruelly twisted her left wrist behind her back. She struggled to hold her tongue but the pain in her arm defeated her.

'Why are you hurting me?' she complained, darting her eyes to see who might have heard.

Tararo read her mind. 'Why should Fletcher know? He might ask why you were standing so close, so intimately. Passion and anger look the same to *popa'a*. He has seen you angry with me before, he will not care, just as no others have. He will want to know what you did to provoke me.

'I am patient, Mauatua. And I am young, younger than you, so I can be very patient. But if I must, I will force you. One day it is us who will rule this island together.'

Tararo had sliced into her head. New, different, disturbing ideas poured from the wound. Since she had known Fletcher, their lives had been full of challenge and novelty. Learning each other's language and thoughts and families. Tubuai. Fucking. Sailing across the Pacific and then back again. They were good together, solved problems, salved wounds.

Tararo made these sustaining thoughts rush from her head and come back a different way.

What would life be like with Fletcher when there were no challenges? When there were no problems to solve, when they would be just living? Was this why Tararo so certain? Could he see into the future?

Of course! That was why he was so confident about their future together, so prepared to be patient. He believed it was foretold. Her mouth tightened and her hands rushed to cover the word she did not want them to say. She could not stop them.

Taputapuatea, that was her real enemy.

As a high noble of Raiatea, the Ma'ohi world's most sacred island, Tararo would have been initiated by the priests of the supreme god Oro into the ritual mysteries of Taputapuatea marae, the most sacred on that most holy island. There was said to be nothing of the past or the future the highest initiates could not be persuaded to tell.

She was pierced by a searing insight of her own. There was only one terrible way to know if Tararo spoke from revelation or from ambition

She was powerless to do anything but wait.

Tararo had laden her with a burden she would have to carry into the future silently and alone.

She sank to the deck, sickened.

Brown drew a map of the island from sketches he had made and Fletcher used this to brief the ship. On the long northerly coast of the island they had found an area previously settled. Although now overgrown, the bush was not as thick as elsewhere and the ground had been levelled in places.

When he could manoeuvre close enough, Fletcher called BOUNTY'S pilgrims to look at their new home from some half mile out to sea from its northern coast.

To their right the highest peak on the island reared almost 1000 ft from the sea, the final flourish of a long thin ridge that tapered back and then rippled away eastwards to their left like a spine along the length of the island. Not far below the peak was a cave entrance and then the land and the sea faces dropped sharply away. A perfect lookout said Quintal, always the most anxious to avoid discovery.

Fletcher asked them follow the tree tops as they dipped smoothly from the long central ridge towards the sea cliffs facing BOUNTY. Running the length of this closest cliff they could then see a long area that seemed less rugged. This was the stretch of liveable land Fletcher's party identified, about a half a mile of it, facing roughly north east.

He pointed out a small bay directly ahead of the ship, an indentation marginally deeper than others, and with a narrow strip of dark sand. The bay and beach were staunchly protected by hostile rocks above and below the surface.

Close to the left of the bay another lower headland, about 700 ft high, had a formation on top that looked like a parrot's head and beak. Beneath that, there was a narrow rocky strip of land that fell quickly into dark, deep water and was thus a possible anchorage.

Behind the little bay, invisible from the sea because of tropical growth, the exploration party discovered a long steep path up the cliff side, probably manmade and that ended at the area recommended as the first camp. But point and tell was all Fletcher could do until the surf subsided.

'Tell you what, boys,' McCoy said. 'With those rocks below and our cannons lined up nicely on those cliffs . . .'

'Too right, mate,' Quintal interrupted. 'No bastard would have a hope in Hades of invading us.'

'If we ever get ourselves on to the bastard,' McCoy worried.

The ennui that struck Fletcher once he found Pitcairn next unpicked the locks into his conscience.

Instead of relaxing with the pleasurable solace of a gratified adventurer, he tossed with the fear and fright Bligh have felt if he were hurled into the sea and then bubbled down to a grave unknown for eternity.

Some of his waking thoughts were laughable at first yet would not disappear. Might it be a good thing to go back to England after all? He had exorcised his most garrulous voices, proven he could lead men at sea the way he challenged Bligh to do. He could believably make suggestions to the Navy Board that would improve the lot of countless other sailors. He would rehearse his distress and disgrace to save others from both.

Salving his conscience like that wouldn't be the end of it. The Navy would still hang him, but he would leave a legacy and through that a sour kind of redemption. It would be a different kind of revolution from the one he planned for Pitcairn. Yes, he sometimes thought, that was settled.

Once Pitcairn was established he would sail to somewhere the Navy would find him and so take him back to Portsmouth and trial. He didn't share this plan. He had found Mauatua a safe home and that was at least one promise kept. Next, he had to get everyone onto the island as soon as the swell settled.

He called Brown and Young to his cabin and closed the door. Mauatua knocked and came in, saying it was better she also knew what was happening so she could explain to the Ma'ohi men and women. The two other men seemed comfortable with her there but Fletcher seemed nervous.

'That bay is the right spot,' he began. 'There are landing places beneath it and a track up to the best place to live.'

'Perfect combination,' Young said, 'but I've not been ashore.'

'Quite. It's not the shore that's the problem. The problem is these seas and then the rocks in the bay. What's going to be the best way to get everything, including us, from BOUNTY to a landing place? Ideas?'

'I take it,' Young said, 'this means running her onto the rocks isn't going to happen, I mean, otherwise that's easily done. Isn't it?'

Fletcher struggled to answer, several times glancing at her, embarrassed by something she thought.

In the tight space, the others had to tip their heads back to see his face.

'Brown, you'll bear me out. The surf and currents are so treacherous a single gust of wind could wreck us on rocks when we are still well away from the shore.'

'Yes, by God you are right, Fletcher. It would be impossible to guarantee we'd get far enough in.'

'Exactly, impossible even to get ourselves ashore safely. Sail all this way and then be stranded on rocks yards from the shore and no safe way of getting off? I hardly think so.'

'Could we get close enough to the rocky ledge under the headland, I mean close enough and parallel, so we could hoist directly onto the ledge?' Brown's voice tapered off, for as he spoke he saw the inherent dangers.

'The margin for error in such close anchoring is just as risky,' Fletcher said. 'We could still lose everything. And maybe everyone.'

He wiped his face vigorously with a camphor-scented handkerchief.

'There's another reason, too, another for not beaching her.' He paused until Mauatua met his eyes. 'I'm not ready to abandon BOUNTY.'

'You mean we might not settle here?' she queried, very quietly but with her heart pumping.

'It's an option for some.' Fletcher turned his back.

Not ready to abandon the ship. So! He was making major decisions without talking to her. Ignoring the others in the cabin, she stalked the few steps to lean over his shoulder.

'An option for *which* 'some'? Who exactly?'

He flinched but she pushed his upraised elbow painfully closer to his head. She saw a sheen of sweat appearing on his brow.

Well it might, she thought, pushing harder as she deliberately collected a sac of venom in her voice.

'Who? Who are these 'some' who might want to go?' she demanded.

He jumped away from her, shivering as though shedding the icy fingers of a ghost. He spoke to her over his shoulder, sounding pained and self righteous.

'You know Tararo wants to go. And there are others. Like me.'

'Like you? You!'

She staggered as far from him as she could in the cabin. Fletcher go? His revelation was incomprehensible. Unable to put into words what she wanted to say, she gabbled insult and outrage into her chest, her head shuddering with wrath.

Fletcher came to take her in his arms. She wasn't some damned kitten to be comforted with a few pats. She slapped him away so violently she hit him hard on the cheek. His head jerked back with blazing eyes but he straightened it looking placatory and wounded.

'You'd stay obviously, and you'll know which women want to go back to Tahiti. That's the way we work, isn't it? I'm trying to be fair about it.'

'Fair?' She was still incapable of responding with coherency and he was pleading like a whining child. The thought of him leaving had thrown her so deep into the furthest pits of her mind she felt she might never climb back. This is madness she screamed in her head. He has driven me mad. She forced herself to breathe slowly, to discover if she could ever speak or speak sense again.

Fletcher recovered his bravado and so turned away from her struggle. He struck a nonchalant stance and flung out an appealing arm to Brown and Young as though nothing of the past minute had happened.

'And what if we were discovered before we had really set ourselves up? We'd need to run for it, wouldn't we? What are your thoughts Mauatua? You look very serious.'

Brown and Young were soundless and she could tell their eyes and thoughts were sympathetic. But what thoughts? Were these two going to desert her, too? This drama was unlikely to be settled quickly or when they were around.

She hardened herself to show the reverse of what she felt. She'd seen Fletcher do that with Bligh, avoid confrontation by saying the opposite of what was expected. It was *ha'avare,* saying what was untrue. He was also good at countering a difficult question with a repetition of its substance. That's what she would do, and thus give nothing away.

'You've told us serious things,' she ventured eventually. As she hoped, there could be no direct answer and he changed the subject.

'Can we anchor off and float everything ashore?' he suggested.

'With just one sound boat?' Brown laughed scornfully. 'Anyway, it'll be a hell of a job getting stuff up that path. Isn't there somewhere else?'

'Well, the west side where we first landed,' Fletcher suggested, 'but then they'd have to haul or carry everything over the island.'

'Rafts? We're back to rafts,' Young declared. Fletcher and Brown both shook their heads. Rafts were too small, too flimsy for the troubled waters of Pitcairn Island. The three men fell silent, shackled by the options open to them.

'Outriggers, a raft with outriggers,' Mauatua said quietly.

Ned understood first. 'Of course, Tahitian style, then it'd be stable in the biggest waves. The sort of rafts we build would be useless and dangerous. We can crane everything from the ship onto a big raft. Even so, in these waters . . .'

'You *popa'a*.' Mauatua's laugh ridiculed them. 'My grandfathers, and their grandfathers forever beyond them, sailed far further in these waters than you have. You should ask those who know about such things.'

She engaged Fletcher directly, poison again in her voice. 'It'll be a big raft, Fletcher. Big enough to sail you back to Tahiti, maybe to England.' She stalked out and closed the door noisily behind her.

The Ma'ohi men were quickly afire with her plan for the outrigger raft, eager to make it their project and to show their skills and knowledge. An hour after she'd walked out on Fletcher, the basic materials were assembled. Empty barrels, spare spars, rope for lashing and binding.

The unseaworthy jolly boat was cannibalised for its clinker planking down to the waterline. The remainder of its 16-ft long hull became a broad back across which the raft was constructed. On top of this the gratings that allowed air into the lower deck provided the platform. With a line of empty barrels lashed on to either side as balancing outriggers, the raft would effectively have three hulls.

Fletcher came on deck to find the entire waist of the ship devoted to building the raft. 'This is amazing, Mauatua,' he said. 'You are a goddess, truly.'

'Don't worry, Fletcher,' she answered. 'BOUNTY will be ship-shape enough for you to sail you home.'

She snapped her fingers under his nose contemptuously.

'You know you can rely on me,' she added and then went below.

Fletcher cursed himself for not discussing his new plans with her, but did she have to take it so seriously?

Tararo struck while Fletcher looked discomfited.

'You better be careful, Titreano. Look. Black man building big raft. And black man know the way to Tahiti. Might leave you behind, eh?' The

Ma'ohi men laughed loudly at Tararo's mockery. Encouraged, Niau added his own tease.

'But we don't need a raft, do we? How many men you think to sail this ship, Tararo?' Tararo ostentatiously counted the fingers of one hand and the thumb of the other. 'I reckon six could do it, if someone knew the way. Anyway, some of the girls would help.'

Mauatua needed the certainty from Fletcher that she had given him. She also needed to know which women were as determined as she to create a new life. It was many weeks since she had talked with Jenny the way friends should.

'Jenny,' she asked when she found her, 'Would it trouble you if we didn't stay at Pitcairn?'

'After all this?'

Mauatua pressed her impatiently. 'Fletcher won't run BOUNTY onto the rocks. He wants to keep her seaworthy, in case he decides to go to Tahiti, or somewhere else.'

'Fletcher go back to Tahiti? Why?'

'He's not been man enough to tell me.'

Jenny thought for some time. 'You'd have to cut your hair, *vahine*. If. .'

'If what?'

'If we went back.'

Mauatua lowered her voice, almost growling. 'You'll never see me going back. No man will ever again tell me what to do, here or there. Now, answer me. If given the chance, would you go back?'

'I might. As you said, sometimes it is better to be a bit unhappy.'

She exploded at the easy acceptance of male domination by her friend.

'That's not what I said. I said it's too easy to confuse happiness with the acceptance of unhappiness.' Then she apologised, aware she had spoken harshly to the woman she trusted as her best future support.

'What about you, Mauatua? You really think Fletcher might go, leave you?'

It was hard for her to say it, but soon she heard the words fall from her lips.

'He knows I would have to stay. That makes him free to go.'

'So what will you do about it?'

'I don't know. I don't. But, how can I ever forget?'

An aching, strangled cry, long, demanding and devouring every last particle of her breath bled from Mauatua's throat.

Jenny held her close to muffle her distress. 'What?' she begged to know. 'Forget what?'

Mauatua bled out her wound to Jenny in a voice thick with pain but firm with resolve.

'How can I forget that he once thought of leaving me?'

CHAPTER 33

'This is Purgatory!'

Fletcher Christian shouted into the wind again and again. BOUNTY had skirted Pitcairn Island for six days and it was still impossible to land. Like any tormented soul he had neither hope of moving on nor a place of retreat. The raft was built and everything was ready to land. But the delay meant more minds turned to Tahiti. He was as torn by that option as any man or woman aboard BOUNTY.

Tahiti would make it easier for him to return to England.

It wasn't enough he had found a refuge for those who had broken the law and followed him, he was equally obliged to expiate his own crimes. There would be something heroic about going back to face the Lords of the Admiralty. Good subject for a painting. The Penitent Mutineer perhaps? Romney and Laurence had painted others in his family.

The outcome would be the same for Mauatua, whether she came with him or not. If he went alone she would be abandoned on Pitcairn.

If she sailed to England with him she would have only his swinging corpse for company.

He'd been mortified when mutineers joined yesterday's laughter about the raft. The last thing he expected was mockery and anyway had no idea how to deal with it. How could the discipline and respect of so many months at sea be so easily swept aside?

He recognised he didn't know what anyone else was thinking, not even Mauatua. It was like being a child again, uncertain of what adults argued about. When he closed his cabin door he put his thumb in his mouth, sorry he had nothing like the stick he once always chewed.

Mauatua didn't stay with him overnight but slept in the greenhouse. They were polite when they saw each other and seemed as bonded as ever when they jointly decided to break the monotony of watching Pitcairn's surf with a banquet of roasted pork and, unusually, roasted chicken too, a quarter per person. Feasting was part of everyone's Pitcairn dream. When freshly caught fish was added, BOUNTY'S galley had rarely served a bigger meal and none was more appreciated.

He waited until very late, but she didn't come to his cabin.

Early next morning, January 20th, the sea and the weather were finally judged calm enough to attempt landing. Fletcher edged BOUNTY to within a few hundred yards of the shore and then positioned her firmly parallel to the proposed landing place beneath the parrot-head headland. BOUNTY held steady with her bow pointing west towards the high lookout point. There were fewer rocks between her and the shore here, but only a shallow ledge of rock for landing.

Ned Young put off in the small cutter with a gang intending to find a way to land on the small beach and then to start setting up the camp. For more than an hour the cutter failed to find its way through the surf-pounded rocks. Ned chose a wave he thought safe but then find the boat turned on its length and hurtling backwards, or he lost confidence at the last second and the cutter hovered dangerously close to rocks that might shatter it. Jeers and ideas from BOUNTY'S deck didn't help and Fletcher angrily ordered these to stop.

Ned finally admitted they were blessed not to have capsized and asked advice from the two Ma'ohi men aboard the cutter. Once valued they told him quietly of how they assessed the currents and the way the rocks of the bay tossed these back and forth. They counted waves and watched the eddies of each, which told them of hazards beneath the surface. Eventually the boat's direction was changed. When it was judged atop the perfect wave, the poised oars were dipped and pulled strongly. The cutter surfed in and landed on the small beach with a thump heard aboard BOUNTY and then the advance party fought up the cliff side with canvas sails that would be used as shelter.

He watched anxiously as the raft was hoisted and gently craned down to the sea. The raft floated evenly and was soon loaded with everything Mauatua and Jenny had gathered as most immediately practical. On this first journey, the raft was paddled and steered with oars. It towed a line from BOUNTY and took another with it. In future it would be secured both ways by this stout rope and pulled back and forth on its journeys.

He ordered the animals off the ship as quickly as possible. This would make more space and the deck could then methodically be sluiced and scrubbed and thus smell less. The slick trotters of the first pigs swung overboard couldn't hold them against the raft's constant movement and in no time they were in the water.

To his amazement, they simply swung their heads to establish where land was and paddled serenely to shore, recovering quickly if they happened to be swirled into a rock. From then on, whenever the raft was on its way to shore, animals were hoisted into the sea and then released to find their way to freedom.

It wasn't as simple for him to leave BOUNTY. No sailor simply walks away from a ship. A ship was called she for the tender feelings she evoked and for the comfort men expected from her, mother to some, wife to others. Friend or foe, a ship's constant companionship became sewn into your skin and mind, its smell lingered on your skin and in your clothes. BOUNTY had been his home since December 1787, for over two years.

It would be hard letting go, as hard as finally throwing away the stick he had chewed for comfort as a child. Next morning, Fletcher and Mauatua went ashore together. The Ma'ohi men agreed good weather and calm seas would last two days or longer. Buoyed by the high mood and good spirits aboard, and seeing how cargo was steadily piling up on land, Fletcher suggested the morning watches might take time off to explore their new home. In the afternoon the teams could swap.

Only Quintal grumbled. 'Them masts stick out like tits in winter.'

'So you are back to wanting her – what? Sunk? Run aground?'

'Something like that, yes.' Quintal pushed belligerently into Fletcher's chest and looked up at him with determination little short of malice.

'We are ashore, Mr Christian. We are now masters of our own fate. We'll not go back to sea again.'

'Indeed, is that so, Matt? What if that's not what I want? Might I remind you of something you said to me in Tubuai? You said, if I remember correctly, that sometimes it was the minority that was right. This time I am the minority. The ship stays safe and seaworthy until I say otherwise.'

Mauatua waited for the others to move well on. Challenging Fletcher would not succeed. Neither would sulking about what he so recently said. This island had to succeed and she determined to make herself so desirable, so crucial to its future, that he would never again think of leaving her. It was vaguely disturbing, like a sad mother forcing a child to love her.

They found the steep path up the cliff side steep was tough, even in the plentiful shade of luscious tropical growth. The red clay soil was deeply rutted where rain must regularly have gushed to the sea in torrents and now these were baked dry so it was difficult safely to land a foot flat.

Her legs were stronger from their months of keeping her upright at sea, but she soon ached from thigh to ankle. She paused at the top of the cliffs to look down at BOUNTY, sucking her chest full of the sweeter clean air.

She picked grasses and pulled bark and broke leaves to smell their juices, excited to be surrounded by greenery and growth again.

They walked only a little further when Fletcher put a finger to her lips. He cocked his head, inviting her to listen. Even here close to the cliff edge the thick foliage muffled the incessant thunder of the surf. The island was silent. He smiled with pleasure but she was chilled. Where Fletcher felt at peace, she felt menaced and vulnerable.

The silence was primeval, the sound of the world before gods thought to add birds and animals, men and women. She shivered, but didn't tell him the reason. The fingers of her right hand patterned on her left breast as she struggled with an awful unbidden thought. Perhaps Pitcairn had no veil of gods and spirits, perhaps there were none to tease her with messages through clattering leaves or the hiss of bending grasses?

If that explained the silence, then Pitcairn was a land gods and spirits didn't care to inhabit. What might this mean for its new settlers?

He wanted to press on, to show her views and gardens his landing party had discovered, but she refused. Pretending she wanted to think more about how their camp should be laid out, she forced him to go ahead. If he didn't see what she was doing, he would never have to lie for her.

She had spied a small ruined marae on the edge of the site, almost overgrown and heralded only by a few upright stones. Tararo could easily clean the marae up and use it again. Determined this would never happen, she pulled off her shift and then looped up her skirt.

Rills of sweat trickled between her breasts as she tugged, pulled and pushed at the upright marae stones, some of which had fallen and cracked. Once she moved them close to the edge of the cliff, she sat behind them. She planted her arms firmly and then she pushed with her newly muscled legs until each stone yielded. One by one they plummeted to smash into the surf and rocks far beneath. Then, on hands and knees, she pulled up as many of the paving stones as she could and did the same. She scuffed the soil, covering the remaining evidence with leaves and branches. There was nothing left to remind BOUNTY'S Ma'ohi men and women of the beliefs that once smothered her.

Anyway, she thought as she rubbed her hands clean with leaves, I will now know for certain if there are gods or spirits on Pitcairn's Island and she steeled herself against any revenge they might exact. Then she laughed. Perhaps the island was silent because it had been saved just for them? She and Fletcher would be its first god and goddess and give the island all the expected deities had not.

More and more amused by both the idea and the danger of this, she looked for the *ahima'a*, the earth-oven site there must have been in the ancient campsite. She was singing loudly while clearing it out when Fletcher returned.

'Come on, I've a reward for you. Quick, before the others come back.'

He held her hand and jogged an arm's length ahead, keeping the other over his head to push through narrow overgrown paths. He stopped her under the soft-shaded umbrella of an enormous banyan tree, whose gnarly roots and aerial suckers marched down a slope for at least the length of BOUNTY. He put a hand over her eyes and carefully guided her around the main trunk of the hoary old tree.

'What do you think,' he asked as he slowly slipped his hand away.

'It's impossible,' she whispered.

It was the edge of a pool of clear sweet water. Blackness beneath the reflections told her of its great depth. At one end shimmers of light revealed a spring feeding the pool. At the other end, tinkling rills ran away to sink in silence beneath high ferns and through bosomy moss.

Above her, lush banana leaves and clattering coconut palms competed with the banyan's arching branches to cool the pool and the air around it. She was amused how spiky pandanus and high-coloured hibiscus had pushed their way forward so their arrogance was better reflected in the pool.

She wriggled her toes on dried leaves but they felt soft, telling her there were many layers of damp, composting ancestors beneath them. The full rich smell was not decay but the sweetness of continuity and future fruitfulness. He released her from her skirt and tilted her forward. When she at last relinquished the cool depths of the pool and swam up gasping for air he was naked beside her.

'This, this I hope, makes it all worthwhile for you?'

'It does, Mr Christian, it does,' she agreed, wondering when he would call her Mrs Christian. They playfully pushed and pulled one another, cleansing themselves profoundly deeper than their skins and then made love with dappled sunlight flickering on their bodies.

An hour before sunset, Fletcher ordered rum and wine served on board. The bright scrubbed decks, free at last of animals, became a promenade for talking and relaxing. BOUNTY's company had never been noisier. As the evening air cooled he encouraged BOUNTY's men and women to talk to him about their first impressions. She shadowed him, listening carefully for what was not being said.

Pitcairn seemed to offer everything they each might have hoped. Some women told of the *aute,* paper mulberry trees to make everyday tapa. The bark of *'ora* the mighty banyan trees made a weather-proof cloth and the bark of breadfruit, *'uru,* also made a useful tapa cloth. There were masses of candlenuts, *tutu'i,* to string and then burn for light at night.

Others were as excited about pandanus and coconut palms for thatching, to make sweepers and baskets, to weave into sun shades or waterproof cloaks against rain. The remains of old gardens were obvious and still bounteous. There must be untold fish in the sea, just as there were oysters and lobsters on the shore.

'We'll still have to work like peasants,' McCoy said sadly.

'But live like kings. And queens,' came the joyful responses.

Fletcher found his explorations had been quickly confirmed by everyone else on deck. The rich, red earth of the proposed settlement was deep and fertile. There was water. They were protected by a wild coastline and could see for almost twenty miles in every direction from the highest peak. The island's geographical position, a little south of the Tropic of Capricorn, made it more temperate than tropical. They would enjoy a mean temperature of about 70°F through the year but there would be more weather variation than on Tahiti.

'Let's be honest,' Ned said. 'It's better than we ever expected. And, as Fletcher also said, it's invisible to the rest of the world. What I say is, three cheers for our captain.'

Mauatua cheered loudest. Pitcairn offered dignity as well as the new home she craved. Yet the enormous tasks before all of them were bound to grow into burdens. She knew there was every likelihood some would be less willing to share their weight.

For now, she was content everyone aboard felt part of a mutually supportive group. She saw the challenge of creating their settlement as like their initial days at sea. They had been alien at first to the Ma'ohi men and women but once the challenges were broken down into small achievable tasks, everything became feasible and then gratifying to have conquered.

Establishing the settlement would be different, the reverse. Little would be a challenge to any of the Ma'ohi. It was the nine white men who had most to learn. She suspected they each saw themselves as some sort of South Seas chief when there wasn't to be even one chief on Pitcairn Island.

Her only real fear was Tararo, still convinced he was to be chief of Pitcairn Island.

CHAPTER 34

On the third morning BOUNTY was anchored Fletcher secured the last of a long rope to a sturdy post at the base of the track up the cliff, so climbers could pull themselves up or use it to stop themselves falling. Brown interrupted him.

'You are a well read man, Fletcher. You must know The Pilgrims Progress. John Bunyan?'

'I know of it. Not a book I've read.'

'Ah, but you will know it is the story of a man called Christian and the challenges he conquers.' Fletcher nodded and Brown went on. 'One of these is a very long hill, arduous it is. It happens to be a verse I remember.

'This Hill, though high, I covet to ascend,
The difficulty will not me offend:
For I perceive the way to life lies here;
Come, pluck up, heart; let's neither faint nor fear:

'You are called Christian, it is a steep hill and at the top is a new life for us all. Bunyan called his Difficulty Hill, or was it . . .? Never mind I think yours should be The Hill of Difficulty, easier on the tongue.'

As more heard it, the name was quickly adopted. Fletcher remembered the great interest there was to name the fort on Tubuai. He looked up at the headland towering over the ship.

'And this, this will be Ship Landing Point.' He pointed towards the highest headland, at the far end of their proposed settlement. 'And that other one, the tallest, that should be Lookout Point. Actually, now we've named it that, I'm damned if we should be keeping watch from the ship. We can't even see around the nearest headlands. From tomorrow we'll put our lookout up there.'

The chore of carrying everything up the Hill of Difficulty was so arduous Fletcher was forced to call a vote that agreed to move only the absolute minimum. The rest was stacked in some order against the cliffs, covered by canvas. There was talk that once the ship was fully unloaded they would arrange some sort of hoist, but that was for the future. Then they'd also want to salvage BOUNTY'S timbers for their houses.

Rock-filled Bounty Bay, seen from high on the left side of Ship Landing Point. The narrow beach once led to the right to the narrow shelf where BOUNTY unloaded. The jetty you see is constantly upgraded but so far no alteration has made the bay safe for boats or ships. The widened red-clay track of the Hill of Difficulty that climbs the cliff has recently been concreted.

His vision of an English village in a tropical setting had never wavered. BOUNTY'S oak was now so seasoned it would be as hard as iron and last them for centuries. It was mutually agreed it would be easier to begin working in the hold, removing the softer, greener timbers of the two new platform decks and their cabins. They would work upwards and outwards through the ship including her inner hull until BOUNTY had only a single oaken skin covered in copper. Eventually, that would be pulled on to the rocks and the copper sheathing salvaged, perhaps to decorate the roofs and there were dozens of ways to reuse the lead sheeting from the greenhouse.

The five leaded windows from the stern and two, three-windowed quarter galleries from either side might be built into some sort of meeting hall. A mast, shortened so it couldn't be seen from sea, would serve as a flag pole and proudly fly the Union flag.

Well, that was the plan if he stayed.

To ensure his safe escape he secreted BOUNTY'S navigational instruments and chronometer in his sea chest with souvenirs of earlier voyages and life.

He'd commissioned the small, camphorwood-lined chest of mahogany in India on his first voyage with the Royal Navy. From the Caribbean he kept trinkets of intricately woven small shells. A set of small porcelain bowls from China, hand painted with fabulous peonies and pheasants, had been given by his Christian great-aunts. They were fearful of the effect of the ruffians he would be obliged to mix with and so gave them as an *aide-memoire* of the elegant, privileged life of manners Fletcher properly shared with them in London and Bath and Cumbria.

Fletcher carried everything of his and of Bligh up the Hill of Difficulty, leading by doing everything he expected others to do. There was to be democracy on Pitcairn, but he'd learned it worked best when there was a clear leader. He thought the trappings of captaincy would help and so toiled through the day to construct and define a space under the canvas awnings that might remind others of Bligh's cabin on BOUNTY.

His goal was order, order upon which he would base his final decision to go or to stay.

It took three days to persuade Teio to leave the ship with her baby. She believed Sully would be dashed from her arms and drowned. She'd often seen the cutter swamped and could barely look at the raft.

Adams suggested putting the baby into a barrel as its own flotation and his idea cut through Teio's fears.

She finally stepped into the cutter, and Sully followed, let down into the boat tied securely into a shallow gang cask.

Once Teio had joined them Mauatua suggested the women might bathe together in the pool under the banyan. The women first giggled and laughed as they splashed and dived or ducked one another.

Once their boisterous pleasures were exhausted they relaxed and began to speak openly. 'I've told Tararo. I'd sail with him tonight if he wanted to go,' Jenny declared.

'You would? You'd prefer Tahiti?' Mauatua found it difficult not to be cross with her friend.

'This place will never be happy. We are different people. And the white men, they drink too much rum. Then they are rough. Demanding.'

'I won't go,' Mauatua said flatly.

'You like this life?'

'No, not yet. But I will,' Mauatua said, her eyes steely with determination. 'And think, one day there will be no more rum for them.'

'That'll be years away. It's not just what's on the island, there's plenty more on the ship.' Jenny turned to the other women in the pool. 'I think we should all go, with Tararo. Why not, when even your Fletcher Christian is thinking of going?'

The startled reaction by the other women allowed Mauatua to continue drying her hair with tapa cloth, keeping her pain to herself until she felt she could sound unconcerned.

'Well, if Fletcher leaves perhaps we should all leave, too,' she laughed. 'Be much safer on BOUNTY than that raft.'

'The raft only needs a mast, and some sort of shelter,' Jenny countered.

'But why would you go, for what?'

'For Tahiti, that's enough.'

Mauatua hung the wet tapa on a bush. She sat with her knees apart, and tipped her hair forward to finish drying and straightening the strands that normally lay against her scalp and neck.

'You think Tahiti is better, do you?' she asked from under her thick screen of hair. 'Do you, Teio, do you really think that?'

Teio held her daughter in her arms in the water, encouraging the baby to splash its arms and legs. 'It is home,' she appealed.

'Yes, you should always be where home is.

'If Tahiti is where you think home is, it will be good to be back. Just as it has always been good for women.'

'We do not get slapped or punched by drunks.'

Mauatua flicked her hair aside and stared at Teio.

'Not so much anyway,' Teio conceded.

Mauatua reminded them of what they had forgotten. That they would not eat as much, or eat what they were now used to eating. They would eat only what men allowed or left for them. They could be divorced on a whim, leftovers from men's other appetites. She reminded them of the inequalities, the unfairness and the exclusions of life on Tahiti. And that they would have only the children that men allowed.

Just as it had always been for women.

'Won't it be the same here?' Teio asked.

'Stupid girl. Fletcher will not allow that and neither will I. What is the point of sailing so far to go back to old ways of life?'

'*Auee!* The point is how *popa'a* behave now they don't need us to sail their ship.' Teio shouted back. 'Demanding this, planning that, telling us what they will do where. Each one of them is a chief already. What does that make us?'

The women stayed quiet, tending one another's cuts and bruises, combing hair or helping with plucking. Each was making their own answers but Mauatua wanted them to think the same way.

'My sisters,' she continued. 'Think more about what Teio has just said. The *popa'a* no longer need our help? That is not true. The ship was their world. This island is our world. None of them knows how to live here.'

She asked if they thought white men could plant at the right time and in the right places or if they knew the secrets of weaving walls or thatching roofs. Did white men know how to catch fish in the Pacific, know which were safe to eat and which might give you strange dreams or belly ache? Could they carve the right hooks for each species from bone, would they know the best part of a human for these? They certainly didn't know which banana to plant on low plains and which on mountains, or how to make *monoi* or which plants knit bones and which leaves will heal flesh.

'And one day they will have no more clothes,' she added, inviting laughter. 'Do white men know how to beat tapa cloth from *aute?*'

Mauatua saw shoulders and backs straighten. Glances of agreement and understanding flickered from face to face. She had won most over. Her voice became conciliatory and soft, so the women had to pay particular attention. Only Jenny was unconvinced and spoke up.

'We are doing the right thing for them. But the more we do to make those men a home here, the further we are from Tahiti.'

'I'm happy with that,' Teio, her mood mercurially changed

'You are?'

'I see what Mauatua tells now. This will be our island, not theirs. And there's that pork. Don't laugh. I like to eat pork. . . '

Jenny was angry at Teio's change of mind. 'We don't have to wait for Tararo or Christian. We are enough women. We can sail that ship ourselves, get back to Tahiti and live with our own names again.'

'I will not allow it,' Mauatua shouted so forcefully some women jumped in fear. She told them she would live on BOUNTY with Fletcher, guarding the ship against them. She would shoot them, any of them who tried to leave.

'What if it was Fletcher who decided to sail? What would you do then?' Jenny demanded.

'I would shoot him too.'

In the awed silence that followed Mauatua declared Pitcairn was now her home and that she would defend it against anyone or anything that was a threat. If anyone went back to Tahiti the world would know about Pitcairn Island and Fletcher's king would send ships to punish those who had sailed with him.

She urged them to think, really to think what there was back in Tahiti for any of them. But she thought too, thought painfully about the look of repulsion that darkened Fletcher's face when she had first called herself Mrs Christian. And how he had thought of leaving her.

She *would* rather shoot him than sail back to Tahiti. She was startled to find she thought so strongly.

'No man is ever going to tell me what I can or can't eat or to cut my hair – or anything!' Tevarua, Quintal's partner, exclaimed falling luxuriously backwards into the pool.

'Tell me, tell the truth.' Jenny stamped her feet with frustration

'Who else wants to go back, who will come back with Tararo and me, or with Fletcher?'

Many of the women were uncomfortable, unable or unwilling to make a decision. Some stayed in the pool. Mauatua took the baby so Teio's mind would fully hear her.

Then, she explained again why each woman would be indispensible, because the white men were incapable of creating a village and living on such an island. Then she drew pictures of the land Pitcairn would be for their children and for their children beyond that.

These were new thoughts. A future as mothers of a gentler fairer society was something none had fully considered.

She spun them deeper into the world she envisioned for Pitcairn's women and their children. They would be mothers of the first children in the South Pacific who were free from their first breath. They would carry their freedoms and equality unthreatened into adulthood, boys and girls who the white men would teach to read and write.

When she felt their minds were softened suitably, she cast before them the potent prize she hoped would trap them in her dreams.

'This is not Paradise, whatever we may joke. Yet, here we will no longer be women who only talk. About problems. Here we can solve difficulties, change things we don't like.'

She pretended to work knots from her hair, tightening the tension around the pool until she was certain each woman was focussed on what she would say next.

'Tonight, for instance, tonight we could ensure Pitcairn was a women's island, a place we would feel proud to bring children into. If we agree, you will have voted to forget the women we have been. You will have been more courageous than other Ma'ohi woman can imagine.

'Tonight, you could vote not for who we are but for the women we might one day become.

'But first you must swear by the stars of *te tauha*, by the ever-watching Southern Cross, that no man will ever know what we do tonight.'

Eleven other hands went up, as Mauatua gambled they must.

CHAPTER 35

January 23RD 1790 – Pitcairn Island

Fletcher Christian was tormented. He couldn't fathom if conscience about the mutiny would outweigh a conscience about leaving her. Which was the better epilogue to his past, which the better prologue to his future? It obviously wasn't the sort of thing to talk about with Mauatua. Ned might laugh at him and make him feel stupid and as for anyone else on board. There was none to ask but BOUNTY, mother BOUNTY, who had comforted him and kept him safe for so many nights.

There was a sharp moon and the stars shone so fiercely their lights bled into scintillating clouds. The Southern Cross was clear, majestic and poised, but tonight unsettling because it highlighted his exile.

At the bottom of the Hill of Difficulty Fletcher faced BOUNTY squarely. The bright light ensured she knew he was there. And even in the moonlight he could see she was not the stout, tight vessel she had been in Portsmouth or in Matavai Bay.

What had once been sleek black or blue paint was peeling and shabby. Her yellow-gold trim was no longer the cheeky conceit of some naval architect's clerk but forlorn, like rain-bleached bunting from a long gone fair. Her rigging was cannibalised and some hung like wind-torn cobwebs. Barrels of rum and casks of salt meat were stacked atop one another on the open deck, a sure sign a ship was home or about to leave.

BOUNTY'S figurehead was aged by the months of pitiless sun and incessant salt water. Yet she remained bold and challenging, perhaps the only touchstone of his life in England. Her blue riding habit conjured images of Ewanrigg, the Cumbrian mansion of his 1st cousin John Christian, where the dressed-stone kennels of the hounds were finer accommodation than enjoyed by most inhabitants of Maryport or Cockermouth. He remembered Isabella Curwen, now John's wife, in riding habit. It was one of his favourite memories of her.

There was no-one else on board who knew or appreciated what his cousin or his brothers, uncles and aunts and cousins did in every vein of law and learning, or in religious and political life in England and abroad. They were why the success of Pitcairn was so important, so he could be counted in this panoply of family pride. Then he shrugged. What was meant to be a laugh became a snort.

He never really belonged to that established sort of life. He was unlikely ever to have the fortune – or good fortune – to marry as well as expected. Would an English woman with her own wealth accept his hands and his sweating and his tattooed buttocks?

The tattoo identified his comfort in the South Seas but not enough to make him fully at home here. He imagined himself happy with Mauatua but knew much of his true personality would have to be submerged to accommodate their cultural differences. There was duty to his family to consider, too. With so many centuries of dispensing Breast Law as Deemsters on the Isle of Man behind them, his family would surely expect him to return and honourably face the consequences of his mutiny. Even his mother would agree with that.

Fletcher turned his ears and eyes fully to BOUNTY. Might she have an answer for him?

He knew BOUNTY'S language as well as his own. He knew all her idioms, her unique way to cut into the sea or fret in high wind. A breeze aimlessly worrying her masts and rigging whistled to him of its sags and shreds. The noises her hull made as she rocked in the sucking and splashing of the waves told him of her demeanour and health. Tonight, he felt anxious for her. There was something sinister about the sounds he heard. Something the ship and her figurehead were trying to say made no sense.

He sat on a rock and dropped his head, aware it looked like penitence. His chin closed into his neck and his thoughts became deeper until he found he was praying, praying for serenity, for the peace he hoped making the right decision would bring.

There was no point praying for serenity, a voice whispered from somewhere. Such reward only came with certainty, it said. Could the voice be BOUNTY, could she be so direct and prescriptive?

BOUNTY now shouted at him with a strange loud series of cracks. It was a new sort of speech, urgent and pained. He understood none of it, but felt he should. His nose twitched. There was smoke in the air. Then he heard splashes. Fish? Fish leaping for the moon?

Cramped, overwhelmed by the weights in his mind, Fletcher turned his back on BOUNTY and walked along the narrow strip of sand and into moon-made shadow. He pulled up his shirt to wipe his face. There was a muffled explosion somewhere and then smoke, acrid and thick, sneaked into the back of his throat. When he coughed, his stinging eyes bled water.

Yet when they cleared he saw only BOUNTY and moonlight on the water. Then the moonlight flickered and danced and became orange and red. One more explosion and he knew.

No moonlight this. BOUNTY was afire.

Smoke suddenly thundered out of her in enormous, blaze-powered columns. BOUNTY, tinder dry and still with much of her cargo of coal and firewood aboard, with kegs of rum and pitch-caulked decks, with barrels of gunpowder and rigging dark with tar, was burning with the fury of the pits of Hell.

Disembowelled by disbelief, Fletcher Christian fell to his knees and howled at the moon.

CHAPTER 36

Fletcher ran to the cutter but BOUNTY was already fatally resigned to the inferno's intent. Others running from the Hill of Difficulty held him back, seeing any rescue attempt was futile.

Flames so urgently digested BOUNTY's anchor lines that the bay's heaving waters had already hauled her further from land and closer to their vast salty vaults. BOUNTY was doomed. No-one then thought to moor the cutter properly. It too was wrenched from Ship Landing Point by surf and then shot through by chunks of burning wood hurled by explosions.

The raft had been moored by its ropes between BOUNTY and the rocks. Brave swimmers went to drag it to shore, but it was pierced by flights of flaming timbers and abandoned.

The cannons and the great stove of the galley fell through the lower deck and stopped only when half way through the double hull and copper sheathing. The ship's bell fell too and once gunpowder exploded the hull was fatally pierced. With flames above and water gushing into her below, BOUNTY was dead.

Mauatua believed Fletcher would be more predictable and compliant away from the sight. Before BOUNTY'S ravaged hull sank, already no more than copper sheathing in some places, she persuaded him back up the Hill of Difficulty.

Fletcher lay with his head in her lap. Even up in the campsite there was enough smoke to irritate his eyes. She gently wiped them, totally at his disposal. It seemed only fair.

She stroked his face and hair and crooned comfort to him.

'You never lied. You never said BOUNTY would take me to England.'

When Fletcher spoke, she couldn't tell if it was to her or some phantasm only he could picture. 'Going back was the only way to know. How many men are dead because I took that ship? Bligh? Fryer? Stewart?'

'Knowing would not make them live again, Fletcher.'

He turned to lay his other cheek in her lap. He pulled his knees up to his chest and clasped his hands under his chin. When he put a thumb in his mouth she pulled it out. She would nurse a man but not a child.

'But I hadn't chosen. There was no proper decision,' he whimpered.

Before she could calculate a safe answer, Quintal and the other mutineers returned noisily, each carrying a musket. They pushed and prodded the sullen Ma'ohi men in front of them. The women followed in small groups. Fletcher leapt from her lap.

'So, Quintal. So, all is to be your will and only yours. Is that it?'

Quintal had been drinking all day but rare good humour masked his usual ill temper. He bowed with a sweeping gesture of his musket.

'So it seems, my dear.'

Tararo rushed forward to fall at their feet. 'Punish him, Titreano. Kill him before he kills us. He is a very bad man.' The mutineers surrounded Tararo, all with muskets pointed at him. Fletcher preferred to believe the mutineers were acting out some fantastic game. He waved them away and reached to help Tararo up and then turned to Quintal again.

'Why, Matt? Why, and why now?'

Quintal stood belligerently with his chest touching Fletcher. The fumes of his breath and the musket in his hands warned Fletcher not to resist but to step back. Quintal followed.

'You thinks I done it?' He stood on his toes so his smoke-curdled eyes were almost level with Fletcher's.

'You wanted it most,' Tararo shouted.

Fletcher held up his hands. 'You do know what this means, don't you?' he asked. His face was stern, yet his lips and voice trembled.

'And what's that, my dear?' Quintal mocked. 'We're all ears, ain't we boys?' Mauatua tapped Quintal's arm, hoping to dissuade him from the derision she heard growing in his voice.

Fletcher eyes were rocket-red from smoke and tears and he spoke with a sob in his voice. 'From today, from January 23rd 1790, there's no way we can be English any more, that's what the fire means. We cannot have houses of oak, we cannot defend ourselves with cannon and shot.

'This is now a Ma'ohi island and we must live like natives. We are at their mercy for shelter and we'll even need them to build canoes before we can fish. It's not the balance I had planned for us.'

'My dear, if the balance is not the way you wanted, then we'll have to change it won't we?' Quintal shook his musket at the Ma'ohi men and women. The mutineers roared their support, enjoying the spectacle of the Ma'ohi men cowering.

And then, strangely placatory, Quintal stepped back.

'Mr Christian. Fletcher, my friend. You can think what you like, but I don't give a bugger. Without a ship you are no longer a captain, certainly not my captain.

'As to who burned the ship - if *any* bastard did – I am not the only bugger who wants to stay here. Perhaps it was the *piskies,* or the spirits our darkie friends fear so much?'

Quintal held up his arms like wings and whistled and hooted the way he thought evil spirits might. No-one reacted. He looked around the camp slowly, his eyes for once merry with taunt rather than malice. The other mutineers, all as jovial as Quintal, shrugged and smirked. Fletcher followed Quintal's confrontations and saw most Ma'ohi turn from him.

Only Mauatua held Quintal's eye, locking on to it. Time seemed to stop. Not a person uttered a sound or moved.

Mauatua tilted her head. Did Quintal suspect what really happened or would his drunkenness keep her secret?

'Fletcher, do we know who burned BOUNTY for sure?' she asked.

He turned slowly. 'You think it wasn't Quintal?'

'Perhaps there were embers in the galley, some accident, a sudden roll of the ship might have. . .'

'So, it doesn't have to be Quintal, is that what you are saying?'

'I'm saying you can't know for certain.' She moved closer so only Fletcher could hear her. 'I think it only a sign our old lives are gone, forever. Nothing from the past. Remember?'

Quintal was bored with not being the centre of attention.

'God's bollocks. This is not time for blame,' he said explosively, standing between Fletcher and Mauatua. 'What's done is done and now we know where we are, so to speak. There's nothing left to do tonight but drinking or sleeping. I'll go without one so I can drink to the sun coming up tomorrow on my new kingdom.'

The mutineers fell in behind him and he gestured evilly at the Ma'ohi men with his musket. 'You boys better stay out of trouble.'

Only the Ma'ohi men and the three women they shared remained. Tararo was puffed up with rage. Mauatua knew the slightest extra humiliation would provoke him beyond control.

'You handled that with great dignity, Tararo,' she said consolingly. 'All of you did. I know some of you are disappointed. You are not alone.

Tonight Pitcairn became a different place. Tomorrow each of us will have to find a new identity. There is nothing here from the past for any of us.'

Tararo took her words as an apology and then led his group away.

She was alone with Fletcher again. 'There are things I have to tell you, Fletcher.' He held his breath, smoke tainted still, and closed his eyes.

'How long has BOUNTY been yours?' she asked.

'Since the end of April last year. What's that, just over eight months?'

'And some women have been on board almost seven of them.' She asked him if there was nothing he thought unusual. When he said there wasn't, Mauatua was certain of her domination.

'Think Fletcher. All that time and no big bellies. No babies.'

'What! You women have been doing things?'

She told him it wasn't right for a woman to bring a baby into the world without knowing where its home would be. And certainly not at sea.

The child's soul would wander forever, looking for the land where his placenta, his *pufenua*, was buried. No spirit was more dangerous or vengeful than that of a child destined never to rest.

'But you said you wanted to get away from, from killing babies.'

'Only when men tell us. These were our decisions. You remember when you said you couldn't tell which woman was bleeding? That was deliberate, so no man would know if his woman was *hapu*, pregnant.'

'But how, what do you do?'

'That is women's business. On this island it is *only* women's business.'

Fletcher was so fragile Mauatua let him pull her to the ground and put his head in her lap. He turned his tear-lined face up to her.

'Do I, can I have any authority now?' She leaned forward to kiss him gently on his trembling lips.

'No-one has more authority than a leader with a son to follow him.'

CHAPTER 37

Mauatua was desperate to clarify her mind.

Was she a woman alone in history? Did ever a woman do what she had done, or face such an unshaped future?

She strode in half light from the campsite and to the headland they had named Ship Landing Point. As the sun heaved itself into the eastern sky she saw charred and scarred relics of planks, spars, steps, walls and doors floating in the sea and wedged into rocks. BOUNTY's ravaged hull sat unmoving beneath the turbulent waters.

To'erau, north
To'o'a o te ra, west
'Apato'a, south
Hiti'a o te ra, east

Whichever way Mauatua faced her eyes were hoaxed into thinking she had not moved. As she spun with her sight on the horizon she was the navel of a seamlessly joined body of sea and sky and she felt the true weight of the compact she and Fletcher had made. The community must become a personal paradise for everyone on the island. There was no escaping her primary responsibility for making this happen.

She scratched the ground, making marks for each of the twenty-seven dreams that must be satisfied, twenty-eight when she included the infant Sully, and then considered how these might be achieved.

Eight of the nine white men wanted to be on the island, were grateful to be there, to escape the noose their necks had earned. Fletcher was the exception and so would be hardest to make happy.

Of the six Ma'ohi men, Tararo was secretly competing with Fletcher for dominance, and for her. There were to be no chiefs or nobles on Pitcairn Island, but Mauatua hoped Pitcairn could find a way to respect Tararo's birth status and learning without demeaning others. At least these six men seemed comfortable sharing three women.

Tararo insisted only on exclusive rights to Toofaiti as a wife. She was from Huahine, a sister island to Raiatea that spoke the same dialect and was considered almost as holy. They would look down on the accent of Tahiti, even hers. The Tubuaians Titahiti and Oha chose Tinafanaea, also from their island. Making a distinct group with their own accent and dialect diluted any sense of being second best. The three other Ma'ohi men were Tahitians and seemed happy to share the Tahitian woman Mareva.

Once land made them self sufficient they would be as settled as the mutineers, who were also divided geographically and by accent.

But who of the Ma'ohi women could she count on to support her view of an island where women were equal to men? Which ones might regret agreeing to last night's secrets. Those uncertainties added to the burden of keeping the secret of Tararo's prediction of the certain failure of Fletcher.

Yet, her most enduring wish had come true. She lived at last where what she thought or did would be valued.

She should be concentrating on her future, but found it easier to slip backwards, to the simpler moments known by all Ma'ohi women, those times they stood breathless and proud before a stretch of bright, white tapa with not a blot, dot, line or image upon it. Old women taught girls that how they placed their first marks on pristine cloth would forever dictate the success or failure of their design.

Wasn't Pitcairn a tapa cloth for her to pattern?

Pitcairn would never be a land as soft and feminine as Tahiti, that was clear. It might be tamed but what might Pitcairn reveal about its new settlers, about the first village of Ma'ohi women with white husbands?

There was no precedent.

Certainly there had been other men here, perhaps women too, beneath the trees sheltering BOUNTY's marooned sailors. They had walked the ridges and made the paths she could make out, had stood where she stood. But the deserted maraes and abandoned stone tools revealed nothing of how they lived, by what laws and agreements and precedents, by what quiet advice from sage, long-dead *tupuna* that shaped their daily custom.

She sat for most of the day on the headland, again willing the island to release its secrets, to open its past. But Pitcairn's history remained locked from her, as silent as its present until the meaning implicit in its silence suddenly shone with dreadful clarity.

The island had no history to give her, none to guide her. Pitcairn Island would never be a land where she could look backwards to then walk more securely into the future. She bit her lip. She couldn't tell if she felt more fright and fear of the unknown past or more for the dread of a future with no boundaries.

Only when the sun had long passed over her head and was dissolving into the western ocean could she simplify the meaning of her day into a single truth.

No te ho'e vahine tei hina'aro mau i te ora, i ni'a i te ho'e fenua api, 'aita e 'ohipa faufa'a 'ore: On an island without a history, there is nothing a woman might not have to do to survive.

She repeated this, chanted it and absorbed it through every pore until it was as deep in her heart as Tahiti had once been.

When this was so, she stood and shouted her covenant with the island, warning whatever gods and spirits that might be listening.

'There is nothing I will not do. *E ora vau.* I will survive.'

Fletcher Christian had no comfort in his new world. He slept badly, every hour increasing his certainty he would one day have fled Pitcairn Island on BOUNTY. Conscience and the honour of his family would then have been served. He had done his duty by the other mutineers. They were as safe from the vengeance of the king as he could make them. He regretted saying he could never live where he may be carried home to be a disgrace to his family. The disgrace was in not returning.

He was not alarmed to discover Mauatua had gone. He had found the promised safe home for her yet it must be frightening to walk in a place once only in her mind. Reality was unkind to dreams.

He stayed alone in a soft muddle of tapa cloth, not eating or drinking, but fighting to clarify his future, accepting he alone would always regret the mutiny.

His more immediate agony was that he would never again have the company of social peers. Ned Young was the only shipmate to ask him about his background or his life between voyages. Ned said he'd asked because Fletcher so often kept one of his Chinese bowls close to him, forever running a hand over its exquisite thinness, holding it up to allow light through it.

He told Ned the gleam reminded him of candle-lit suppers in gilded rooms with looking glasses the height of two men, of the bosoms of women in powdered hair made taller with nodding egret feathers.

Ned prompted him to describe family picnics on Belle Isle, Isabella Curwen's round house on an island in Lake Windermere, and to tell of excursions to Milntown, the ancient family mansion at Lezayre on the Isle of Man. He relived horn-led hunts and masked balls at Ewanrigg and in the

Home Counties and told of candle-lit parties and all-night dancing and splendid dinners at great houses in London and Bath.

Ned recognised none of the families, none of their vast houses. He knew only Fortnum and Mason, the Society food emporium on Piccadilly. He too had bought *bohea* tea there.

It was hardly the basis of an intimate friendship.

Fletcher's fragile consolation was that his mutiny was not a conscious act. A sort of madness had come over him and then left him as quickly. Bligh, whom he had always managed before, was cast adrift in the middle of the South Pacific, and so were many other men who had considered him a friend. It was wrong, as bad a thing as any sailor could do. Yet, he was the only one on Pitcairn concerned.

After a morning of sleeping away the excitements and disappointments of the burning ship, the men and women of the camp were busy. He overheard couples speak loudly of moving further along the cliff, to make more private arrangements. Others pretended to think of the community but he suspected they thought only of how best to take advantage of the division of all that had come from BOUNTY. This would have to be settled quickly or jealousies would stalk every action, footstep and word.

Matt Quintal was sanguine about what had been burned, saying you couldn't miss what you never had. Bumpkin thinking, Fletcher muttered. Of course they had once owned everything now on the bottom of the bay.

He ticked off what else was being achieved that first day. Ned was searching for a site that would become a central village square. Brown began a communal compost heap, turning together the waste of the animals kept in the campsite with the camp's vegetable leftovers.

Most animals had been set free to fatten on Pitcairn's bounty, later to provide sport when they were hunted.

McCoy, hot, dirty and stripped only to a loincloth interrupted him with five other men, white and Ma'ohi.

'That's the dunnikins dug,' he said with pride.

'Dunnikins?'

'Aye. Where I came from that's what we called them, the long drops. We've dug two, three yards deep and close to the cliff edge so drainage won't threaten our water. There's something different about them, too.'

He walked with them on a new path to two huts with walls of loosely woven coconut leaf and with doors that had to be lifted in and out of place.

The surprise was the width of each dunnikin. This was what amused the men, too.

An entrepreneur had removed some of the pierced planks attached to BOUNTY's cats' heads, where more than one man could squat or sit to evacuate at the same time. Pitcairn's first buildings had been designed to their dimensions, and each could accommodate two people, side by side.

Already the women's tongues had reduced dunnikins to duncans, and Fletcher agreed that's what they were. Duncan was another new word for the island's language.

Fletcher escaped and went wearily back to his bed. Niau was waiting.

'Titreano, I know you are anxious. I have been left alone by Tararo. He is with Toofaiti. I will play for you.'

'Play? I don't need noise.'

'Not noise, Titreano, my nose flute, gentle and sweet. I will sit where you cannot see me and play bad and sad things out of your mind.'

In spite of his scepticism Fletcher fell into untroubled sleep, entertained by fluttering airs that swirled in and out of his consciousness, music as far removed from his memories of Handel and Mozart as was possible.

He dreamed only of good things and woke as Mauatua returned, sensing her before she spoke and at a glance they agreed one day of introspection was enough.

They agreed a schedule for the next day and then for many more after that, their low voices weaving into the flute's soft notes.

CHAPTER 38

There was no working tomorrow for either. Fletcher's anxieties erupted as days of furious fevers. Mauatua tended him night and day with massages and aromatic oils. Jenny helped and together they gave him small doses of laudanum. He was most tranquil when the narcotic coincided with Niau's flute playing.

For the other Pitcairners there was much to do and to her keen eye all seemed willing and industrious. Brown organised chains of men and women to bring up the potted plants from the bottom of the Hill of Difficulty. They were taken to land cleared by the big pool, now called Brown's Water, where each was heeled in to acclimatise and strengthen before being shared out. A runnel from the pool irrigated them.

Some of the white men complained they didn't like the thought of water in which the women might have bathed, especially if they had used BOUNTY's harsh yellow soap.

'We'd happily go second if you used soap at all,' she jested. Yet the objection was voted sound and so a narrow canal was dug and a smaller shallower pool was created, just for the women. When this overflowed, its water joined the irrigation system.

Tararo and his companions offered to discover where was best and safest for fishing from the rocks and to select timber to make canoes. They experimented on Pitcairn's tallest straightest trees with the many traditional stone tools found abandoned on Pitcairn's ground, but quickly changed to adzes and axes of steel.

While Fletcher was in his fever, Mauatua organised two more votes. The first agreed to ban fires during the day, so smoke would not give away their hideout. The second was more difficult. Adams pointed out that the yapping of dogs carried so well it would also let ships know their island was inhabited. The Ma'ohi at first bristled, saying their dogs had been silent until they bred with European ones, but they soon accepted the problem. Their reward was several nights of feasting until there were no more dogs on Pitcairn.

'I've found it, the perfect place for our square,' Ned announced. The site was well back from the sea cliffs and above the old path that divided the strip of the proposed settlement. It sloped slightly from top to bottom and in the upper right hand corner an ancient banyan tree marked a natural boundary with high screens of aerial roots, making it an easily spotted landmark for the square.

Pitcairn's men and women soon had the land cleared, agreeing the bigger trees and thicker undergrowth that divided the path from the clearing were reserved, so the square was shielded from the sea.

Once Fletcher was well enough he and Mauatua were given the task of first defining the broad stretch of the first settlement and then dividing the land. The plots were different shapes and sizes but each was the same area, big enough for a house and gardens for everyday use. Brown checked each plot had a fair share of good soil and drainage. Some Pitcairners would need to carry water further than others but the distances were not arduous and everyone would collect plenty in the expected rainier season.

The day arrived when the land plots were to be allocated by ballot. Mauatua followed Fletcher proudly as he walked solemnly across the village square to the shade of the banyan tree. She told him to walk like an *ari'i*, like the chief Pitcairn was not to have, and he remembered. She had lightly oiled his long hair so it stayed in place. He wore breeches and a white shirt and carried a hat upside down holding all that he needed.

Even with the bare feet that were universal the effect of his demeanour, his straight back and squared shoulders showed this was his island, their island, and others moved out of their path.

She was ecstatic inside but kept a solemn face so she didn't demean the proceedings or seem to dominate him.

To underpin the ceremony's significance Fletcher sat on a high naked root of the banyan and another made a makeshift table. From his hat he took ink and a quill. Beside these he carefully placed a map drawn by Ned Young and William Brown and a Bible he hoped would give further gravity to the ceremony.

The mutineers stood close to one another, looking suspicious others would take some advantage but the Ma'ohi men stood apart. None of the men, white or Ma'ohi, wanted their women beside them and so they watched from a nervous, separate huddle.

She felt uneasy when Ned spoke in Brown's ear and then pushed him forward. Brown had an ill-look, because of a scar said to be from scrofula. It malformed his eyelid and then ran across his cheek and down his throat. But he was the best spoken of the other mutineers on Pitcairn. She hoped this is why he had been chosen to represent them. Brown sought reassurance from the other mutineers and when he turned back she was comforted there was no challenge in his expression.

'Mr Christian, we are aware of the debt we owe you for bringing us safely to this invisible island. You say we will have no chiefs, but you have certainly been our chief, our captain and our leader until now. We believe this should be rewarded and that it would not be fitting for you to be in the ballot for land.'

The white men cheered and clapped. She joined in, uncertain if she should, but there was no protest.

'Sir, we believe you should have what we think is the finest plot.'

'It's the most westerly, Fletcher,' Ned explained, pointing it out on the map. 'Runs right to the cliff edge and there is flat land with a pool and a path that leads towards Lookout Point.'

Fletcher scratched his head, smiling and bewildered.

'I know it, we know it.' Mauatua stood behind him with a hand on his shoulder. 'We accept, thank you,' she said, hearing tears in her voice. It was an island of equals but it was possible only because of Fletcher's skills and leadership. He deserved this recognition.

He remained with his head bowed, hiding a broad smile. With a loud clearing of his throat to settle his emotions, he stood up and then smartly saluted the gathering. Involuntarily, eight others saluted in return.

'Better write your name on it,' Ned said pushing the map towards him. 'You know what these buggers are like.'

Fletcher dipped the quill in ink and wrote CHRISTIAN on the outlined plot of land, numbered 6. When he turned to her with a beaming smile Mauatua knew a defining moment had past. Land ownership meant status and dignity wherever it was and she sensed some of his doubts withering about his imprisonment on Pitcairn.

Then he got on with the business of the gathering.

'Gentlemen and ladies. We will do this the Navy way. Mr Young will pick out a piece of paper on which I have written a number that corresponds with the map. Before each piece is opened, I will say the name of the new owner.

'Now, let us begin.'

Ned dipped his hand into the hat and held a small folded slip high in the air. 'Who shall have this piece of land?'

Fletcher put one hand on his Bible. 'Adams,' he said. Ned dropped his hand, unfolded the paper and then gave it to Fletcher.

'By God, Adams - Number 7, the flat plot above mine. That's luck.' Adams danced a small jig. Fletcher wrote his name on the map and Ned dipped his hand into the hat again.

'Who shall have this piece of land?'

Fletcher hesitated a little and then held up his Bible and called Niau's name. Ned turned bright red and turned away from him.

Quintal marched up to the table and thumped it, followed by the other mutineers, all shouting.

'This is not right! He can't have land. You can't do that if there are only nine slips in there.'

'Nine? There are fifteen, one for each man, one for each plot,' he shouted back. 'I put them there myself.'

Quintal rounded on the others. 'God's balls, has none of youse buggers had the bollocks to tell him?' Quintal met only shifting eyes and shuffling feet. He turned back to Fletcher Christian.

'Remember you said the balance was changed, that since BOUNTY burned Pitcairn was a native island?'

'Well, we done something to change that back. We've had a vote, ain't we boys? All nice and proper, like. We decided the island will be divided just between the English boys, BOUNTY's boys. That sorts out any question of balance.'

Fletcher was infuriated and stood to shout back at Quintal.

'Balance? By God we are *all* BOUNTY's men. The Ma'ohi men *must* have land. Who voted? Who?'

He swept the hat and everything else off the banyan root.

'BOUNTY's men. The majority, the English men,' said Quintal.

'But NOT me. And what about the women? Did you ask them?'

'Why would we? You wanted the old balance back, Mr Christian. We done it for you.'

'Not for me you didn't. Tararo is a high noble, Niau has noble kin lines, Titahiti is a chief's brother. Ned, you will support me. This unkindness, this greed, it's bullying, everything we mutinied against.'

Ned's face was immobile. 'You mutinied,' he said. 'I followed.'

Defeated on that side Fletcher turned to Mauatua. She was as startled as Fletcher, and dared say nothing. She spread her hands to declare her bafflement.

'First the ship, and now this. It is insupportable!' Fletcher cried, his face turned up to the clouds.

'The ship was too easily seen. We were not safe,' Quintal reminded.

'That's what you thought, Quintal. What about what I thought? Is *nothing* to be what I want?'

He marched to the gang of mutineers, now standing further apart from one another, hoping to avoid notice or blame. He spread his arms and held them high. His lips were tight, too tight to allow shouting.

He growled, his voice rasping with rage as each word was pushed out into Pitcairn's silent air.

'Is nothing to be what *I* want?'

'You'll have to blame that voting business, I expects,' Quintal sneered. Fletcher tipped back his head slowly. His eyes narrowed and his lips clenched tighter. There was nothing low enough to say. When he'd reduced Quintal's mockery to fear he strode back to confront Ned Young.

'What could I do, Fletcher?' Ned countered. 'It was a vote. You were ill. Anyway, what could only two of us do?'

'We'll never know! Did it occur to you not to vote at all, or to wait until . . . No, I can see it did not.' Fletcher thumped his fist hard on the root, again and again and again. His voice was fierce but soft and she hoped he kept it like that, otherwise it would crack and sound feeble.

He stood and looked directly ahead to the Pacific Ocean, and did not move his head when he finally put words together again.

'This is against everything I have done for you. The whole point of Pitcairn is for everyone to have a vote. Every man is supposed to have land. If Tararo and the others do not have land, they will have no equal voice. They will be nothing more than slaves.'

She felt Pitcairn was crumbling into the sea beneath her. For a moment she wished it would.

If such treachery blocked an equal society why had Fletcher put himself through so much to find these men a haven? She could tell he was fighting to conceal mortal pain as he bent to pick up his hat.

He shook the folded slips onto the ground and lashed out at them with his bare foot. Then he kicked the Bible into the banyan's roots. Looking at no-one, he walked away, still erect and officer like.

He turned and shouted back along the track.

'You should have voted to burn me with that wretched ship. Damn the lot of you. *Damn* you all, for all time!'

CHAPTER 39

Mauatua was as shocked as Fletcher by the unfair division of the island. But her day on Ship Landing Point had prepared her. However Fletcher suffered or avoided reality, she had to face problems and then solve them. If not, she would not survive and then Pitcairn would founder.

Fletcher wallowed in deep depression, silent except for dismal mourning that if Pitcairn was not to be a vanguard of enlightened co-operation, there was even less reason for him to be there, and that he was doomed never to pay out his debt of sin. She found no way to comfort him but for the sake of the infant community she ensured he shared the public workload and prepared the earth for gardens on their plot. Pitcairn's settlers soon learned conversation with Fletcher was painful for him and difficult for them.

She went to the Ma'ohi men and the women living with them. Tararo was collected and reserved, saying nothing helpful but fighting, she thought, to keep some semblance of dignity when little or none had been allowed him. Reciting the lands you owned was as important as your ancestor lineage and without land Tararo would never feel he belonged on the island. She feared he would be more likely than not to lead some sort of mutiny against Fletcher.

The other Ma'ohi men were wounded but content for the moment. They were the ones carving the canoes and that kept them optimistic of escaping one day.

'We don't have to do a thing to crush the white men,' Tararo said into her ear as she was leaving. 'They will do that themselves, just as I foretold. And then, Mauatua, my noble cousin, and then the island will be ours, it will be ours to rule.'

'You are a dreamer, Tararo.'

She had laughed at him but her mind was tortured.

With Fletcher no longer able to believe in his new society, every day made it more likely Tararo's prediction would prevail.

Her goal was for the island to prosper without further confrontation. She worked through the women so she never appeared to be dictating to the white men. Soon there were rules, agreed by voting or because of their good sense. Fruit-bearing trees or coconut groves away from the proposed village were each branded with the mark of this or that owner. Anyone could pick and eat while standing under the tree but no-one could take fruit away unless they had permission from the owner.

Stripping the bark from *aute,* paper mulberry, or breadfruit trees on common land to make tapa cloth also had to be negotiated.

A catch of fish that would feed more than four was always to be shared, balloted in lots on the village square if really big.

Well before permanent homes were considered on each plot, the women ensured pens were constructed for animals and rules were made for reparation if one person's animal escaped and caused damage to another's gardens

Every day and in every direction she walked Mauatua saw order being imposed on Pitcairn. Fletcher's mood of defeat made it easy to manage him and he did whatever she suggested.

As for the rest of the white men, she knew a time would come when being shipwrecked on a Pacific island with a compliant woman would no longer be a novelty, and that then the work pace would slacken. In the meantime she encouraged couples to call one other husband and wife, hoping this would foster more respect, perhaps even loyalty or love.

Twenty-seven adults and one infant ate a great deal every day and awareness quickly grew of the need for forward planning. Preparing and planting public gardens was given precedence and the first were made on the land Fletcher thought would be the Ma'ohi men's.

The women insisted on planting communally owned *aute* trees, for unless they could one day make tapa cloth they felt a vital part of their persona would be absent. There was no need to make any for the moment. BOUNTY had been given huge amounts, but the tradition was at least as important as the product. The rhythmic beating to felt the bark, the old songs that were sung and the warm sisterhood that developed over tapa making, had always helped women deal better with their demeaned status and with the loss of unborns and newborns.

She determined that when the time came for tapa-making on Pitcairn it would celebrate a new freer sisterhood.

Everything left at the Landing Place was hauled to the square and shared or stored under canvas in the shade of the banyan tree. Canvas and rum, candles and cooking utensils were carefully divided. Already, those keeping watch at Lookout Point tended to trek back to the village at night, bored with the inactivity and nervous they might be missing out on something shared or given. There was a general bad-tempered feeling they should have landed BOUNTY's bell first, so everyone could be summoned when decisions were being taken.

By the middle of March everyone was living and cooking for themselves on their own land in a temporary Polynesian-style shelter constructed by the Ma'ohi men and women. Private duncans were dug only after the agreement of Brown, who judged the likelihood of the contents draining to contaminate common water or another's land.

Mauatua's greatest difficulty was to negotiate Tararo's position. The mutineers agreed he and his party could live together close to the top of the Hill of Difficulty, a place generally called The Edge. But they would not live independent of the white settlers. They were to have no gardens of their own, were given only a small amount of rum and could keep no animals and thus they relied on the white men for their daily food. More and more they became dependent servants, little more than hard working drudges in the gardens.

She was not prepared to countenance Tahitian men and women as slaves to white men. The price others paid for her freedom should never have been that high. Yet the impetus towards that seemed to increase daily. Tararo's prediction became the opposite of reality because the white men were crushing the Ma'ohi men.

Mauatua expected the white men to now embrace the simple good life and to be grateful for it. Yet, nothing seemed to satisfy them. Rum and a growing feeling of superiority over the Ma'ohi men spilled the cauldrons of cruelty in the worst of them and encouraged unconcern in the others.

The Ma'ohi men complained about being struck or whipped with little reason by Quintal or McCoy.

Most white men called their women wife but treated them like whores. More and more the night air was rent by furious argument and commonly one or more of the women could not bear her blood and injuries to be seen by other women at their pool.

When Fletcher was persuaded to talk about it at all, he sourly told Mauatua why she should expect more of this. Young and Brown might be exceptions, but without the discipline and routine of a ship, none of the other six white men was capable of injecting structure or ambition into their daily lives.

In England they had no prospect of advancement and if they did would drink it away. There was no tradition of land or property ownership behind them and they were always likely to have been more servant than master anywhere else in the world.

'There's something else to remember, even in Young's case,' Fletcher reminded her. Until they came to Tahiti, these men had only seen or heard of natives as servants and slaves.

However little education they had, they will have yarned in bars and in messes and know Britain had built an empire of sugar in the Caribbean on the backs of slaves from Africa, and that black slaves were the key to the success of America's wealth and exports.

'You think that is what they plan here?'

'They'll certainly have an ingrained sense of superiority. Now they are landowners, something beyond their most insane hopes.'

The women tried to reduce the risks. Tevarua, the bravest for merely living with Quintal, was caught pouring away rum. She dragged herself to Jenny for treatment of her vicious penalty and this time Jenny was so sickened that she sent others in secret to assemble all the women at their pool.

At first no-one talked. As women bathed or had their wounds tended, they glanced, lifted a chin or an eyebrow. Each unspoken message of pain or sympathy increased the sombre weight of misery. Mauatua passed no opinions as she soothed the cuts and bruises most women brought with them. She cried out just once, when Jenny led in Tevarua.

Tevarua's entire body was as black and blue as her tattoos, one wrist twisted and as swollen as a small breadfruit, fingers in her right hand broken, hanks of hair wrenched from her bleeding scalp, both eyes so swollen she needed a guide on the most familiar tracks.

'He didn't mean it,' Tevarua burbled through her bleeding lips, she alone blind to how battered she was. 'Matt says he loves me. It's the drink, not him. He's promised not to . . .' Tevarua's voice faltered when she heard none of the others believed her. 'He won't do it again, he swears.'

Mauatua knew nothing she could say would prise Tevarua from Matt Quintal. It was as well they had found one another to feast on. The comfort of discomfort, she muttered.

'This is not what you promised, is it?' Jenny's tone was not accusatory.

'No, it's not. It's not . . . Who could know what those men would become?' Mauatua took Jenny's hands in hers and they absorbed the warmth and familiarity of the other.

The group agreed nothing would be better until the rum is gone.

'To stay safe we must play a game that lets them think they are masters,' Mauatua said.

'From time to time we'll remind them they might not be, but in the meantime, we must not become lazy and slip down to their level. We must take pride in having clean floors and neat thatch and a tidy garden. It is good to wear flowers and to be happy. We must all learn to cook over open fires in their metal pots every day, for none of them will.

'When we do such things and do them well, they cannot complain.

'Most men on Pitcairn are not bright enough to know this but, however often they call you a princess, what they really want is to drag you down to their level. To see you drunk and dirty.

'That way there can be no blame on them.

'Remember, we voted to stay here for the sake of the women we might become. That must be a journey with a slope that leads only upwards, only upwards. Perhaps there are some other things you might like to consider.'

Before Mauatua could continue, Jenny giggled.

'I have just thought of another day that will come. One day their *popa'a* clothes will get too many holes. They will be naked and then the sun will really turn their *kokoro* pink. *Aueeeeee!*'

'If if it can get through their hairy bums and balls,' Tevarua cried. The image smashed the tension.

With no care they might be discovered, all twelve women jumped back into the pool and splashed and played as though they were carefree girls in the streams and waterfalls of Tahiti again.

CHAPTER 40

Fletcher Christian steeled himself and then walked on to the public square for a sharing of fish. It had taken him many hours of faltering resolve but he was determined to beat his depression and to regain respect and authority. That afternoon, most of the men had taken time off to catch fish from the rocks and now their haul was displayed on banana leaves on the ground.

All the mutineers other than Fletcher now tied their leather mugs from BOUNTY to their waists, determined to protect them from theft and because they agreed none should be seen drinking from coconut shells, like blacks. As they carried their mugs anyway, more and more thought of drinking from them exactly where and when they wanted. Four of the men on the square had their mugs in their fists and were already drunk.

Adams was on his hands and knees, dividing the fish and lobsters into even piles on banana leaves for the ballot. He straightened up and stretched his back and then raised his mug.

'Your health, my lords.'

Quintal bowed extravagantly. 'Too kind, my duke of the Flatlands. And you Brown, your lordship, an earl I believe.'

'Just one of many titled owners of great estates, m'lord Quintal.' Brown fluttered his hand.

'Aye. Ain't that right?' Quintal said. 'Jack Tars we was back there but here, here we are lords.'

'Just look at this, boys. Grand, ain't it?' Adams said, marvelling at the catch before him. He ducked his head into the mounds of fish. 'You can smell the sea on them, and all for free. Weren't like this in 'ackney where I was brought up, I can tell you. We are lords indeed, lords of Paradise.'

'Hah! This is Paradise? You treat us like animals.'

Tararo had arrived with the men from The Edge in time to hear the self-congratulatory boasting and saw there were only nine piles. He ran up and kicked the closest, spilling its scintillating colours onto the bare red earth. He scattered a second pile of fish and then the tallest men, Mills and Martin, knocked Tararo on his chest so hard with their flattened hands he staggered back. One foot crunched onto a mound of fish and he slithered uncontrollably until he landed on his back, across the rest of the catch.

The Ma'ohi men were as tightly wound as Tararo and equally unable to absorb a single insult more. They responded as Tararo struggled to get up.

There was a battle, Ma'ohi men against white, fist into face, blood-bursting skin splattered with rum from flailed mugs. Quintal and Niau exchanged punches fuelled by such hatred

Fletcher couldn't resist. He easily dragged them apart and held them there until he felt their rage subside.

Mauatua shouted as she ran in to separate the men '*A fa'a'ore i te reira ohipa!* Stop behaving like this, stop! *Fa'a'ore!*' The other women, still damp from the pool, struggled to calm and to extract their men.

The men shuffled back into their factions, still nudging, hard-shouldering and muttering threats. None could stand still. Bruised hands clenched and unclenched. Fingers explored jaws for permanent damage. Clenched fists swiped eyes free of blood, noses of snot. Both mingled with tears of rage or outrage.

The hot sweat of terror and of anger swirled through the air and carried with it sweet-sharp messages of spilt blood. Ned, too, had stood back.

'This has the reek of war,' he said to Mauatua. She turned to face the hard-breathing men with as much brightness as she could summon.

'We have something to say.'

'Who has?' Quintal asked, his face red and swollen.

'We have, the women.' She beckoned the women to stand with her. Quintal snorted derision and turned away. Mauatua shrugged her shoulders. She saw glitters of amusement in the eyes of some of the men. It was good to know there was not universal support for his boorish conduct

'We have settled something, something that will be good for everyone on *Fenua Maitai.*'

'What the hell is that?' Quintal yelled.

'Here, this island. When men came here to make stone tools it was called *Hiti au reva reva.*'

'And what the hell does that mean?'

'Land of the Passing Clouds.'

'So? Pitcairn does for us, darling,' Quintal cackled and looked to his mates for support. There was little.

'No,' Mauatua said. 'Those names will not do. Both those were names given by men who did not really live here. We have a better name. *Fenua Maitai*. It means, The Good Land.'

McCoy lumbered forward. 'Who gave you the say?'

She stopped him with her outstretched arm. 'We did. We voted, the *twelve* black women. Just like you *eight* white men voted about sharing the land.' McCoy turned away, contemptuous as he sought to retrieve dignity.

'There's something else, too,' Mauatua said. 'Much more important.' She waited until she had as much of their attention as she could expect.

'We are going to have babies now.'

The announcement was received in silence. The confusion told her the white men never considered women had such a choice. Quintal lurched to Mauatua and put his arm around her waist.

'Well, we can help you there, my lovely. Can't we boys?' He looked up from her breast level. 'I'm ready when you are, Mrs Christian my lovely, right now if you like.'

Mauatua wriggled easily out of his grip and shouted louder over the uncertain chatter of the mutineers. 'Fletcher will be the first father.'

Quintal laughed hard enough to change his face to purple. He pointed at Fletcher as he doubled over catching his breath.

'Does she tell you when to shit, too?'

Mauatua's face furrowed and her eyes narrowed. She glared at Fletcher, daring him not to ignore Quintal. He held his hair back with one hand and put the other on Quintal's shoulder.

'Matt. We need to speak to each other better than this. I want things to be different on the island.'

'Oh, they'll be different. Very.' Matt struggled to stop laughing and then to catch his breath. 'What we've decided, what we *men* have decided is that it's about time we lived like the lords we are.'

He ducked, easily releasing himself from Fletcher's hand, and then held himself as erect as his inebriation could manage.

'Come, my lords,' he said to his ship mates. 'Let's decide what sort of palaces those black bastards will build for us.'

Mauatua, Fletcher and Tararo watched stiffly as the five most obnoxious mutineers left with many ostentatious courtesies and bows

'Why does it have to be like this?' Fletcher asked Mauatua, his voice clouded with misery. She stood back from him before answering.

'It doesn't,' she said coldly. 'Believe me.'

CHAPTER 41

'Mr Christian, Mr Christian. Where are they?' Fletcher was shaken awake by Quintal and surrounded by a surly crowd of men.

'Where's who?' Fletcher demanded, half asleep and frightened. 'What's the matter? Mauatua, where are you, Mauatua?'

'That's what we want to know. The bitches have jumped ship.'

When each man woke up the morning after the fight, they found their wife had gone. No amount of calling had revealed a single one of the Ma'ohi women.

'Even ours have gone,' Tararo said. The Ma'ohi men's shared indignation eased the belligerence of the last night. Fletcher calmed down and asked the obvious, if the men had checked the pools, the gardens. Perhaps the women were fishing from the rocks or collecting birds' eggs from the cliff? They were nowhere.

Fletcher searched Mauatua's likely hiding places for her bag of medicines and cures, and, when he could not find them, agreed with the men.

'You're right. We seem to have been abandoned.'

'Mutiny, that's mutiny, Mr Christian!'

'That damned Mauatua. That's who it will be if there's a bloody mutiny.' Quintal looked as though he would strike Fletcher. Fletcher grabbed the initiative from him, saying they must search at once. What, he warned, what if there really were wild men living in secret places on the island? Or might men have come in a boat and kidnapped them during the night? He had had a few drinks himself and so would have heard nothing.

Fletcher hurried Tararo and the Ma'ohi men to circle the village and look for clues and told the others to get themselves armed. When they had gone, he checked once more. He hadn't told the others what he suspected. Five minutes later he was certain. Mauatua had taken a musket.

She had plotted the revolt for some time and had chosen an elevated site close to the cliff edge on the southern coast. The women carried flag stones from a marae and made them into a low secure wall. It gave protection against gun fire if they were flat behind it, and provided sheltered but unobstructed views over all possible approaches.

Some women stayed on guard, others she sent to cut long poles and palm leaves. They made screens from these that they dug in and then further anchored against the wall with smaller rocks. An eye close to the screens could see through without being seen. When the men came they would hear the women but not be able to see them.

The women easily burst into laughter at the adventure and undoubted supremacy of their fortress. If they were to stay for more than a few days, their lair would have to expand. For now, they were content to wait.

'We must sound happy to be away from them,' she plotted with the women. 'We will sing happy songs and tell funny stories.'

It was well into the next day before Fletcher shouted for her. The women laughed at how long it had taken. Each left a false trail out of the village and the men must have spent many fruitless hours following them one by one. Now the men were hot, dirty and bad tempered.

'Let's start as we mean to go on,' Mauatua said and fired her musket over the men's heads. 'We've more than enough ammunition to shoot you one by one,' she shouted. They ducked and ran, stopping and turning only when the noise of laughing women overwhelmed the rushing blood in their ears. The men shook what muskets they had been left. Quintal put up his to aim.

'Hey, Quintal! I shouldn't do that. Kill any of us and you'll be back to bums, to *pa'i'a*, like the useless bugger you are anyway. If anyone would let you.'

Once again the sound of twelve women laughing shamed the men's ears. Fletcher put both hands on the musket until Quintal reluctantly lowered it. The men huddled and talked.

'Alright, but no more shooting,' Fletcher called. 'Tell us why you are all up here.'

'No.' Mauatua shouted. 'We want to hear this from your mouths.'

'We can't talk to you if we can't bloody well see you,' Quintal yelled, furious at being restrained by Fletcher. 'Come out and talk like . . .'

'Men? Talk like men? Is that it, Matt? You want us to show you how to behave like men?' Fletcher was first to laugh at Mauatua's taunt. When the men heard nothing else from the women, Quintal pulled himself away and walked closer to their den.

'Tevarua, Tevarua, princess. I'm sorry. I've promised. Come on now, be a good girlie and come back with me now.'

Mauatua put a hand over Tevarua's mouth, pushed her to the back of the women and threatened her with a raised finger to stay silent. Then she went back to the screen and fired once more. Quintal fell backwards and scuttled to safety like a crab, his eyes rolling with terror.

'That's the only thing your princess wants to say,' Mauatua called when the echoes of the shot had rolled away.

The women lit a small fire to roast fish and breadfruit knowing the cooking smells would torment the men, who had brought no food.

Fletcher tried once more. 'The men are asking me say this has gone far enough, Mauatua. Will you come back with us now?'

'We stay here until you tell us why we are here.'

'That'll be a bloody long time then,' McCoy said.

'The longer the better. Each day will sharpen your minds. And each night will harden something else.' The women laughed louder than ever. The subject that most amused them kept the men most silent.

'And, by the way. We've got more than one musket, as well as these.' With a frightening yell, the women pushed long sharpened sticks through the screen. The more a man used his bulk to rush the women the more he would be injured.

'So,' Mauatua taunted. 'We are eating and drinking and waiting for you to say something. What are you doing?'

She heard only mumbling from the men until once again Fletcher spoke up, sounding as conciliatory as he could manage. 'We are going back to get something to eat. We'll be back tomorrow morning, very early.'

'More time to think about your speeches.' Mauatua shouted.

She knew they would do little but drink rum and arrive back in an even worse state. Good, she thought, the longer it took, the more the men would be ready to negotiate.

'You think they'll really go back?' Jenny asked her.

'Now they've realised their dicks will get no attention, they'll want to give their stomachs plenty of it. But I wouldn't put it past one or two of them to hang about. There are sleepless nights ahead for us, *vahine*.'

There was still an hour before nightfall and so while some women kept watch, others went in careful groups to cut many more long thick poles. They pushed these into the ground to make a palisade down the slope some way in front of the screens and stone wall. Tomorrow they would finish it and thread it with brush and leaves and then have more space and more protection.

Mauatua wasn't often in this part of the island and used the last of the sunlight to search out useful herbs and leaves and seeds for her medicine bag. The bush and undergrowth were summer-dry and crackled and hissed as she swept her searching hand back and forth allowing no other sounds to be heard. Her shock was absolute when she was grabbed around the throat and a man pressed his body to her back. His other hand clamped tight over her mouth. Then he yanked her around to face him.

It was Tararo and he was naked.

She responded immediately to his excited scents. He was a superb looking man, but there was no possibility of it going further. She laughed loudly to hide her guilty feelings.

'No joke, Mauatua.' He grabbed her long hair tightly and bent her forward, forcing her face close to his erection. However Mauatua fought to free herself, Tararo was able to counter her.

'You see? See what your power does to me. I can no longer ignore this.'

Her face was forced against his engorged sex, already stinking with anticipation. He constantly smeared her cheeks and brow with the lubricant that streamed from him.

'There was never a woman like you. You look like a goddess. Yet you think and act like a god. I've never been so excited by a woman's defiance.'

'Keep your excitement to yourself,' Mauatua screamed back at him, hoping to attract attention. Tararo smacked a hand over her mouth.

'This island will be ours. The best of Tahiti and of Raiatea. Oro will triumph here. We will dedicate this island to the supreme god Oro and worship no other.'

He forced Mauatua's right arm up her back. She bent away from him, to relieve the scorching pain. Tararo ripped at Mauatua's clothes and as he saw more of her body, his breath became shorter and shallower. He released her arm but grabbed both wrists and pinned them to her sides. He bent her back, his huge hands almost spanning her waist between them.

'What about Fletcher?' Mauatua protested.

'He is nothing, merely a man to get us to *our* island. You think he will be first father? What if it is me?'

Mauatua's head turned away, her face acidic with disdain and repulsion. 'Too late. Fletcher's baby is already in me.'

'You sure?' Tararo taunted her. 'You will never know if it is Fletcher's baby or mine. Not until too late. And what will be said if Pitcairn's first baby is black? Then he will finally know. No part of him rules on Pitcairn, not even his skinny white man's dick.'

Tararo shoved his erection along the tight furrow between Mauatua's closed legs, teasing her like a cruel child with a kitten. She was helpless to struggle any more than twisting in his hands. Then, content with looking at his prey, he leaned over her and started to thrust.

'*Aueeee!*'

'Don't move, Tararo, not a muscle.' Mauatua recognised Jenny's voice.

Tararo dropped Mauatua to the ground. He tried to stand straight. He yelled with pain again and stood on his toes, pulling at his buttocks.

'Not a muscle, Tararo. Not a muscle.' Jenny said again. Her free hand came from behind him, holding a bunch of dry, pointed grasses to his face. The man who had been a sex-fuelled beast stood like a carved idol, his eyes widening ever further when he saw what was in her hand.

'Yes, these made the pain. Here it is again.'

With her other hand Jenny rammed stiff grasses further into the soft flower of his anus.

'You know what we do with these grasses?' Jenny hissed at him 'That's right, we kill babies. You know what else these grasses can do? If I ram them hard enough up your arse and pierce your bowels, you would die in agony, poisoned by your own *tuta'e,* your own shit.'

Mauatua had recovered. 'Hmmm – good girl.'

She pushed her face into Tararo's. 'Some of those sailors are bad,' she said. 'They rape instead of making love, but would not call it that. Yet they have very strong views about right and wrong in others.

'What do you think they would call this, a black man raping the wife of a white man?'

The women knew he could have stood the pain for an extraordinary time, for that was how Ma'ohi men and women were brought up. But dealing with emotional stress was beyond the capability of most. That was why he had not struggled to escape. Being caught trying to rape her was enough shame to render him childlike and the promise of future humiliation exploded all sense of masculine superiority.

Tararo fell at her feet and held her ankles in supplication.

'We will say nothing of this,' she said. 'Your gods will have seen this insult by a noble to a *ra'atira* woman from his own family. It is an insult to them, too. They will punish you in the next life. And in *this* life you will always fear we might tell Fletcher. He would send you to those avenging gods before the sun had moved in the sky.'

She had balanced Tararo's threat of a future without white men. But was it good to have peace only because the island's men were bound by fear and threats of revenge?

No answer came as she wiped her face clean.

CHAPTER 42

Fletcher led the men back to the women's fortress in the middle of the next morning. 'We know you are angry with us,' he shouted up.

'Our pigs know that,' Mauatua mocked. 'You must say why.'

Fletcher glanced back at the other mutineers before he continued. They nodded encouragement and some pushed at him. He spoke the words he had promised to say.

'We are angry too and you must agree not to make us angry anymore.'

Three muskets fired from behind the palm leaf screen. They ricocheted off rocks and sprayed the men with splinters.

'You will never be angrier than we are. Start by telling us why we are here or go home.' She banged a screen. The women shook others to make a threatening rattle and screamed and screeched with as much scariness as they could without laughing. Fletcher threw up his hands and then cupped them to his mouth to focus his messages.

'We agree. We have been bad to our women.' He was nudged. 'Some of us have been. Sometimes. And to each other.'

Mauatua walked into the open. 'If you are not men enough to admit what you do wrong, I will do it for you. Put down your muskets.' Not a man moved.

'I said, put them down!' When there was no response, she waved a hand behind her and a shot winged the upper arm of Quintal.

'That is so you know, Quintal. When you beat Tevarua, you beat all women. From now, like that shot, you will never know where the revenge comes from. Not even Tevarua will know. But it will come.

'I am telling you one last time. There are too many men on this island. We will not mind shooting one.'

When the muskets had been dropped she made the women's demands.

'I want to see hands. I want those who agree they will stop beating their wives to put up their hands. If you do not beat your wife then you must promise to stop the other men doing it. There should be fifteen hands.'

Quintal's hand shot up first and he feverishly bid the others to do the same. Tararo encouraged the Ma'ohi men.

'Good. It seems you do know what we are talking about. What we are angry about. So here are the other things you must agree.'

The men groaned loudly but she raised her voice over them.

'Or we stay here until you do.'

Mauatua strutted back and forth in long, certain strides. She emphasised points with her hands and sometimes stopped to stare deep into a man's eyes, until he could bear it no longer. She told them they must agree not to drink rum during the day, that if they wanted sex they must first wash the beards they all wore and also wash their foreskins. The mutineers laughed out loud but she knew from their eyes it was from embarrassment.

'You expect your wives to be clean and fresh. You must give them the same pleasures and respect,' she commanded.

Then she told them this was only one example of the consideration they must show. There must be no more name calling between Ma'ohi and white. They must settle disagreements by talking rather than fighting. It was not acceptable for white men to beat the Ma'ohi men. Whatever they had heard about the Caribbean or the Southern States of America, Ma'ohi men on Pitcairn were not slaves.

She softened her tone, for by now the men were listening intently.

'You see? We are not asking for the impossible. We do not ask you to behave like English lords or Ma'ohi chiefs. We simply ask you to treat us and one another with dignity and respect. Just as each of you expects, and then you will get the same.'

Fletcher took a step ahead of the others. His face was alive with pleasure and admiration. She had clearly said words he should have spoken, but which would not have carried as much authority. She was grateful for his goodwill but she hadn't finished.

'There is one more thing you must agree. We will dance only when we are happy and we want to dance. We will no longer dance because you hope to fire up your drunken *kokoro*. I am waiting to see you agree.' Not even her eyes moved until all hands were raised.

'We might come back today,' she announced. 'But it might be tomorrow. We expect our houses to be as we left them.'

'Well, when you do, we have made a decision too.' Quintal held his wound and sounded peevish.

'Aye, well, if you are bad to us, if you leave us again we have agreed not to speak to you, no man will speak to any of you girlies.'

She mocked him. She trembled her legs and body as fiercely as any dancing warrior. She rolled her eyes pretending to be afraid and spat on the ground to dismiss his threat and then went back behind the screen where the women sang and danced, creating a bonded world men would never enter and share.

When the men had gone, the women sprawled in the sunshine.

'And how long do you think this will last?'

'Until the day after tomorrow.'

'And then we will play another game.'

'Should we be having any babies when it is like this?'

All eyes turned to Toofaiti. Mauatua told her she had been thinking about this a lot.

'These men are not likely to become the men *they* might be. They have no vision. But our children can be different. The first with white and Ma'ohi blood mixed together.'

'Then what about me, and the other two?' Toofaiti pointed at the others who lived with the Ma'ohi men, Tinafanea and Mareva.

'No babies for you three.' The women fell into a keening plea for sympathy. If land was vital to men, the prospect of motherhood was as important to them.

'Not with Ma'ohi fathers. You saw how Tararo behaved yesterday and he is a noble, supposedly with virtue in his thinking and actions. My fear is that if Ma'ohi men father children, they will encourage them in the old ways. Those children would know they were different, even if their fathers didn't do that. We would have division on the island.'

'And the white men, what about their children?'

'Can you imagine them being interested in how they are brought up? We will have their children but bring them up a new way, with no fear, no pain, no differences. There will be no divisions because they will all be the same. It would only mean trouble if we had Ma'ohi children on the island.'

'You take a long view, Mauatua.'

'Is that not what children are, a long view on our success as mothers?'

'Will the men know this?'

'Only if a woman tells them.'

'Are we really staying here tonight?' Tevarua stood, fidgety and anxious. 'I think I'd better go back. It would be nice for Matt.'

'What about you? What would be nice for you?' Mauatua asked.

'I would feel better, if I knew what he was doing.'

'Brown is not so bad, he never really hits me,' Teatuahitea stood. 'I think I should go back to him, it's not fair.'

'I think Matt will be good now,' Tevarua said convincing only herself.

Mauatua sighed. 'Well, I think you are all being silly, *vahine*. They will think we are scared if anyone goes back now. Who else thinks we should stay another night, to prove a point?'

Her hand went up but only two others followed.

'If that's the feeling, we'll go.. Might surprise them into being nice.'

Before they left, Jenny gave Toofaiti and Mareva and Tinafanea some of the long stiff grasses and made circular massaging movements with her hand, ensuring the women knew the choices they had for aborting.

CHAPTER 43

Below Fletcher the sheer cliff fell away for hundreds of feet to the settlement. His view from the shallow ledge in front of the cave beneath Lookout Point was like sitting on a cloud. The height was dizzying, but he felt safe up here and could let his mind wander more freely than anywhere else on the island.

A brown smudge in the foliage below showed the thatched roof of his house, well, he corrected himself, the first building that looked anything like what he would call a house.

It was agreed each cottage would be built by joint labour rather than by individuals and theirs had been built first because of Mauatua's pregnancy. The co-operation had pleased him and created a comforting atmosphere.

The Ma'ohi men showed the white men how they made planks from trees by splitting them with wedges of stone, and so the enormous effort of pit-sawing was avoided.

Jack Williams was unable to forge hinges, so the white men copied Tahiti's sliding windows and doors but strengthened them with cross-braced timbers fastened with copper nails from BOUNTY.

When the house was finished Fletcher built a large bed base, a platform raised from the floor. It was more like something seen in better Tahitian *fare* than the beds on legs of Moorland Close and Ewanrigg. But Tahitians slept on and under woven mats. He used needle and thread from his naval hussif to stitch tapa cloth together to make pillows and a mattress and stuffed these with banana leaves. Then he chose the finest, whitest tapa to make bed sheets as superior as the best pure Irish linen.

'You see,' he said displaying his bed. 'It is possible for us to be civilised on this island.'

Fletcher called the triangular scoop behind him a cave but it wasn't, not even deep enough to be an all-weather shelter. He'd hoped it would be a hideout if the island was discovered by the King's Navy. It was no secret refuge, but the long steep climb to get there across the steep face of the headland made it infinitely defensible. He sat there often, brooding his shipmates called it, and he had no answer to that. He did brood. He'd done the same in Cumbria, sitting with rock-warmed buttocks to look over the lakes. From those heights he knew which narrow road led to which house and which family lived there, which coach was on a last stage to Carlisle or to Cockermouth.

When he looked down over Cumbria there was certainty. On Pitcairn he faced only uncertainty. Mauatua thought the cave made Fletcher's mental state worse. He agreed but found it irresistible. Misery and his troubled conscience were comforting familiars.

A scrabbling clatter of tumbling gravel warned Fletcher someone was climbing to the cave. He waited with his musket primed until he saw Tararo's face.

'Can I come and talk to you, Titreano?' The noble seemed relaxed and asking permission sincerely.

'Of course. Go the other side of that big rock. It's easier.'

Tararo reached the ledge and sat panting. The day was hot and the climb relentless. Tararo's golden skin was sun-darkened now from his forced work in the gardens and the sheen of sweat made it shine like a fine old saddle. The wind sweeping up the cliff face chilled him and he shivered as he rubbed his arms vigorously to counter it.

Fletcher allowed him time to recover but it was Tararo who spoke first.

'We have the same problem, Titreano my friend.'

Fletcher turned so he could give him more attention.

'We are both men alone, Titreano. We have no-one who is the same.'

'But you have relatives at least. Niau and Mauatua. They are family and they understand your status.'

'Young, Brown understand your status, Titreano. But understanding is not the same, is it? Not the same as sharing it.

'You think about this when you hold up your bowl so the light shines through,' Tararo said

'What? How do you know that?'

'I see it in your eyes.' Tararo fiddled with stones on the cave floor and shifted several times. 'You know they call this Christian's Cave now?'

'No, I didn't.'

Tararo clenched his lips and looked into the distance.

'I have been looking at the women.' Fletcher didn't understand. Tararo seemed sorry he had started and for no reason checked they were not overheard. 'It's Faahotu, *vahine* of Williams. She is thin. Her neck . . .'

'Look, I don't see much,' Fletcher admitted. 'What about her neck?'

'It is swelling.'

This is one of the two Chinese bowls that belonged to Fletcher Christian on BOUNTY and Pitcairn Island. Given to Captain Matthew Folger, who discovered the community in 1808, they are owned and displayed by the Nantucket Historical Association, who also kindly gave permission to use this image.

A high wailing call distracted them. There were so few noises on Pitcairn and this was unfamiliar. Both men twisted to look in the skies and on the cliff faces for a strange bird. Then they realised the shout was from high above them, from Mills and Jenny who were the week's lookouts.

'Fletcher. Your baby,' they called down.

'My baby, what do they mean?' Fletcher asked Tararo. Tararo pointed down to the village. Below, tiny figures waved white cloth to attract his attention from the middle of the village square.

Fletcher clasped his head in his hands.

'Of course. She said it would happen any day. I promised to stay close. Tararo, I'll have to go.'

The loose surface of the slopes scratched and cut his hands and he prayed sincere haste and a little blood would make up for not being there when he should. Tararo followed, trying to slow Fletcher, saying there was nothing he could do by being there faster.

'I promised, I promised. This is something momentous. The first child. Everyone should be there.'

Tararo screwed up his face. 'Nothing I want to see, my friend.'

'No, not watch. I meant, just being close. Damn and blast not being there. One more thing for me to regret.'

Fletcher ran through Lookout Point's low skirt of bush and onto the twisting track along the coast and through his gardens.

Ned was walking to meet him.

'Too late, my friend. Too late, no need to run.'

'Too late? You mean, what's happened? Is Mauatua . . .?'

Ned clasped his shoulders to reassure him. 'Both of them are fine.'

'Is it . . .?'

'You'd better see for yourself.'

He found Mauatua resting on the shaded step into their house, suckling their son. The women sat close, crooning in low voices to soothe mother and baby. He bent to kiss her and thought he caught the baby's attention.

She told him his son couldn't see yet but had recognised something familiar in his father's voice or smell.

'Do you realise, Ned? Just as she promised, a son almost nine months to the day since she said it. It's uncanny. Sometimes I wonder who's really in charge on this island, I really do.'

He didn't see Mauatua turn her face away.

'You know what your son means?' Ned asked. 'He means we belong here now. He's like an anchor.'

'Not to me. Not to me, Ned. He reminds me of everything I have lost,' Fletcher cried. 'He makes me think of my mother and my brothers and sister. My family. On top of everything else I've produced a half-native relative for them.'

Ned grabbed Fletcher and walked away a few steps. 'That's looking backwards, Fletcher. This is the time to look forward.'

'I think I have more to look back at than you. I'm sorry Ned, that's unbelievably rude. Forgive me?'

Ned ducked the question. 'Do you have a name for him?'

'Nothing Tahitian, that's been decided.'

'Won't you name him for your father, Fletcher?'

'I have insulted my family enough.'

'The first true Pitcairner should have a special name.'

'He will, Ned, he will.'

Fletcher bent his thumb to gnaw at the joint. A son told him more than ever he was forged to this god-forsaken rock in the middle of the South Pacific. Sweat poured off his head and body.

His voices taunted him and he answered them back, once more cursing the infernal ship that brought him to Pitcairn.

'What day is it Ned, the day of the week? You have been keeping a diary, haven't you.'

'Thursday.'

'Then that shall be his name.'

He stood by his wife and son again. He let the baby grip a finger. 'The boy's name is Thursday, Thursday October.'

'Fletcher you can't. That's cruel,' Young protested. 'That's what slaves in the West Indies do to their children. You know that. They refuse to give them African names until they are free again.'

'Well?'

'Aren't you free? Isn't Pitcairn the ultimate freedom?'

He prised his finger from his son's grip. 'Pitcairn is a prison for me.'

He turned to Mauatua. 'I'm sorry. There is one more thing. I take it you will not bind his head, to make it pointed like yours.'

'Your son is a Pitcairner, Fletcher,' Mauatua said.

Tararo grabbed his arm. 'You see, Faahotu is not here.'

CHAPTER 44

It was an effort for him to take an interest in Thursday. The Ma'ohi men were more likely to pick him up or to tickle and amuse him. Yet, when Mauatua put Thursday into his arms and his son lay there smiling and calm he knew something heart warming was inevitable.

Holding his son made the future seem more positive, suggested there might be something to build towards on Pitcairn.

Such thoughts did not linger.

Tapa-cloth sheets would never make a house like he remembered and aspired to, with fires in stone hearths and marble surrounds, with Persian carpets, burnished brass chandeliers and a cook in a generous scrubbed kitchen and polished furniture that smelled of beeswax.

There weren't even bees here.

Months later, when they had been on the island over a year, Thursday's lungs were lustier and his crying more insistent. Fletcher couldn't bear the sound, even from the gardens. He tramped around other houses and gardens waving or nodding at anyone he saw, convincing himself he was doing something more positive than escaping his son's noise. Something deep in his brain resented the boy.

Thursday was an anchor to Pitcairn he didn't want.

He had more than once fought voices that insisted he would be happier if the boy was not around.

Today his expedition was to see Faahotu without her knowing. Mauatua reassured him all was well, but people seemed to tell him untrue things. If Faahotu was so healthy why did she always wear a high wrap about her neck?

He hid behind bushes as Faahotu came out of the house she shared with Williams. She glanced about before taking the cloth from her neck and then with some difficulty cornered a large cockerel amid much censure from his fat, blustering hens. She threw the cloth over him, lunged bravely and quickly had him in her arms. It was a struggle to close the run behind her but rather than help her Fletcher looked carefully at her neck.

There was a definite bulge, bigger than a fist. It trembled a little when she moved. The skin was evil-looking, swirled and blotched with purple, scrofulous he thought. And then, struggling to hold the infuriated rooster, Faahotu slipped in a patch of mud. She landed on the bird. Blinded by the cloth and now injured it struggled violently. The bird's legs flailed and their vicious spurs and claws slashed deep into Faahotu's face and neck. She released it, screaming as loudly as the infuriated fowl, which ran for the bushes, directly at Fletcher.

He made one sweep with his musket and the bird's head bounced to the ground. Then he ran to help Faahotu. She covered her neck with the cloth but the hot blood kept it slipping away. He helped her to lie in shade and then asked what he should do.

'Mauatua,' she sobbed hoarsely. 'Mauatua *ana'e*. Only her.'

His wild run to fetch her alerted others from their houses and gardens and by the time she found Jenny and reached the injured woman, half of the island was standing outside Faahotu's house.

The two women needed none of their specialist knowledge to recognise the danger. The cockerel's spurs and claws were thick with farmyard filth, and they had plunged deep into Faahotu's neck and face.

They quickly worked to clean what they could, hoping her pumping blood had rinsed away much of the contamination. When the bleeding stopped they smeared her facial wounds with healing oils and then bound oils and herbs to her neck.

Faahuto's husband Jack Williams was the last to arrive. He had put down his forge tools go fishing and it took time for him to hear the calls.

'Mon dieu. Ces femmes noirs damnées!' he exclaimed in the French of his early life on Guernsey, immediately pouring himself rum. Mauatua tried to explain the accident but Williams found only blame in his wife.

'I can't talk to her, she won't listen.'

She smashed the mug of rum from his hand. 'No. It is you who will not listen. Your wife has been sick for many months and you . . .'

'Of course you will say that. You women, you stick together.' Mauatua's steel-cold look silenced him and the other women stood closer to her. 'Yes, Jack, because we are flesh and blood and we have feelings.'

'Not for me she doesn't.'

'It's not feelings she doesn't give you, mate' Quintal and McCoy were drunk although it was only mid-morning. She attacked them.

'Would you want an unwashed *animal* stinking of rum pounding on top of you if you were dying?'

The Pitcairners tracked back to their chores, disturbed to hear her so angry and chastened by what they had seen of Faahotu's wounds.

'Dark clouds gather, *tane*,' Tararo warned Fletcher.

Three days later Mauatua saw what she most feared. There was poison in Faahotu's veins and her temperature soared. When her level of pain rose unbearably Fletcher agreed she should be allowed laudanum, saying to everyone this was the least he could do for a woman who had hoped for a better life by following him.

Everyone agreed it was proper Faahuto's death was honoured the Tahitian way. Tararo chanted and prayed her soul would find its way to her *pufenua* on Tahiti, where gods and spirits would welcome her.

Once the ceremonies were over, the Ma'ohi immediately became animated and happy again, as was their tradition.

Jack Williams was fidgety, bored or derisive throughout. He was not looking for manly sympathy when he cornered Fletcher and Mauatua.

'I can't be the only one without a wife.'

'What can I do about that, Jack?' Fletcher begged.

'That's not for me to say. But you better do something, Mr Christian.'

'She's barely cold,' Mauatua said. 'Have a heart.'

'It's not my heart that needs the wife. *Comprenez*? I want a new wife and I want one now. *Immediatement. Il y a quelques mois. Mois!*'

Tararo nodded his head with sombre slowness. He pointed up into the sky and then circled his head with his hand, making the shape bigger and bigger until he was circling his shoulders.

She wondered if her heart would ever start beating again. Was Tararo's warning about the dark cloud coming true so soon?

If so, what about his prediction he would one day rule Pitcairn?

Days later Mauatua led Fletcher and Jack Williams to where the six Ma'ohi men were working in the common gardens with their three wives.

On the way she had tried to dissuade Jack once more but he refused to share a woman. 'Then there is no other wife for you,' she contended.

'Sully is the only possibility,' Fletcher pleaded, perhaps for the hundredth time. Jack dismissed the idea. '*Non*. She's not even two years old.'

'You would have to wait.'

'Not so long in these parts maybe, but too long for me. *C'est impossible.*'

'Those black buggers won't care.' Jack walked on, cackling defiance.

The Ma'ohi were playing with an old work song, begging the gods and spirits to reward their labours with fine harvests.

Sometimes they tossed the words back and forth between men and women, or from one row of garden to another, accenting words or melody by the rhythm of their digging or weeding.

She was relieved there was a good mood but when she called Tararo the men straightened at once and not one dropped his tool.

'Tell him Fletcher. Tell him,' said Jack, jiggling with excitement.

Tararo would never share Toofaiti but she pointed at the two others, Mareva and Tinafanaea. 'Would you share one of those, Jack?'

Jack spat. 'Plough the same furrow as some black?'

'That's really your last word?' Fletcher asked, putting his hand on Jack's shoulder. It was shaken away. 'Well, if that's the situation and the blacks are not agreeing, there will have to be a draw.'

Jack thought about this and then nodded his agreement.

She was grateful that Ned sauntered in and Jack welcomed him, too.

'Neddy is the one to do it,' he agreed gleefully.

Ned bent to pick blades of grass. He broke two pieces into different lengths, thought for a few seconds and then added a third.

Mauatua slapped his hand. 'You cannot include Toofaiti. Tararo won't let you do such a wicked thing.'

'We must,' Ned argued.

'Even you? We women are just *what* to you?'

'You have a better idea?'

'Fewer men,' Mauatua said, running a finger across her throat.

For an instant she thought Fletcher agreed. He could shoot Jack Williams and the problem was solved. But no-one else really understood forging and metal work, largely because Jack refused to share his secrets.

Ned agreed with Jack which blade of grass meant which woman and then turned his back, rearranging them in his fist so each looked the same length. Jack treated it like a party game. He made a drama of humming and hawing, all the time ogling the women, his tongue rippling back and forward between his lips. He clasped both hands over his crutch, closed his eyes and then suddenly grabbed a blade of grass and pulled.

When Ned opened his fist to show which were left, Jack punched the air. '*Bien. Tres bien.* That's a result. C'm 'ere my beauty.'

Tararo didn't move when Jack strode to him, took Toofaiti by the arm and walked back with her. But his face thundered when he saw Toofaiti smile at Jack with no apparent regret at leaving.

She was defiant even to Mauatua.

'Now, I can have babies, too,' she jeered.

'If this is to be then I demand another woman.' Tararo kicked plants and soil in every direction. 'It is proper for my rank and she should be too. You Mauatua.' He grabbed her arm.

No-one moved for each feared what might come next. The tension was broken by Matt Quintal, who had chanced upon the confrontation.

'You need another woman, Tararo? I'm surprised. Not after what I seen you up to with your pretty boy there.'

Niau turned his head away. 'Aye, that's the one,' Quintal sneered. 'Right seeing to he was getting, I can tell you.'

Tararo took his hand from Mauatua. 'Hah, what would you know that is not made of rum?'

He called Niau to come to him. 'It is an honour for Niau.'

'We'll remember that honour the next time one of our girls have a headache, won't we, Mr Christian?'

Quintal minced a few steps, flicking his wrist and batting his eyelids.

Tararo's anger left him, replaced by powerful dignity. 'We do not prance like cheap women or *mahu*. Or like the boys I have seen on *popa'a* ships, the ones you pretend to dislike but then give pennies to fondle and suck you.' He waited until he saw Niau had recovered his pride.

'We get and give pleasures only men can give or get from another man.' Tararo leant into Quintal's face. 'You have to be a man to understand this.'

Matt was totally unperturbed. 'I'll tells you what I understand, mate,' he shouted, with a wink at Fletcher. 'I understand your boy is a bit of delicious. I could have some of that, yeah, very nice.' He clapped his dirt-engrained hands onto Niau's pectorals and roughly rubbed them in circles, making vulgar noises.

He pinched the youth's nipples with two great flourishes and then slapped Niau on a buttock and held his hand there firmly as he thrust his body against him.

Niau looked directly ahead, his expression unchanging.

Tararo grabbed Quintal around his chest and brandished his shovel above his prisoner's head. Fletcher and Ned cocked the pistols they now carried all the time.

'By the time those things strike a spark and then light a powder, if they work at all, he will be dead,' Tararo vowed.

Tararo squeezed Matt's chest again and again, each time eliciting a pained grunt. 'Why is it everything you do reminds me of a pig, Quintal?'

Even Matt Quintal would know this was a ruse to get him to call Tararo a pig. Calling a Ma'ohi man or woman a pig was declaring your death sentence. Wars had been fought over the insult. With the dull sense of self-preservation thugs rely on to survive, Quintal for once kept his mouth shut.

Encouraged this silence meant his imminent victory, Tararo declared himself. 'I am the only high noble on this island. I should be ruling. And to rule I need a woman beside me. That woman can only be Mauatua.'

She knew he had the strength to kill his hostage with one strike but waited until the impasse lasted long enough for the frisson of its novelty to wear off. Then she lunged forward and wrenched the shovel from Tararo.

'There are no nobles on this island. We want none of that Ma'ohi nonsense here. Now go, go away, you are being silly.' She shooed him, flapping her hands as though he were a troublesome infant.

'You should not talk to a man this way,' he sulked.

She lost the last threads of good temper. 'Go, go before I tell more of your secrets.' She spat on the ground in front of Tararo.

'You would need no woman then. Or boy.'

Her threat pierced Tararo's shell of conceit and he released Quintal.

'You want status, the best of Tahiti and Raiatea? You want, Oro? Want, want. That's all I hear from men,' she bellowed. 'Well here's what I want. Here's all you'll get from me, Tararo.'

She turned, bared her tattooed buttocks and loins to him and then leaned forward in the *tipou*. She reached behind and slapped one buttock after the other.

'There, that's Tahiti. And that's Raiatea. And that's your god Oro between them, with all the *tuta'e* I can make.'

Tararo recoiled but his face stayed impassive. The white men understood the insult, but there was something of a schoolboy prank about showing a bum and they couldn't help giggling.

Their amusement tipped Tararo's determination. He grabbed Toofaiti from Jack Williams and was in the bush with her before anyone could budge. The Tubuaian Oha, the only Ma'ohi with outraged tears in his eyes, scampered high-kneed through the undergrowth after him.

Mauatua put up her hands before anyone could pursue them. 'There are better ways,' she said.

Tararo stopped his flight long enough to crow like a rooster three derisive times from the bush, reminding them of how the debacle had begun. And then another cry was heard on the wind. As it wasted into the hot, late summer day she turned to see it chilled Fletcher as much as it frightened her.

They ran to the village and Jenny told them Puarai had fallen from the cliffs at the end of their garden. 'Is she alive?' Mauatua asked.

'No-one's heard anything, not for a long time,' Jenny said.

'Tie a line to a tree. I'll go down,' Fletcher offered. Mauatua put her hands over her face as she visualised what he might find. There were only rocks to land on, vicious surf-pounded rocks. The fall was countless times the height of Pitcairn's tallest tree, which was why Puarai's scream had lasted so long.

Dead or alive when she landed, she would have been mauled by crashing waves and then sucked away by pitiless currents. She told Fletcher not to risk it.

'Adams, does he know?' she asked. Jenny nodded to the banana palms to her left. Adams stood in their shadows. It was a struggle for him to speak. When he could, he mumbled, 'It was for me. She was getting birds' eggs for me.

'There'll be no trouble, Mauatua, not like Jack William's been giving. I'm used to being on my own, have been all my life. The last year with Puarai was more pleasure and comfort than I ever expected in a lifetime.'

He shook his head slowly from side to side. She watched as he stopped and started, imagining he was rearranging his mind to his new solitude.

Not long before the sun went down he took a deep breath and sighed, saying

'I think I'll go home and take a bit of a nap.'

CHAPTER 45

Fletcher felt constantly harried by Mauatua and she didn't stop when he swooned into sweating. Why she nagged he couldn't imagine. He knew perfectly well that Tararo had stolen Toofaiti and that it wasn't right. But couldn't she do something about it? Or someone, *anyone* else? Why was it always supposed to be me he asked again and again?

On top of that Jack moaned to him about getting Toofaiti back, Adams moaned that he'd already had enough of celibacy and Thursday grizzled all the time. She said he was cutting an early tooth but he saw her do damned little about it.

One night when their son was at last asleep Mauatua told him something quite new. She told him she didn't believe Tararo had hoped to make friends with him in the cave.

'He wants you to feel more isolated.'

He put down his book, puzzled. 'Why? Does he think that will weaken my position on the island?'

'And strengthen his, yes. He still wants to rule this island.'

He didn't trust the way she was talking with her eyes down. Suspicious, he thought and he couldn't stop airing a thought he knew would be better kept to himself.

'With you?'

'Yes, with me.' She looked him directly in the eyes, obviously alert to his dangerous implication.

'But how? Has he ever tried anything, forced . . .?'

'You know what he's like. I ignore him.'

He couldn't bear the voices and images that crowded into his mind, each clamouring for special attention. Did her equivocal reply mean Tararo had pushed more than his ambition on to her? Could she have given in, perhaps dismissing it as something meaningless to her? Perhaps thinking it was a privilege because of his rank?

Surely she would have told him? An Englishwoman would have. And there he saw the flaw in this thinking. His sweating started but he didn't leave. There was more to hear or to say.

'Look, this is not about Tararo,' she said, combing her hair, provocatively he thought. 'I want Toofaiti back here. How that happens, what that costs, Fletcher, I don't really care.'

Her careful proposition calmed him. She had handed him the baton of leadership. 'I'll organise search parties tomorrow,' he said. 'So we know what the situation is. I'll only frighten him, that's all I'll do.'

'The girls from The Edge, they say he goes to a cave.'

His voices started again. What if Tararo *had* succeeded? What if she was not telling him the truth? What if Tararo was the father of the second baby Mauatua was expecting? He turned his face to the wall, hoping pity for the rivers of sweat streaming from his scalp and body would somehow force her to take back his offer to frighten Tararo tomorrow.

Mauatua expected 1791 would probably pass without other births. In spite of the agreement at the pool, the other women were not having babies. The excuse she heard was worry over the safety of children around the drunken and often violent mutineers. She understood this but begged them to ignore it. They could protect the children, even if it meant living separately on the island.

Without children there would be no point to Pitcairn. Its women would wither and die, leaving nothing but a bitter legacy of envy and regret.

She asked each woman discreetly to estimate how much rum was left in each mutineer's possession. Most men were drinking many more times the daily grog ration they would at sea, and so it was reckoned the last of it would go by the end of this year. With discreet siphoning and then replacing just some of the rum with water they hoped to hasten even that.

They were less forthcoming on whether their men's sobriety might then lead to more babies.

Tevarua gave birth to a son but after the first day Matt Quintal had forbidden visitors to the house and she was rarely allowed to leave it. Mauatua and Jenny insisted on burying the placenta properly and after that insisted on seeing her on the pretence there was secret women's business to settle after the birth of a son and heir. They found Tevarua constantly in tears. They couldn't say if it was the doldrums that could come after birth or living with Quintal.

He had insisted on intercourse two hours after his son's birth and punched her because she was not as tight as he remembered. He turned her, ignoring her protests about the haemorrhoids caused by pregnancy.

Mauatua weaned Thursday early and he thrived on a pap of baked breadfruit and coconut milk. This also meant Thursday was easier to leave with any one of the women, something she later realised a few thought a better arrangement than having a child of their own. With her milk dried, she hoped she would soon fall and she had. But was it the right thing?

Fletcher hadn't warmed to Thursday and seemed even touchier about a second. Still, perhaps it would be a daughter and he could call her Mary after the sister he appeared to love so much.

He resolved to make a personal plea to Tararo. He left at first light because he wanted time to himself before the confrontation. Mauatua's view of Pitcairn Island was wrong, he saw that. It would never be a place where men and women were equal, because that was not what men or women wanted.

Some men and women were leaders. Some preferred to do what other men and women decided. He saw this as no barrier to equality but as the basis on which it worked. The key was for everyone to be where they wanted to be, and that there was no bullying by one stratum to make its life easier by exploiting another. That's what equality meant, that everyone was where they wanted to be.

It confirmed the way of the Navy, that many men functioned more comfortably under a figurehead of authority but even this worked only if the commander was at ease in his role and respected for it.

Social theorists in London didn't understand this, but then, none of them was marooned on a Pacific Island with men and women of different class and colour.

Who else would take on his role on Pitcairn? No-one other than Tararo seemed the least interested in that sort of responsibility. Unless, but no, whatever her qualities, and there were many, surely Mauatua would not want such a role, not with an infant who was barely walking and another on the way.

Another on the way?

The thought of the new baby started up the chattering in his head. It told him he should be killing Tararo, not negotiating. Just as he might have shot Jack Williams. Once one of them was dead, all would be well on the island. But was this the way the island should work? Was violence its solution to resistance?

He caught and stilled the voices before they inebriated him for the day. He'd find Tararo and Toofaiti and bring them back. Mauatua would be pleased. She might even tell him the truth about the new baby.

He knew approximately where the cave was on the west coast. He walked slowly, close to the cliff edge, until he heard voices swept up to him by the wind that always blew over the island's rim. There was bantering laughter too, so he believed the atmosphere in the camp was relaxed and that the trio thought they were safe. He lay flat on his belly.

The mouth of the cave was lower but more or less at a right angle to him in a ridge face. The few hardy wind-bent plants hid his head so he had a sharp, oblique view and a quick push backwards would get him out of sight swiftly if necessary.

The cave was like a smaller version of his beneath Lookout Point but the triangular shape was narrower, more compressed. It pierced the sharp side of a narrow-topped ridge that ran down from the cliff path to become another impregnable tower in Pitcairn's coastal defence. The cave's opening sloped towards the sea, one corner pulled down like a disenchanted mouth. It was two or three men's height below the ridge crest but access could only be by rope.

The direct approach was a broad steep slope of loose shingle and low scrubby plants that then fell away so abruptly the land looked as though it met the sea, but this was a dangerous illusion. The slope was less severe at the cave's mouth but only for a man's length.

There was no cover and nothing to break or stop a fall. Gravity and his weight would be his executioners, pulling and pushing him over and down the slope and over the edge and onto the rocks.

Anyway, quiet approach was impossible because of the noisy shingle and any attempt to rush the cave would mean the attackers slipping and falling. The cave was a brilliant choice by Tararo. There was no easy escape but there was also no way the occupants could be surprised.

He pushed forward on the cliff path until he could see further into the cave. Tararo was pawing Toofaiti as she was lighting a fire.

She liked the attention quite as much as she complained, giggling and slapping Tararo in turn.

Would Manatua have giggled too, making protestations she didn't mean? His chest contracted and he felt anger rise through his gorge and explode into his head. He stood and fired directly at Tararo.

Oha scampered deeper into the cover of the cave and Tararo flung Toofaiti to one side

'Hah!' Tararo mocked. 'Can't even shoot straight.'

Fletcher was appalled he had shot at Tararo, that he had shot to kill. 'They're blanks,' he lied. 'I'm not trying to kill you, just want to talk.'

'You useless, Titreano, useless.' Tararo pulled Toofaiti under his left arm. Then he saluted mockingly, pushing out his chest.

Fletcher panicked. Nothing was happening the way it should.

His pistols had charges in them. Unable to clear his head of imagining Mauatua with Tararo he shot off a pistol and heard the ball ricochet from the mouth of the cave. Tararo didn't flinch but Toofaiti twisted into his chest, her arm over her head.

He had been a fool. Anger was not going to help. Yet anger was all he had. He shouted what he should have said calmly.

'I don't want to hurt you or kill you. I only wanted to frighten you, so you will talk to me.'

'Better spend your time watching your back, Titreano. No use talking to me. You know what I say.'

'That you want this island to be yours? Over my dead body.'

His bluster couldn't hide his bungling. He was dangerously exposed. Tararo was amused rather than aggressive, but that might not last.

He noticed Oha slyly assembling a pile of small rocks. They might have sling shots. Withdrawal was the better move.

He'd make something up on his way back. and then tell Mauatua whatever he wanted. She never need know the truth.

'I'll not miss next time, Tararo. And it won't be just me.'

On his way back he told Jack Williams that if he wanted to shoot Tararo he had his backing.

He wasn't surprised Jack wouldn't put himself at risk.

He wrestled unsuccessfully to create a false version of what happened. Instead, he simply told Mauatua Toofaiti seemed happy and that Tararo was defiant. He could see no short term solution.

'What do you think Tararo meant, why should I be watching my back? Is someone trying to kill me?' he demanded of her.

'Don't be silly, Fletcher. We all need you. Your boy certainly does.'

'And what about the other?'

'Other what?'

'The new baby. Is it mine or Tararo's?'

Mauatua hurled a coconut at him, but missed.

'Answer! If it is going to be a black bastard you'd better kill it now.'

'Black? *If* it is black?'

'I'll be able to tell.'

'How would you tell? By skin colour? Might I remind you, Mr Fletcher Christian, that you are many times naturally darker than Tararo?'

Her riposte made things worse. It was true. Whatever its colour the baby could have been fathered by either of them.

He'd never know the truth.

He left and ran. He ran and ran through their gardens and climbed to his cave faster than he had done before. He was exhausted, hungry and thirsty.

But mostly he was appalled that he and Mauatua had rowed.

Throughout every challenge she had been there and supported him and now he doubted her. She was the only Pitcairner who thought the same way he did, who could leap forward in conversation the way no-one else on the island seemed able to do. Well, Ned of course, and when Fletcher thought about the way *he* sometimes looked at Mauatua, he wondered if they had thoughts of setting up together.

He lay on his cave's floor and gave in to the rushing voices. He knew they would continue through the night. Most would tire and he would wake with only one or two of them. These were usually optimistic.

That was how he survived, knowing how ever bad life seemed at night he woke up hopeful. If ever that gift disappeared . . . This new fear became another voice added to the dozens already rattling around in his head.

He closed his eyes and so wholly abandoned himself to the chattering it smothered any sense of solitude or physical need.

He would be better in the morning, and up here in the cave Mauatua and Thursday had not been forced to share his anguish.

That thought was his sole comfort.

CHAPTER 46

Late in 1791 little had changed for Mauatua other than her second pregnancy becoming more obvious. Next year McCoy's Teio would have a brother or sister for Sully, the girl she had brought ashore in the barrel. John Mills and Vahineatua expected a child about the same time. Then it would be time for her second.

It was common knowledge Toofaiti stole back into the village to visit Jack Williams. Without having to see Tararo he ignored his distaste for sharing Toofaiti. The improvement her visits made to Jack's mood and work ethic were so marked there was a general agreement not to comment.

The biggest change Mauatua saw was Fletcher's mental state, burrowing deeper into depression and moodiness. She no longer argued or challenged him for fear of shattering one more of the fragile hopes he clung to for his sanity.

In mid-December she trudged back from the gardens laden with baskets of fruit and vegetables. Thursday was suddenly precocious and able to walk strongly on legs that showed nothing of his father's bandiness. His walking was a mixed blessing. With the weight of the food she carried, trying to curb her son's inveterate curiosity and with the effects of her advanced pregnancy, she was annoyed that her life was so dreary, repetitive and draining.

She was the only woman on Pitcairn with the demands of a child, and the only one whose husband was so emotionally dependent. It was like having two sons, she confided to Jenny.

Fletcher had been in a black mood for weeks and still wondered about the new baby, however hard he said he tried not to think that way. He hadn't moved from the stoop of their house since she left for the gardens hours ago. His hair, longer than hers, was lank and unwashed, his beard matted and tangled. He had a musket across his knees. One index finger tapped it continuously, beating a descant to the chattering voices he said he always heard in his head.

Still, at least she knew where she was with him and he never erupted into blind rages like most of the other mutineers.

Thursday ran ahead to climb on his father's knee. Fletcher used his arm to frustrate the boy. Thinking it a game, Thursday laughed and tried once more. Fletcher knocked the boy aside with his musket. Thursday tumbled backwards and then yelling his frustration reached forward and accidentally pulled the musket from Fletcher's knee, bruising his forehead with it. Fletcher raised his arm with a clenched fist.

Mauatua dropped the food baskets and mirrored Fletcher's raised fist over him, sweeping Thursday into her other arm.

Fletcher waited dumbly for her blow but she couldn't deliver it. Instead, she used her raised arm to pacify Thursday. He stopped crying and then struggled, pointing behind her.

The four Ma'ohi men from The Edge stood with their heads bowed, uncomfortable at witnessing the scene. She put Thursday down and stepped forward as though it were she they had come to visit.

'They want to tell you something,' she then said, lapsing into the deceit Fletcher was head of the household.

'They do?' Fletcher turned away despondently. He didn't see her signal Niau to speak. The youth moved forward.

'We have come to say we agree with you, Mr Christian.'

'Who cares what I think anymore?' he responded. At a further discreet sign from Mauatua Niau stepped closer and spoke more confidently.

'It is not right for Tararo to steal Toofaiti. It is not right they eat from our gardens without having worked in them.'

'It's been bloody months and you buggers haven't done a thing about it. Why come moaning to me now?'

'Can't do anything without muskets,' Niau said. 'And you didn't use yours when . . .'

'Fletcher couldn't surprise them like you could, Niau,' Mauatua said soothingly. 'Tararo would trust you.'

She put a hand on Fletcher's shoulder as though she were a conduit for his thoughts. She said Toofaiti shouldn't belong to Tararo but should be Jack's wife now. That made Tararo a trouble maker and Fletcher thought all troublemakers should be shot.

There was a long awkward pause until she squeezed his shoulder and Fletcher understood he was expected to agree. He sat straighter and spoke without knowing he was repeating what he had been groomed to say.

'It's time. If you do not do what I want, you will be troublemakers, too. And then, it will be me shooting. First you.'

He pulled a pistol from his waistband and aimed it at Niau. In spite of his decrepit appearance he retained his physical strength and his raised arm and hand were firm. He moved the pistol to each of the men in turn. 'And then you. And you. And you. Until every trouble maker is dead, and there are no black men on my island.'

He lowered the pistol, reached for the musket and threw it at Niau's feet. 'This is to shoot Tararo and Oha.' Niau hesitated.

Mauatua reassured him. 'You would then have Tararo's chiefly status.'

'There are no chiefs on my island,' Fletcher roared.

'I know Fletcher, but still . . .' She smiled complicitly at Niau, who picked up the musket, watching Fletcher anxiously.

Niau stepped closer. 'Toofaiti will be Williams' wife. And as the highest noble, I . . .'

Mauatua put her finger to her lips. '*Mamoo*, Niau, *mamoo*.'

Within an hour everyone else on the island was crowded into her house, shocked a black man had been given a musket.

'Jack's moving in with me, safer for both of us,' Adams blustered. Safety was what everyone bristled about.

'Us having the muskets was how we kept them bastards down,' Quintal declared, his hands trembling his mug of rum.

'Now it's us buggers at risk.'

'And if Niau does what we've asked?'

She waited for an answer. Gradually there was a shuffling agreement that it would solve what seemed insoluble.

'In that case, I suggest you all go home.'

When they were still in earshot she called after them.

'I've still not heard a single volunteer among you who would do the job instead of Niau.'

She brought Fletcher food at the simple table he had made for their house. The Tahitian style of serving food was the same as he was used to in Georgian England. Every dish was put onto the table at the same time, so an eager eye or swift arm could ensure the better portion of what the stomach would most enjoy. Sweet could precede savoury or both could be devoured at the same time.

He insisted she ate seated at the table but she refused to sit until he had finished. Men and women always ate separately in Tahiti and she never felt comfortable sitting so close she could hear food in someone else's mouth. On BOUNTY waves pounding on the hull had drowned the noise, but in the stillness of Pitcairn it was unbearable.

He dined daily off the fine plates Bligh was supplied for entertaining on BOUNTY and used a knife and fork of Christian family silver engraved with their unicorn-head crest.

Two of his painted Chinese bowls always sat on the table and today she had crammed them with luminous hibiscus blooms.

He half closed his eyes to smell the flowers. The hibiscus had no scent but pleasure danced on his lips and his head moved slowly as he dipped from blossom to blossom. He took one endless, luxurious breath, held and then exploded it. He pushed the hibiscus away. 'Ah, roses,' he said into them. 'The scent of English roses in summer . . .'

When the first distant shot was heard Quintal rushed through their door without greeting.

He was stopped by a second shot and then shook a fist in the air.

'We'll soon be rid of all those black buggers at this rate.'

'It's only the troublemakers,' Fletcher protested.

'They are all bloody trouble makers. I want men to work for me by day and women to play by night and, by God, I ain't getting neither.'

'What's in your pocket Matt, show me?' Mauatua demanded.

Quintal didn't move.

'I'll tell you, shall I, Matt? Salt. That's what's there. You carry salt. You rub it into the cuts after you've lashed a man in the gardens but before he has recovered enough to resist. Salt, Matt, so the sting it makes in those fresh stripes makes men faint with the pain. That's why so many men and women do anything to avoid you, day or night.'

'I didn't know that,' Fletcher said softly. 'That's not right, Matt.'

'Look, I didn't come here to be criticised.' Quintal was uncomfortable and she took advantage.

'No, you came here to criticise others when the problem is you. Your wife doesn't like the dirty sort of games you like.'

'But you might, mightn't you Mauatua?' She turned her head away as Matt reached up to stroke her hair.

'You're a pleasure I still haven't had.' He laughed low in his throat.

Fletcher hardly moved. 'Come on, Matt,' he roused himself to protest.

'She shouldn't mind, Fletcher. The other girls don't. It's only fair.'

'Fair is not in it anymore,' Fletcher protested.

'Aye, ain't that the truth, m'dear.' Quintal rounded on him. 'It's not fair there should be two girls with them four black bastards when there are two of your shipmates without even one between them. Something will have to be done, Mr Christian.'

'What do you think those shots mean, Matt? Tararo and Oha are dead and Toofaiti will be back.'

'I know that's what they *should* mean. But now the blacks can get their hands on muskets, well, who knows? Anyone could be on the wrong end of one, even you. And when you've gone . . .' Quintal roughly slid his foot under Thursday's buttocks. 'There'd be no reason for him to be around either. We could start again, Mauatua m'dear.' He tipped the boy over so his bruised forehead split and bled.

She rushed Quintal out of the house, hurling dishes and food from the table. She shouted loudly enough for the entire village to hear. She swore and cursed him off their plot, swearing she would kill him if he ever touched her son again.

When she came back inside Thursday was whimpering on the floor and Fletcher was silently eating and reading.

The new baby was still weeks away and she was dozing lightly on her stoop, listless in the heavy afternoon heat. Her sleepy mind had been ambling through what she could do to bring her second child into a calmer village. Adams interrupted her.

'You knows what I said about my time with Puarai? Well, now I think, well I reckon I'd like more of the same. If Jack can have a woman from the blacks, it's fair I should have one too.'

She couldn't tell if the baby had kicked furiously or her stomach had shrunk with dread. It took time for the pain to resolve and for her to respond. 'Fair? That's not what I think.'

She took time to rearrange her loose draperies of tapa cloth, flapping them so cool breezes reached her swollen abdomen.

'You saw the trouble it caused when Toofaiti was given to Jack.'

'Because it wasn't voted on properly.'

'You think voting would solve it?'

'Isn't that the point?' Adams stalked away, muttering.

She'd never seen him as a trouble maker or even as a man with determined views. Yet every one of the mutineers changed once they became landowners and all nine houses had been built. They were still young men and, she supposed, exploding with sexual energy.

And all had too much time on their hands.

CHAPTER 47

When Mauatua called to Fletcher for advice about the last obstacles up to his cave, he panicked.

'My God,' he said, 'you won't have the baby here will you?'

'I'm trying not to, Fletcher.'

It must have taken her all morning to manage the slick slopes and rock outcrops. Her face was red and her voice weak with exhaustion. He had to pull her up the final steep ledge and when she was over that they both fell, unbalanced by the bulk of her pregnancy. Incapable of knowing what to say or how to revive her, he concentrated on finding her a comfortable sitting position.

'Did you know what they did, before you came here this morning?' she asked, once she had slowly eaten the ripe banana he offered her. There was nothing else to give her, no cool water or refreshing coconut.

'How could I?' He regretted his sharp tone but his fear for her condition defeated his finer feelings. She didn't seem to notice or mind.

'Your shipmates have had another vote.'

He put a hand to his forehead. He braced himself but couldn't look at her. 'Tinafanea has been taken from The Edge. She's living with Adams. They said it was to help in his gardens.'

He thought quickly. That left Titahiti and the three Tahitian men to share only Mareva.

Up in the cave with only the faint whistle of wind worrying at their thoughts, it didn't seem possible that far below them a skeleton settlement with fewer than thirty men and women harboured the injustice, jealousy and injured senses of a big city. In less than two years two men and two women were dead. Death threats had been made by most men against most others and Mauatua's threat to Quintal wasn't the only one by women against the white men.

'There's more,' Mauatua sighed. 'Jenny's pulling boards off her house to build a boat and some of the men have agreed to help. Even Quintal.'

'Why would he do that?'

'He says life on Pitcairn would be easier without 'that bitch's tongue' in the village.'

'Would it help if we gave the black men land now?'

'Then they'd work only for themselves.'

'Exactly. And so?'

'Your old shipmates would then have to work harder and they won't. We are the only ones who have never used black men, except for building the house.'

He still clung perilously to his belief everything could be solved with talk and compromise. But now he sat silent, cast adrift because the way he and Mauatua wanted to live was not the way of others.

He still hoped Pitcairn was not his future yet he knew she saw it as her only future. 'I know it's difficult for you, me and my moods. It's why I come up here, why I stay out of your way.'

He paused until she met his eye. 'You really are the world to me. Without you I wouldn't have a world.'

She squeezed his hand and once more Fletcher was grateful she found this comfortable. 'The baby is yours, Fletcher.'

'I know, I do know that.' Fletcher leaned forward to kiss her on the brow. And then she told him about Tararo's attempt to rape her and how he had predicted he would rule the island with her. His death had meant a great weight was lifted from her mind.

'Is that what you wanted to tell me?'

'About the baby, yes. And to ask you what you thought we should do.'

'Ask me? I'm useless. Since BOUNTY burned, nothing has been what I wanted or expected.'

'I know. Not even your son.'

He was stung by her direct criticism but up here in the cave it was somehow easier to admit he behaved badly after Thursday was born. His rejection of his son as a 'native' disturbed everyone on Pitcairn. But that was then. He thought of a clear way to show he had changed.

'We'll call this baby after my family. It's the proper thing to do.'

'What names, Fletcher?'

'Charles, after my father and brother. Or Mary for my sister. Perhaps Mary Ann. Ann is my mother's name.'

She murmured the names. She suddenly pitched forward. Fletcher grabbed her. 'What happened, are you all right?'

'A very big kick I think, or cramp from sitting like this.' He helped her stand and she stretched her back. She felt her abdomen and told him her womb was noticeably lower.

'Is it time?' he asked anxiously. He had no idea what to do if the baby decided to be born up here.

'I'm not certain, but, thank you. I wanted to hear you say you knew it was your baby. Up here you could have said anything and only we would have known.'

They held each other tight enough for Fletcher to feel their baby struggling against the walls of its mother.

He laughed, suddenly caught up in the wonder of birth and parenthood, remembering the joy on the faces of his mother and father at Moorland Close when his younger siblings were born.

'I think I should get you back down.'

'That should give it a hurry up.'

They laughed again and this new high mood continued. For much of the way Mauatua slid on her bottom, with Fletcher as an obstacle at her feet. It was more comfortable if she leaned back so she saw the sky rather than the sea or the sharp slope.

Once they were down on the cliff-top path, she stopped and stood splay legged. 'There's is a leak, look my legs are wet.'

She rubbed her inner thigh and sniffed her hand. She put fingers under his nose. It was startling, like the waft of a Society woman's smelling salts.

'What's that?'

'The water that holds the baby safe. It's a first message, like a song heard over many hills to say a visitor is coming. But this one will stay, gods willing.'

'You still believe in them?'

'You told me about your relative, William Christian. What was it he said before he died?'

'Before he was executed, yes, he said: There is but a thin veil between life and death.'

'Gods or not, when a baby comes that veil is thinner than a spider's web but stronger. Sometimes it cannot be broken whatever we want . . . ah!' Mauatua's face crumpled at the pain of a strong contraction.

'You'd better get me home.'

She had negotiated for months to give birth on the bed where the baby was conceived, just as Fletcher said he had been born on the bed where he was conceived. The black men and most of the women tried to dissuade her over many weeks, reminding her of the traditional *tapu* and fears surrounding child birth, how nothing of it should ever be seen where men might walk and certainly not in a house. These Tahitian ways had been sacrosanct for so many generations it was difficult for any Ma'ohi to adopt a different way without fear of its consequences but Fletcher supported her against the others.

They wanted Pitcairn to abandon belief in the 'old ways'.

Jenny was first to say she understood her belief in a birth where there had been conception. It was the completion of a natural cycle she agreed and there should be no offence in that. She offered to help birth the child if the old ways were honoured for the placenta, so the child's spirit would know where in the world it was anchored. It was only good sense and Fletcher was certain he'd heard such customs in Cumberland.

He had built a dividing wall in their house to create a bedroom. He left her in what she assured him was a comfortable position, squatting on her heels between the thighs and against the body of Teraura. Teraura had her arms around her and clasped her hands over her swollen abdomen so she could help bear down on the baby.

Back in Matavai it was often a man who supported a woman giving birth, so other Tahitian men could be certain correct procedures would be followed if the baby was not to join them.

On Pitcairn birthing was a woman's thing and Teraura, the youngest of the Tahitian women, needed to learn about it.

He heard few sounds of pain or strain through the wall for although Mauatua was slim, she had broad hips and birth was neither dangerous nor specially painful for her.

'A boy,' Jenny shouted. And then she screamed. Screamed and shouted, "*avae hape, 'avae hape, 'avae hape*!'

The horror in her voice brought Fletcher running. The boy was still attached to his umbilical cord but not moving between Mauatua's legs.

Jenny pointed.

Fletcher's intake of breath came slowly, in short shuddered gasps. He covered his mouth and his voice shook behind his hands.

'Club foot! What have I done?'

He retched and then reeled to the wall for support. He couldn't stand but turned and slid to the floor.

'Not you, Fletcher, not you,' Mauatua said, her voice dark and haunted. 'Me. Many Ma'ohi babies are born like this.'

'I never saw one.'

'They have never been allowed to live.'

Jenny held a pad of tapa close to the baby's face, waiting to smother the baby's first attempt to breathe or open his eyes. She looked to Mauatua for permission. Mauatua lunged and slapped it from Jenny's hand. She fell forward so she was kneeling. She held the still infant up by his ankles and slapped his buttocks.

'This one will live. He is a Pitcairner. He is my son. *Our* son, Fletcher.'

Mauatua shivered impatiently as Jenny urgently cut and tied the umbilical cord. The boy turned blue under his golden skin and hung from his uneven feet like thin-skinned game kill. She smacked her son's buttocks and whispered without cease, cleaning his mouth and eyes and ears with her tongue and finger tips.

She tumbled words of loving welcome into his ears between soft sea-like sounds, sounds he must have known in her womb. She kissed his folded foot, reassuring him it was no obstacle to her love. She spanked him again, twice, three times. She whispered louder, pushing her will for him to live deeper and deeper into her son's head.

Nothing encouraged the boy to join this world.

He twitched once but this was worse than the stillness. The start or the end? No-one could tell. The silence that followed was ageless. And then without further notice, he opened his eyes and his mouth, shuddered the full length of his body and howled. She turned him up the right way.

'This is Charles, my son Charles Christian. Welcome him.'

Charles opened his eyes and stared interminably only at his father. Then he put his thumb in his mouth and snuggled into his mother.

Fletcher's mind was a turmoil of conflict. Everyone in the room had tears but tears of what, happiness or pain? Now he had another native son, this time with a club foot. A cripple all his life, whose first act was to challenge him. If there was a god of any kind, he played with spiteful and heartless vengeance.

Ned had followed Fletcher into the room when Jenny screamed. 'That's a remarkable thing Mauatua has done, Fletcher,' he said in a whisper, leading him out of the room and away from the house.

'Can you imagine the change of mind-set it took for a Tahitian woman to allow this baby to live? That's untold centuries of custom turned on its head in less than a minute. I can't begin to understand the daring and the courage this took.'

'I can't either, Ned. More's the pity.'

'You must support her decision, treat them both as though there is nothing different about the boy. If you don't he will know and hate you for it. If you don't treat Charles as an equal he will be bullied and excluded because he will expect it.'

Jenny overheard the men as she was organising the ceremonies to bury Charles' placenta. 'That is why such babies never joined us,' she agreed. 'They would probably have been killed in what other boys called games. The old way, not letting them join us, was an act of kindness. Your wife is very brave, Fletcher.'

'The boy will have to be braver.'

'Boy?'

'You are right, I'm sorry. My son, Charles, will have to be braver.'

'If he is to listen to you, to know it is you who will teach him this bravery, he must know your scents.

'You should hold him and welcome him.

'He's waiting for you, Fletcher.'

CHAPTER 48

Mauatua's decision to let club-footed Charles live was a point of no return for Pitcairn's women. From then they knew that a resolute mind could challenge any rule men had once determined their lives should follow. She saw each was kindled to accept fewer small insults on their paths towards greater respect and freedom but even such determination was little defence against drunken brutality.

What passed for peace on Pitcairn was a fragile balance of demand and cruelty by the men and of quiet resolution by the women.

She seemed alone in being totally free of physical bullying and she thought this was because she and Fletcher were the only couple who had freely chosen the other.

She accepted Fletcher's increasing inability to interact with her was not a spiteful decision but the inevitable result of his continuing descent into the sullen silence of depression. He had a battering conscience about Bligh, and because he could no longer remember all the names of the other men he had cast onto the South Pacific. Were they alive or dead?

He had once prided himself he took BOUNTY without a drop of blood being spilt. But since then? It was not necessary to draw blood directly to have killed a man.

The new Pitcairners Mauatua expected had been born in 1792. McCoy and Teio had a son and then John Mills and Vahineatua presented Pitcairn its first daughter, Elizabeth, called Betsy from her earliest days. That made only five children in two years and she'd borne two of them.

She grudgingly recognised the lack of children gave the women more time to themselves and now their gardens were well established there was a certain comfort to life and time to sit. She couldn't resent the others their pleasures, but she wished there were more Pitcairners and told them so at every opportunity.

Fletcher was comfortable using his still formidable strength to dig and then to dig over gardens. The gentler attentions of watering or weeding or harvesting gave his mind too much opportunity to wander and so these tasks were never completed. She persuaded him to make up the time he should have been fishing or in gardens by spending it with his sons, so she might labour in his place.

As long as the boys' reasonable demands were gratified, they were as accepting of him as they were of her. He enervated his unused strength by walking a great deal. She'd help tie the two to him with lengths of tapa, slung fore and aft, and others told her that as they went he talked to them incessantly, teaching them words and names, showing them every corner of Pitcairn and telling them what was beyond the horizon. She thought this was more for his comfort than for their education. Sometimes he took them to the cave, even though she begged him not to do this.

She listened without comment when he confessed that the demands of his sons fought loudly with his voices. He learned to enjoy this clash because, like violent lovers when each battle was over, the outcome was a heightened sense of well-being. His sons' company made him a gentler man and she and Fletcher reaped the benefits in greater companionship and a tender loving sensuality that constantly grew and changed.

It was a curious triangle in which his children gave him much of the comfort and strengths she had once done but everyone benefited. Mauatua reminded him of an old Tahitian saying: *E ha'apua'i te here mau, i te pua'i o na ta'ata e piti.* Love is only true when it makes both lovers bigger.

None of this was how she had visualised her life with Fletcher Christian, yet only one thing really worried her. Fletcher seemed to think Bligh had survived and would lead an expedition to find him. She'd heard him mumbling he expected his old captain to arrive any day.

By the end of 1792 Mauatua encouraged the women to use their free time to make tapa cloth because this was first noticeable shortage on Pitcairn. The mutineers maintained their elevated status as landowners with tapa sheets and pillows on their beds. Curtains, wall hangings and even carpets were made from tapa. The cotton, linen, silken and woollen trappings of a fine life in England were answered by the different grades and thicknesses of tapa cloth. Yet, by now the huge store BOUNTY had brought to Pitcairn was dwindling and even the men would have to wear it.

Pitcairn soon echoed to the regular beat of *e'e*, the long, squared batons of wood that flattened and felted sticky inner bark into tapa cloth. She believed the daily dull thumping of tapa by women bound the Ma'ohi islands of the Pacific more assuredly than men's war cries or the worship of Oro. It certainly created high spirits and greater cohesion among Pitcairn's women. Soon she was hearing white men mutter that tapa-making seemed like a club that excluded them. Because the men were stupid enough to have complained, the women spent more time at tapa making than was strictly necessary.

Mauatua's hands and eyes didn't readily fall to traditional patterns when she decorated her first length of Pitcairn tapa. Instead, she and the other women created designs that celebrated their difference, just as their foremothers had done for generations each time a canoe brought women and tapa-making to hundreds of new islands of the Ma'ohi world.

It was pointless to travel and then to do what had been done before, stupidly celebrating what was left behind.

The women were united. Creating Pitcairn's new designs would give their daughters and their daughters after them a heritage of design based on the freedoms and wild beauty of Pitcairn. Anyway, Mauatua reminded them, Pitcairn's women had a unique story to tell, for all their children carried European blood and that had to be recorded.

There was a feast of inspiration when she led them to harvest patterns from the *popa'a* world. The peculiar birds and flowers on Fletcher's Chinese bowls were a totally new language of colour and line. BOUNTY carried lengths of cloth from England for trade and gifts, printed with posies of flowers they'd never imagined.

The white men's memories were ploughed for favourite images of their homes on the other side of the world.

She and Jenny were experts in finding familiar and new plants for dyes on Pitcairn. Soon dried blossoms were also pressed into patterns, sometimes in fragile, decorative tapa that was as transparent as morning mist. Fletcher said these ephemeral tapa were as sumptuous as silks he had seen in India, each length so frail they could be worn only for an hour and only by the most favoured and inflaming beauty in a *zenana*, the forbidden women's quarter of a palace.

Gossip and tattle-telling enlivened tapa-making and Mauatua added this to what she heard at the pool. She used the skills that had once stored her English words to now catalogue the mutineers again.

It was the only way she felt she could protect her sons and Pitcairn's other children from sudden drama or danger. For as the women became more resolute and defiant, she saw the men, all of them, target the island's vulnerable and trusting children.

Sometimes it was mockery and verbal abuse, but just as often it was cuffs or pushes or swipes with a switch for no reason but ill temper. She was treating the cuts and bruises of bullied and abused children as often as she was salving their mothers. It took a long time for the women to accept the depth of cruelty to their children, for none of them could imagine such a thing. Even Mauatua thought they might be wrong until Quintal had assaulted Thursday.

That's when she began assessing reality rather than hope.

Brown, the once gentle gardener, had become a surly and brutal drunk who fell into the ease of continuing his bad temper when sober. Dismissive of Ma'ohi wisdom he would kick and dig over what Ma'ohi men planted or insist on harvests being collected too early or too late. As they noticed this the women added extra of the ruined crops to their home patches.

Mills insulted everyone with his sharp, shrewish tongue. Vahineatua said he felt lessened because he fathered a daughter rather than a son and so made an industry of demeaning everything and everyone. He hadn't spoken to her for weeks and hit out every time his daughter was brought near him, injuring one or the other and always putting both in danger. She repeatedly berated him with behaving like an angry woman rather than a man and that hadn't helped. But once drunk his many dislikes so overwhelmed his senses he sank into surly, silent discontent.

'Lucky you,' Mauatua sympathised.

Jenny's gossiping revealed Martin as a confused man. He had been a confident and happy sailor for he liked order and easily admitted he was all at sea on land. Yet, when Jenny tried to instil order and rules into their household he became less secure. If Fletcher had a bigger house he would happily have lived with him, as a sort of servant, because this would give him the manly sense of structure he needed. Living independently and with a wife was beyond him.

Ned Young was more likely to criticise than to command but the Negro blood he carried made Pitcairn more rather than less to his taste. Nevertheless, he had been brought up with a natural disdain for coloured skins and sometimes it showed. But he was frank about it and so Pitcairn's women accepted it.

In spite of his ugliness and the malevolence of his breath and mouth Ned had the most charm and flirted outrageously, to the great pleasure of all the women. She and Jenny lessened the effect of his mouth once they agreed his foul breath came mainly from food rotting between his teeth. He was introduced to the Ma'ohi habit of picking teeth after eating and then rinsing his mouth and this made him a more popular companion to all. He was especially interested in the welfare of the children, for their mixed blood was something he knew might one day cause them problems and that alone recommended him above other men.

Adams remained grateful for the taste of domestic life he told her he had never experienced as a child and had never expected in later life.

Now he was undemanding and loyal to Tinafanea but once drunk he was too eager to egg on other mutineers in whatever mischief or unkindness he found them.

He explained this to Mauatua as the way he survived in the poorhouse where he had been brought up since an infant. You never led any violence he said, but you always made certain you were seen to be on the side of those who did.

Jack Williams was liked less than any of the white men. His status as the blacksmith was less important now the island was more settled. He maintained rather than made new tools and more than one man watched closely with the thought of taking over. Everyone hated the way he spoke constantly in graphic detail about his sexual life and to compare his succession of Ma'ohi women, not just their enthusiasms but this or that private feature.

He lost the respect of Ma'ohi and white, men and women, when he hoped to do the opposite, but he never believed this. Mauatua knew this because she made a point of telling him the truth and was always ruthlessly mocked and dismissed.

Quintal was as violent and demanding to Tevarua as ever and whenever her son had been kicked or swiped out of Quintal's drunken way she fled and left him for his safety with the Christians. Quintal was the first to discover his rum supplies were almost gone. Cutting his daily intake made him more irritable and uneasy. Sometimes even McCoy avoided him and the Scot had taken to disappearing into the hills somewhere for days.

Whenever McCoy went away his wife Teio blossomed and with daughter Sully beside her and her son on her hip was in and out of every house, filling it with laughter and song as she dismissed the cuts and bruises they all wore.

Mauatua led the women to flee in the night several more times and once they lived apart from the men for more than a month.

The symptoms of the men's withdrawal from alcohol seemed worse than those of drinking.

The Ma'ohi men from The Edge contributed to their own safety and to the peace of the island by working in the public gardens very early in the mornings, when Brown, Quintal or McCoy were less likely to be about. They spent much time fishing from their canoes and by their generous sharing of the catch earned grudging thanks and respect. The mutineers fished only from rocks, because none could swim.

Eventually, Jenny's boat was complete and tied up to bushes beneath Ship Landing Point and she loaded it with food and finely woven sheets of waterproof coconut fibre. Everyone but Fletcher trekked down the Hill of Difficulty to wish her Godspeed. He pleaded not to leave the house, and instead cared for the island's five children.

And then Toofaiti and Tevarua disclosed they were sailing too. Williams accepted Toofaiti's revelation with apparent equanimity, bragging he now expected Mareva to leave The Edge for his bed. There was greater surprise at Tevarua's decision for she would be leaving her vulnerable son. She said it was for his sake she was going. Pride had overcome her comfort at being the target for Quintal's manic lusts.

'Your son will be safe with me,' Mauatua called to her.

As Ma'ohi women there was no need to say such a thing, but she thought the white men needed to hear it said. The women were quickly in the boat, although Tevarua had to fight Matt Quintal's last rough attempts to deflect her. He stood away from her only when the women crowded him. The boat had a mast and a finely woven sail and once it cast off the women helped it on its way with paddles.

'We'll tell the king,' Jenny called back. 'We'll bring back the British Navy and you drunken buggers will hang and we'll live happily ever after without you.'

Mauatua's hands flew to her mouth as the bay's wicked cross currents spun the boat at their idle will. Barely five or six men's length from the shore, the boat capsized. At once it was clear to her from the white men's loud laughter this is what had been pled. They bragged how, with neither outrigger nor a proper keel, they ensured the craft was totally unsuited to the swirling waves of Pitcairn's inner waters, let alone the open ocean.

The women were strong swimmers, but disappointment, anger and the confusing currents exhausted them quickly and she saw fear in their eyes.

She ran to the edge of the rocks to encourage the women's struggles, but when they were close enough to scramble up onto them Quintal and McCoy stamped on their fingers with their bare-feet and pushed them back into the water.

Tragedy was an eye-blink away and then Mills and Williams joined the torment. Adams clapped and pranced like a court jester.

When the Ma'ohi men protested, the white men bundled two of them into the water. But this meant the women were safer, and soon being helped out of the water by them.

She was suspicious when Quintal congratulated Tevarua on her decision to return to him. He clasped her hand when she was half out of the water and in one strong movement pulled her onto land and took the credit for her rescue. He held his wife's sopping body tight to him and swirled his hands over her back.

'My lovely, my sweet lovely. You wouldn't leave your Matt, would you? You wouldn't really want him hanged, would you?'

Tevarua fell into his trap, at once contrite and agreeing with everything he said, just as Mauatua knew she might. She sidled closer, her mouth dry with dread, and heard Quintal's threats.

'Who else would put up with such a worthless, ungrateful bitch, eh, eh? You're lucky to have any man, you black whore. Think you'd get away from Matt, did ye? Never!'

Mauatua's stomach churned as Quintal's tongue teased Tevarua's ear while she giggled and struggled to get away, protesting this sort of intimacy should be private. And then Tevarua yelped, high and short. She seemed paralysed but her face told of shocked agony.

Mauatua battered Matt's head with flattened palms until he disengaged himself. His mouth was foaming with blood and Tevarua had blood pouring from her head. Matt leaned to spit something into the sea.

He had bitten off most of Tevarua's ear. He wiped his mouth.

'There now. That's a white man's tattoo. You wear my mark now. Bitch! Get your black arse up that hill and back home where you belong.'

Everyone else feared what Quintal might do if they did or said a thing but Mauatua's pent up anger at Jenny's impossible plan had no more reason to stay imprisoned. She grabbed Tevarua from Quintal just as the initial anaesthetised shock flooded away and she swayed with faintness.

Quintal was shocked at the malevolence in Mauatua's face as she deliberately towered over him. He shrunk away, spitting onto the ground.

'Pathetic,' Mauatua said of those empty gestures of supposed manliness. Her heart still thudded, as sickened by the thought of Tevarua's pain as she was at Quintal's switch from bully to coward.

She shouted into the fear-filled silence.

'None of you men will have a wife if you do not treat them well. Why should women put up with this?' Mauatua turned Tevarua around so they saw exactly her bloody injury.

'Do not think yourself free of blame, Tevarua. Did you think what would happen to your son if your expedition failed? If your boat had sunk in an hour or a day instead of just a few minutes? He would be safe on Pitcairn, yes, but he would no longer know you, or hear your voice, or learn all you promised to teach him.

'Our children did not choose to be here. Did you forget that? Yet they might be all that will make being on this island worthwhile.'

'There'll be plenty more of them if you don't like the ones you've got, won't there, m'shipmates?' said Quintal laughing and thrusting his hips.

'Laugh while you can, *popa'a*.' Mauatua waited until the white men were quiet again. 'What would your lives be if we did leave you?

'Do any of you know for sure what to plant and when? Do you know how to make fish hooks or catch fish, or know which fish are safe to eat?

'Not one of you could build a house.'

Tevarua whimpered with pain and shock. Mauatua helped her to the bottom of the Hill of Difficulty.

She had one more thing to say before they started up.

'I've said it before and it is still a truth.

'We women can live here without you. You cannot live without us. The same goes for the Ma'ohi men. You could not live here without them.'

CHAPTER 49

When Mauatua brought in Tevarua, the children in Fletcher's care were wailing or crying. The floor was littered with half-eaten bananas and pools of breadfruit pap, most of which were being licked by kittens or cats. He sat despondently at the table, his hands over his ears.

Tevarua's spilled blood caked her hair and shoulders and so frightened her son he scuttled to Fletcher and hid his face between his legs. Mauatua's sons pushed their faces into her thighs, blinding themselves to their first encounter with bloody violence. Fletcher disinterestedly patted Tevarua's son and then looked up wearily, as Mauatua told him what happened. He nodded, unsurprised.

'Didn't work? Oh, well. Back to the good old days.'

Tevarua wouldn't let Mauatua treat and dress her ear, anxious not to upset Matt Quintal further. She swiftly rinsed away the worst of the blood, changed into one of Mauatua's shifts and left with her son.

Fletcher called her back and she took the Mills girl and Teio's children too, promising to deliver them, hoping Quintal wouldn't mind. She might still be home before him, she called as she hurried out.

Mauatua heard only conflict through the open door and windows of their house as infuriated mutineers and their resistant or pleading wives returned to the village. She held her sons to her on the floor, creating an enfolding sanctuary of love. With a sigh of defeat Fletcher joined his family. Like any child exhausted beyond understanding he lowered his head onto her lap between those of his sons, and closed his eyes.

'Forgive me. I can't help you. I can't stop any of this. This makes me as bad as any of them.'

She sat straight backed for many hours, until the tropical night came, bringing moonlight and soft scents that dissolved the smell of blood in her nostrils. Once, out loud, she begged time to stand still as her husband and sons slept on her lap. If she moved she would acknowledge the present and thus invite in the future, and the future terrified her.

She understood isolation for the first time, never before imagining she could feel so alone surrounded by those she loved.

Fletcher was the first to stir. The moon's brilliance cruelly showed his fragility for he at once began to tremble. But she knew the time was past for unbound sympathy. She wanted a clearer picture of what might become of her and her sons, whatever that might be.

'Will you ever be happy here?' she asked him, her voice low, unashamed to reveal her fears.

He lifted his head a little and turned to her and opened his eyes, but nothing changed in the sad light there. When he bowed his head back into her lap she was certain she felt the last of Fletcher's willpower ebbing from him. Later, she heard Fletcher mention Bligh again, but he could have been dreaming.

'This is not why we burned the ship,' Jenny said, her feet and fingers tattooing constant patterns of frustration as she watched Mauatua put a dressing onto Tevarua's ear. None of the other women at the pool added more than a disappointed murmur but they all turned to Mauatua. She spread her hands.

'I am only one voice,' she said. 'Tell me your stories.'

Unexpectedly, Tevarua complained first. 'We dig in the gardens when that is men's work, we fish, we climb cliffs for eggs, we thatch and repair thatch – and we have children. I have never known what it is to be loved by Quintal. It is, well, it has to be a sort of rape or he can't.'

Others were not confident enough to admit they shared this experience, but Mauatua did not need them to voice it.

Jenny supported Tevarua. 'Martin is a rough man but I am not beaten or raped. I am cut by his tongue. He complains about everything I do, everything I cook or make or put somewhere is wrong and used to make me less of a woman.'

There was a sense Jenny might be exaggerating, for she was expected always to have an ache or pain. Then she told of her worst injury.

'He speaks more kindly to cats than to me.' She sobbed, the first time they had seen or heard this. 'He calls for the cat when he comes in, for the cat. And talks to her, the cat, before he has even looked to see if I am alive or dead.'

Mauatua listened silently and inside her head a faint idea became stronger and louder. She was careful to keep her voice calm and thoughtful.

'Why tell my ears things they know?'

She saw the invitation behind her simple words strike and the women in the pool think more deeply.

'My ears are anxious to hear you, but only to hear what I do not know, or have not thought.'

There was a very long pause, solemn with expectation and fear. She recognised many eyes alight with sparks of revolt. When the most forthcoming women spoke, they took their cue from her and there was formality in their speeches. They knew they were speaking of portentous subjects in a clandestine way.

Once only men would have argued such serious matters, speaking secretly on a marae and protected by spells and spirits.

Some looked over their shoulders but for most women almost four years on Pitcairn had allowed their ears to forget old beliefs that bushes and trees were the voices and the ears of gods and spirits. Some dared to believe there were none there anyway.

'*Vahine*, the question is simple. Are we unhappy to be on Pitcairn – or unhappy with the men on Pitcairn? This is what we should discuss.'

'That is wise and just. What sort of woman would choose to live as we once lived, suffering like our mothers and their mothers before them.'

'Your thinking is wise and correct. Is this island still a place we can be the women we might be? And when might this be? I seek your views.'

'It can't. Not with these men.'

'Our sons could make Pitcairn a place for women, for future women.'

Mauatua steered the women closer to the course she wanted them to take. 'We must not talk only about the future. For there to be a future these days have first to be correct. Today *and* tomorrow.

'If Pitcairn's sons are not brought into a safe and settled world they will learn the mistakes of their fathers, just as it was on Tahiti. How could that make our sons better men than their fathers?'

She waited for another woman to take up her argument, but none did.

'If you feel there is a problem, perhaps there is but one question,' she went on. 'Forgive me if my tongue takes the place of yours. I say this only to assist the paths of your minds, of all our minds. Perhaps the question we should ask is this. This is my suggestion, if you will forgive me.

'What will we do about it?'

When no-one answered, Teio started a new thread.

'*Vahine*, we have not spoken of our daughters. We also have the burden of ensuring they are happier than us. My daughter Sully and those who come after her must have husbands who are better men than our husbands.'

'*Auuee!* My daughter must not have a husband like I do.' Vahineatua, mother of Betsy Mills, supported Teio.

Mauatua sensed the women becoming keener to join the journey she was opening before them. 'But who will teach our sons to be these better men, better husbands for our daughters?'

'With men like these, there is no knowing what the future of Pitcairn will be for our children.'

'This is a truth we all must accept, heavy though it is.'

'That is also wise and just. Yet, there is another troubling fact our minds and tongues must consider. Without these men we would have no daughters. Or sons.'

'As is the case with most of us, and after so much time.'

The absolute silence that followed told Mauatua the time was ripe for her to ask what no woman in Pitcairn had dared to offer.

'Forgive me if what I ask offends. Please correct my mind if it is in error. It begs me to ask if fears for their safety are why Pitcairn has so few children. It is almost four years and we are ten women.

'Show me your hands if you do not want to speak. There is no shame in wishing to protect your unborn children.'

Most women in the pool kept their eyes down but put up their hand. She felt her guts churn and fought to keep her face unmoved. Her suspicions were correct.

Yet without children there would be no future here. Fletcher's sacrifices and struggles would be for nothing. Her resolve strengthened, but the idea had to come from the women, not her.

She softened her body, making herself look less tall, less like a chief demanding obedience. She waited, wanting all that had proceeded to spawn and force the women to the conclusion she believed they wanted as much as she. Jenny caught her eye. Mauatua encouraged her with a discreet blink.

'Perhaps there is another question we should ask?' Jenny suggested.

'*Vahine*, that is wisely said and just.' Mauatua supported her before anyone else might. 'I believe I know the question that will stop this talking. I will say it for us all. It would be only wise and proper and just for us to ask it. This is the question I believe we should ask.

'If we are to protect our sons and daughters, to give them a better example of what men should be, what will we do about the men presently on this island?'

Jenny understood what she was implying. 'Forgive my mind. It is slow and has been much exercised today. Do you suggest we do something, something well, permanent about certain of these men, or about all men?'

Mauatua took a deep breath of resolution and put into the women's ears the pledge that many suspected but that none had heard.

'Here is what I believe. *No te ho'e vahine tei hina'aro mau i te ora, i ni'a i te ho'e fenua api, 'aita e 'ohipa faufa'a 'ore.* On an island without a history, there is nothing a woman might not have to do to survive.'

She raised her hand as slowly as the shadow of a cloud drifting over the island. Silently, other women joined her.

When ten arms were raised, Mauatua knew the time had come to honour her pact with the island. This time she was supported by the sisterhood that first swore to act together under the Southern Cross. This generated a calmness so rooted in certain strength she straightened her back again and relit fire in her eyes. As she did, she felt the walls of her womb kicked furiously.

She made herself yet another promise, a vow her anxious third child would be born into a safer world.

There was less than a month to achieve this.

CHAPTER 50

Fletcher couldn't say when he first knew. Facts were more important than stuff like that. Someone, he forgot who, whispered the secret into his ear. Bligh had survived and so Bligh was coming to Pitcairn. Bligh would take him back to Britain.

On their voyage back to Britain Fletcher could cajole and flatter him. They would share the blame for the mutiny. Fletcher knew he would be hanged, there was no defence. But it was fair Bligh shared some of the blame and that the Lords of the Admiralty saw and heard this. It was the law they should hear both sides and whatever the law said was what Bligh always did, not a word more or less. Bligh would have to defend himself. That way, the truth would be known.

Whenever his black moods lifted a little, the thought his commander would be on Pitcairn energised Fletcher and he seemed to be everywhere, totally in command once more. He dealt powerfully with men who disobeyed him or abused their women or bullied children, reminding them they were sailors in His Majesty's Navy. Things would go better for them if all was ship-shape, including their relations with their wives.

He didn't tell them who was expected on the island. He wanted Bligh to see he could command a ship without insults and prejudice.

The last thing he did before leaving his house and the first thing he did on returning was to straighten, tidy, dust or polish. Ship-shape, ship-shape he kept saying. Pitcairn was now a ship to him and all who lived here were its company.

BOUNTY's chronometer was polished and wound and his nautical compasses and telescopes and sextants were neatly displayed high above Bligh's many books, so no accident could befall them.

He became passionate about the state of his garden. There was confusion in his mind about how his previous ship had carried a garden inside a cabin for which he had responsibility. That ship had burned if he remembered correctly. With hard work his new ship's gardens would be just as neat and flourishing as the old ones.

Mauatua humoured Fletcher until she found he was less than honest about the attention he gave to his sons when she left them in his care. Once she hid as he berated them for being half native. He told the boys he would be ashamed to present them to Bligh, especially the crippled one.

There was no point taxing Fletcher on this, although it was the most difficult hardship of all to conceal. She kept her sons closer and they slept with her. Fletcher had turned out an old hammock and slept in that.

Only two of Fletcher's shipmates spoke to Mauatua about him. Adams stood outside, not wanting to intrude. He wanted her to know he would help protect her children if anything happened to Fletcher.

'Won't that depend on how much rum you've drunk?' Adams hung his head and then shuffled away.

Ned had something different to say. He spoke about his life and the constant confusion of having family of different colours. He said he would watch very carefully that none of Pitcairn's children ever fought the same battles. Mauatua reminded him no Pitcairn child would face such battles for all would have white fathers and Ma'ohi mothers.

'Where do the Ma'ohi men fit in with that, the black men?' Ned asked. 'I thought you'd want lots of black children, to grow up and work for us.'

'What, as slaves? What would you call the mothers of these slaves?'

Before Ned could defend his thought Fletcher returned.

'Better smarten up, Ned,' he said flicking his hand through Ned's untidy shoulder-length hair. 'Not long now. C'mon lads. Ship-shape, ship-shape. Pick these things up or it'll be the lash.' He stepped over his sons on the floor and went into the second room, calling, 'You too, cripple.'

Mauatua was distraught that Ned had seen Fletcher's madness but said and did nothing until Fletcher returned and his face crumpled into a rage.

'What did I say, cripple?' He kicked Charles and then Thursday hard enough to send them across the room and into the wall. Mauatua was there almost as fast and huddled herself between her sons and their father. Fletcher stood over them.

'That won't always work, Mauatua. Ship-shape is the way things must be. I will not be shamed by your native children or by you.'

He sat at the table and peered about, as though expecting food to be delivered. He pointed at her belly.

'We'll not be needing that one. Get rid of it. Sooner the better don't you think? Tidier all round.' And then he turned to his right. 'Now Captain Bligh, you were saying . . .'

Fletcher woke early. It was more than half way through September and the sun was already warmer as the southern summer came closer. It was the perfect time to be digging and planting. It had been correct to take his hammock to the gardens and sleep there. Someone had to set an example.

By the time the sun rose he worked furiously in an uncleared patch. He was angry he had not noticed its untidiness before. This was exactly the detail Bligh would see at once. With his commander due any day there was not a minute to be spared. A new taro patch would do the job.

He was determined Bligh would not find a single thing to criticise aboard his new ship. As long as he didn't see him dressed like this, bare footed and with only tapa cloth around his buttocks, like a black. What if he landed today? Better get the garden dug quickly.

It must have been the middle of the morning when Mauatua called him. She carried an eye-shade and a drinking coconut. As well she might, he thought, anything to deflect attention from her coloured children and what was the name of the fellow who played the nose flute, Niau that was it. He was with her. Handsome, as they said, but not the sort you wanted on a ship if what they said was true.

It was right to get rid of the older man they said was his lover. Tararo, that was the one, supposed to be a chief or something. No more competition from him now. Imagine, a native who thought he should be chief of an island rather than a white man.

Mauatua and Niau each held a naked boy and stood some way from him. He was certain he saw fear in their eyes. He laughed loudly. Fear, that would be right. Everyone on this ship feared hard work except him. Still, a cold drink. He put out his hand for it.

Mauatua gave the coconut to the older boy. Fletcher turned away. The boy didn't understand he was not wanted. He stumbled over the rough diggings and because Fletcher kept his hands clasped put the coconut at his feet. Fletcher picked up the coconut but pushed the boy away every time he irritated him by holding on to his leg or reaching for his hands.

The woman, who ever she was, ran up and grabbed the boy into her arms. About time, Fletcher thought. No idea of discipline.

'Fletcher, Niau wants to be nice, to do something nice for you.'

Outraged, Fletcher hurled the coconut at Niau.

'I don't do that dirty stuff.' Stupid woman. How could she think he would want to, but he wasn't given much time to put her right, because she shouted at him again.

'Don't say that, Fletcher. Niau has offered to help with your new garden. He knows you want it finished quickly.' Then the young man called to him.

'And, the boys, the boys from The Edge want to give everyone a feast. We'll shoot one of the wild pigs, Fletcher.'

'Mr Christian to you. I don't want your kind of hands in my soil. Go away, get off my land.'

When even black boys called him by his first name, what sort of ship-shape was that? And why did everyone shout at him? Once he saw the black had left, Fletcher turned to the woman. What was her name? It didn't matter. Doing nothing useful, just holding on to the two boys, both as bare-skinned as the day they were born.

But what else could you expect from natives?

He jabbed at her stomach with the spade in his hand. The blade just missed her clinging children. She fell back, landing heavily on the newly dug soil and brought the boys down with her.

He had to keep his advantage. There was only black or white with Bligh and he had to be just as determined. He straddled her putting the blade onto her swollen stomach and pressing so hard the woman seemed to have trouble breathing. Well, that might make her listen to sense. If she could hear anything above the horrific noise of those brats.

He'd have to shout, too.

'I've told you. No more cripples.'

The woman's eyes looked wildly about her but no-one came. Just as well. No one to contradict him. There'd been too much of that to make a happy ship. He jabbed the spade a couple more times, beating time to what he was saying.

'You know how to fix these things. All you women can do it.'

He pushed the spade deep enough for the woman to cry out. Good, she finally got the message.

But there was no need for those boys to be carrying on. He tripped and pushed them until both were face down in the earth again. He smiled. That's the way to keep their mouths quiet, full of dirt.

Well, he decided, can't stand here giving orders. He turned away from the woman and children and went back to digging. He'd have to dig faster now, to catch up. Blast them.

The woman held her stomach as though frightened her new cripple would fall out of it. Be a simple solution that would, but she was slow about it. He would make her get on with things.

If no-one followed orders, where would his ship be?

'Tell me when you've done it. I'll be here. Bligh knows where to find me, too. We'll both know if you have disobeyed orders.'

He didn't turn to her but spoke as he dug, each few words grunted between the sounds of his efforts.

'Discipline and ship-shape. Ha! You'll know about that when Bligh gets here.' From the corner of his eye he saw the woman use a bush finally to pull herself up. She and the children watched with curious limp mouths and crinkled eyes, but said nothing.

Waiting for me to dismiss them he supposed. Right, bit of order at last. He shoved the spade deep into the red earth and slapped his stomach.

'Woman's work that sort of thing. But don't think I couldn't do it.'

He showed them what he meant by miming a cutlass stroke across his midriff. 'See? Easy.'

He repeated the action twice, so there could be no doubt.

'And then, no more cripples for Bligh to see.'

The thought of Bligh immediately turned his mind back to his responsibilities. He dug furiously. He didn't stop although blinded by sweat. Who needed to see to dig? When he finished turning the soil for another row he swiped his eyes clean.

The woman and her children had been joined by others at the far end of the gardens. The group looked very strange to him, standing in a huddle and holding each other. Had they never seen a man working properly before? Probably hadn't.

He needed to be certain the native woman understood her orders before he went back to his demonstration of how things could be ship-shape in a garden. Better if others knew them, too.

'I'll sort it out if you don't,' he promised.

He marked his naked torso twice with the edge of his spade. Pitcairn's soil and his sweat smeared into a muddy red cross across his abdomen.

'No more cripples!'

CHAPTER 51

September 20th 1793, Pitcairn Island

The women and children sped out of the village early, lying that it was time to collect wild crops from the other side of the island. Only Mauatua and her children remained. She stood by her door, listening through the slight opening she allowed.

'Uncle Ned will be here soon.' Thursday waved at her and put an arm around his brother Charles and then their heads were once more together as they chattered in their own language.

She fretted until she heard a low whistle and then went outside to Niau and Teimua. The men proudly showed the two muskets they had stolen.

The white men were in their fields early this time of the year. The Ma'ohi had hidden even earlier so they weren't forced into the gardens by any of them.

The two men were nervous, jigging and encouraging each other with slaps and punches. She had seen this before when men prepared for battle. They heard footsteps and stood in a protecting triangle.

It was Ned Young at last. She waved him into the house.

Soon afterwards Titahiti ran up. He waved a musket high above his head and was about to whoop, when Mauatua silenced him.

'Any problems?'

'None,' Titahiti boasted. 'I told Martin we boys wanted to give the white men a treat, to say sorry for all the bad things we done in the past.' The men giggled at this unlikelihood.

'So, he thinks you are shooting a pig?' Mauatua was tempted to compare their real targets but the time for mockery was well past.

'Have you decided?' The three men nodded in unison.

'Williams,' said Niau. 'He was the first *popa'a* to treat one of our women like a dog.'

Teimua and Titahiti picked young branches and pushed them into their hair to help camouflage their movements. Mauatua kept Niau back. In case there is a problem, she confided.

A single shot shredded Pitcairn's shroud of silence. She listened for what sounds followed in its echoes. There were none, so none of the other mutineers was suspicious.

The three men came back, fighting to contain their excitement.

'It was so easy, just one shot. Why didn't we do it before?'

Manarii, the fourth man from The Edge, had been collected before dawn by Mills, they said, but he'd not be safe now a white man was dead.

'We'll say you just shot a pig and ask if he can help you carry it,' Mauatua suggested. 'Only two of you go, the third better stay hidden in the bush with a musket.'

The men made much of adding camouflage to Niau's head, but then Mauatua thought better of the plan. To ensure their success, she would accompany them. They took the leaves from their heads, twice asking Mauatua if she was sure they should.

She walked into Mills' garden with Niau and Titahiti. Teimua kept out of sight. McCoy watched Manarii working, slowly running a thick knotted rope through his fist. Mills had little interest in either.

'Nice morning, Mills.'

Manarii looked up at her voice and McCoy jumped to his feet and threatened him with the rope.

'No need for that McCoy,' she said. 'I've got a better job he'll do in a hurry. A couple of the boys shot one of the wild pigs – you hear the noise? They need Manarii to help them carry it back.

'Big *pua'a* feed tonight, eh boys?'

Mills and McCoy grinned at one another. McCoy winked and said, 'Tell you what, you tell Mr Christian to bring along some of that rum he hides away, and you can have Manarii as long as you like. That a deal?'

'You'll have no worries about rum tonight,' she said. 'I promise you.'

McCoy moved swiftly and swiped Manarii's buttocks hard with the rope. 'Go on y'black bastard. As long as you're working for us somehow, I don't care what you bloody well do. On your way.'

He aimed another blow but Manarii jumped fast enough to avoid it. She moved swiftly between the men and steered Manarii out of the garden.

'Now come on, before someone finds Williams,' she warned.

The four men jogged. Mauatua could barely keep up. Since Fletcher had bruised her with the spade, the child within her had been restless, forever kicking and bucking.

Revenge, she thought, the child wants to get out and wreak revenge.

She promised her baby that when it was born there would be no need for revenge on Pitcairn Island.

The next garden the men stopped at was Fletcher's. They hadn't asked her and she couldn't shout without alarming other men. She heard Fletcher's voice, plaintive and apologetic.

'Captain, Captain Bligh, is that you?'

As she reached the garden, his hands supported his waist and he bent back to stretch his spine. He was burning the weeds and undergrowth he had slashed on previous days.

The smoke stung her eyes and she had to blink continuously to clear them. How strong he looks she thought, admiring the play of muscle down his back. Before she could say a word to the others two muskets exploded.

His bruised and mangled flesh splattered as blood erupted from his naked back like the bursting of carbuncles.

The force of the balls tumbled him forward and after a few faltering steps, he fell into his freshly turned soil. He called once, a long questioning howl that faded like a cry into a gale.

She stumbled, too, swooning because she couldn't absorb what she had seen. Should she have stopped them? Could she have? Did her admiration for his body condemn Fletcher? The smoke from his fire twisted and fell to the ground searching for a breeze and she lost sight of him.

'He'll be dead, won't he?' she asked, hopelessly adrift in a whirlpool of unfamiliar emotions and feelings.

'We'll make sure.'

'No, no. Leave him, please.' As she pleaded she recognised her child had chosen to come into the world that day.

She bit her lip at the first real contraction but fought for a semblance of normality, trying to steer a path for her mind between the shock of her shot husband and her insistent womb.

The men chose McCoy as their next victim. Manarii wanted revenge for the stinging mark on his buttocks and for all the others that preceded it. Niau supported Mauatua for she would not be left behind, but his thought for Mauatua did not include missing any of the promised carnage.

He pulled her along at an awkward trot. She turned her head but smoke veiled what they had last done. When they caught up, Niau was chosen to warn McCoy that the other Ma'ohi men were in his house and stealing. She was astonished how quickly McCoy moved when he was threatened.

It wasn't far to McCoy's house from Mills' garden. McCoy made the final approach quietly, believing he was unexpected. He carefully chose from the axe handles by his door. His hesitations gave Mauatua and Niau enough time to get close and watch McCoy burst into his house.

Two shots from inside broke the island's silence but then McCoy ran out, unharmed. Titahiti bounded after him and they fought. The Tubuaian was bigger than McCoy, but terror gave the smaller man super powers and Titahiti was thrown into the muck of a pig pen.

McCoy ran off into the bush, gibbering with fright.

'He's going back to Mills. Quick,' Manarii warned, finally coming out of the house. Before they left, the men each picked up hatchets and hand-whittled axe handles McCoy had lying about his yard.

'Have to be sure, Mauatua,' Teimua grinned.

Suddenly she felt vulnerable, unattached when she had expected to feel grounded and certain. Where should she be? Was her place with Fletcher, in case he was still living, or was her contract with the island and its children more important than him?

Before the men hunted down Mills, she made them swear they would report back to her before going after another white man and then waited with Niau in the bushes near McCoy's house.

Niau was frustrated at not being part of the bloodletting. He compensated by making much of protecting her, forever starting at imagined sounds, ducking, bobbing, and whistling through closed teeth and taut lips. His free hand worked ceaselessly inside his loin cloth, too. Why not, she thought, blood-letting and sex were the only highpoints of most men's life.

In the sun-heated bush, the citric freshness of Niau's youthful perspiration reminded her of Tararo's attack, and of the instant she was excited by his scents. She'd not been this close to a Ma'ohi man since. She had no doubt she could succumb in some way to the youth, with no concern for her unborn child. The child's kick startled her back to sense.

How dare she criticise the men for their excitements. How easily she too descended to life's rawest levels when bloodlust and revenge and fright were about and busy.

They heard crashing. Someone was running through the bush, ignoring the paths. How many? Which way were they headed?

Mauatua made Niau put up his musket and stood with her back to his so they would not be surprised.

McCoy was back where he began and insane with fear, seeing and hearing nothing. When he collided at speed with another desperate runner the impact hurled both men on to their backs. They yelled hoarsely to scare the other, both disoriented and blinded by fear. They flipped into a crouch barely daring to open their eyes, each with an arm over his head and ready to fight. Their wild eyes recognised the other before their fists landed. Their tongues were thick and dry in their mouths and they stumbled over their words.

'They're killing us, Matt,' McCoy said. 'I seen Mills dead.'

'And Mr Christian. Flat on his face,' Quintal told him

Mauatua stopped Niau from firing. With only one musket they were hardly safe against two such fear-deranged men. Hadn't two muskets just misfired at close range in McCoy's house?

Niau dropped the musket and pulled aside his loin cloth to roll his erection back and forth against his thigh. She looked away but her body tensed and an unrecognised sensation mounted inside her.

'We'd better get out of here,' Quintal said.

'You got a musket or pistol?' asked McCoy.

'No, and I ain't risking getting one, neither.'

'C'mon. There's a bit of a cave I know. Been working on something.'

More running men were coming. Quintal and McCoy fled as though pursued by every denizen of hell. Breathless with excitement the posse returned, with Teimua bragging.

'We got Mills, two shots. And then we made sure.'

Manarii swung a hatchet above his head. Its gruesome cargo of thickening blood and matted hair and bone splinters was so hefty gobbets still flew off as he rehearsed his triumph.

'Chopped his head off. One, two, three. And off.' He looked at the others, his face serious. 'We think he's dead.'

The men's laughter was too loud, too uninhibited. Mauatua raised her voice, for the first time recognizing the danger she could be in from these men. 'But Quintal and McCoy have escaped and they're the worst.'

The men hardly noticed she had spoken. She cursed herself for her mistake. She should never have let these men choose who they wanted to kill first but that had been the bargain.

'You'll have to be quieter and more careful or it will be you who has no head,' she counselled.

'Not us. Not now. Our blood is up and that makes our senses keener.' Their chests heaved and their eyes glittered. She thought they were seeing what they had done rather than what was in front of them. Niau leant over, his hand still working.

'This is why we seek war and battle,' he confided. 'For those hours you feel like a god.'

Without a word more they ran. In minutes they were back and telling her Martin was dead. Once again their aim was bad and so they battered him with their hatchets and axe handles.

'But he is dead, that's for sure.'

They held up their gore-crusted weapons. The sun reflected from Martin's clotting blood on their hands and forearms.

Titahiti pointed as Niau ejaculated without touching himself, his teeth grinding and his eyes narrowed in ecstasy. That made them laugh more.

She was grateful. It took the focus from her. Her head was pounding, as though she were in the womb with her kicking child.

Birth had always been something calm for her, a time of fragrant ferns and sweet scents and gentle massage. Now she was surrounded by blood spattered men, one of them stinking of a pig pen and all elated by the ending of life rather than its beginning.

This was not what she had promised her child.

She couldn't regain control of her tensed body. Her mind's eye would not clear. It saw only blackening blood and assaulted human flesh and the obscene eruptions on Fletcher's back.

Niau's rapture at the bloody weapons and limbs shattered her last constraints of decency and privacy.

After panting quickly, she held her breath as long as she could until with one exquisite shuddering sensation she at last understood what her body had been screaming to tell her. She released a flood of birth water.

Pitcairn's red soil sucked it down as greedily as Fletcher's blood.

CHAPTER 52

Had she seen blood running from his wounds before the smoke descended? Didn't running blood mean Fletcher was still alive then, might still be alive now? There were things she should do, or could do if he was alive, but how could she make such decisions?

Every time she tried to think ahead her body rebelled and fought to bring her back to the moment, arguing to bring her baby into the day. She couldn't. She had promised. The world wasn't ready.

Pleading the urgent murder of Brown, the men left her. Ma'ohi men were mortally afraid of the powerful *tapu* around birth and none of Pitcairn's had grown less pious.

She could think in the silence this brought. She thought she had an hour at least, probably more. If only the men would kill Quintal and McCoy. Instead, they were back and laughing at the joke they played on Brown.

He had deserved more than a simple death for the torment he wreaked. He never appreciated the importance gardens had for Ma'ohi men. When he kicked and uprooted, chopped or cut down or burned, he wounded their pride more painfully than when other men marked their body.

Titahiti had gone on ahead to warn Brown. He said he would only pretend to shoot him and then he must lie down and play at being dead and promised to tell him when it was safe. Brown fell convincingly, turning onto his front so the supposed wound could not be seen.

Titahiti joined the others to watch from the bush and it wasn't long before Brown moved his head to make it more comfortable. They charged out of the bush yelling Brown's hated phrase.

'That's not the way to do it!' He was stoned and clubbed to death, until his brains were indistinguishable from the ruddy earth.

The last man would be Adams. Laughing like innocent children they ran out of sight and on to his house. They approached stealthily and found him just as cautious, hoping to escape with a basket of food. They fired and a musket ball went through his shoulder and out through his throat.

Adams fell gargling blood but fought to ward off the musket butts battering him. One blow snapped a finger but he got up, terror overtaking the handicap of his girth. Titahiti held another musket to his head. It too misfired. In the surprise Adams escaped but soon fell heavily again.

She was close enough to see everything but dared not call out or be seen by Adams. Titahiti saw her and with a comic slap to his face remembered what had been agreed the night before. She said they were supposed to save Adams.

Manarii and Teimua helped Adams up, dragged him her house and then ran back. 'Now,' she said, 'go back to The Edge. Stay there until tomorrow. No *pua'a* tonight. Tomorrow.'

Niau looked anxious for her but the companionship of his blooded companions had a more potent pull. The four men ran, finally whooping and leaping, slapping and jumping together in hugs, celebrating the way they had wanted to do all morning.

She leaned against a tree, hoping to calm the urgency of her contractions. If she sat she'd never get up and no baby of hers would be born like a feral cub.

The sun had barely moved further up into the sky but in that short journey she had rewritten the future for Pitcairn's children.

She'd kept her promise and her new baby would be safe.

Titahiti came back. They thought they'd seen Fletcher move as they passed his gardens. So they had chopped into his neck and shoulders.

'He'll be dead now,' he laughed. He leaped into the air with a cry of victory and then bounded and jumped back to his companions.

She wouldn't look into the smoke clouds in their garden but staggered with her arms under her belly and her eyes straight ahead until she turned into the path to her house. She was surprised to see Jenny tending to Adams on the ground.

The women had been too frightened to be outside when they heard the shots and voted to hurry back to her house. Ned rushed to her but she refused to tell him a thing. Just keep them here, all of them, until I come back again, she insisted.

'See, I am safe, Mrs Christian,' Adams called to her. 'Ned says he's going to teach Pitcairn's children to read and write. I'm having some of that, too.' The pain and shock of his injuries suddenly grabbed him. The low laugh he started became a pleading groan. His cry brought back the image of Fletcher's raped back.

Her breath came in shallow anxious pants as she retrieved her medicine bag and then confided in Thursday. She told him she had a very big job for him, a job only her oldest boy could do. Would he be able to do that, she asked.

Jenny took her hand. 'The baby, is it coming?'

'False alarms, that's all.'

Jenny sniffed and pointed at her feet where the dust on them had clearly been splashed. 'No secrets from you, *vahine*. I'll call if I need you. We'll be in the gardens somewhere.'

She couldn't see Fletcher. Her heart seized. The cleared patch was airless and so the thick yellow smoke, choking with the smoulder of half-dried vegetation, lazed close to the ground. She ran in heavy swaying steps, dragging Thursday to the spot she thought Fletcher had fallen.

She bent as far as her unborn baby would allow and waved away enough smoke for her stinging eyes to find a wide slick, crusted with blood-soaked soil.

Had he dragged himself away or did the four men pull him somewhere else, perhaps onto the fire? She retched painfully and was grateful she had eaten nothing that morning.

Those next footsteps were the hardest she ever took, wanting both to run to Fletcher and to escape from what she might find.

Thursday saw him through the smoke first. He tried to flee but she gripped him. Ignoring the boy's whimpering, she leaned on his shoulder and held a bush for extra support as she tipped forward to look at Fletcher.

He had pulled himself into some shade beside the pool in their garden and was lying on his side, facing them so they could not see the bullet wounds in his back, unlike those in his neck and shoulders. These were flayed by atrocious axe-chops that exposed bones and flesh never meant to be seen by the sun. The depth and tone of his shoulder muscles had saved him from faster death.

He was not moving, but she recognised his wounds showed the colour only life could give. His breathing was irregular and shallow. Its sporadic bubbling sounds turned her stomach. But Fletcher was alive and her mission might be possible after all.

Thursday was traumatised, as breathless as his father, but she had to keep him here. It would be to his ultimate advantage.

She had to half fall and then roll on one thigh and hip so she could sit by Fletcher. Just once she cried out, cursing and then begging the child within her to be still. Thursday kneeled beside her, swaying ceaselessly from side to side and mewling into the hands he clamped over his face.

Fletcher's face was uninjured. For the first time in weeks he was neither drenched in sweat from work nor from his affliction. He was sun darkened from the years on Pitcairn, but had always looked blacker than her. She never minded this and now her wonderful brave, strong, ambitious Fletcher was there for her eyes to feast on once more.

It was better he was unlikely to speak. She could forget the confused Fletcher of the last months and instead remember him on the sands of Matavai, when he was so virile and all seemed possible for them both.

Was it really only four years ago? Against her instincts she thanked whatever heavenly deity there might be that she could be with him.

She took water from the pool to wipe his face clean, tracing the lines of his strong nose and eyebrows and the cushions of his beautiful lips hidden beneath his long moustache and beard. She untangled and combed these and then cleaned his ears of blood and tidied back his hair, all the time murmuring to him in Tahitian. She knew he understood.

Didn't they say hearing was the last sense that left you, so the last thing you knew of life might be words of love?

Her conscience suddenly arrested her with an awful rehearsal of the litany of blame she knew she'd hear the rest of her life. She had no doubt. She had done the right thing. If she could have told Fletcher she would.

Then she realised where her conscience was leading her and that this is what she must do. So she revealed to Fletcher all that had sped back and forth through her mind and the events that brought the two of them to this, a few days before his thirtieth year would begin.

Thursday's hands dropped from his face as he heard what had been done for his sake.

When she had said all she had to say, she felt he was calmer too. His vestigial warmth revived the essentials of the oil she rubbed onto his brow and temples. Their tropical intensity had always soothed him. Their opulence wove a cocoon about the two of them again, the protective bower where they once discovered the peaks of sensual adventuring. A smile of sweet remembrance came to her, and tears for their lost joy finally fell.

Had he really once thought of leaving her? Her rancour hadn't lasted long. It dissolved when he said he felt he had kept his most important promise to her, to find her a safe place to be a new sort of woman. If that was all there was to be of them, it was infinitely more than most women ever had from a man.

Mauatua struggled to make his right shoulder more comfortable, so he was lying on the front of it. That is how he slept, what he preferred. This turned his back further towards them, making his wounds more obvious but Thursday didn't seem to notice.

She briefly left Fletcher in the care of his son and found the eye shade he had worn. Thursday waved it to keep smoke from his father's face.

She brushed away the remainders of the threatening muddy cross from what she could see of his abdomen and then she thought of something else she should do for him. She pulled away his loin cloth and massaged oil into his tattoo.

How staunch and confident it was, leaping and swooping over the buttocks he so liked to be admired. She traced each soot-bruised arch over his loins remembering what each had promised him.

And hadn't most of it been true?

He had protected her and all those others, as many as 50 sometimes, for as long as they needed. He kept them safe on sea and land and had then brought them to this invisible place. Giving light and lustre to his tattoo brought Fletcher's energy and optimism back to her.

Toa, warrior, she whispered, *toa,* just as she had when they first admired the completed tattoo.

Thursday judged there was no risk to him in this place. He reached out to trace the tattoo. She quietly told him what each symbol meant. Thursday would never be marked like that but knowing the significance of his father's images might embolden him one day.

She sat quietly with her son, he with his head against her. He put one of Fletcher's hands onto the swollen hiding place of the new baby and then slipped his into his father's other palm. He whispered to his mother, surprised to be able to tell her it was warm and dry.

When her head once fell forward, scorching tears as big and luminous as Tahitian pearls fell onto Fletcher's eyelids. One eye opened. She saw life lingering, in a soft, lucent point far, far further away than any star. She smiled and raised a fist of triumph for him to see. As more tears splashed, his other eye opened. Did he have tears? She couldn't tell, but she thought of the comfort it must be for his eyes to be soothed and so she wept them for Fletcher. Her tears fell onto his lashes with a soft, even rhythm.

Like the tick of his time keeper, each drop signalled the death of another instant in this world and the inevitable arrival of the last.

Her contractions became faster and more intense as Fletcher's breath slowed and became fainter. A sudden fiercer demand for release made her cry out. Fletcher's eyes snapped shut as if it had been his pain.

It was time for them both.

Fighting her body's spasms she balanced splay-legged across him, awkwardly tilted forward by the weight and movements of the fretting baby. She turned his face to the sky. Then she held Thursday by his armpits and put his face close to his father's.

Uncomprehending, he screamed again and again, primeval sounds of fear she'd hoped no child of hers would know.

What she would soon do was against everything that had brought her to Pitcairn. But what if it were true? At the instant she thought Fletcher's last gurgling breath was leaving his body she pushed Thursday's open mouth onto his father's, smothering his cries.

'*Ha'u!* Breathe in,' she urged. 'Take daddy's breath in. All of it. *Ha'u, ha'u!*' Then she convulsed, coughing with smoke in her throat. She lost her balance and let Thursday drop.

When Jenny at last appeared through the pungent clouds in search of them, Thursday was unconscious on his father's chest. Beside them Mauatua was suckling Fletcher Christian's daughter.

'Take them home,' she entreated her. 'Take them away from this.'

CHAPTER 53

She stayed in her bed for a week, exhausted in every way, and treating Thursday with the same care she gave her new daughter, suckling him, too, so both children wallowed in her love. She had lost Tamahere as the price of her determination there was a better way for Ma'ohi women to live. And now Fletcher was dead, too.

Had any woman paid such a price for her children's future?

Charles was two by now. He felt important rather than jealous and happily served whatever errands were asked of him. From the first he rarely relied on swaying from one longer leg to the shorter one but interrupted this to hop to run messages and deliver food. By the end of the first week of his sister's life he earned the nickname he carried the rest of his life, Hoppa. The girl was Mary Ann, as Fletcher wanted.

Ned Young assumed he was next in command as the only other officer from BOUNTY and for the moment she was comforted by that and flattered him by asking his advice.

'Can you think how to get Quintal and McCoy back into the village, Ned?' she asked. 'Do you think they'll behave better now women outnumber them?'

'Those men will never change, unless they are bullied into it.'

'Then that's what you must do. You've watched them enough to know how to do it.'

'I've found him!' Tevarua danced into Mauatua's bedroom with her news. Quintal and McCoy were hiding in a shallow cave off one of the less used cliff paths to Lookout Point. They were too drunk to talk any sense, even so early in the morning. They were pissing in the cave, too, like animals. The sharp stink had disgusted her.

'I'm sure Matt will behave better now, after what, well, you know.' Tevarua shifted uncomfortably on the bed.

Mauatua shrugged and turned away from her. The Ma'ohi men were more keenly on Mauatua's mind than the cave dwellers.

Four of them with muskets made them a new power on the island especially when only Adams and Ned Young of the four surviving white men lived in the village.

The killers were still highly charged when they came to sit on the floor around her bed. At first she used her *ra'atira* rank to tell them what she wanted. She found that turned against her, forgetting Niau believed he had inherited Tararo's greater status. They told her what they wanted, considering fate had finally turned in their favour. The rewards they wanted for their patience, and as payment for their bloodletting, were simple. They expected to move into the houses of the men they killed and then choose from the widows they'd created.

Niau considered he was Mauatua's only possible husband now Tararo was dead. Titahiti might be a chief's brother but he was only from Tubuai and his kin lines had none of the dignity of those from Raiatea. She said she'd give Niau's offer great thought, reminding him she was more than ten years older than he was. So we must hurry, he insisted, pointing out her age meant less time for them to make many babies.

She sent him away with a laugh, which he took as flirtatious and was soon heard bragging about the village, warning others he would soon be chief of Pitcairn.

One by one the women came to her bed to say they welcomed the company of their countrymen but all agreed that what had been done in the name of their born and unborn children had to be protected.

No woman made a permanent place in her bed for any of the black men. No love was declared, no promises made. None felt instantly unchained or cheered by the deaths. Like Mauatua they had wounds in their minds to heal and they needed to weave new patterns of trust. Mauatua persuaded the Ma'ohi men to continue living at The Edge until the women judged themselves recovered.

There was one point of disagreement. She was told this to her face. Quintal and McCoy were supposed to have been shot first and her role by omission in their survival was not appreciated.

Only Tevarua was happy about this.

The Ma'ohi men didn't help their cause. They bullied convalescent Adams to give them rum and then became aggressive and abusive, determined that as they had muskets and were twice the number of white men in the village they held the balance of power.

She hoped she'd not have to intervene, that all would swiftly settle into a comfortable resolution. Love for her children was all she wanted to contemplate or manage because after the murders she felt emotionally dumb.

Events were too dramatic to ignore. Pitcairn risked becoming the Ma'ohi community Tararo had predicted.

Sense forced confrontation on her, chattering at her with the sort of incessant voices Fletcher complained about.

Did she regret the murders? Did she have a conscience about sending so many to their white God before their time? She didn't think so, not when she held her children close and slept safely with them in the bed Fletcher had built.

But what would the murders mean when Pitcairn was discovered? No ship had been seen for four years and it seemed impossible their luck would last much longer.

The first ship, whatever port or kingdom it came from, might mean the end of Pitcairn Island unless the truth could be hidden.

A ship might bring new men, different white men, who would lighten and dilute memories of the wickedness of Pitcairn's first white men. Except, they might not do either of these if they knew the truth. What if the four Ma'ohi men told visitors the truth? If they explained why they shot the white men she was likely to be dragged off the island and executed, even though all the women had voted in favour.

She couldn't allow her children to see that.

The women around her bed hoped that when the reality and the reasons for the murders sank in, the remaining four Ma'ohi and four white men would pull themselves together.

Reason and reality had no place among Pitcairn's men. The Ma'ohi men fought one another for the rights to this or to that woman. Fuelled by rum and with muskets in their hands they behaved the way they believed was the norm on Pitcairn, the way drunken, armed white men did when frustrated in their wants.

The belief in their superiority created a dangerous sense of unchallenged victory in each of the four Ma'ohi men. Their main objective was to be fathers, and they shouted that about the village. Their impatience was a discomforting partner to their rum and muskets.

She had no choice.

She rose from mourning for Fletcher to continue the bloody path towards making Fenua Maitai a safer world for his children.

CHAPTER 54

The women around the pool said they were more afraid of their enraged countrymen than they'd been of their husbands. Mauatua agreed she should persuade Quintal and McCoy back into the village, so the number of white men equalled those of black.

Ned failed to persuade them and so Adams was sent. He went several times before he found them sober enough to speak. Their answer was chilling. They would not come back to the village until there were no Ma'ohi men.

Adams told the women he'd also discovered the cave's special attraction. McCoy had used his experience at a distillery in Scotland to build a small still, and was successfully producing a spirit by fermenting and distilling the long sugary root of the *ti* plant. He confirmed Tevarua's story that they pissed where they were and ate almost nothing.

Mauatua saw a defining decision looming, as important as voting to burn BOUNTY or the murders. Did they still want Quintal and McCoy dead? If they did, what should they do about the Ma'ohi men? Which were they more afraid about, the white or the black?

The children recognised their mothers' fear and hid from the Ma'ohi men or burst into tears when they saw one. Mauatua found Thursday and Charles scrapping and shouting and when she pulled them apart the boys said they weren't really fighting, just playing at being black men.

She summoned the women to the pool once again but they were too frightened by the fury and determination of the Ma'ohi men to generate proper discussion. Instead, she summed up their situation as she saw it.

'These are our countrymen, and their skills make it easier to live here. But they insist on becoming fathers. My belief is that Ma'ohi children are a future threat we should not allow. Of course, these thoughts are only my suggestions, and not what you must think.'

No-one else spoke and she struggled not to say outright what she wanted to happen. She composed herself to speak without emotion and to present only facts. Her arguments had to be balanced, so none could retract or pretend she didn't understand. Besides, one day they would have to tell others, perhaps even explain to their children.

'White men mean more work for us, for none can do what Ma'ohi can in the fields, or fishing or caring for animals. Our burden will be heavier. And I say nothing about their drinking. But that is today.

'We are ten women, all young enough to have children. *Popa'a* men mean my vision, your vision too I hope, could come true. The more children with white fathers there are, the safer the island will be. The safer these children's future, the more we will be rewarded for all we have done. The more children there are, the more comfortable our old age will be.

'What we cannot do is to vote for some white men and some Ma'ohi, no matter who we like or love. That way our turmoil would never end, our children would never be safe and we might not be – ever.

'Pitcairn's men must be one or the other. Ma'ohi. Or white. This is my view. I have no other.'

Forcing the issue seemed the only way. To reinforce how she wanted them to vote, she created images for the women's mind, for these were always understood better than plain words.

'Once more, *vahine*, we stand balanced on a sharp mountain ridge and must jump into the void of one of the unseen valleys on either side. But we must all jump together.

'We are voting to save the Ma'ohi or to save the *popa'a*. First, who thinks we should save the Ma'ohi men?'

It was agreed she and Jenny or Adams and Young would always be walking about the village armed, so the Ma'ohi knew they were watched.

Two days after the vote Mauatua heard black men arguing furiously, counterclaiming promises they said had been made by Teraura.

Teraura was young and naive, not even 20, and enjoyed such competition for her, but it put her most at risk, made her the most liable to precipitate disorder.

Jenny turned the corner first, just as there was a loud explosion. She fell back onto Mauatua, spattered with blood. When no answering fire came, Mauatua sidled to peek around the corner, hoping there really had been only two men.

Teraura was almost hysterical on the ground. Manarii swayed, drunk of course, the musket in his hands, blue smoke curling from its barrel. Between the two Teimua was dead, his head exploded with the violence of the point blank shot.

'You are an animal,' Mauatua shouted. Manarii was shocked by what he had done and at his discovery by the women. Mauatua coldly judged she had time. She aimed very carefully at his heart.

The charge didn't catch. Manarii came to his senses, turned and fled.

'Follow him' Mauatua commanded 'I want to know where he goes. If the blacks have a secret hideaway, that's where he'll be going. We need to know before they all go there.'

Young didn't get back until after dark. 'You won't believe it.'

He took a long time to regain his breath. The wheezing that had slowly got worse on Pitcairn sometimes seemed almost to stop his lungs working.

'Where did he go? What won't we believe?' Mauatua pleaded.

Ned's whistling gasps were loud enough to mask the spluttering candlenuts. It was hard not to insist he answered anyway. She'd tried that once before but his anxiety made the condition worse and so it took longer to hear what she wanted.

She planted herself before him, desperate to sound sweet and caring. Her patience was close to being exhausted and she was frightened.

Ned looked up pitifully, his eyes wet with, with what? Pain? Fear? Or with some awful truth?

She could have forced Fletcher to tell her, but he wasn't likely to suffocate from her pressure. Ned whispered a single word. She didn't hear it.

'Ned, just once, try just once more and speak up.' She leaned closer.

'Cave, cave,' he huffed out.

'Yes, but which one, where?'

Ned closed his eyes, concentrating on pushing enough breath from his lungs to answer. 'Cave. With Quintal and McCoy.' The effort finally exhausted him. He sank to the floor with his back to the wall.

With Quintal and McCoy? The idea was ludicrous, as though a rat had run to dogs for safety. But Mauatua quickly saw an opportunity.

Here was a chance to share the burden of the island's bloodletting. She'd be safer if more hands than hers were guilty.

Adams was her messenger again, told to separate Quintal and McCoy from Manarii long enough to tell them that if they killed Manarii, the village would kill the other two Ma'ohi men at once.

Next morning Manarii's severed hands wrapped in banana leaf were outside Adams' house. He took them to Mauatua, shielding them with difficulty from her children, who thought he was bringing them a gift.

She now told the women to smile and flirt with Titahiti and Niau, the last two Ma'ohi men, pretending Manarii's murder was deserved for what he had done.

Jenny invited the two to dinner in her house and Mauatua led the other women to join them. They sang and danced to underpin a sense of happy optimism. When Titahiti was drunk and sexually excited, Brown's widow Teatuahitea led him to her bed.

The giggling Niau was persuaded outside by Ned.

Mauatua uncovered an axe she had sharpened and handed it to Teraura who had offered to atone for her earlier silliness with Teimua and Manarii.

They waited until they were certain Titahiti was fully engaged in love-making and then sang and clapped loudly so nothing could be overheard of his passion.

Teraura crept in and it seemed only seconds before she returned saying she'd chopped into Titatihi's neck and split open his head. She was splattered with a second Ma'ohi man's blood but not as badly as Teatuahitea, who had to slide from beneath the hacked man.

Teatuahitea demanded a drink, explaining when she could that she didn't think Teraura would aim well enough to kill Titahiti without also chopping into her. She almost rolled off the bed with Titahiti when she saw the axe strokes coming towards her over his shoulder.

The women wanted to comfort and clean Teraura and Teatuahitea, but Mauatua didn't dare alert Niau and insisted they continue singing and dancing. She went to the door and nodded at Ned.

He was showing Niau the finer points of putting a charge into a musket, so it would always explode reliably.

He stood back and shot Niau at close range.

Quintal and McCoy wouldn't take Adams' word. Gagging and shivering with the horror, Adams carried a basket with the heads and hands of the last two Ma'ohi men to the cave.

He returned flushed and in an unexpectedly high mood.

'I was rewarded. I've tasted McCoy's Pitcairn whisky. It's excellent, my dears. There'll be happy days ahead.'

Mauatua stalked away and into her gardens. She bellowed up at the Southern Cross, demanding to know when Pitcairn's women would get their reward. They had contracted by that constellation to burn BOUNTY and to make this a woman's island that was safe for their children. Yet Pitcairn was still poisoned by men and by their slavery to alcohol.

She filled her hands with Pitcairn's soil and crushed it in her palms as she once again vowed there was nothing she might not do. But what else *could* she do, she cried to the heavens, and when would it end?

As the last of the red earth fell back to the island from her fingers she collapsed to her knees.

What more could there possibly be for her to do?

CHAPTER 55

Quintal and McCoy returned to the village cockier and more brutal because they had survived the massacre. She saw nothing in their eyes but arrogant belief in their superiority and more determination than ever to drag Pitcairn's women down to their level of hygiene and behaviour.

The whisky still was constantly in her mind. She could destroy it, but what would the result be? She listened to the others and reluctantly agreed they would be in more danger of violence and retribution. They remembered how badly the men reacted when they had little or no rum to drink and so the still remained and became the poisonous focus of island life.

She conspired with the others to keep the men busy in a ragged, edgy and unreliable rhythm of gardening and fishing by day and with entertainment and sex at night.

Ned and Adams often drank as much as Quintal and McCoy and sometimes the women joined them but none ever became addicted.

Whenever one of the men was unacceptably disruptive, or a woman could no longer bear the strain of being so constantly on watch for the safety of their child, Mauatua sped the women and children from the village and sometimes they lived apart for months.

She believed in these 'holidays' for Pitcairn's children, so they knew a life other than day after day centred on alcohol-fuelled bullying, confrontation and fear. In many ways life with just four white men was little different from life with nine of them and six Ma'ohi men.

Even so, her essential objective was being reached and her ideal seemed more possible. More babies were being born.

Between 1794 and 1799 12 children were born. Mauatua had three children by Ned Young, who also had four by Toofaiti. Quintal and Tevarua had three more and Adams fathered three daughters by Vahineatua. McCoy produced a single daughter by Teio. Five of the Ma'ohi women never fell pregnant, or decided not to let their babies take their first gulp of Pitcairn's air.

Mauatua wondered how many would have liked children but had been too injured by earlier abortions on Tahiti or aboard BOUNTY.

McCoy's ti-root spirit was as potent as Navy rum but more poisonous. Even so, it took five more agonising years for McCoy to addle his brain and then, maddened by its toxins, he flung himself off a cliff.

And so did Tevarua.

Tevarua's death was a mystery. Mauatua was never sure if she threw herself from the cliff, finally driven beyond tolerance of Quintal, or if he had pushed her. Quintal insisted she fell gathering birds' eggs when she was drunk. His foul mouth was dismissive, saying the way she died was less important than the outcome for him.

He spent no time mourning her but farmed his children to other houses and reverted to his claim that Mauatua should be his concubine at least.

Uglier and more brutal than ever because of McCoy's *ti*-whisky, he repeated his threat to kill Mauatua's children if she didn't agree.

She found him teasing them cruelly, threatening to toss them over the cliff one by one. There was only one question about what to do when the women gathered. Who would do it?

None of them felt strong enough to risk Matt's temper and strength.

Mauatua persuaded Adams and Young to invite Quintal for a drink, ensured he drank more than they did, and when he was suitably fuddled both men swung at him with an axe.

Thursday and Charles were told they imagined the amount of blood they later saw in the room. But they were eight and seven and with minds of their own, and Sully who was a year older agreed it was real. The three of them and Betsy Mills helped younger children scramble up the outside wall to see through the window for themselves. Their mothers treated their gory stories the way they did their dreams and other fantasies until the children got bored with the conflict and slowly forgot what they had seen.

She was happy to bear Ned Young's three children. He was a gentle man who loved and welcomed his children by her but he wasn't the true and equal partner Fletcher had been.

Ned's problem was his health and he was as much an invalid during her years with him as not. What began as an occasional wheeze developed into permanent asthma. Nothing she or Jenny knew could open his chest to help with the agony of breathing out or could pacify the urgency of gulping air back.

She carried him out to greet the sun on the first day of the new century, but from then he rarely left his bed and had long been incapable of love making. Her children spent as much time with other mothers as she nursed him but she welcomed this opportunity for them to escape his suffering.

On Christmas Day 1800 she held him until the pitiful breaths he could manage no longer supported even his emaciated and tortured body.

She was more distraught than she expected. Ned was the first forefather not to die by another man's hand or from alcohol-related delirium, yet perhaps he'd been in more pain and distress.

Her deeper regret was that Pitcairn's children had seen death only associated with pain, suffering, accident or murder.

Ned's intellect and background were what she'd specially valued, hoping he would teach Pitcairners more than mere writing or reading.

He could have taught them about the world none had yet begun to wonder about.

There was a struggle to choose which of his children should take his dying breath, to receive his trove of wisdom, but she decided none would have it. With such insignificant breath to pass there would be little learning to bequeath.

She despaired more about Adams, Pitcairn's last man. He veered between avuncular teacher and drunken menace. Ned's promise to teach Pitcairners to read and write had been well honoured and he had taught Adams, too. She insisted Adams passed this on when he was capable.

Mostly he distilled and drank, drank and distilled, eating almost nothing and largely incapable of speech or thought.

When he was lucid he remembered the brutal fates of the other Pitcairn men and began the cycle again. The women considered breaking his still, but were too frightened at the murderous effect it might have on him, and who his subsequent victims would be.

Sometime early in the first years of the century Thursday and Charles ran shouting to their mother.

'Father Adams,' they jabbered, 'he's gone funny.'

Most of Pitcairn's women and children were watching, trying not to laugh but also wanting to, so they might hide their fright. Adams was pale as a ghost, unshaven, dribbling and quivering. His arms flailed insanely as he stumbled about the village square. He leaped and dived, sometimes covering his head and sometimes rolled into a ball on the ground.

When he shouted coherently between his screams of agony and shrieks of atonement he swore the Archangel Michael pursued him, shooting flaming darts into him for his sins and all the sins of Pitcairn. His arms were stick thin and his body emaciated and poisoned, but his hallucinations made him superhumanly strong and he easily fought off Mauatua and Jenny and any of the young men who tried to capture him.

They waited until he collapsed, whining and snorting with self pity, blood-flecked snot mixing with tears and saliva that turned dirt into mud on his face and in his beard. His corrupted body gave up so completely he twitched in puddles of excrement and urine.

They sluiced him clean and then carried him to his house.

She insisted the women vote outside Adams' house, choosing whether it was worth carrying him inside. They could let him die and finally rid the island's children of his threat or they could save him and hope he would recover enough to continue teaching the children what reading and writing he knew. He might even father more children.

They treated him the way they rehabilitated kava addicts on Tahiti. They tied him to his bed and took it in turns to make him drink water and to force-feed him purees of banana and baked breadfruit into which they added pounded fish and chicken and the herbs they thought would help.

When he was finally well, perhaps in better health than ever in his life, he broke the still, picked up the Bible and converted them all to Christianity as he remembered it.

Mauatua was first besieged or shunned by the other women, who suspected this was a plot by her to become all powerful, perhaps to be worshipped. Now Ned was dead she called herself Mrs Christian, so none forgot what Fletcher had endured to bring them to the island.

The quarrel was about the confusion of this name and the name of the religion and once they accepted she was not demanding to be a goddess Christianity was welcomed because it included them. They and their daughters could worship beside the sons who would one day be Pitcairn's new sort of man.

Here was an inclusive religion that enfolded them into a single family based on loving and personal responsibility, a religion far removed from the imprisoning traditions of Tahiti.

None of the women disagreed with her on the importance to Pitcairn's children of Adams' teaching. Like her they recognised the Bible he taught was a simple morality based on the Ten Commandments, with little true spirituality or requirement to suspend belief and accept reincarnation.

If their sons and daughters grew up believing these simple lessons Pitcairn would indeed be special.

When Adams also taught them hymns, singing became a daily pleasure, as it had always been on Tahiti. He claimed his reward from Jesus and His Father was his new son by Teio. George Adams was his only son.

The years of terror from drunken men were finally over. This was no guarantee of uninterrupted pleasure for her children and a sunny future, and she felt safer now she wasn't the only one with bloody hands. At some point Adams, Ned, McCoy, Quintal and Teraura all had bloodied hands and the rest of the women were complicit.

There was much to do if Pitcairn was to survive until its sons and daughters were able fully to share the work and the decision making. The greatest danger would come from the outside world, from whoever the men were on the first ship that discovered them.

The solution was a vote that agreed to resuscitate the Tahitian custom of *ha'avare,* scrupulous lying to outsiders even though they would have to teach their children to lie, too, something that clashed with the Christian message but was essential for the island's future.

They justified *ha'avare* because Tahiti's culture of playful lying would not be for amusement or because there was nothing else to do.

On Pitcairn Island it was the only way the island's women could insulate their children from any revenge the outside world might take on their mothers.

CHAPTER 56

February 6th 1808: The Edge, Pitcairn Island

Mauatua held Jenny's hand tightly as they stood between the palms at The Edge and watched two canoes fighting their way against the surf. She had no idea where this ship was from, but she was certain Great Britain's flag wasn't made of stars and stripes.

In this new century no ship could possibly miss the signs of Pitcairn's occupation. Smoking fires were the least clue. The neat rows and shapes of their gardens and plantations showed Pitcairn was inhabited. When she went out to fish from a canoe she could even see houses from the sea. Flaunting their presence on the island gave a kick to what had become a comfortable but uneventful life, agreed by the remaining Ma'ohi women as worth all the earlier unpleasantness.

Each one of them came to her at some time to thank her, to show their gratitude for being rescued from their due on Tahiti or Huahine or Tubuai.

It was so long since the women first rehearsed lies about Pitcairn's past some hardly remembered the truth.

Today the truth would have to be buried as never before to protect themselves and their children, 24 of them now.

She couldn't be sure what the young Pitcairners knew or might say about their island's bloody past. Some said they remembered horrible events and frightened younger children with stories of axes and blood on walls but their mothers insisted these were imagination, not memories.

She calculated on her fingers, using Fletcher's counting of the years. His mutiny was 1789, they had arrived on Pitcairn early in January of 1790, and this was February in 1808, so just over 18 years to be exact. Even so, how could she possibly know how long and determined the arm of a British king might be?

Pitcairn's children certainly wouldn't begin to understand the concept of crime against a crown or of regal retribution. All they knew was a simple life of kindness and honesty in the name of Jesus.

When news of the ship spread around the village, she gathered everyone in the square for a prayer meeting and Adams begged Jesus and His Father to protect them and their island. Mauatua prayed hard too, but for all she believed in Jesus' care and mercy, she knew Pitcairn's secrets might no longer be safe. No-one on Pitcairn had any need to lie in their daily lives yet now they had to remember that the truth about the past was their greatest enemy. She couldn't afford to let Pitcairn's young men and women repeat what they thought they'd seen and heard.

Yet, didn't they deserve to know about other worlds, just as she had yearned to do on Tahiti? Wouldn't those with her blood be as rebellious and as curious as she was? And now her sons were about to board a ship. She hoped it was from a country that didn't speak English so that Thursday October, already the father of two sons, would quickly paddle back with his brother Charles and Quintal's tall eldest boy, Matthew.

Jenny watched through a telescope and interpreted what she thought happened on the deck of the ship riding in what they now called Bounty Bay. The boys were welcomed and then disappeared into the ship. That would be nasty she said to Mauatua. It would be, for even up here they could smell this was a hunter, too small to be hunting whales they thought, but some dead marine creature gave off a nauseating fishy stink.

Mauatua jumped when Adams put his hand on her shoulder. Father Adams had first hidden in his house, crippled with fear of being taken and punished for his part in the mutiny and not at all certain his piety would help. He had reconsidered, acknowledging that as nominal father to the island, as patriarch and unofficial church minister, he should set an example to the young ones and face this danger manfully, trusting in Jesus.

He was quite bald on the front half of his head now, and had twisted the grey hair that grew further back into a sailor's pigtail. He wore the remains of an old sea cap and had swathed his increasingly rotund hips in new white tapa cloth so the many tattoos on his arms and chest and legs showed, except time and the sun had rather faded them, as though they'd never really been meant.

She wondered if it was embarrassment at other white men seeing him half swaddled that might really have kept him in his house that morning.

'They'll be American sealers, I reckon,' he said. 'Not the Royal Navy anyway, I swear.'

Would that be better or worse for her boys, Mauatua worried.

It was an excruciating hour before the boys come back on deck but then only Thursday paddled back to shore. There was a rush down the Hill of Difficulty to welcome him back. None of the 24 native Pitcairners had met anyone not born on the island. Some wept constantly, two had vomited with fear and there was much discussion of whether these visitors would be God's children or heathens.

Mary Ann Christian warned the younger children they would be safe as long as there were no black men. Black men were very bad men and likely to kill them all. That's one of the facts everyone knew. Their mothers had told them that for as long as they could remember.

Had they? Mauatua wasn't certain where this idea had started. The women hoped it would disappear like so many childish enthusiasms. It hadn't, it had flourished. Why didn't their children see that the rest of the world would call their mothers black, too?

Thursday was incandescent with excitement.

'The captain, Captain Folger, wants Father Adams to come on board,' he shouted breathlessly as he beached his canoe. 'I'll take you in a few minutes, when I get my breath back.'

Adams objected firmly.

'Tell 'em very politely I'll not be boarding any ship. There's no knowing who they might be and if I might be sailed away.'

His flock tearfully begged Thursday to tell the Captain he could not have their Father but should return Charles and Matthew at once and then sail away. Instead, Mauatua told Thursday to invite the captain and officers, no more than six of them, on to the island, for a feast. No sailor in the centre of the Pacific, so many weeks away from fresh water or food, could possibly refuse.

Thursday thought everyone would want to come ashore but Mauatua said this wasn't possible. She hoped that with just a few of them on shore she would more easily control what was said and learn what was thought about Pitcairn and Fletcher's mutiny.

He couldn't believe sailors on the ship, called TOPAZ, knew so much about BOUNTY and his first father.

'They wanted to know about you,' he told his mother.

'And?'

'I said you were dead.'

'Good boy, that's the way.'

Everyone laughed with her and she hoped this would set the mood for the rest of the day. They'd all promised to say their mothers couldn't speak English and that seemed to engage them. Her plan was to keep the island's focus on the novelty of the ship and its sailors.

The sailors mustn't be allowed to ask about Pitcairn and its past. If they did, what might Pitcairn's children ask after the ship sailed?

Thursday said the ship had doors that swung open down one side. He'd felt very foolish trying to slide one. He couldn't blame the men on board for making fun of him but it wasn't nice and they also laughed at him when he told them his name. He protested no-one mocked another on Pitcairn because the Bible said it was wrong. That seemed to work and there was no more unkindness.

They were from America, Thursday said, and he made everyone laugh as he imitated the curious way they pronounced their words.

He recounted how the Captain was amazed he said Grace before and after the food they offered and he'd declared he was amazed they didn't do the same, saying Father Adams had taught them it was the proper way.

When something they called a hound appeared and barked at him he had jumped back into the Captain and almost knocked him from his feet.

All in all, Thursday thought his first visit to a ship like his first father once sailed had not been pleasant.

'But were there any black men, did you get frightened by black men?' his sister begged, perhaps, Mauatua thought, hoping it was true.

There was one, Thursday told the hushed group, and this was when he was most frightened. He hid behind the captain, whispering he knew black men were bad and would kill him. The captain told him to look about. The men on the deck had lived with the black man for months and were still alive. And then he suggested Thursday had darker coloured skin than the man he called black.

'I told him this was very confusing and that I would have to ask Father Adams what I thought. After that the black man kept away from me.'

'Better not bring him back,' Mary Ann said. 'But I don't expect he's an officer, is he?'

When her boys paddled back from the ship, guiding a rowing boat with officers aboard, Mauatua took Jenny's hand again.

Everything they had done to make Pitcairn safe for children might be discovered. The worst thing would be to act suspiciously or not to be welcoming. If they were found wanting, the island's next generations could be sentenced to a lesser life. They prayed together quickly and were encouraged by a chorus of Amen from the children who had noticed.

Mauatua suggested Betsy Mills and Mary Ann help the younger ones to pick flowers and make garlands and posies for the visitors. She agreed Adams should greet the visitors at the bottom of the Hill of Difficulty and many of the older youths said they would too, all trying to outdo the others with promises of what punishment they would inflict if these Americans tried to take Father Adams or anyone else from Pitcairn.

'Do you think . . .? Jenny wondered. Mauatua understood immediately and nodded. The older girls could keep their chests bare. Might be a help she laughed, but then silently asked Jesus for forgiveness as she did whenever she was a bit rude or behaved like a Tahitian.

'I think we'd better keep out of the way, *vahine.*'

Adams had also promised to say none of the Ma'ohi women spoke English, agreeing this wasn't really lying but protecting the truth. That made the women laugh. Some whispered to her it was good to be telling stories again, remembering it as one of the few pleasures they had been freely allowed in the old islands.

There were four different versions of Pitcairn's history they and their children had agreed and no doubt others would occur during the tellings.

The Ma'ohi women agreed that to be at home and busily pounding or grating would be the most natural way to be found. If all was well, much of the proposed feast would then be on its way.

Mauatua led Jenny to stand in the shadows of the roots of the banyan tree at the top of the village square. There, they clasped their four hands together in a tight knot of fear and waited for the outside world to step onto Pitcairn.

Adams led the Americans across the square to the shade of the banyan tree where the two women were concealed. All the visitors had flowers behind their ears and around their necks. The younger children skipped around them, clasping and releasing their hands, completely enchanting and enchanted.

'*Aueee!*' Mauatua slapped her hands on her cheeks and shook her head. 'We must look like heathen savages to them.'

Her older boys wore the *tiputa* of Tahiti, a folded tapa cloth length with a slit for the head to go through, so it hung evenly back and front. Each was a showpiece for the brightness of the yellow, black and red-ochre patterns created on Pitcairn. Some of the sailors pointed at the startling patches and strips of abstract patterns pasted over the designs.

What did these people from America really think? Were Pitcairn's colours and patterns vulgar to their eyes, comical even?

'They must think our boys are very rude,' she whispered to Jenny. Jenny nodded thoughtfully and smiled a little. Many of their waist-length *tiputa* tapered to a point just below the navel, something they recognised for the first time as deliberately provocative.

Below that, all males wore the *maro,* a length of tapa wound low around their hips and then between their legs, ending in a small apron in front, leaving the lower torso bare and their hips and buttocks naked.

'There's so much of them on show,' Mauatua worried, comparing her sons' skimpy covering to the visitors' sober trousers and shirts and jackets.

'They are more interested in the *vahine*,' Jenny said. Now they were so close Mauatua could see the sailors' eyes fighting not to ravish the naked breasts of the younger women.

'*Aueee, Aueeeee!*' she cried with her eyes turned to the heavens. How wrong she was to let the younger ones go naked on top. She'd forgotten how hungry BOUNTY's men were for such sights after weeks at sea.

No matter where they'd been in the Pacific these sailors would never have seen breasts like these, breasts on girls who would seem more European than Ma'ohi, more like those they expected to see only in secret once in their home ports.

Even so, the similarities between the tanned sailors and Pitcairn's men were more obvious than the differences their dress made. Swap their clothes and they could change places.

Jenny agreed. Pitcairners combined the height and bearing of their mothers with profiles that remembered their English fathers and many had pale skins, too.

The girls and women who had covered their breasts wore a fuller, unshaped version of the *tiputa* over their skirt, which hung from their shoulders to below their hips. They at least were discreet, as modest as Jesus-fearing women should be. As for the rest, Jenny agreed it might have been a better decision to lock up their daughters.

'We'll have to keep our eyes peeled.'

'And open them behind us, too,' Jenny laughed, too loudly.

Mauatua nervously pushed her further into the shadows, hearing general relief as one by one the sailors flopped to the ground after the stiff climb up the Hill of Difficulty and the stroll to the square. It was February after all, sometimes the hottest month, and not a single cloud diminished the tropical sun.

By now most of Pitcairn's young men were relaxed enough to strip to their *maro* and invited the sailors to remove their shirts. She could scarcely look at the almost naked young men, whose bodies seemed as interesting to the sailors as the girls' breasts.

It was relief when the sailors refused even to take off their jackets because Captain Folger was still in his, and with a tie around his neck and a cap on his head. Perhaps their clothes would imprison any baser thoughts and ideas?

The older Pitcairn boys brought spring water and green coconuts to offer the visitors and conversation lulled as they took these refreshments.

Mauatua and Jenny worked their way back through the gloom of the banyan's high tangle of sucker roots until they could more clearly hear the visitors as they murmured among themselves, not certain if they were always understood. Some discussed the curious stillness of Pitcairn while others cast admiring or lustful opinions about the Pitcairners or rehearsed what they thought they knew about the mutiny on BOUNTY.

Mary Ann asked the first difficult question. She had been rebellious and spiteful from the moment she could speak. There were tears in her eyes as she took the hand of the captain, but Mauatua knew too well she could summon tears to ask what was for dinner.

'Captain, have you come to take Father Adams away?'

'Now why would I want to do that?'

'Because my first father took one of the king's ships.'

Adams bustled forward.

'The captain doesn't know about that old stuff.'

Mary adopted the look of injured innocence Mauatua so disliked. She was almost 15 but innocent she most certainly was not.

'But you always said, you *said*.' Mary Ann stopped to sob a little. 'You said if we asked for the truth it would always be given.' Pitcairn's children clamoured support for Mary Ann.

'Hush. Hush now all of ye. Hush.' Adams told them what he must have confirmed on the way up from Bounty Bay. 'These gentlemen are not from the king of England. They haven't come to take me away. They will all sail away on their ship tonight, but I will stay here with you.'

Mauatua felt proud as the children of Pitcairn fell to their knees and prayed, giving loud thanks. Why would any visitor imagine there was something sensational to know about the island's past?

'Bye and bye, we'll have a public dinner for you,' Adams promised.

One of Folger's officers immediately pulled out a bottle of rum and Adams grabbed it eagerly.

'That'll help the party,' the captain said. She ran from the shadows to take the bottle. She shouted at Adams in Tahitian and mimed to the captain that rum was not allowed on Pitcairn.

'What? A jolly Jack Tar who doesn't drink rum?' The captain laughed. She turned quickly to take the bottle out of Adams sight. As she did she saw something that made her feel she had fallen through the earth of Pitcairn and into another world. She checked quickly. Only five of the sailors were under the banyan tree. And now the sixth had arrived.

Tamahere, the son she had thrown into Matavai Bay, stood staring at her from the far edge of the square.

She forced the bottle back into the hands of the captain and ran back to Jenny. The sting of a very long, very cold needle raced painfully down her spine. She was half laughing, half crying but neither sound came out of her struggling body. Was she having visions, like those saints and prophets in the Bible? Had Jesus chosen her above other women?

She couldn't be in some other world. What she had seen was of this world and if she turned her head she would see Tamahere again. The son she had abandoned for Fletcher had found her.

'Now my lovelies,' Father Adams said to the Pitcairners, rubbing his hands together. 'Plenty to do. Polly, you get sweet potatoes from Matt's patch. Thursday, you and Matt go fish out some big lobsters.

'Next, you Mary Ann, get some girls to bring extra firewood from down Fletcher's place.

'Use a barrow to bring it back to this one, the village pit. We'll need a big fire to heat these stones, so we eat sooner rather than later.

'Daniel and Arthur, you butcher up that pig we killed yesterday. Small pieces but with plenty fat on them. They'll cook faster. That's another wheelbarrow from somewhere you'll need. Charles, you be the breadfruit man and take the little 'uns to carry them for you.'

She watched Tamahere silently take this in. He was clearly used to being sidelined, even by his fellow officers. His face was impassive, expressionless, until he saw Charles hop away. Then his lip curled with open disgust.

The anger and hatred she felt for Tahitian men spewed up into her throat. She contained it but as she gasped for breath through the flood of acid her mind tumbled with outrage.

Tamahere was her son, her flesh and blood, yet personified everything ugly about Tahiti. He'd confirmed it before he'd said a word. Tahitian men were as evil as ever. Her emotions raged. To be so dismissive of Charles, Charles of all people. Like his father Fletcher, Charles was the one everyone turned to for advice and comfort and leadership. She rebuked herself. Tamahere wouldn't know that, or that Charles was his brother.

'Come gentlemen,' Adams said. 'While our dinner is cooking, let me show you our little paradise.'

'In a minute, if you please,' the captain asked. 'I'd like to sit a bit longer and perhaps, well I suppose you are longing to know the news from the rest of the world, Mr Adams?'

'Some, some, but not much. We have done very well without it for these many years.'

'The rest of the world certainly wants to know about you and BOUNTY and the other mutineers.'

'I was never a mutineer,' Adams said emphatically.

'But at the trials it was said you were.'

'Trials?'

'Yes, Captain Bligh - of course, you don't know. Bligh survived. He sailed that open boat more than 3500 miles to the Dutch East Indies.'

Mauatua felt her world stop again. If Bligh had got back to England, he would have been determined to punish Fletcher. She felt that little man's vindictive temper settle like a shroud over the island.

They had never been safe and now never would be.

'When he got back to England, the king sent a ship to search for the mutineers. They caught most of those who had stayed behind on Tahiti, and then lost many of them when the ship sank off Australia. PANDORA she was called I remember. But some were taken back and three of those were hanged.'

'Can you remember names, any names?' Adams entreated.

'Let me see, Heywood is the only one I recollect. Peter was it? He was pardoned, and went on to become a naval captain. Met him once.'

That was good news for Mauatua. If Peter survived he would have taken the message to Fletcher's mother, and perhaps told others a different version from the one Bligh was bound to have concocted. Mauatua willed Adams to ask the questions she wanted to ask.

'Was Bligh punished?'

'He was exonerated by the Admiralty. But he wasn't at the trial of the mutineers. By then he was on a second breadfruit voyage to Tahiti.'

Adams heaved himself to his feet, fulminating at this injustice.

'Bligh not at their trial? Infamy! Then he cannot have been questioned properly. That's supposed to be the way at mutiny trials. Sometimes, that was how the captain was punished instead of the sailors.'

He caught a glimpse of Mauatua and Jenny, who encouraged him with a shunt of their hands.

'Bligh not at the trial? That was wrong. That was not justice, certainly not British justice.'

He fell back to the ground again, his jaw working with fury.

'Perhaps, if I might repeat what has been said to me?' Folger offered. 'It might not have been British justice, but it was naval justice.'

'Not for Fletcher,' Mauatua said to Jenny.

Adams leaned close to Folger, who inclined his head. She had to read his lips. 'I *was* not, *am* not a mutineer, not to the children on this island,' Adams said and put a finger to the side of his nose.

Folger changed the subject. 'So, you don't want to know about the rest of the world?'

'Would it affect us here? England is still there, ain't she?'

'She is, and a few years ago, 1805, she defeated France off Cape Trafalgar on the Spanish Coast. Close to Cadiz, I believe. That war is finally over.' Adams rose and swung his cap three times over his head calling out, 'Old England forever. Huzzah! Huzzah!'

'I have to ask. Where are the other BOUNTY men? What I mean to say is, is Fletcher Christian on the island? I was hoping to speak to him.'

'Why would that be, Captain Folger? Who would be interested in what happened him so long ago?'

'The whole world, that's who. It's probably the most famous mutiny in history. No blood spilled on the day, South Seas, native women, Bligh's journey and then you disappeared for, well, until now. There'll not be a sailor in the world who doesn't have an opinion about it. Bligh wrote about it, of course.

'Y'know, Fletcher Christian, is supposed to have been seen in England, around Lake Windermere and at Devonport in Plymouth. It was that Heywood, Peter Heywood who said that. There's even been a book, two I believe, supposed to be letters written by Fletcher Christian, saying he escaped to South America.'

'He was a great navigator,' Adams said mischievously.

'Ah yes, a British naval man told me that. With a compass and, of course, BOUNTY had that chronometer. But that's not possible, surely?'

'It might be,' Adams agreed pretending serious concern. 'Ain't seen that thing for years. Or the compass. Or him come to that.'

'So you are saying, what, does that mean he did escape the island?'

Adams leaned back to him again and put a hand on his shoulder. 'Captain, Sir. Captain Folger, is it? As a visitor to this island you are welcome. But as someone with these sorts of questions . . . It would not be kind to disturb the minds of our children with such matters.' He winked at the captain and nodded conspiratorially.

Certain Adams was not spilling their secrets, Mauatua had only half listened to the conversation for her eyes were fixed on Tamahere. Her oldest son, on the island and wanting what? He couldn't have known she was here, so how, why?

'Have you told Adams the truth about Massacre Day?' Jenny wondered.

Mauatua was adamant. 'I have always told him nothing.'

'Can we trust Adams to tell lies to Folger?'

'He's afraid enough. Afraid for his neck.'

'About the mutiny, you mean?' Jenny asked.

'And the rest.'

'He'd better keep *mamoo* – and we had, too.'

'We'll be alright if everyone pretends we don't speak English,' Mauatua assured her.

'We didn't mutiny.'

'You think? And there are too many dead men on this island,' she curtly reminded Jenny.

'I had forgotten them,' Jenny replied, her eyes suddenly downcast.

Mauatua saw only evil in Tamahere's stern expression. Was he here for revenge of some kind? Of course, that would be it. He was a Tahitian and would want revenge in this world, in this life time. And yet, she thought she saw something fragile too, so there was an urge to take him in her arms. Which was right, and what was right, she couldn't tell.

Surely there were no more costs to pay for her freedom? She shook her head wildly, hoping for insight but discovering only dizziness. Her legs buckled and she reached for Jenny so she did not fall.

'You've forgotten more than you think, *vahine*,' she warned her friend.

This rather awkward drawing is the only portrait there is of Thursday October Christian, the first-born Pitcairner and the oldest son of Mauatua and Fletcher Christian.

CHAPTER 57

Dinner was served from the square's great pit oven as a Pitcairn-style feast, on sheets of tapa cloth spread on the ground, with the men seated and eating while the women served them. She had no choice but to be one of them and tried to keep out of Tamahere's eye line. He must have been the black man who frightened Thursday on the ship. That was why they sat at opposite ends of the feast.

'You don't enjoy the female sex at dinner?' Captain Folger asked.

'This is the proper way,' Thursday assured him, tapping the treasured book beside him. 'The Bible tells us God created men first, so men must be first in everything else in this world.'

'Nonsense.'

Every Pitcairner turned to Tamahere, whose deep, angry voice they heard for the first time. 'This is not a Christian custom. It is the old way of Tahiti, where men and women never ate together.'

There were cries of 'Bad man' 'You telling stories against the Bible' and 'Black men don't know such things.'

Mauatua caught Thursday's eye and he took his cue. 'We know nothing of such heathen ways here. We are all Christians.'

Tamahere grunted derisively. He shouted back. 'How would you know what Christians are, locked away on your little island like this?

'Anyway,' he went on, ignoring signals from his captain, 'I heard some of you speaking of one of the old women as Mrs Christian.'

No-one answered him but Tamahere was not deterred.

'Was that Mrs Christian once called Mauatua?'

Thursday was flustered. 'Father Adams says my mother is dead. I told you that on the ship.'

'If Mauatua is dead, then who is the Mrs Christian who looks like a Tahitian and who must have come on BOUNTY?'

'I cannot speak of my neighbour, black man. It will do you no good and I will do her no harm.'

Tamahere jumped to his feet. 'If you say your mother is dead, then who is that there?'

He turned to point at her but she had gone. Father Adams hauled himself to his feet and, after a look of apology to the captain, pronounced to Tamahere over the feasting men and boys.

'Mauatua, his heathen Tahitian mother, is dead, that is true. Mrs Christian is alive, born again through the blood of Jesus.'

'Alleluia,' Thursday and Charles cried together.

Tamahere threw down the food in his hands and walked slowly away from the feast and into the roots of the banyan tree.

She had heard the exchange and waited and listened as Tamahere stumbled in the gloom. He found her and stood an arm's length away. Both faced directly ahead but in opposite directions.

It was her responsibility to speak first she thought, but could not grasp what might be most acceptable. In the corner of her eye Tamahere unbuttoned his shirt. He pulled it away to show a long thin scar from his shoulder down to his hip.

'I know it is you,' she said in a small, low voice.

They both choked back a sob and their eyes filled but both steadfastly looked ahead.

'Why did you not greet me?' Tamahere was at last able to ask.

'Did you greet me?'

She relented and looked at him, but saw only a profile. There was silence and Mauatua felt obliged to explain.

'I wasn't sure. It's so many years, almost 20 since . . .'

'Since you abandoned me,' Tamahere spluttered softly, finally turning to look his mother full in the face. She searched for any sign of forgiveness or understanding. There was none. If she was to survive this confrontation she'd have to match his tough attitude. She cast her eyes down before she spoke, hoping this would lessen the effect of her question.

'Why have you come?'

She didn't see his face change but his voice did.

A boy spoke to her from the body of this huge, aggressive man, taller than her by a hand's breadth.

'I have been looking for so many years, on so many ships, as soon as I was able to go to sea. Finding Pitcairn is my reward.'

She thought him weak and plaintive. 'Men and their rewards. That is not how the world works. You did not need me as a mother. My mothers and sisters were all your mothers. It is the way of Tahiti.'

She turned away, thinking this was the only way she could dominate him. But then Tamahere touched her. He put a hand on each of her shoulders. She turned to face him again, struggling not to cover his huge hands with hers.

'That *was* the way,' Tamahere said. 'Tahiti is another place now, where Europeans burn our gods and beat us for not being born to their beliefs.'

No longer able to resist she put a hand up to her angry son's cheek.

'But you have noble blood.' The childish softness of his skin had become something harsh, with nothing to remind her of closeness or love.

'Hah!' he said, brushing his mother's hand from his face. 'That is *why* the missionaries beat me, until I would say it was not true, so I would say Jesus was the only lord on this earth.'

Her heart raced. She wanted to leave and hear no more but Tamahere grabbed her so she had to listen.

'They beat me every time I said you had sailed away to live with gods. I believed Fletcher was at least a noble, if not a god, because he knew his lands and could say his grandfathers for so many generations.' He was shaking her as he spoke and she couldn't disguise the fear in her voice.

'That was all true, Tamahere. Did it count for nothing?' She tried to wriggle free but he held her firmer, forcing her to hear every word.

'The missionaries called him a criminal, a sinner who would taint anyone who had anything to do with him. They said he would be hanged. When I told them I had exchanged names with him, then, well then they conveniently chose to believe in Tahitian customs.'

He hung his head compressing his lips, but the memory would not be silenced. Relaxing his grip he then slowly dripped his past to her in sad, soft words, finally holding her hands in his.

The priests had said he should be punished as if he was Fletcher Christian. So for years he was threatened with being hanged, but as a boy how did he know if this was going to happen or not?

'Priests dictated children could live only with their real mothers and fathers, and they had to be married in their church. Tahitian culture was so destroyed we were left with only the priests' imported beliefs and rum.

'The missionaries didn't care about the drinking as long as we did nothing Tahitian and could be counted in their churches once a week. Our lovely life, our laughing and happiness that worshipped gods and spirits every minute of the day, we were told all that was wrong and bad. Everything we were was thrown aside for an hour in their church, as though our lives were dung, as though we had no right to a culture or heritage.'

Mauatua pulled her hands from him and turned her back as his words added to her burden of guilt and disgust, telling her in awful detail how white priests fought each other for the right to sack and burn traditional *fare* and their family totems, competed to chop up and feed blazes with sacred objects and statues, and argued to be first to desecrate maraes with hammers and pickaxes.

'Once I shouted at them,' Tamahere persisted in to the back of her bowed head. 'I said I *was* a Christian, I was *Fletcher* Christian.

'I was locked away by myself for over a year for that, except when I had to cook or clean for them. I was punished as though I really was Fletcher Christian.'

'Jesus forgive them. I didn't know. How could I have known?' she wept, forgiving herself because she knew her son would never do that.

'It is they who must apologise, they who must change things, not me.'

'They will never do that. It is too late for Tahiti, too late for me. I was made to feel a nothing, not a child, not even a Tahitian. Those men who said they were doing the work of Jesus even made me doubt I was a man.'

Her tear-shone face contorted with dread at what might come next. She turned to see Tamahere pulling at his shirt and trousers.

'But when I was a man, I chose. I chose the life I knew, not the life I did not know. It was very dangerous. These were forbidden.'

Tamahere yanked his arms from his sleeves and revealed a mantle of magnificent tattoos that covered his back, snaked over his shoulders and chest, over his biceps and on to his forearms. He pulled down his trousers to show his buttocks and legs were as completely covered.

In the luminous shadows and sharp scents of the tree Tamahere's golden skin and blue-black tattoos conjured him into a pagan god striding in to her Christian world.

His effect was visceral, as challenging as it was meant to be. Not just a display of birthright but of belligerent, controlling manhood. He flexed and strained to show his tattooed body to maximum effect but his marks and their messages were alien to everything she had come to believe on Pitcairn. Her son was assaulting her with a bullying demand to acknowledge their common Tahitian heritage, perhaps even to return to it.

She turned away her head again and put up her hands to shield her eyes and her mind. Averting the image did nothing to lessen the resonance of the passion she'd seen in Tamahere's eyes and she thought of Fletcher. He would have cheered her son's fight to be his own man, just as he had done for himself, just as he had admired her battle for freedom.

'Someone must remember Tahiti, must fight for the old ways,' Tamahere declared.

She collected herself, drawing power from the certain convictions of her life on Pitcairn and her belief in Jesus. She dropped her hands to growl a response.

'No-one here wants to remember the old ways of Tahiti. They were wicked in ways you would never know.' For an instant Mauatua thought she saw acceptance of this in Tamahere's eyes but then he diverted to a different track.

'Will you tell them I am your son?'

It was another challenge, cunning and brutal. Tamahere stood for everything she had abandoned and that had cost her so much. What would acknowledging Tamahere do to her gentle unmarked Pitcairn sons?

'All Pitcairn's children have English fathers and are brought up to be English and to believe in Jesus. You cannot be my son on Pitcairn.'

She choked on the words, ripped apart inside because she knew she had to say them but really wanted to hold him tight, to hold him until she'd poured 18 years of missed love back into her son.

Now there was nothing more each could say to the other Mauatua was relieved to see Jenny walk in. She went directly to Tamahere.

'It is good to know what became of you,' she said softly, stroking his tattoos as she spoke.

'That is no concern now.' He turned Jenny away, his arm around her shoulders. 'Jenny, perhaps you are the one to tell me what happened to everyone.' Jenny glanced over at Mauatua.

'We do not speak of such things.'

'Why not, if there are no secrets. Where are the other women? BOUNTY sailed with how many?'

'We were only 12 on Pitcairn. Now we are nine. The others died, some naturally, others by accidents.'

'But that can't be what happened to so many men, can it? How many? Nine white men and I don't know how many Ma'ohi men. What happened to them?'

Jenny tried to escape. Tamahere grabbed her back roughly. 'I was hoping to talk to Fletcher,' he said menacingly.

A curious sound interrupted them. Thursday slumped on a high root, whimpering with small sounds of protest. His pupils were upturned showing only their whites and he shivered.

Mauatua rushed to him and once he was in her arms his eyes focused and he faced Tamahere.

'I saw you talking to my mother. You made her angry.'

'I used to know her.'

'Before my first father's ship came here?'

'I have been searching for her for a long time, and for Fletcher.' Thursday twitched and then closed his eyes. His mother held him tighter, commanding with a raised hand that Tamahere and Jenny said nothing. Thursday recovered and continued. 'My real first father, yes. You knew him too?'

'And? You would not conceal a truth from me?'

'No. That is forbidden.'

'Is Fletcher alive or dead?' Tamahere asked, losing his patience.

'Don't say his name!' Mauatua pleaded.

Thursday had once again cut himself off from the world. In seconds he was back. 'I do not think I know that answer.' He turned to his mother, barely an inch taller than he. 'Do I?'

'Think, think. Why only *think*?' Tamahere bellowed.

She wanted desperately to challenge Tamahere's malevolence but he got in before she found the right words.

'How many Pitcairners are your brothers and sisters?' he demanded.

This time she butted in quickly. 'All of them. They are all my children.

'All Pitcairn is my family.'

'But not me,' Tamahere said.

'Why should you be? Why should you be in our family?' Thursday moved to stand protectively in front of his mother. She thanked him with a brief nod and felt secure enough in his protection to walk forward and to poke Tamahere's chest emphatically as she spoke.

'I will tell you one last time, Tamahere,' Mauatua warned.

'Pitcairn wants nothing from the past. And that includes you.'

CHAPTER 58

Tamahere tossed his head and marched out of the banyan roots, attempting to dress as he did. A swirl of visitors and Pitcairners rushed up the slope to the tree, kicking balls and playing tag. Charles was playing aggressively and as he competed for a ball he stumbled and fell at Tamahere's feet.

'Cripples weren't allowed to live on Tahiti,' he proclaimed.

Thursday pulled Charles to his feet and stood with a protective arm around him, too shocked to respond. Mauatua grabbed Tamahere by the collar. She dragged his head down to her and with as much threat as she could summon spoke directly into his ear.

'You certainly are a Tahitian man, aren't you? Only a Tahitian man could think of saying such a thing. You disgust me.'

She pushed Tamahere from her and was at once arrested by what Thursday was saying. 'Those are the marks of our mother.'

Tamahere's disarranged shirt had ridden up and Thursday pointed to the tattooed geckoes he could see.

'I remembered them,' Tamahere said.

'From Tahiti? You knew her?'

Mauatua wanted to stop the discussion but Jenny interrupted her, swiftly convincing her there might be a better outcome if the three worked things out man to man.

'I know I must tell the truth on this island,' Tamahere said with sneering disdain. 'Yes, I knew your mother on Tahiti and I do belong to your Pitcairn family. That is because Mauatua/Mrs Christian is my mother, too.'

Before Tamahere could respond, Mary Ann interrupted.

'That's a horrid thing to say. Come away from him.' Her mother pulled her back, warning her not to say another word.

'Yes, I'd expect you to stick up for another black.'

Mary Ann's malice was clear but Mauatua pushed her away to avoid feeding the spat.

Charles and Thursday chattered to one another in low voices, as they had since infancy. Very quickly they nodded agreement.

'So you are my brother, our brother,' Charles said.

'Your older brother,' Tamahere corrected.

Thursday and Charles again threw up an invisible curtain. Their whispers rose in volume as they came to their conclusion.

'You must mean half brother. We have those on Pitcairn, too. But why did our mother never tell us? She must have forgotten you.'

'She did not forget me!' Tamahere stamped like a petulant child and the Christian brothers laughed at him.

'It must be because you are a black man.'

'I am a *Tahitian* man.'

'You certainly can't be a Christian man, not with so many tattoos.'

'Your mother has tattoos and so did Fletcher.' Thursday clamped both hands over his face and his head shook but his reaction lasted only seconds.

'Don't say that name to him, please,' Charles waited until he was certain Thursday had recovered. 'My mother had tattoos before she was a Christian.'

'Or a Mrs Christian. You know,' Tamahere said, walking around the young men, who wore no *tiputa*, 'there are many who would think what you wear is not Christian. So much bare flesh.' He slapped the brothers on their bare buttocks.

'These are heathen. This is the way of old Tahiti, the Tahiti our mother says was so wicked.'

'Does it say this in the Bible?' Thursday asked.

'About bare *tohe*? Don't you know?'

'We can all read a little but we mainly know what Father Adams reads to us. And then he tells us what it means.'

'I would say the Bible means just what Father Adams wants it to mean.' Tamahere laughed coarsely.

'That is a wicked thing to say. God will punish you,' the brothers said.

Tamahere looked up to the sky. 'I am waiting.'

Tamahere walked around her sons once more. Mauatua was intrigued as he compared his arms to theirs, his legs and thighs, the girth of his chest, his shoulders and height.

There was no question he was a bigger, stronger man, but all three were pale-skinned where the sun had not coloured them. Her Pitcairn sons were both straight backed like her and broad shouldered like their father. They had worked outdoors all their life, not needing to protect their skin to convince others of bloodline superiority. But they were not fully grown and their voices and bearings were gentle.

Perhaps there was something less manly about them compared to men from the rest of the world. Yet with no comparisons to make, this had never been noticed or criticised on Pitcairn. In her eyes they lacked nothing Tamahere flaunted except tattoos. Now she had the chance to compare she thought their untouched skins were preferable.

When Charles stood straight on his good foot her sons were about the same height and because there was only a year between them they appeared to be twins.

They certainly had an uncanny ability to understand one another without as many words as other men used.

'Do you shoot arrows, make spears?' Tamahere asked them.

'We don't know how.'

'That is what men do.'

'But we have no men to teach us.'

'That's why you hold your brother's hand and don't walk like men.'

Of course. Without men, without fathers, none of Pitcairn's sons might ever be men. Mauatua immediately dismissed her thought. Who was to say what a man should be? The important thing was that they were not like the drunken bullies BOUNTY had brought to Pitcairn. They were part of the better generation the women promised their daughters under the Southern Cross

Adams barely counted. Almost everything Pitcairn's youths knew, other than Adam's introduction to reading and reassurance after their discovery of masturbation, had been taught them by women. Tamahere was threatening her sons' confidence as much as he threatened her and that would have to stop soon.

Tamahere demanded the young men put out their hands. The brothers did this, shrugging their shoulders at one another and not understanding the reason behind the command.

'You see. That is the woman's way, the tops of your arms close to your body, your elbows in. Look, this is the way of a man.'

When Tamahere put out his arm, his elbows were crooked and his upper arms held away from his body. Thursday and Charles quickly perfected this. They strutted at each other, proud of this new thing with their arms.

Mauatua appealed silently to Jesus when she saw them also walk with their knees turned out. It was the swaggering walk Adams defended as the walk of sailors used to rolling decks. Fletcher disagreed, saying it was the walk of low, unconfident men who wanted to look bigger and bolder, like roosters fighting for precedence over squabbling hens.

She remembered much of that walk on BOUNTY, but never among the nobles of Tahiti. Fletcher's great regret was that his knees stood out, so most would call him bow-legged. He tried to walk with straighter legs than was easy for him, the correct walk, he said, of a gentleman.

Simply by adjusting their arms and the way they walked her sons now looked aggressive and bullying. Memories of the most belligerent mutineers, Quintal and McCoy and Mills, crowded into her mind, all of them bearing down on her with swaggering walks and arms held far from their sides. Now her sons were strutting like the dead men she wanted to forget.

'You will never really be men if everything you know is taught by women,' Tamahere said, too critical to praise them. 'And you won't be a chief, Thursday.'

'We don't have chiefs.'

'This is also why the gods sent me here. To teach you the things a man must know but your mothers can not teach you. And then to be your chief.'

Her sons glanced to their mother for guidance. Conscious of Jenny's firm hold on her arm, she flicked her hand to say they should stand up to Tamahere.

'I *am* a man,' Thursday said. 'I have a wife and two children. Do you have a wife or children to come after you?' The brothers were surprised Tamahere said nothing. They conferred, to build she hoped, on what they judged was success.

'We have been thinking, Tamahere. You are a very bad man, even for a black man who does not want to kill us. We are the way we are because that is the way chosen by our mothers. Our mothers have told us that is why they came here, so Tahitian men did not tell them what to do.'

Thursday turned anxiously to his mother for reassurance. She hoped her expression of pride would be encouragement enough.

'What you say about chiefs is settled, Tamahere,' Thursday continued. 'I am the next after Adams, so I will be the next leader, but I will not be a chief. I will be the next *father* of Pitcairn.'

Thursday put his arm around Charles.

'Tamahere, we thank you for thinking kindly of us, for wanting to teach the things you know. We do not need to learn more than we learn on Pitcairn. We do not need you or your ideas on Pitcairn.'

Mauatua hugged Jenny, because without her insistence she would have interfered and then never heard such speeches from Thursday.

Tamahere hadn't listened.

'When I have taught you, Thursday, when you know how to be a man and a warrior, there must be a battle between us to decide who is chief on Pitcairn Island.'

'If you beat Thursday, then you will have to fight me,' Charles asserted. 'I am next.' Charles whispered with Thursday and they quickly agreed. 'We will fight you now, Tamahere. Then you must sail away and never come back.'

'It wouldn't be fair,' Tamahere answered, surprising his small audience. 'You are not ready. It wouldn't be suitable. There is another way. Our mother will arrange it.'

The Christian brothers were puzzled by what Tamahere said. Each reached for the other's hand and their heads met in close debate.

It didn't take them long to realise Tamahere must mean they were going to vote rather than fight.

Mauatua confirmed this but pretended not to hear when they asked how a visitor knew about such Pitcairn ways.

CHAPTER 59

Certain there would be no fisticuffs, she strode away to Captain Folger who was dozing in the shade on the far side of the square. She took him to Adams, who had kept as far away from the conflict as he dared without seeming cowardly. Mauatua spoke to Adams in Tahitian.

'Ask the captain if he has a long voyage ahead of him.'

Adams relayed the answer in his excellent Tahitian. It would be many months before TOPAZ was home in Nantucket and Boston, and they must round Cape Horn to get there.

She told Adams to offer the captain water and fresh provisions, live young pigs, goats for milking and chickens, too. The captain protested they were not a rich ship but she told Adams to make it clear everything would be a gift, but with one stipulation. Captain Folger should promise to spread the message that the Pitcairners were loyal to their king, and were faithful English men and women.

Captain Folger agreed and then she asked the American to follow her, saying she wanted to return some of the king's property.

Two officers joined their captain as she led them to the bottom of the square and turned left.

Inevitably Mary Ann tagged along, but whether it was to keep within sight of the first marriageable white men she had met or to pry into her mother's business, she couldn't yet tell.

Mauatua led the small party past another banyan that overflowed and filled a hollow on the right of the path and then she turned into the house she had shared with Fletcher and she now shared with Thursday October and his family.

He had insisted nothing was changed because it was what his father knew and that was all he would know of his father.

It was only when his father's name, his first name, was mentioned that Thursday had the difficulties his mother had never explained and that no-one else understood.

She needed help, gladly given by Folger. She pointed at bundles, tightly wrapped in tapa cloth on a high shelf, above shelves of books she said once belonged to Captain Bligh. The ragged ends of the wrappings of each parcel had been sealed with the sap of the breadfruit tree, so they were safe from the few insects on Pitcairn, and from inquisitive fingers. In fact the bundles had been there so long no-one who lived there or visited noticed them anymore.

'Something else I haven't been told about,' Mary Ann couldn't resist saying. Mauatua ignored her.

For almost 15 years nothing had stopped Mary Ann's sharp tongue wanting to destroy or turn everything to her interest. Pitcairn's women agreed about what she most needed, but Mary Ann said she would marry only a white man, a proper white man not a Pitcairner with pale skin.

With great care Mauatua unwrapped and revealed BOUNTY's azimuth compass and the box that held the chronometer. The chronometer had not been wound for many years. She'd fallen out of the habit because it wasn't important for her life on Pitcairn.

She felt it somehow dead and worthless and so apologised but then saw Folger seem to stagger when he opened the box. He obviously valued it immensely, more perhaps than she could understand.

Folger wound the chronometer a little so the thin second-hand once more swept around the dial. She thought he might have cried if there were not other men present. He told his officers he knew where it had been before Bligh took it to the South Seas, mentioning the Arctic and the North American Station and Africa, just as Fletcher had done.

He caressed it as though something holy, and then passed it to one of the officers. Folger cautioned him that his life was many times less valuable than the chronometer.

She explained through Adams that the chronometer and the compass were not gifts but were to go back to the king of Great Britain, to demonstrate Pitcairners were not thieves.

'Fairly much proves Fletcher Christian didn't sail away, I'd say, not without these,' Folger said, once he could bring himself to speak.

She forgot she was not supposed to speak English. 'What, what did you say?' she exclaimed.

Adams covered for her. 'One of the questions these women ask all the time, but they never understand the answers. It was mentioning Fletcher.' Folger was pacified but she saw he now watched her more intently.

Then she gave him the last two of Fletcher's Chinese bowls and the small mahogany chest in which he used to keep his handkerchiefs. She opened this to empty out the treasures inside. On top was Fletcher's naval hussif, something all the mutineers once had, with buttons and needles, thread and scissors. Over the years she had added other keepsakes to the chest, her sons' earliest curls and some shells they once valued. The penetrating scent of the camphor wood interior wafted so many memories of Fletcher into her mind that she closed the lid.

'Nothing there from his daughter, I see,' Mary Ann sniped. If she dared answer Mauatua would have reminded Mary Ann she only ever wanted what others had and that these had all been returned if she had not destroyed them.

Folger remarked on what she thought were the greatest treasures, Fletcher's once shiny knife and fork were now blackened but you could still see each had somehow been cut into with the head of that animal with a head like a horse, but with a horn and a beard. She could never remember its name. Speaking through Adams she made certain Folger understood Fletcher always used these to eat, saying he was brought up a gentleman and that living with bare feet under a palm-thatched roof could not change that. Tell Fletcher's family we are not pagans and savages, she said, unwrapping Fletcher's small Bible, which she wanted to keep in the house.

'This was given to him by his mother. I will keep it for her grandchildren, but the bowls and chest are for her if she is still alive. Tell her to be proud of her son.

'He inspired us as women and gave our sons and daughters, her grandchildren, the dignity to live as free human beings.'

The resonance of what she said astonished everyone in the room. Even so, she couldn't bear the thought the visitors might dismiss her words.

'Few women have ever had the right to say something so thrilling about a son,' she added, holding Folger's gaze until Adams had translated.

Folger faltered and looked away and this time she was certain he had tears in his eyes.

Tamahere wanted the island to vote on his plan to become chief of Pitcairn, something he had seen so effective when he was a boy on BOUNTY and on Tubuai. She couldn't say no.

Thursday, Charles and Adams organised Pitcairn's gifts of food and animals to the ship and the women and children took these to The Edge. The ship's sailors had to get everything down The Hill of Difficulty and on board and Captain Folger said their gain was worth the effort. It would take many hours and he was sure his sailors could handle the surf and the rocks. In any case, it would be a clear moonlit night and so they could work well past sunset.

Remembering Tamahere's comment about her sons' nakedness, she suggested Adams ask if the ship might give some trousers and shirts or jackets, not as a payment, but as a gift.

'That would be a good time to tell Folger what he wants to know.'

'Everything?'

'No, Father Adams. Nothing. Remember, it's your *tohe* you are helping to save, too.

'Tell the captain anything you'd most like him to believe.

'You know, *ha'avare*.'

Word about the voting spread and the Pitcairners were seated on the ground when she walked on to the square with Tamahere. She had helped him prepare, a sop to maternal feelings for a son she feared would soon suffer great humiliation.

Her greatest gift was white tapa, as fine and luminous as the silk of Fletcher's handkerchiefs and which she had made as a gift for the 30th birthday he never lived to celebrate.

Tamahere wore the tapa in voluminous drapes, the way Fletcher believed an old Roman or Greek might have done, but which was also the way of the nobles of Tahiti. His hair was oiled, coiled and decorated with two long narrow, feathers from the red-tailed tropicbird.

While she was doing this for him, he had made a bow and some arrows and then whittled a straight javelin. He bound them to finely worked stone arrow and spear heads that otherwise lay anonymously on Pitcairn.

Tamahere's appearance caused a mix of fear and awe for, whatever their mothers had warned them, she knew most Pitcairners carried a romantic image of what black men might be. The sexual and amorous fantasies of those amidst or past puberty might be painfully ripened. When Adams arrived, she handed him one of Pitcairn's remaining Bibles.

'I'll say something,' Adams began.

She ignored him and taking the stance of an orator, her back straight, her chin up and her hands on her hips, she addressed the Pitcairners in a loud, stern voice none had known from her before.

'The decision to follow Jesus, to be English, was made before many of you were born, certainly before most could understand what this meant.

'You will soon hear the words of Tamahere, a Tahitian man who wants to come and live amongst us, to be chief of Pitcairn Island. Tamahere is also my son, my Tahitian son.' She paused while this was discussed but her expression and stance did not falter. 'He thinks you should live like Tahitians because that is where your mothers come from. He and I believe it is fair you should decide for yourselves how you will live in the future.

'So, Tamahere will speak and then you will hear me speak and then anyone else who wishes to speak.

'And then you will vote for his gods and Tahiti, or for Jesus and Pitcairn Island.'

Introducing Tamahere as her son was as much new information as most young minds could cope with in a single day. And now her flock of Pitcairners had to decide what they wanted to believe and what their future might be, too.

Well, perhaps it was time they learned the world and its challenges didn't come in easy stages, didn't come only when they might be ready.

Tamahere strutted the way men did on a marae, his head held high, seeming to hold the world in little regard. Mauatua's sons were impressed, and she understood why. Tamahere was a kind of man they could never have imagined from what they knew on Pitcairn, and yet he was their brother. Would they be diminished by him or fired up to emulate him?

'You see.' He paused a long time, to ensure all minds were opened to possible answers. His mother recognised it as traditional orator's technique and on the innocents of Pitcairn it worked like magic.

They would believe whatever he said next.

'Choosing? Voting? Pah! These ideas from other worlds confuse you. Tahitian men make decisions and their women are grateful. They have other things to do, with children and food gathering and tapa making. And, most of all, with being obedient to the men who make those decisions.'

Thursday and Charles nudged Matt Quintal and the other young men who sat close to them. Their mothers' stern faces quickly changed their expressions back to serious concentration.

'Think. You Thursday, and you Charles, my brothers with the same noble blood of our mother. Think what it means to be a man on this island. Women's ways and women's work and women's things. No archery. No javelin competitions and no war games. This is because you have no men to teach you what is proper, no one to make you into real men. Real men do not hold hands. Did you see the men from TOPAZ holding hands? Only a man can teach men.'

He turned to face Adams. Adams thought he was being complimented, but Tamahere turned away with a low, sour laugh. Tamahere lifted his bow and his javelin high. 'This is men's work. These are their tools. These and war are the only way to make strong men.'

He turned to show his profile and the bound shape of his head to best advantage and, without seeming to think, hurled the javelin. It flew straight and pierced the bark to lodge firmly in a high branch of the banyan with a loud thud.

The cries of admiration for this entirely unsuspected thing were followed by louder ones as he quickly fired arrows that flew to quiver in the branch, each only a finger's width from the javelin. The men and boys clapped and cheered and most girls did too. Tamahere posed and posed again, showing profile and then profile until there was silence.

'When your men can do these things, when they are men *and* warriors, only then will they belong to the blood that flows in their veins, belong to the gods who created this island, to the gods of the land and the sea and the air and the sun that are in every breath you take. These things have been denied you. Because you have been brought up by women, women who did not understand the value of them.

'I will give you back what your white Jesus took from you. Jesus? Who is Jesus to tell you anything? Jesus never walked on this land or fished in these seas. Jesus does not live in the flowers and trees and water of this island. He lives only in the land of sand in that book.'

Tamahere swung and hit the Bible out of Adams' hand so it arced into the air and tumbled into the Pitcairners. They shouted at him. 'You bad man.' 'You bad black man' 'Jesus will punish you.' 'Jesus' father will send you to Hell.'

Tamahere grinned defiantly as Adams scrabbled to get the Bible.

'It was not Jesus who put you on this island. It was Fletcher Christian. A man. A man I knew. We liked each other. We became *taio* and exchanged names, a Tahitian thing to do.

'He did this even though I was just a boy because he knew that when he died men would follow me the way men followed him.'

She fought her inclination to counter such a lie. Tamahere's name change with Fletcher was different, very different from that fabrication.

'Now he is dead, everything that was once his is now mine. That is the way of Tahiti. Yes, Mauatua, even you, you are mine if I wish.'

Thursday jumped to his feet.

'She is your mother. That is all you can have of her. You cannot take her from us.'

Tamahere dismissed the interruption with a sweep of his hand.

'Oro and the gods of the Ma'ohi, the gods of the great sea that surrounds you, it was they who sent me here to be your leader. It is what your father wanted.'

The deliberate, determined style of Tamahere's oration hypnotised the Pitcairners. Any thought of mocking her new-found brother had drained from Mary Ann. Mauatua listened carefully, constructing her response. Suddenly, Tamahere turned his back and stamped. In a few dramatic swirls he removed his robes completely, exposing the tattoos on this back, arms, buttocks and upper legs.

It was the first time native Pitcairners had seen a fully tattooed man. Nothing they had seen on their mothers or on Adams had prepared them for such assault.

Tamahere had oiled his body and the rich, red light of the setting sun appeared to give the inky tattoos independent life as he rippled his muscles in a well rehearsed ritual. No sound broke Pitcairn's silence as the Pitcairners struggled to appreciate the intricate play of swirls and whorls, the zig zags and circles, the fine lines, the dotted lines, the shark's teeth and his solid black buttocks.

Mauatua shivered. It was again as though a primal presence had slithered onto Pitcairn, striking dumb everyone who looked at Tamahere. No wonder Jesus' priests in Tahiti were afraid of tattoos.

Tamahere shouted over his shoulder, demanding a response as raw and direct as his challenge.

'Look closely. These are your marks. The marks you should wear. They are the marks of your ancestor fathers. The tattoos of your Tahitian mothers and of their fathers and mothers for generations beyond telling. It is these that tell you who you are and who you should once more be.'

Few Pitcairners restrained their admiration. Until today's visitors none had seen a man in his prime, and certainly not a muscular, tattooed Tahitian man. They jostled for a better look, too awed to move close or to think of touching him. Mauatua turned away when she saw the other

Ma'ohi women disguising their admiration with downturned mouths. Their vivid eyes told the truth.

A gasp from the crowd turned her back. Tamahere had dropped the tapa cloth and turned bare-skinned to his audience with his hands held high and his face in the sun. It was shameless confrontation that demanded no possibility of indifference. Adams rushed forward and crouching in fear of violence held the Bible over Tamahere's genitals.

Tamahere kept his arms up but his eyes slowly turned down to the Bible. Mauatua had never seen a man show such contempt with so little expression on his face. Adams was humiliated. Unable even to stand straight he skulked away broken backed, like a rejected boar.

Tamahere slowly dropped his arms, and then aimed a trembling fist at the crowd. 'You are not people who belong to someone in a book.'

Many moved closer to their mothers but found little comfort there and no explanations. Tamahere stepped to his right so the last redder rays of the setting sun further inflamed the pallor of his skin and then he startled them again.

He strode through the Pitcairners, touching them, challenging, turning heads to face him.

'You belong to the gods I speak to you of, the gods who live here, every day and night,' he said into one upturned face after the other.

Tamahere's presence was so defiant it demanded responses, but no Pitcairner had learned the language of confrontation or of religious debate. A naked Tamahere at such close quarters sowed only discomfort and self doubt. Thursday passed his newborn son back to his wife, Teraura.

'The only true gods are the gods who live where you are born. And I will lead you back to them.'

He posed with his arms flung out straight. His feet were crossed, his head tilted to one side and he couldn't stop a smile on his lips.

He was a derisive nude Ma'ohi crucifix, intended to disengage every young brain for whom Jesus was the only object of ambition or optimism.

As the image wormed its way into minds too innocent to protect themselves from such malice, Mauatua lost her intention to keep the debate free of anger or personal attack.

'Enough! Tamahere that is enough. You were invited to honour your gods, not to dishonour ours.'

CHAPTER 60

She followed the paths Tamahere had forced among the Pitcairners, calming with soft words and cupped cheeks, whispering as she stroked their hair and answering fears as best she could.

Only when she joined the other women did she stand erect, still taller and straighter than any other Pitcairn Islander.

'Tamahere's is a thrilling picture. But it is a thrilling future only for warriors, for those like the noble Tamahere. And that is all it is – a future for *some* men.' She left the women and stood where Tamahere had spoken.

'If I lived as a Tahitian, if your mothers lived as Tahitian women, did you know most of you might not be here with us?'

She let the Pitcairners puzzle this while she walked to Charles. She leaned forward to take his hand, so he stood up beside her.

'Charles is a good friend to you all. But on Tahiti he would have been beaten to death the moment he left my body. Beaten or smothered by the man who sat behind me as I gave birth. Why? Just because Hoppa's foot is not perfect. That is all. Because of that small thing we never notice we might never have known his laugh and his kindness. Or his hops.'

Mauatua knew words struck harder when minds were diverted by amusement and attacked before the giggling melted away.

'Yes. On Tahiti there is a custom of killing unborn or newborn children, hard as that might be to imagine. Sometimes this was because it was what we women wanted. That is also true. It was usually done because it was what men wanted. But Charles is here because I chose to be a Pitcairn woman, because I chose not to be a Tahitian women like Tamahere thinks I should be.'

She let their eyes follow her as far as she dared and then spun and shouted at them. 'On Tahiti, babies who might have been your uncles and aunts, your cousins, even your brothers and sisters, were killed. Killed because it was what Tahitian men wanted.' She looked across to the women for support.

'That is why we women were so few on Tahiti,' Jenny added tearfully.

'Only the finest were permitted to live, only those who would grow tallest and straightest. Some men would only be seen with daughters of the palest skin.'

Mauatua took over again.

'Was that so we would make more beautiful wives for men? No! The most perfect girl babies were chosen so men would one day have finer sons by them, warrior sons, who would fight in some silly inter-island war and might be killed before they were really men.

'That's not all, when our fine sons were strong and handsome and tattooed like this . . .' She ripped away Tamahere's robes leaving him nude again but this time he was embarrassed and turned away.

'When a mother had a fine son like this, muscled and tattooed and good and kind to his mother, well then, she never knew when the priests might kill him, sacrifice him to those gods of theirs who do not exist there, and certainly do not exist on Pitcairn. It was yet another way a mother could lose a son.

'Can you imagine seeing a son like this killed by the priests of gods who do not exist? As though . . .' She pushed hard at Tamahere so, unprepared, he stumbled and looked foolish. 'As though he was worthless? Yet that was what mothers of sons were expected to endure and to accept. And he might have been your brother. He might have been you.'

She used the swell of dismay as reason to speak louder. She heightened the distress, saying, 'Were daughters luckier? The few permitted to live? They were. But their mothers were not. A mother was a slave to a daughter.' She waited until there was absolute silence.

'A daughter could eat only food gathered and cooked by her mother, by no other hands than her mother's. She had to enter the house through a new door, sometimes had to live in a separate house, built so men would never meet such a horrible thing as a baby girl or anything to do with her.

'On Tahiti Mary Ann might not have been a sister for her brothers because her father might think her too short or too black. Or because her mother didn't want the bother.'

Her sons were eager to comment but she stopped them with a flicked glance. 'On Tahiti, you or the person sitting beside you or behind you, might never have been allowed to be your best friend, to pick you up when you fell, to give you the best piece of pork.

'Oh yes. I almost forgot, if you were a woman, you were not allowed to eat pork, or shark or tuna or turtle.'

This was the most shocking thing she said and even the youngest understood but found it hard to believe this could be true.

'But look about you. Pitcairn has no men like that. Pitcairn has gentle men who love women, who love children, who love one another. Pitcairn does not need gods or men who kill babies and imprison mothers and sacrifice sons and kill each other in constant battles and wars.'

Tamahere and Adams shook their heads, her son displaying disbelief any Tahitian women dare speak like this, Adams' face crumpling with fear of what would ensue, mainly from Tamahere she guessed.

She felt no fear. She remembered discussing these things with Fletcher, who understood how much she wanted to turn her back on them. He would have applauded her convictions, praised her for telling the same unchanging story to the children they had made possible. It was grisly and there would be nightmares. Her Pitcairners saw nothing of violence, or poverty, of neglect, or idleness.

Now the world had come to the island's innocents it was her duty to tell the next generation why their mothers believed so much in Pitcairn. Telling them publicly and at the same time meant they had others to turn to and talk about it.

There was one more thing she had to say. She knew it could change Pitcairn more profoundly than anything she or Tamahere had yet said. She stood squarely to confront him and waited until he looked her in the eyes.

'As for owning me, owning me because you once exchanged names with Fletcher Christian,' she said, and then turning to the Pitcairners, she explained, 'by which he means his mother should be his wife...'

She waved a hand in disgust and marched away, enjoying the sounds of outrage she had aroused. Then she copied Tamahere's trembling, extended fist, but aimed hers only at him.

'But first my son, my Tahitian son Tamahere, before you own me or any other part of Pitcairn Island, first you would have to prove that he is dead, that Fletcher is not alive somewhere you do not know.

'Can you do that? Can anyone here?'

Tamahere's eyes rolled back in his head. He staggered and would have fallen if Adams had not braced him.

Yes, Mauatua rejoiced, even a Tahitian warrior fears ghosts, and he'd be even more frightened to think a living Fletcher might have heard him, or could be watching him.

Tamahere and Adams looked fearfully into the shadows about them but who clung to whom more fiercely she could not tell. She did not need to look to know the Ma'ohi women and many of their children were doing the same thing.

Others were supposed to speak now but only Mary Ann did. 'If you married Tamahere I would leave the island. Even if I had to walk.'

'So, you do think you are Jesus,' her brothers piped together.

Mauatua tapped Adams on the shoulder.

'Who? Who is voting?' he asked.

'Everyone old enough to have a worthwhile opinion. You and the women, of course. And every one born in the last century, twenty I make that. I will not and Tamahere will not.'

Tamahere blew himself up to protest but Mauatua knew what he was thinking. 'Some will be only eight or so? You thought yourself important and wise enough to change names with Fletcher when you were six. Do you think Pitcairners less worthwhile than you were?'

'Jesus. You didn't mention Jesus, how Jesus' blood and love saved us, that this is what they should vote for.' Adams held up the Bible.

'If you have done what is right all these years, and if the Bible is true, then Jesus will be in their hearts. Young people vote with their hearts, don't you find, Father Adams?'

'So, what you are saying is, let me get this right, Mrs Christian, is, if they don't vote for you, it will be my fault? Is that right?'

'Isn't that what you would think?'

The cold light of the high white moon shone as brightly as the last of the ebbed sun yet she found it hard to read the faces of those who voted, before or after they went behind a banyan root to pick up a black or white shell and then to put it into the proper basket. She hoped the privacy would encourage them to search deeper and vote truthfully.

Jenny was the last to vote. Once the quick musical note of her dropped shell was heard, Tamahere and Mauatua agreed everyone had voted and none had voted twice. She sent Adams to collect the two baskets. He poured the basket of black shells at Tamahere's feet and then that of white ones in front of her.

She hardly had time to cry Alleluia before greater cries went up from the youthful voters.

'Jesus has won.' 'Jesus is our captain.' 'Alleluia, Pitcairn is saved.'

With these and many more shouts the young voters went on to their knees and continued to give thanks, including many who must have voted for Tamahere. She was conciliatory and took Tamahere's hand.

'Will you join us? Will you be another son of Pitcairn? You would be welcomed.' Tamahere answered with chilling determination.

'Your truths are not my truths, Mauatua. If I cannot follow my true gods in this world, then perhaps I will be permitted in the next.'

'Plenty of time before that,' Thursday said, wrapping an arm around Tamahere. 'Stay here, be our brother. We will teach you the ways of Pitcairn and Jesus, we will all be Pitcairn brothers.'

Tamahere unpicked himself from the arms of his brother.

'No. There is *not* time. I hear different drums, drums telling me the time to discover the truth is when the question burns most brightly.'

Thursday and Charles had not the slightest idea what Tamahere might mean. Before they could ask, a call from the edge of the square told them the last boat to TOPAZ was loaded and ready to row away.

Mauatua saw resolution in Tamahere's eyes. She hoped he was finding the words to say good bye.

Instead, Tamahere told her he would not be leaving.

'I cannot meet my gods at sea. I must meet them on land, this land.'

CHAPTER 61

When Tamahere refused to return to TOPAZ, Mauatua asked Thursday to canoe out to the ship to collect his brother's belongings, and that kindness soothed Tamahere. He told her once more that he had chosen to die, took his drum from his sea chest and then walked away from her.

Tamahere's drumming continued throughout the night, troubling the sleepers in every house on a night when it was too hot to slide the wooden windows closed.

Mauatua took her other sons to find Tamahere at first light. He sat cross-legged close to the cliff side at The Edge, naked except for a garland of flowers he had made for his head. His drumming had eased him into a trance. Her arrival didn't interrupt the incessant beating of his fingers or break his unfocussed stare.

Far below, she could see activity on TOPAZ, but the anchors were in place. Captain Folger was so grateful for the provisions he had agreed to put off sailing until early this next morning.

'Could he really do it,' Thursday asked his mother. 'I mean, just lie down and die?'

'I have never seen it, but I have heard about it on Tahiti. It should be done on the marae where his *pufenua* is buried.'

'He'd never be allowed to do that on Tahiti, not from what he told us,' Thursday said.

'If what he has told us of Tahiti is true. Can you believe missionaries would do such things?' Charles asked.

Mauatua dismissed her sons' cares. 'After the night, after the drumming, his mind will think more clearly I am sure.'

She kneeled and leaned forward to *ho'i* but Tamahere held his breath for as long as her nose touched his and did not interrupt his drumming. It was insulting but she admired his determination.

'Tamahere, my son. When I greet your gods on this new day I hear voices that tell me they do not want you. They think it cruel for you to join them before you live the full life of a man, without knowing the comfort of a wife and the pride of children to follow you.

'I have listened carefully in the correct trees and bushes and cannot hear them saying it is your time and that they want you with them.

'Tamahere, the ship down there is a better escape from what you feel in this new world on Pitcairn.'

His drumming continued loud in her ears, weaving rhythms of increasing violence and volume until with an explosive last beat there was sudden louder silence. Eventually, he spoke without looking at his mother.

'I will leave if you come too.'

Mauatua recoiled and overbalanced but when her sons rushed to her she pushed them away, putting a finger to her lips.

'Help me win Tahiti back from the missionaries,' Tamahere begged. 'They destroy our music, our maraes, our gods, everything.'

'And your evil traditions too, I hope. Good for them,' Mauatua said standing over him. 'Jesus will be the saviour of Tahiti, just as he brought peace on Pitcairn.' Her sons said Amen.

'I will not go if you do not come,' Tamahere said. Mauatua moved behind him and gently massaged his shoulders, hoping that because he had not slept he would be more easily persuaded by gentleness.

'There are ways you could stay here with dignity. You could teach your brothers the good things about being a Ma'ohi man, fishing and carving, drumming and games.'

'We should be teaching the young men of Tahiti,' Tamahere insisted. 'We could make a new Tahiti. We'll do what you did here, creating something new out of everything old.'

'And they'd listen? Who would believe a Tahitian woman had succeeded where white men failed?' She heard the edge of anger creeping into her voice and took her hands from his shoulders so he did not feel their tension.

'Come with me. Or I die here,' Tamahere repeated in a low flat voice.

'What sort of son would ask that of a mother?' As soon as she said it, she knew what Tamahere's answer would be.

'What sort of mother would do what you did to me?'

She slapped him as easily as she would any child who was petulant for the sake of attention. Pitcairn mothers were allowed to chastise and criticise and punish. It was the way in England, Fletcher had insisted.

Thursday and Charles ran back to guard her again. She regretted they had heard Tamahere's criticism or seen her slap him. They had no tools to deal with the emotions that would be raised in them, nothing but the simple beliefs of their remote island.

'He must love you,' Thursday said.

'He spent so long looking for you,' Charles added. 'He thought you'd forgotten him.'

'Yes, he just wanted you to remember him,' Thursday agreed.

'Remember!' Mauatua whirled onto her feet, a hand up to threaten her other sons. Her mind raced as fast as Tamahere's drumming had done. There was one other way that might save her son, yet it was something she hoped to share with him in a moment of love.

It was never to have been dragged out of her, never used to defend herself as though she had done something wrong. Anything but that.

Yet, perhaps it was all she had left to save him, perhaps this was the way it was meant to be used?

Even Fletcher had never known this secret, because she was afraid he would think her pointlessly sentimental. The gentle words she had shaped and saved so very long for Tamahere fled from her tongue. She lowered her hand and pulled at one of the small woven containers she wore on the sash around her waist. She mumbled 'remember' furiously as she struggled to open it and then she flung the dried remains of his blooded *he'i* at Tamahere, the one he wore before she threw him back into Tahiti's care so long ago.

'Remember?' she cried again. 'Remembering is all some mothers ever have. Mothers *do* remember their lost children, every one of them, dead or alive. I did. I do.' She stood over Tamahere, so angry that he cowered.

'Why do you think all my sons and daughter were allowed to live on Pitcairn? It was not to spite Tahitian men, but because I *remembered*. I vowed never to lose another child just because I would not live as a Tahitian woman.'

Then she focussed on Thursday and Charles.

'I once had to make a choice, a terrible choice in seconds. If I had not, there would be no Pitcairn, no you Thursday and no you Charles. One day you will judge if that was right or wrong. 'But never, not one of you, ever tell me I did not remember.'

She spun back and pointed directly at Tamahere, now as alert as his two Pitcairner brothers.

'Your brothers and sisters here, Christian or Young, *every* child living on Pitcairn, all are proof I remembered you, Tamahere. I remembered, I did, I did, every day.'

Her voice faltered and drained lifelessly into the silence. She crumpled but Thursday and Charles dived and held her.

Hanging limp and defeated between them she wept hot silent tears, unable to imagine how she might ever take her first step from the unholy agony of this place.

Tamahere ignored them. He collected the dead and desiccated flowers of the *he'i*, which crumbled more as he touched them.

He put their rough dust to his lips and it turned to paste as his tongue tasted for the lost fragrances.

A long cry came from the ship. He ran to the cliff edge and swung his arm in great swoops, telling the ship she should sail. Then picking up as many of the old dead flowers of his boyhood *he'i* as he could hold in one hand, he gathered his drum in the other arm and turned to walk back into the village.

The anchors were raised and sails unfurled almost at once. TOPAZ saluted with a single cannon shot.

Mauatua and her Pitcairn sons prayed the ship would safely take news of them to the king and to Fletcher's family. And then, not knowing what to say about all they had seen and heard, they followed Tamahere.

After just a few steps she ran back to collect her son's clothes.

CHAPTER 62

She got up with the sun and took water and mashed banana to Fletcher's old gardens for the seventh time. Tamahere was lying in a long pit, not much deeper than an earth oven but clearly grave-like. Kind but frightened Pitcairners added fresh flowers to it each day.

Tamahere withered with these in the tropical February heat, even in the shaded place he had chosen close to the pool. The only signs of life he gave to relieve her misery were occasional movements of his eyes beneath their lids, like the distraught dreaming of an unhappy child.

How had it come to this? Her son so distressed and confused that his only solution was to will himself to death? She could lose him forever this time, and the only solution was for him to change his mind. She could not abandon Pitcairn and go to Tahiti with him. She begged him, but after three days she lost her will to battle with him.

His determination to die was invulnerable.

Day after day she saw his body weaken and as it did his tattoos lost their power. Her warrior son looked more and more like a very old man morbidly painted to look fierce. As the tattoos lost their voices to frighten or inspire, fewer Pitcairners came to sit with Mauatua and her dying son.

She regularly crouched to dribble water onto his lips until the least tip of his tongue spread it and took some inside his mouth. He didn't resist when she used her finger to moisten his tongue and teeth. When she spread banana mashed with coconut milk across his lips, they tightened. She wiped it away, far past any thought of force.

Thursday and Charles arrived to keep her company, as they had done every day. 'There's time, there's still time, isn't there. Have you told him?'

She shook her head and Thursday strode up to the pit. He couldn't sit or kneel by his dying brother even though he couldn't explain why not.

'I'll go. I'll go to Tahiti with you the next time a ship comes. I'll help you, like a brother should.'

He turned to his mother. 'I like having a big brother and if he is my brother, he can't be a bad man, can he?' he wondered.

'No point talking to her.'

Mary Ann had followed her brothers. She had no sympathy for Tamahere yet rather than stay away she chose to use him against her mother. Mauatua couldn't understand her daughter's poisonous mind or why she had been so deeply jealous from her earliest days.

Was she still looking for revenge for the bruising she suffered in the womb? Or did she think her life would be better if she were a boy? How could she think that on Pitcairn?

'No point,' Mary Ann continued with as little gravity as if she was discussing dinner. 'She's made up her mind and she wants him dead. Always knows best, doesn't she? Well, I think this so-called brother of mine needs to hear other things.' She moved closer, tormenting her mother by speaking loud enough for any passerby to hear.

'She likes to think she freed us even though we have never been to Tahiti or other islands to choose for ourselves, to see if what she says is true. She thinks this makes her a saint. Well, it's true, she has given me the same choices as men. But how? How did she give me these choices? Blood, that's how.'

Mauatua shrugged and showed her sons they must not interrupt. There had been such an outpouring of secrets and opinions since Tamahere landed on Pitcairn. Mary Ann was due her turn.

'The only thing that's really Christian on Pitcairn is a few names, and even hers is a lie. She should be Mrs Young. He was her last husband.' For the first time a slight noise came from Tamahere.

'You see, he agrees with me.' Mary Ann flounced away flashing an ugly mask of triumph.

Mauatua recognised Tamahere's feeble call as a signal he knew death was finally near. She searched quickly and picked a leafy twig from a bush thought sacred by Tahitians, a bush she remembered was the most potent carrier of messages to and from their gods. She kneeled beside him and leaned forward over Tamahere's head.

'Don't, don't do that,' Thursday cried, clamping his hands to his head. 'Stand up. Stand up.'

She couldn't ignore Thursday's distress. This time he might remember why seeing her kneel over a dying man caused him such distress and why he couldn't bear hearing Fletcher's name.

'Take him away, Charles, look after him,' she begged her younger son.

Thursday struggled against Charles but agreed to be led to a tree he could sit behind with his hands over his eyes. When Fletcher's sons were settled she knelt to Tamahere again. She leaned close, so her other children couldn't hear.

'For the second time you are at the thin veil between life and death. But this time it is not for me to say if you live or do not. I insisted you took your first breath but the last one is yours to choose.'

She dropped more water onto his lips but there was no reaction.

'This time you are choosing to abandon me. I ask you one more time. Please stay. Teach Thursday to be a man so he can be a better father to Pitcairn's children.'

Tamahere's eyes opened and his lips moved. What? What did he want? It didn't matter, getting some reaction was all she wanted. She offered him water and he took more than he had for days. Encouraged, she put mashed banana on his lips. He worked some of it across his tongue until he could swallow it and this easing of his throat meant he could take more from her. She tipped a palmful piteously slowly from her cupped hand, praying to Jesus and to the Tahitian gods he believed in that he had chosen life.

Tamahere's lips continued to move and she put her head right beside his mouth before she understood he was asking for Charles.

Charles stood close to her for comfort and constantly glanced back at his brother. Thursday still had bastions over his eyes. When Tamahere blinked to say he recognised Charles was there, she prodded Charles and he spoke as nervously and quickly as she had spoken softly and slowly.

'You should stay, Tam. You could, even if it is only until the next ship. Think of the things you could do here with your brothers, think of the things you could teach us, like you said Fletcher taught you.'

Charles flicked a look at Thursday but he had heard nothing.

Tamahere opened his eyes very wide and lifted his right hand a little. He turned and moved it enough to beckon Charles closer.

She was torn between Thursday seeing Charles leaning over his dying brother and ignoring what might be Tamahere's last wish. Thursday was still closing himself off. She knelt and pulled Charles down, encouraging him to lean his head in to Tamahere.

Tamahere pricked his thumb on a sharp point on a stem in his bower and showed he wanted Charles to do the same. He found the strength to croak out a speech he must have foreseen for days.

'Your foot made you the most valued one, Charles. Choosing to let you live was the greatest gift our mother gave any of her sons. You are the chosen son, Hoppa. Not me, not Thursday, but you. So, I choose you to be my *taio*. And then I will teach you all I know.'

With surprising strength he found Charles' hand and turned it so the blood on their thumbs mixed. Charles and his mother smiled, for they thought Tamahere had changed his mind. Tamahere was not finished.

'So, now I am Charles. And you, you will . . .'

Even the whisper became too much for him and he fell silent but they could see his chest moving.

'Am I Tamahere now?' Charles looked to his mother expecting permission to leave but she returned his head to Tamahere. Her son in the pit rallied to speak.

'Yes, you are Tamahere. But that really means you will be Fletcher. You will have his spirit in you and be the vessel of his wisdom.'

Charles turned to ask his mother what this meant but with another enormous effort Tamahere reached up to clasp him behind his neck and pulled Charles closer to his face. She recognised what he was doing and pushed on Charles' neck until his mouth hovered over Tamahere's cracked and bleeding lips.

Tamahere gasped, breathy and urgent, and then his grip became imperative. He pulled Charles' mouth onto his lips and through them expelled his last breath.

For an eternity, Mauatua, Charles and Tamahere were as rigid as death. She turned only when she heard Thursday. He had seen his brother on Tamahere's mouth. He staggered, clutching his throat but struggling to say something. Mary Ann was spinning on the spot and screaming.

'He kissed him. He kissed him!'

Thursday collided with Mary Ann. The physical shock broke his dumbness. 'It was Daddy, Daddy. I remember she made me kiss Daddy like that,' he cried.

Mary Ann fell heavily but begged no sympathy. She picked herself up and ran from the gardens.

Mauatua pulled Tamahere's dead arm off Charles and then dragged Charles to Thursday, hoping to catch him before he dropped to the ground. She managed to reach him but the weight of her two grown boys was too much. She fell with them.

She sat profoundly alone with one dead son before her and two more with heavy, dumb heads in her lap. She knew neither Thursday nor Charles was sleeping. One had fainted to protect his sanity from the memory of what she had forced him to do in these gardens fifteen years ago. The other was paralysed and mute for what she had forced him to do minutes ago.

She was uncertain if the day's end would find her with only one sane son or two, or none. Would she have the chance to tell them they shared the most flattering and profound of Tahitian traditions? If it were true, one of her sons was now the true inheritor of Fletcher's soul and wisdom.

A clamour of voices and running feet came closer. Mary Ann had not abandoned them but brought anxious women. They stopped short of Mauatua and stared. Even though more and more Pitcairners confronted the tragic tableau not one could find words that were adequate.

Only Mary Ann voiced her views, and she had no thought of solace. She bundled together every whisper and rumour she had heard.

'It looks like Mauatua has been killing again.'

CHAPTER 63

The rain was heavy and insistent. Mauatua led the Ma'ohi women in a slow procession, each wearing a protective woven cloak of coconut fibre. Water churned through the village and around their feet, making every pathway a culvert and every exposed measure of Pitcairn into clinging red sludge. On all their heads were garlands of flowers, picked and made up during the night and already sodden and sad. She carried a small branch and shook it as the women chanted incantations of intercession and mercy to the gods and spirits.

She had asked for some time before the rest of the Pitcairners arrived, so the women could offer ancient prayers Tamahere would know. As they reached Tamahere's dying place, young men finished piling earth and stones over his body and strewed the poignant mound with flowers.

The rain bore petals away in long coloured strands over the sodden ground, as though the flowers were weeping with her.

The rain eased as Adams led in the other Pitcairners, singing together with bright, thin voices. Today she found their Christian hymns disturbing and shrill, for Pitcairners' harmonies rang more truthfully of their Ma'ohi heritage than of any message from Jesus. Yet even their Christian beliefs had not united them.

As they struggled with words of saving and redemption it was obvious the past week had taken a ragged toll on the minds of Pitcairners. It was sad to see that each walked and huddled only with those who interpreted events their way.

Adams showed her he had a Bible.

'Would you like me to lead prayers?'

She nodded but found it hard to listen. Both Pitcairner sons and Mary Ann had stayed away, feverish and unable to eat or drink.

Adams prayed and then sang again in a loud, brave voice. The Pitcairners joined in lustily, moving close for the joy of hearing their voices multiplied and harmonised but their Ma'ohi mothers gathered apart from them, at the head of the grave, and defiantly keened and chanted in their Mother Tahitian.

Mauatua stood steadfast beside Adams singing about Jesus, but nothing in the Christian messages reflected what was in her heart.

The honours and compliments she heard the women give, commending Tamahere to his Ma'ohi gods and spirits, were more telling, more personal, more relevant.

She might have been able to resist if Adams had not held the Bible up to block her vision. She pushed him and the Bible aside and ran to the head of Tamahere's grave.

She turned her face to the grey sky and welcomed the rain that spilled again. and pulled out the rough wooden cross suspended around her neck. Her sons had made it for her many years ago. Adams protested it was too Catholic and unsuitable for worshipping his Jesus but she couldn't agree.

She shouted at him. Jesus was love, and her sons had made the cross with love for Jesus and for her. Where was the sin?

If Fletcher's sons and daughter were there she might not have done this, but without them she could no longer resist. She beat her forehead and scalp, striking harder and harder with the wooden cross until blood, rain and tears combined.

Through the sudden red pall she saw Adams was horrified by this unholy collision of Christian and pagan but it was the only way she could say what she wanted. She added loud, long keening and chanted words to the rhythm of her blows, telling every hill and valley, cave and mountain, field and garden and patch of weeds that she had lost one son and feared for the others.

Her desperate pleading easily penetrated Pitcairn's canopy and she saw birds fly from the trees, ignoring the rain.

Might they be flying with Tamahere's soul?

The hymn singing faltered and died. Adams scurried the Pitcairners away until only the Ma'ohi women remained to share her grief. Soon, even their chanting stopped and instead she heard low murmurs of concern.

When she cleared her eyes of blood she saw Thursday, Charles and Mary Ann standing at the foot of the grave, each of them pale and distressed. Charles skipped to her and flung the clotted cross from her.

'You are still Tahitian. That's all he wanted to be.'

Thursday shouted over the grave to her.

'You lied. You lied to him and now he's dead because of you.'

'I am honouring my dead Tahitian son the correct way. He is your brother, have some respect for who he was.'

'It's who *you* are, that's what we want to know,' Mary Ann whined.

Mauatua's mind seized. She had no more arguments to give them. She had only emotions and these were focussed on her grief at losing Tamahere a second time.

Fletcher's children would each want something different from her but she was incapable of giving a single word more of comfort.

She was the one in need.

She pushed past them to pick up her cross and then hurried as fast as she could from the gardens but this was leaving Tamahere too soon. She looked back with every few steps, sending placatory words.

Thursday ran to keep up with her but Charles struggled in the thick red mud churned by the fleeing Pitcairners. Thursday went back to lend him a shoulder and they struggled three-legged to catch her. Mary Ann walked a shorter route through the undergrowth and gardens.

Mauatua's foot turned on a rock and she fell. Thursday instinctively reached to help her, but when he let go of Charles the impetus of their interrupted chase overbalanced them and Charles fell. Thursday hesitated and so helped neither.

Thursday ran to stand four-square over her and to stop her going further. She wanted to go home she moaned, and as they struggled both ended up on the path, both blooded from her head.

Too exhausted to walk, she crawled on hands and knees to get away. She tried not to think what she must look like to her children, with so much blood and red mud smearing her body. She pulled off her diadem of flowers and dropped it into a puddle. Its bloodstains dissolved away in the muddy, ruddy water. Was that a portent of the end of a life? Whose blood could possibly be next?

She turned, still on all fours, threw back her head and sighed before creasing her eyes with the effort it took her to speak. Her lips were tense and her teeth barely apart. 'I did tell him, I told him he could have both worlds. He could have belonged to both.'

'Is that what you have always done without telling us, Mummy, lived in both worlds?' Charles asked. 'Have you always been lying to me, to all of us, Mummy?'

It had been years since he'd used that childhood word for her. It inspired a revelation, an insight that Pitcairn's first generation was bound to think and act as children at heart. How could they be anything else?

'Are you really a Christian, or only a Mrs Christian? Or just a Tahitian called Mauatua?' Mary Ann called from behind a bush. Her eyes were shining, feeding her hatred with the sight of her mother overwhelmed and gripping a painful ankle.

'Are you doing what our Daddy wanted? Is that it? Or is it what he still tells you to do. Where is he? Is he still alive?'

There it was. The question she hoped never to be asked by her children, even when at her strongest. She stumbled to stand, straightened her shoulders and limped away, no longer knowing if she was looking through blood, tears or mud. Even now, she couldn't stop the fight in her mind, forever balancing self-blame against self-justification.

She cursed Pitcairn for not giving her a single precedent to use for judging what was right. How *could* she have done anything else?

A stone hit her head and she staggered into a tree. Charles was still on the ground with his arm raised. 'Where is Daddy?!'

She had never seen him so angry and confused. When she said nothing he picked up another stone and this time hit her on the shoulder.

Why was Thursday letting him do this?

'What did you do to him?' Thursday moved to stand between her and Charles but only so he could challenge her more directly.

'Tell us. Tell some truth at last.'

The bruising pain in her head and shoulders was besieged by memories of his crying, '*It was Daddy, Daddy. I remember she made me kiss Daddy like that.*'

Of course Thursday said Daddy. Of course Charles threw stones and called her Mummy. Her sons would be 20 in a few years but could be nothing more than children on Pitcairn and without warning they had been pushed into confronting searing different realities.

Each of them wore only a thin green bark of maturity and Tamahere's traumatic death had stripped that. There could be no logical, adult discussion. Just shouting and challenging stares, the way Thursday was doing now. It was pitiful to know he was plumped with sadness only for himself but not for her.

Suddenly she knew why Pitcairn was so silent. It did have a past and it was too awful to tell. There were spirits here, but only of malevolence and envy and violence.

They were too cunning to attack her earlier. They waited until the burden of her deeds was so great her sacrifice to them was inevitable.

The soil of Pitcairn, its red soil, was true master and mistress of this island, red for its centuries of feasting on blood and now aching for hers

She resigned herself to dying at her children's hands.

She had never been an independent woman here but a mindless vassal of the island's gory greed. Pitcairn had edged its desires for as long as it could bear and now she would gratify them with the greatest prize of sin and regret the island had ever known. Its predatory soil would be well sustained until it chose another to bleed into its bowels.

She prayed to no god but waited for whatever any of her children might do. Instead, her fears of pain and death subsided and her mind cleared of the past. For a blissful moment she knew serenity.

When nothing more and no-one else struck her, the small voice that always rescued her from dark moments bubbled through her inertia. They were her children, it said, and she should not be their victim. That was not the proper role of children. She picked up a stone, a bigger one than had hit her, and weighed it in her hand. She stood.

'I know,' Thursday said, defying the rock 'I know some of it. I remember.' He turned to Charles. 'I will tell you.'

It was a relief. His attention was no longer focussed on her. She felt strength trickling back into her legs. Thursday's offer encouraged Mary Ann out of the bushes. Drenched to the skin, weak with the shock of the last twenty four hours, her three children by Fletcher stood separated from her by the secret she kept locked furthest away from them.

She had done it to ensure they lived with pride and now the secret was destroying their bonds.

She dropped the rock. She turned her back on them and began to walk home, her head throbbing in time with each careful step. This was a secret too big for the telling.

She knew their immature minds could justify killing her in the way they defended killing an injured bird or animal.

It no longer mattered. Killing her would ensure the last secret about their father was never told and then the benefits to her children could never be stolen from them. Thursday might well begin to tell the story of Fletcher. What mattered most to her, more than life itself, was that her children never knew the end of their father's story.

CHAPTER 64

March 1st 1831: Pitcairn Island

How had 1831 come so quickly? And why should the entire island be expected to board a ship with so little notice and then sail from Pitcairn forever? Mauatua chose her usual solution when there was a big decision to be made. She walked alone to her bath on the hill. It took so much longer these days, with her stiffer hips and knees and having to manage the walking pole she used to keep her balance.

The pool had been Fletcher's greatest surprise and his greatest pride. It was the shape of a bathtub in England he said, long and rounded at each end. He secretly carved it for her into living rock, across the slope of a long hill that then shattered into sheer cliffs.

The slope saw the sun most of the day. A small reliable spring further up the hill ran into the bath and because it dawdled it took as much heat from the rock and the sun as was offered. It trickled to overflow from the lower side so there was always clear, warm water to sit in and think. The inclination at one end faced the sun, so she could lie back under a shade and rarely feel chilled.

Over 80 lived on Pitcairn now, including three Englishmen who had found their way to the island, Nobbs, Buffett and Evans. Thursday was the oldest true Pitcairner at 40 and still married to Teraura, the youngest of the Tahitian women who had come with her on BOUNTY but 16 years older than him. He had four children at home but his eldest boy Charles II and his 15-year old wife had made him a grandfather, less than a year ago. She was a great-grandmother.

Charles married Sully, the Tahitian baby girl who landed from BOUNTY in a barrel, but she died young four years ago leaving him with six children aged from 20 down to almost six.

What would Fletcher think if he knew both sons had married older Tahitian women from BOUNTY and that his grandchildren were all three-quarters native blood? They were the only such Pitcairners for the rest were half Ma'ohi and half white, and when these married their children were the same.

And then there was Mary Ann, the spinster. She'd dismissed her doubts about Christianity and considered herself married to Jesus as the ideal white man, and to any unpleasantness she could create with her tongue.

Only three years after Folger discovered them a poem was written about her in England by some woman with a long name. What was it? Something like Mary Russell Mitford? Mitford called Mary Ann *The Fair Maid of the South Seas*.

No-one would deny she was strikingly beautiful. Or had been then. 38 years of spleen and jealousy was beginning to show. And yet, her very busyness and nosiness was useful. It was Mary Ann who noisily instructed every family on the island what to take and what to leave and how to pack. Frankly, it took a load off her and there were plenty of capable men on the island, anyway.

The three Englishmen might argue about who was the better teacher of this or that, but they would lend a willing hand and a broader view of the world in any crisis.

Half the families wanted to go but she couldn't decide. She was over 70 now, as far as she knew. These days her skin was wrinkled before she soaked in the pool. The question was not simply to go or stay. It was what was best for Pitcairn's children. She took an involuntary deep breath and her body shuddered under the water. Children. They were the basis of most decisions in Pitcairn's history and would have to be again.

Jesus certainly ruled Pitcairners' lives and had made Pitcairn safer. But he was a different Jesus from the one Adams taught. Adams and his last wife Teio had both died in 1829, he first and she just nine days later. Thanks to the three Englishmen she now saw what nonsense Adams had believed. Imagine insisting Pitcairners fast on Wednesdays and Fridays yet still demand they worked in the gardens or fished on those days. Children fainted from hunger as they toiled, yet were assured this was part of Jesus' teaching and love. Once ships began to call she quickly sorted that out and Adams accepted it with bad grace.

One captain, she forgot which, had called Pitcairn's earlier Christianity 'nauseating'. He'd also complained it was not possible to get the same version of any story from more than one person. 'Each seemed incapable of agreeing with another, even to the point of what their name might be.'

The truth in that still made her laugh.

He wasn't the only one who was confused. Pitcairners had always played with visitors by telling them tall tales, *ha'avare*

They'd even invented a Pitkern word for it. Hypocriting.

The worst thing a doubting visitor could do was to tell a Pitcairner that the word didn't exist.

'Yes it does, my friend,' Charles would say. 'We just existed it.'

Anyway, it wasn't as though visitors knew it all. The rest of the world seemed to believe Father Adams was singlehandedly responsible for Pitcairn's climb from bloodshed to Bible and harmony. He wouldn't have been alive to take to the Bible if she and Jenny hadn't brought him back from the edge of death.

Oh well, that was the way of the white world, perhaps of the world in general. Just like the priesthood in Tahiti, the male-dominated Anglican Church never believed women capable of anything but motherhood.

Mareva, Teatuahitea and Tinafanaea had all died childless. Jenny had sailed away on SULTAN in 1817. She'd never been a mother but had spirit enough to know she should be using her skills to do greater things in this life than care for other women's children on Pitcairn.

She'd wanted more of the world when she sailed on BOUNTY and Pitcairn was not enough of it for her.

She wondered if Jenny would tell the truth to anyone, but even by 1817 hypocriting was established enough for her to be uncertain of the past. Now there were just four Ma'ohi women who could tell the truths of what happened before Pitcairn was rediscovered in 1808.

Even if they remembered the truth, the survivors Toofaiti and Vahineatua would never put their children at risk and Teraura had become a loving wife to Thursday. Why would she tell anyone she wielded the axe that beheaded Titahiti when he had been deceitfully lured to bed?

She judged Fletcher's bath had worked its magic. There were problems on Pitcairn, mainly with water supply but they could be fixed. A few days' public works would easily make another reservoir.

On the other hand Pitcairn's youngsters should see more of the world, as she had. If they left Pitcairn now their memories would be of a lush, abundant and safe island.

Just like a handsome man or beautiful woman who died in their prime was remembered that way for ever. Just as she remembered Fletcher.

Of course they should all go to Tahiti and join the greater 19th century world. Tahiti was ruled by a queen now, granddaughter of the child Tu she remembered, and it was said England might soon have a queen.

Perhaps the world was finally a place for women with opinions? On balance, she looked forward to seeing Matavai and Tahiti again, in spite of the changes she had been warned about.

When Mauatua announced she would go the Pitcairners who still dithered agreed to join her.

In 1980, Tom Christian rediscovered and excavated Mauatua's pool, reputedly dug by Fletcher for her as a substitute for Tahiti's running streams and falls of fresh water.

CHAPTER 65

March 7th, 1831 – leaving Pitcairn Island

LUCY ANN and COMET headed into the Pacific and she marvelled again that BOUNTY ever found the island. It was so tiny, so remote. No wonder it had been eighteen years before others discovered it was their home. From the sea it looked less a home and more a clumsily mounded memorial for the many bodies unmarked in its soil. Only Adams had a tombstone on Pitcairn and that was the way she thought it best.

Reminders of the past helped no-one.

Only now did she think that in the rush to live in Tahiti, no-one had given much thought to *why* they had been offered this exodus. What had moved others to take them from their home, and why had they thought it was their business? Not even the English newcomers to Pitcairners had seemed inclined to ask.

Buffet arrived in CYRUS in 1823. His offer to help with teaching the children was accepted and he also started a register of the ships that called at Pitcairn and of the island's births and deaths. He attempted to record the dates of events before the island had been found by Captain Folger but of course no-one told him the truth.

Even so, when she managed to read some of the journal she was shocked to learn he reinterpreted what he was told. He expressed no surprise Jenny's boat had capsized, writing *'for what could a few ignorant women have done for themselves drifting upon the waves'.*

Ignorant women? The boat foundered because ignorant white men like Quintal built it to fail.

She didn't let him know she knew about that entry but since then she'd not trusted him. Anyway, he didn't seem to have that many reservations about life with 'ignorant' women. He'd married her daughter Dolly by Edward Young and also had a child by Thursday's daughter Mary.

Evans was an altogether simpler man, who kept to himself with his wife Rachel Adams and their two boys.

Nobbs arrived in 1828 and was welcomed to stay when he offered to be both schoolmaster and unordained pastor. He soon married Charles' daughter Sarah. With Nobbs married to a granddaughter and Buffett to a daughter, she was obliged to see both Englishmen often and was closer to island affairs than she wished.

Her opinion was constantly sought and her answers were as much like Fletcher Christian would have given as she could manage. But she really wanted only to spend time with her grandchildren.

Why did these Englishmen so readily agree to go to Tahiti? Had the thrill of living on such a remote island with 'ignorant' native women palled for them?

The two ships were sent by Britain's Governor Darling in New South Wales, Australia, she knew that much. Samuel Henry, the son of a missionary once based in Tahiti, was in charge and supported by a Captain Walpole of HM 39th Regiment. How much was all this costing?

She privately wagered it was more than enough to have solved Pitcairn's problems and still kept them all in their homes.

She made a point of befriending Samuel Henry and through him discovered the ships carried a swag of goods intended for 'Chiefs and Natives' and for 'strengthening that good disposition which the Natives have always evinced for the English'. There were tools, cloth, food, beads and two umbrellas.

'And who are the 'Chiefs and Natives' these goods are intended for?' she asked. 'Is this what the British in Australia think of Pitcairners, or do they mean Tahitians when they write that?'

Mr Henry couldn't or wouldn't answer. He diverted her by asking, 'Did you know Mr Adams wrote to London requesting the Pitcairners be transported to Australia?' She did know.

The arguments had been fierce. Adams gloomily predicted the island would run short of timber, perhaps even of water, and thus be unable to support itself but she had disagreed.

Samuel Henry said the letter was considered at length by the Foreign Office, the Colonial Office and the Admiralty.

Meanwhile Henry Nott, another who had been in Tahiti with The London Missionary Society, convinced the Colonial Office the Pitcairners would be better removed to Tahiti. Letters were exchanged and the then king of Tahiti offered the Pitcairners hospitality.

At the same time several naval visitors to Pitcairn contradicted Adams' views, believing life was sustainable there and that the island could actually support a bigger population. Apparently no-one thought to pass this on to the Colonial Office or to Mr Nott.

'Mr Nott's view was that Pitcairners would become useful missionaries throughout the Pacific,' Samuel Henry explained. 'It would be a way of showing gratitude for your new home if you took the story of your conversion and saved other natives.'

'We are not breeding stock for missionaries, Mr Henry,' Mauatua protested, banging her pole into the deck. 'And we do not need a new home. We have brought up children and grandchildren, great grandchildren now, and built houses and made gardens on Pitcairn.

'We did not do this to be spread like manure to sprout other Christians. We have our own world, our own language. We are Christians, yes, but we are Pitcairners first. The Christian religion is an extra.'

'It was thought by the Mission that you would welcome the opportunity to spread God's Word,' Herbert dumbly repeated.

'The Mission might have asked us first. Is it because Pitcairners are not pure white we can be so disregarded? Do they think us second class somehow? Hardly a Christian way of thinking, I would have thought.'

Henry had more to reveal. Yet another missionary from Tahiti had called on Governor Darling of New South Wales. Named Crook, he convinced Darling there was no reason to delay a move to Tahiti and so the ships were despatched.

Missionaries! Why hadn't she asked these questions before they were at sea? Why hadn't anyone?

Herbert huffed and puffed like a badly stoked fire, so she drove her point further, making it quite clear they might be taken to Tahiti, but neither missionaries nor Governor Darling could make them stay there.

'I see that, Mrs Christian. I see that.'

She stalked up into the bow to stand where she and Fletcher so often stood on BOUNTY. Her excitement at seeing Tahiti after 40 years vanished, replaced by anger at herself and by fear for the Pitcairners.

The Tahitian nation couldn't protect itself from Europeans or from their religions. Tahitian culture was destroyed while the preaching invaders fought among themselves. What chance did her few Pitcairners have?

She was furious at letting the next generations agree so readily to the move. She wasn't chief of Pitcairn Island, didn't want to be. Her days were filled with grandchildren and surely at her age she should be able to trust others to make the right decisions? But a few words from her might have made the difference if she had known the truth. If she had asked the right questions. If anyone had.

Why didn't those interfering missionaries stay at home? They had plenty to do there. Look at the sort of Englishmen that sailed the ships that called at Pitcairn, even those of the British Navy. Foul-mouthed, ill educated and certainly not Christians. Why not target Englishmen first?

And why had anyone listened to Adams?

He was an unpunished mutineer and reformed drunk, saved only by Pitcairn's women. He would never have become a leader anywhere else on earth. His influence was largely paternal and over a community of children with no way to judge him.

Her sons had been child-like at 20 and today's Pitcairners weren't very much more advanced. Adams had only ever done or said what the women wanted, but the world had seen it the other way round. By 'world' she meant other men.

She welcomed it when Pitcairners questioned Adams and the Bible as they became older. It was a good sign, as long as the Bible's central message was never lost.

She wanted Pitcairners to live by its sense of morality rather than any strict belief in an unlikely story of reincarnation supposed to have happened in a world they would never see and that might not even be true.

'Did they hypocrite us?' Thursday asked when she relectantly revealed her discoveries to him.

'Yes, son. We have been hypocrited by missionaries.'

CHAPTER 66

Perhaps Tahiti still wanted revenge for her bared buttocks? Perhaps it was the old gods of Tahiti rather than Jesus filling the sails?

If she were alone she could bear it, but there were so many others now, and they were so young. More than half the 87 Pitcairners afloat on the Pacific were under 15. Surely children didn't deserve to share whatever punishment she was due?

Their arrival was not what she promised the Pitcairners, nothing like the celebrations she remembered of almost half a century ago, when ships were greeted by double canoes of chanting priests with long banners, by howling conch shells and hypnotising drums and flowers and gifts of food. Matavai wasn't even the main landing place.

Now it was Papeete to the west, where the lagoon was deep right up to the shore. Wooden jetties stuck out from the land and other sailing ships were moored there. Papeete looked broken, ramshackle and impermanent, not in any way as though Europeans had brought advancement.

When they were closer to the settlement dozens of canoes raced out to the ships. More than 50 brawling women clambered aboard to sell themselves and to beg for presents. Dishevelled, dirty, stinking of alcohol and tobacco and sweat, they fought for customers, not caring about the age or able to imagine the innocence of the Pitcairners. Exposing their breasts and their private parts, forcing the hands of Pitcairn men onto and into them, they created such a shock no-one could first think what to do.

Samuel Herbert and Captain Walpole began the fight back, followed by Buffett and Nobbs and Evans. They shamed the eager sailors to think better than of immediate sexual gratification.

As soon as the women had been bundled overboard, the Pitcairners battered Mauatua with questions about returning home.

Then Captain Herbert welcomed two men in black over the side. He introduced them as George Pritchard, head of The London Missionary Society in Tahiti and a Mr Henry Nott. Nott? The missionary who thought Pitcairners were only worthwhile as messengers of Jesus? The Pitcairners pushed her forward.

'Mr Nott, I believe we have you to thank for being in Tahiti.'

The man she confronted was thin and wiry and wore a permanent smile of condescension. His head was bent patronisingly to one side and he spoke slowly.

'It was my plan, yes, inspired by our Lord and Saviour Jesus Christ, yes indeed, but since then I reflected and advised against it.'

'Too late, Mr Nott,' she snapped, still calming the youngest Pitcairners tears from their fright at the scenes they had just witnessed.

'It seems Christ had other plans,' Nott said with a sickly smile of certainty that she wanted to slap.

'That might be so, but I hope *you* have plans to get us back to Pitcairn if we are not happy here.' She took two steps closer to him, punctuated loudly by her pole. She leaned it towards him.

'Many have already demanded to go back,' she said, taunting him with her pole. Nott swayed and swallowed his smile.

George Pritchard interrupted. 'You may be sure the welfare of the Pitcairners is my greatest concern. And now, we will show you your home, at least for the present.'

Mr Pritchard seemed an altogether better sort of man. He was tall and dark-haired with a straight back and broad shoulders. He was reserved but had welcoming, encompassing kindness in his eyes rather than the disdain and dismissal she saw in Nott.

But he was a missionary and she resolved not to be taken in.

The ships sailed eastwards in the lagoon. The Tahitian monarch, Queen Pomare IV, had arranged accommodation for them at Outuaiai, on the peninsula at the opposite end of Matavai Bay from Venus Point.

They were to live looking across the lagoon to where Fletcher's breadfruit camp had been.

Their first homes were the houses of men who had fled to take part in a civil war that still threatened to explode. The owners would not be back for some weeks and by then the Pitcairners were promised they would be settled on land of their own. Contracts were awarded to supply the Pitcairners with meat and other provisions for six months. Pitcairn's self-sufficient community was beholden to charity and many had already walked into Papeete to The London Missionary Society insistent on passage back to Pitcairn Island.

It took less than a week for her to understand that, apart from the supplies, she and the Pitcairners were essentially abandoned.

Britain had no official representation or authority and thus no budget that might be used for repatriation. Pritchard and the missionaries pleaded poverty and no responsibility. They expected only to take advantage of Pitcairn's migration at the British Government's expense.

Her community had been dumped into the care of the Tahitian administration and what there was of that was more concerned with civil warring and the waywardness of their new young queen. The Pitcairners were alone in a foreign country, unsupported except for the promises of the dismissed courtiers of a dead Tahitian king.

They were also surrounded by unimagined temptation.

The first dissemblance Pitcairners ever learned was confusing their parents or partners about their intentions before they left and then later lying about where they had been.

They bragged that Papeete's waterfront was a kingdom within a kingdom. Law and order were virtually unknown because its population of anarchic crews from whaling, sealing and trading ships constantly changed. The missionaries described these men to her as drunken serpents in what the rest of the world thought was a benign paradise.

Her sons – even her daughter - soon swanked to her they had no need of money, for everything they wanted was given them in return for allowing themselves to be the butt of ribaldry or for telling the story of their island and what they knew about the mutiny.

'Hypocriting works here, too,' Thursday giggled to his mother through rum-fumed breath.

She welcomed the few Tahitians who visited the Pitcairn village, even though they too wanted only to mourn the ill effect of the missionaries. All celebrations of the body, including traditional dancing and tattooing were now associated with the devil and with punishment. When new examples were discovered, they were hailed by the more egregious missionaries, for it fed their squalid belief they were saving these people from sin.

'None of these things were sins until you said so,' she complained to Pritchard and Notts.

'They were to Jesus and his Father,' they answered, making pious pyramids of their fingertips.

She had expected difficulties of adjustment but the depth of her personal discomfort was depressing and disappointing. Tahiti's water was as blue, the peaks as tall, the foliage as striking and green, the air as balmy. But the joy of living, the *pleasures* of Tahiti were forbidden.

What could the missionaries achieve by such joylessness, when even the *he'i* was no longer worn to celebrate Tahiti's natural abundance?

Her only practical help came from the Belgian merchant Jacques-Antoine Moerenhout, who was settled in Tahiti with a young Peruvian wife. He had visited Pitcairn and was well liked by them all. He or his wife constantly brought or sent home drunken or wounded Pitcairners from Papeete and the men who worked for them were told constantly to watch out for any in trouble.

Moerenhout chastened Nobbs, Buffet and Evans for turning their heads from the Pitcairners' abandonment. It didn't lead to much action and she wondered if they secretly preferred the 'civilisation' of Tahiti to the peace of Pitcairn.

Finally, George Pritchard announced the embattled queen had negotiated an agreement with her relatives for a tract of land at Papaoa. This was tucked into the south west corner of Matavai Bay, part of the huge expanse owned by the queen and the royal family that stretched from Matavai almost to Papeete.

The land was superb, rich with luscious fruits and tumbling flowers, shaded by productive breadfruit trees and coconut palms. It was close to the black sands and lagoon and there was a stream.

Building was promised to start very soon and the Pitcairners looked forward to helping. It was said all to be free but the cost turned out to be enormous. Until their houses were built the Pitcairners were billeted in local households and were thus no longer protected from the degraded life the missionaries allowed to Tahitians.

The royal family's generosity confronted the Pitcairners with a situation even further beyond their simple experiences.

The casual enjoyment of sex that had been as uncomplicated as daily washing, and that Mauatua had hoped to combine on Pitcairn with some responsibility for its outcomes, had become dirty and furtive for Tahitians, fuelled by alcohol, boredom or a determination to defy the missionaries.

Babies were no longer killed before birth or before they took their first breath. Instead, unwanted new-borns were abandoned under trees or thrown into streams or into the lagoon while still breathing.

There were no extended families, so children of unwilling parents ran wild, dirty and hungry.

Where some members of a family hosting Pitcairners had become Christians, they shunned and insulted those who had not. When she asked about Jesus' message of encompassing love for all she was told the missionaries were adamant. It was only possible to love others who had accepted Jesus Christ as their Lord and Saviour.

Shamed by what they were daily forced to confront, embarrassed to ask for the hospitality that once would have been given freely, Pitcairners watched Tahitians supposed to be their hosts and observant Christians steal from their supplies of meat and vegetables.

She tried to convince them this was a small price if it meant they were left alone to pray and to mourn for their homeland. Thus it seemed a good thing when the queen acknowledged their continuing unhappiness and offered them use of a large house in Papeete.

There the 87 Pitcairners trudged to live together once more as a self-contained camp of Pitcairn piety.

The dirt streets of the ramshackle settlement of Papeete behind the waterfront assailed her with a totally new language of sight and sound. In every street her flock was mocked for their ragged, hand-me-down clothes and for their accents and the words they used if they could find a common language. Most of all Pitcairners were mocked for their laughing.

They laughed at the noise and smell of horses, they laughed at carts and carriages that moved people and goods so quickly, they laughed at defecating horses and the stink of their droppings in the street, and at the stench of decomposing human urine and worse in doorways. They laughed and laughed because they had never seen or imagined such things. They laughed to discover some didn't even like the colour of their skins.

'Sometimes nigger means they like me, sometimes they want to fight,' Charles moaned as Mauatua soothed his knuckles and cheeks.

She found it hard to learn to look before she crossed a street and couldn't conceive a greeting might precede begging, for Pitcairners brought no sense of money with them.

The young men were loathe to admit they were offered free alcohol because others wanted to laugh at them and their cast-offs and their awkward, unaccustomed drunkenness.

Older Pitcairners sought the worst of Papeete's waterfront as 'characters', unable to picture how bad and immoral they were. Some were soon caught in their nets and taught everything they had once been unable even to imagine. But the men were universally protective of their women and girls and not one of these got into trouble for anything more than unwise flirting.

She stopped weeping for Tahiti and for what was happening to Pitcairners there, because tears brought no solution. What could she do to get Pitcairners back home?

Every avenue she explored led to the same distasteful resolution.

She would have to beg, beg to make Pitcairn's children safe again. She knew she could do that. Begging would be nothing compared to what she'd done for Pitcairn's children in the past.

She'd start with Queen Pomare.

Patronising officials at the palace attempted to teach her how to curtsy but she couldn't lock one of her old knees behind the other. That was the secret, they insisted, that would stop her falling and ensure she could rise again, but she still wobbled and felt very insecure even with her walking pole.

She bowed from the waist when she was ushered into the queen's presence, praying she would be forgiven and the 18-year old queen of Tahiti greeted her with a beaming smile, clearly unconcerned about the lack of a curtsey. Mauatua liked her at once.

Queen Pomare carried herself with the innate poise and dignity that was the essence of *ari'i* bearing and superiority, but she could see that under her regal facade this ebullient young woman wanted to skip and dance and speak freely.

Papeete buzzed with rumours the queen was separating from her husband to whom she was married when nine. She had become a follower of a local man who thought he was Jesus Christ and shared the same expansive free views as her on life, sex and society.

Oh dear, she laughed to herself, how those dratted missionaries had their work cut out to mould her.

The queen led her to two chairs by a small table in what she called a drawing room. The chairs were padded with something softer and quieter than banana leaves and covered in a cloth that shone like new cobwebs. Some of the chairs appeared to be joined together, so there was space for two or three to sit side by side. The queen sat with no part of her touching the upright back of her chair. It was easy to copy her straight back and posture, but she wondered why they had bothered to put the backs there in the first place.

There was so much furniture, so many chairs, cabinets with windows into their shelves, chests of drawers, big tables and small tables, all with curly edging of the same sunny metal. Gold, was it? The polished floor was muted by many small bright carpets with complicated patterns and white fringes, of wool she thought.

The walls were covered in what looked like tapa but might be paper. Someone had painted curious birds and animals and flowers on it that reminded her of those on Fletcher's bowls. She didn't recognise any of them and hoped it would be a compliment if she asked the queen about the images. The queen laughed loudly, aggravating the hovering missionaries.

'They say it is from China, but how would I know?'

The queen continued in a soft voice, so it would not carry. When her grandfather Tu was made Tahiti's first king there was no precedent for a single monarch of the island. Since then everything had to be different for her family, including living in a European house of wood with glass windows and there was a plan to build her a grand palace with many floors and a clock tower. The queen noticed Mauatua's discomfort in the room and suggested they move to the deep verandah that encircled the house.

'They'll find it harder to listen to us outside.'

Pomare strode ahead, and Mauatua looked at her more carefully. Tall, broad and well fleshed, she was as big as Thursday and Charles put together. Her skin was glowing and pale, like the sweet, fully ripened bananas *ari'i* once ate ritually to fatten their bodies into supposed greater sanctity. Her hair was in two long plaits that hung in front of each of her wide shoulders. Her dress was floor length and simple and could have been made of tapa, but it moved and sounded like something different. No-one had flattened her nose or bound her head and she wore a wide frame woven with Tahitian gardenia from ear to ear, so she was wreathed in its high fragrance.

As they passed a long reflecting glass Mauatua looked quickly at herself. She was still slim when she pulled herself erect. Her skin had lightened a little in the time she had been away from Pitcairn and her long hair was only just starting to go grey, in this light anyway. It looked less grey in the single thick plait she wore. She could be the queen's mother rather than being old enough to be her grandmother. Or great grandmother.

'We will have green coconuts,' the queen ordered. Mauatua admired the way she commanded without looking at those she expected to act.

The queen shuffled off her shoes, upsetting the hovering courtiers and missionaries. Mauatua could have hugged the girl, would have if she had not been a queen. Pomare leaned close and confided they had a lot in common. The arms given by Fletcher to the sailors staying in Tahiti were used to 'help' her family gain supreme authority over the island, forever changing the political and social structure after centuries of individual competing chiefdoms.

'BOUNTY is responsible for us both being who we are,' Pomare said.

They had still not got around to the Pitcairners adversity when shouting distracted them. A badly-dressed, long-haired man struggled with guards at the gateway to the palace.

He broke free and stumbled awkwardly towards the palace.

It was Hoppa.

Mauatua ran along the verandah, down its steps and across the grounds to meet him.

He fell into her arms, exhausted and barely able to draw breath.

The queen ordered servants to hurry and to hold shades over the pair.

'Thursday, quick, quick. He might be dying,' Charles managed to gasp.

The sun seemed to disappear from Mauatua's sky. She stood immobile and shocked, not knowing what to do, which way to move.

There was an infection ravishing Papeete and Thursday had not been well. But dying?

Queen Pomare put a comforting arm around her shoulder and ordered a carriage brought round, the quickest to harness up and with the fastest horses she had.

CHAPTER 67

April 21st, 1831 – Papeete, Tahiti

Her son *was* dying. Thursday's breathing was painful even to watch. His lungs were flooding with mucous that suffocated life from him. It didn't help that so many were crowded into his room, most kneeling in prayer. She scolded them for taking the air that should keep him alive and shooed them out.

Only his wife Teraura stayed and Mauatua prayed she would understand what had to be done.

Who should have Thursday's last breath? Thursday had taken Fletcher's breath when she thought he was dying, so Thursday should have inherited Fletcher's wisdom. But Tamahere believed he was Fletcher's true inheritor because of their name change. He had pushed his last breath into Charles believing he was passing on Fletcher's legacy.

Which of them was truly Fletcher's heir? Was it Thursday or was it Charles through Tamahere?

There was no-one to ask now, no aged *tupuna* or learned *tohu'a*. Even discussing such matters was punished on Tahiti. The cross of Jesus on her breast made her nervous. Might it interfere with something so, what was that word the missionaries used . . . so pagan?

Thursday groaned. Water, she'd give him some water. If Fletcher's wisdom was in Thursday perhaps the refreshment would help him find some way to guide her. A man who had taken another's last breath was supposed to look at the world though the dead man's eyes. Were Fletcher's eyes willing to give her a clue? Perhaps it should be her? Could she take her son's last breath and then have Fletcher's spirit inside her?

She called Mary Ann to get water and then to keep Thursday and Teraura company, thinking she would appreciate this chance to demonstrate her piety.

Mauatua wanted the nourishment of clattering palm fronds and a soft warm breeze that would bring the richness of Tahiti to her. There was only the stink and filth and dusty weeds of the town, with hardly a flower to be seen, no sense of the sea, nothing of Tahiti but a few forlorn palms. These had surly horses tethered to them, forever kicking at flies.

Once her resolution was firm she prayed briefly and hurried inside as fast as her legs would allow. Mary Ann looked tearful.

'He doesn't want me there,' she said. 'Too much praying he said and called it mumbo jumbo. He hurt me.'

She patted her daughter, amazed at her ability to turn even the death of her brother to her interest. And then Charles returned, cooler now and restored after his epic journey to find her. Charles, yes it had to be.

He would be Fletcher's unquestioned heir if Thursday's last breath was added to the one from Tamahere.

'Charles, come and say good bye to your brother.'

In the few minutes she left him Thursday had become more wretched. He pushed himself up to slouch against the wall hoping this would help him prevail over the miasma in his lungs but his head dropped onto his chest and his breathing became even more difficult.

Charles knelt by his brother's bed. His quiet, sincere praying calmed Thursday and he put his hand on Charles' head. They had always been able to talk with few words and Charles's back straightened. Was Thursday silently passing the mantle to him? Might that be enough?

Thursday shook with paroxysms of coughing, but these couldn't get enough sustaining air to his lungs. He collapsed, his body twisted so his head hung backwards over the edge of the bed. This was the moment. When she thought Thursday was about to take his last breath she pulled the wooden cross from her neck and threw it to the floor. She pushed Charles closer to his brother.

Charles thought he was meant to kiss his fevered brother and did so again and again with such endearing fervour and sincerity she knew there were few in the world who would not weep for his sorrow.

Teraura knelt on the bed by her husband's chest and leaned forward to support her husband's neck so he could more comfortably receive his brother's kisses. The kisses on his face encouraged Thursday to open his eyes. Charles was too close for him to recognise.

'No,' he croaked, 'No, I don't want to kiss Daddy again. No.'

They were the last words he said.

She wanted her son to die with pleasure on his face but it was too late. Teraura still didn't understand what was happening, but continued to support Thursday. Again he opened his eyes to see the hateful image he thought was his father, Fletcher. He gathered the last air he had in his lungs to scream. Mauatua smothered it with Charles' mouth.

'*Ha'u ha'u*, breathe it all in, Charles.'

Teraura understood. Her prayers to Jesus stopped and with invocations to the gods of Tahiti she pulled against the back of Thursday's neck with both hands so not the least whisper of breath should be lost between Thursday's mouth and his brother's.

Teraura fled to her now fatherless children and Charles went to his motherless ones. She straightened Thursday on the bed. He was dead and had died pleading for mercy, for relief from the terrifying image of what he thought was his dying father's face and mouth. She had forced Charles to take the breath of a dying brother for the second time. What if it were true she asked, yet again.

What if a man's soul and wisdom was transferred in his last breath?

If it were true, Charles was now the unquestioned repository of Fletcher's soul and wisdom and should see the world through Fletcher's eyes. His spirit would come to Charles in his sleep to impart his knowledge and instruct him how best to use it.

It had been believed for more generations than she could number.

White men didn't know everything. How was that possible when Catholics and Anglicans couldn't agree how to worship Jesus?

Her thoughts for Charles' future were replaced by a growing sense of loss. Thursday was dead, the first Pitcairner was dead. Fletcher's oldest son. His heir. Their son. Her son Thursday was dead.

She called retribution on every god in Tahitian and in Pitkern and in English. And then she raised a fist to the mountains she could see over the town's rusty tin roofs. She damned Tahiti's peaks to every hell imaginable.

She told them she was glad the Tahiti she had once known lay destroyed, stinking and rotten at their feet and would never rise again.

She vowed Pitcairn would never join Tahiti in such shame, whatever the price. Pitcairn would prevail, no matter what was rained down on her people, no matter what happened to the land or the sea around it. Good, gentle Pitcairn would survive. There was nothing she would not do.

The Pitcairners gathered in the grimy shadows of the inner staircase and hallway, drawn together by confusion about what to do next.

'It is enough,' she seethed, without a thought of voting. 'We will return to Fenua Maitai.'

It was not enough. Thursday had barely been buried when John Buffet announced he'd found a schooner prepared to take a small party back to

Pitcairn, escaping both the influenza and the iniquities of Papeete. Eight of her blood were preparing to leave.

Buffet's wife was her daughter Dolly by Ned Young and they were taking their four children, her grandchildren. Also going were Ned Young's son Robert, Thursday's son Joseph, Charles' sons Edward and Little Charlie, and young Matt Quintal III.

She kissed and held her daughter and her seven grandchildren and promised it would not be long before all the Pitcairners were home.

Three days later the oldest Pitcairner's death was followed by the loss of the youngest Pitcairner. Lucy Ann Quintal had been born on board during the voyage to Papeete.

Soon someone in every room and hallway and verandah of the mansion was fevered with aching joints and heads and with fierce coughs fighting to clear congested lungs. Jenny wasn't here to help, and she had little experience of affliction on this scale.

She prayed for some intervention that would lift this burden of suffering from the Pitcairners but prayer wasn't enough, she knew that. Surely the Europeans had a sort of medicine to ease them?

Whenever she ventured out to search for relief she was ostracised, as though she was the sole source of the dread disease. Her family of Pitcairners was piteously marooned, more forsaken than if they were still on their remote island.

On April 29th she watched Vahineatua perish as painfully as Thursday. She was mother to Pitcairn's first daughter, by Mills, and to three more daughters by John Adams.

On May 6th, Mauatua's stepson George Young died aged about 34. He was mourned by his mother Toofaiti and his widow, who was mourning her mother Vahineatua.

Some days more Pitcairners were ill than were well enough to care for the others. Feeding more than 70 every day was a greater task than anything she had done on Tubuai or BOUNTY. Whoever was well enough, including children, helped to make soups in large vats from whatever meat and vegetables had been delivered. There were days when even preparing this was beyond the stricken community. Then they relied on spoiled fruit that traders from the market left at their door and bakers sometimes left bread they couldn't sell.

These discards made their plight more evident. Sick or well, Pitcairners wept as they struggled to eat such pitiful charity.

She couldn't bear to see it and constantly mourned that somehow Pitcairn's children were paying for sins she had committed.

Kitty Quintal was 12 when she died on May 15$^{th.}$ The next day 17-year old Polly died. She was Thursday's daughter and had married Edward Young, one of her sons by Ned Young, so was both granddaughter and daughter in law. A day later 9-year old Jane McCoy died. On the 8th Catherine Quintal died, aged 31.

The day after that Mauatua began to strike her head and only Charles could stop her. Toofaiti had died, first partner of Tararo and later mother of three sons and a daughter by Edward Young. She was wrapped in tapa made in Pitcairn and quickly taken away.

Now there were only two of BOUNTY's Ma'ohi women left, herself and Teraura, Thursday's widow.

Some thought living so closely with one another encouraged influenza and that was judged to be why such an epidemic was unknown back home. They lived in rooms with windows closed against infection from Papeete's foul air. Others kept them open day and night, hoping any sea breezes brisk enough to navigate Papeete's sad streets would somehow sweep the contagion away. But no-one knew for certain what they should do and no-one came with advice or assistance.

Their regular food supplies were dumped at their door, as though they were a Biblical colony of lepers.

Before June ended another of Thursday's children died, his son Charles II aged 23. So did 17-year old Daniel McCoy, followed a day later by his brother Hugh, five years younger.

In less than ten weeks 12 Pitcairners had died, more than one in seven. First was her oldest Pitcairn son, two were her grandchildren, and two were women she had shared over four decades of life with on Pitcairn.

She wept ceaselessly, not just for herself but for the grieving Pitcairners and for Pitcairn, Pitcairn the safer, simpler home none of them should ever have left. The Pitcairners shrank from great grief to absolute silence.

Mr Nobbs made an effort to be a leader and to offer comfort. They asked him to explain how Jesus could possibly allow something so monstrous to happen to them. Hadn't they always been good?

His opaque sermons about some greater plan by Jesus and his Father were dismissed. Yet none dared abandon Jesus completely, for then who would they be, who could they cry to for help? And help was what they needed, for in every room of the house there was illness and suffering such as they had known only from the Bible's stories of plague and pestilence.

It was all so much more frightening when not one of them could find sins in their past that deserved such foul destiny. Someone might have stolen an orange, or pretended to be sick rather than go to church, or lied about a sore back when they didn't want to hoe or dig or rake.

On Tahiti some might have been drunk or fought or committed fornication but other than that, we are just Pitcairners, they cried.

She walked about Papeete all day every day, pleading for a means of escape. The queen and George Pritchard harried public opinion to help raise money for the Pitcairners to charter a ship to take them back to Pitcairn but other than that believed they had done what they could.

Even God seemed set against the Pitcairners and so church, crown and government stood back in case His wrath splashed back onto them.

Only Moerenhout did anything. The schooner that took the Buffets away was hit by a storm and the party marooned on Lord Hood's Island. He paid for another ship to rescue them and take them on to Pitcairn. Then Moerenhout offered to buy a schooner called THE MESSENGER OF PEACE for the remaining Pitcairners. In return he asked if some of the Pitcairn men would dive for pearls and pearl shells on the way, to which they quickly agreed for this would help defray some of his costs.

The missionary owners of the schooner refused a generous price for the ship. Mauatua despaired, saying the missionaries must be messengers for some other Jesus than hers, and many others agreed, even the non-believers in bars and stews on the waterfront.

After this refusal the shopkeepers and publicans of Papeete, the brawling sailors, the abandoned whalers and sealers who had enjoyed demeaning and degrading Pitcairn's men and women, and even simple local farmers and fishermen started a fund for the Pitcairners.

She told the distraught Pitcairners all this but they cheered only when they heard Nott, Simpson and Wilson from The London Missionary Society contributed.

She stopped some of the older Pitcairners confronting them with the demand they should be paying for all the islanders' repatriation. She knew those men's vision of Christian charity was not what might be expected and anyway they didn't feel the Pitcairners were their responsibility.

The British Government had brought them to Tahiti. The British Government should take them home. But the British didn't even have a consul in Papeete, let alone an emergency budget.

The desperate Pitcairners sold as much as they could of the provisions Governor Darling had sent for 'the Chiefs and Natives'. To this they added caches of copper nails and other bulk items from BOUNTY that Mauatua had first collected on the ship and that Mary Ann had thought to include in the baggage they brought to Tahiti.

Captain Driver of the CHARLES DOGGETT, an American whaler from Salem, Massachusetts, took pity on them and accepted $650 Spanish dollars for taking more than 60 passengers back to Pitcairn. It wasn't a bad price, less than they had expected.

The Pitcairners were all aboard. On the broad wooden slats of the wharf she was saying a final farewell to Mourenhout and his wife and to the black clack from The London Missionary Society when she heard a clatter of hooves and iron-clad wheels. The queen had come to say goodbye.

Her open carriage stopped away from the small crowd. She tipped back her parasol and did not alight, instead sending her coach man to ask Mauatua to sit with her.

'There are things I want to tell you,' the queen said. When Mauatua tried to speak the queen lifted her hand.

'If you say anything, the sorrows and envy I have inside will show. I am not allowed such weakness.'

CHAPTER 68

'I know you have rejected or changed many of the old ways of Tahiti, as have I,' Pomare said. 'But you left here a pure Tahitian woman, a woman from the time before missionaries and guns changed Tahiti forever. You changed because you found better ways inside you.

'You and the Ma'ohi women of Pitcairn are the only Tahitian women who have not been forced to become a white man's version of a Tahitian.' The queen sighed heavily and kicked at her discarded shoes.

'I wish I could be like you. You know who you are and what you are. You have been allowed to find yourself.'

Mauatua was pleased she had been forbidden to speak. She had thought the queen would be the happiest and most envied of all Tahitians.

Yet the girl was jealous of her, she who had never owned a pair of shoes to discard.

'I cannot think of myself as truly Tahitian or as queen. I am a creation of others. How can I be a Tahitian queen when I was crowned in an English church with white people singing Christian hymns? How did that make me Queen of Tahiti? Men are punished for baring their shoulders when I am present. They are no longer allowed to carry me on their shoulders, and yet many wish to do so.

'When people saw their *ari'i nui* flying on the shoulders of others they were reassured. Someone superior lived amongst them whose duty it was to care for them, to ensure they had food in times of famine or war.

'I am their queen but I have no idea what crop is thriving and which is failing, which fish to protect or which fruit to share. And I must eat at the same table as missionaries and other men, hearing the noises they make and with no space for a whisk to keep away the flies. Tahitians say the only thing to tell them I am queen is the big house I live in.

'There is wisdom in their words.'

Mauatua thought of a thousand other wise words to cheer the queen. Pomare stopped her before she opened her mouth, telling Mauatua she had a truer claim to call herself queen.

Mauatua was well born and tall and fair skinned of course, but she had something more, freely given love and respect from her people.

The queen said any love or respect she had was because white men ordered it to be given.

'The Pitcairners follow you because their hearts tell them it is the right thing. Here it is not hearts that make me 'Her Majesty' but the laws and the religion of white men. *'A haere*, Mauatua. *Araua'e*. I will remember you and hope you can forget the harm Tahiti has done to your family.'

Pomare sighed painfully and was silent so long Mauatua became uncomfortable, uncertain if she was breaking some regal nicety that made it imperative for her to speak first. She shifted in her seat to do so but the queen checked her with a slightly raised finger.

'If it were possible I would sail with you and live with bare feet again.'

There were tears in her eyes. Mauatua didn't know if it was acceptable but she leaned across to *ho'i*. The queen granted it and below the low carriage door, where no one could see, she took her hand and squeezed it tightly. Mauatua lifted her face only when the pressure on her fingers lessened. She wished she could have given the girl the motherly embraces she really needed.

When her feet were back on the ground, Mauatua ripped her shift to bare her shoulders and enjoyed the ripple of outrage from the black-clad men on the dock. She lifted her head and spoke loudly.

'Your Majesty's kindness to us will never be forgotten. We leave our lost children in your loving hands. Fenua Maitai will always welcome and honour you as another mother to our island.'

She bowed deeply and walked backwards for six steps before turning to board the CHARLES DOGGETT.

Tahitians had formed a protective cordon around their queen's carriage. Nott stood outside it, praying ostentatiously, his hands clasped, his head back and his eyes closed. Nott! The missionary whose interference persuaded the Colonial Office the Pitcairners should go to Tahiti and help convert South Seas Ma'ohi.

'Yes, you might well pray Mr Nott.'

He shuffled backwards, a coward's elbow up as though she might beat him with her pole. She followed him step for step until he halted and then she sweetened her voice to confuse him, saying there were things she must say to him and that the Pitcairners would like to hear them too.

She led Nott to the ship, where the Pitcairners were gathered at the rail. Nott fluttered with insincere modesty, and she hoped he was expecting paeans of praise from her.

'Pray as much as you like, Mr Nott. The deaths of the Pitcairners in Tahiti are your doing. My son, my grandchildren, my friends. Mothers, fathers, sons, daughters. Infants, too, Mr Nott. Your hands are forever stained with their blood. Jesus' blood won't wash that sin away.'

The Pitcairners said loud Amens, and when Nobbs and Evans tried to silence them they were hustled to the back.

'We once worshipped a gentle Jesus, a Jesus we understood and who never let us down. Your Jesus is different. Not loving and gentle at all.

'You banned human sacrifice in Tahiti, saying Jesus was nailed onto the cross so men never need be sacrificed again. If that is true, then why did your mission in Tahiti need the sacrifice of my son and grandchildren? What worldly sins have their blood cleansed?'

Pritchard moved to calm her. She challenged him with the same question. He retired, hurried by a low disturbing mumble from the Pitcairners.

'We were the most religious of people, Mr Nott, and now I fear many will never want to hear the name of Jesus again, not even the gentle Jesus of Pitcairn. Jesus will have fewer worshippers rather than more.

'How does that make you a good missionary, Mr Nott? How is that the work of Jesus?'

Nott clasped his hands lightly, put his head further to the side and spoke gently. 'Dear lady, you are upset and we understand. Sometimes Jesus works in ways . . .'

'We will have none of that.' she cried and then cried louder. 'Those are weak words that mean nothing to us, nothing, except that you have no answer to my question.'

The Pitcairners clapped noisily and Nott blanched. She stepped closer.

'Let me ask you this, Mr Missionary Nott. If life is a gift from God, anybody's God, surely he intends us to worship every second of it? How can the point of life be to give life no value?

'Why should we poison today with what might *not* come afterwards?

'My son Tamahere once asked this, he asked how could your Jesus know what was better for us, who lived and spoke and ate and laughed and danced a different way? How could he know what was right for Tahitians when he came from a land of sand where there were no coconuts, no breadfruit, no *tiare Tahiti*?

'It is still a good question.' She banged her pole to emphasise she was finished and then marched away.

She regretted Mourenhout and Pritchard had to hear her questions to Nott. Without those two they might all have been buried in Tahiti.

'I thank you Mr Moerenhout and Mr Pritchard for all you have done so we can go home.' Neither resisted when she approached them to *ho'i*.

Once more she fixed on Nott. 'Look to your own backyard, Mr Henry Nott. Then when that is in order, be a good neighbour to mine rather than wanting to add it to yours.'

The reaction from the ship and the wharf was noisy and uninhibited, unexpectedly so. She turned and saw the reason. Queen Pomare had allowed her carriage to roll forward. She stood and bowed her head deeply to Mauatua and kept it there until there was no doubt the furious missionaries had seen her.

She ordered the coachman to unfold her carriage's steps and then put down her parasol and picked up a traditional fly whisk. Some at the front of the crowd bent their heads before the queen was out of the carriage. When her bare feet touched the ground they immediately knelt and others quickly followed. Those kneeling ripped their clothing from their shoulders. The missionaries pulled some of them to their feet but they were slapped away and threatened.

Mauatua attempted to kneel too, but her knees and hips couldn't oblige. She stopped awkwardly, half way down, supported uneasily by her pole. The queen hurried forward and pulled her up with one hand.

Mary Ann called from the ship, 'Careful, she'll think she is a queen, too.' Pomare appeared to ignore her, but the crowd that had gathered from Papeete's ships and bars and streets quietened, expecting a sharp response.

'*Think* she is a queen?' Pomare's eyes swept the wharf and the ship for any who might contradict her.

'She *is* a queen,' she declared magisterially in her deep, dark voice of authority. She stepped backwards and pulled at her neckline and bowed low to Mauatua.

'I salute you, Mauatua *vahine ari'i Pitkern. A haere 'oe. Ia ha'amaita'ihia.* Good bye, Queen Mauatua of Pitcairn Island, and may you be blessed for the rest of your life.'

She walked back to her carriage, a royal, one-woman procession, tall, distant, looking neither right nor left but slowly waving her fly whisk.

She was majestic and the crowd was transfixed.

With a rap on the carriage door the two horses at once moved forward.

Ma'ohi and Europeans cheered and applauded and some ran with the carriage, shouting good wishes to the girl who'd acted like the monarch they wanted, like a Tahitian monarch. Queen Pomare sat resolutely upright and nodding regally, but Mauatua saw a smile threatening. There might be few of those for the girl in future. Did her courtier-missionaries even know where she was?

Mauatua boarded and Mary Ann ostentatiously handed her the wooden cross she had thrown off as Thursday died.

'Hard to know if you want this now,' she said sourly.

Captain Driver shouted for the gangplank to be raised, the final lines were cast off and the rowers who waited patiently in small boats towed the ship away from the dock and pulled her to the open sea through the coral reef. She led the sweet harmonies of Pitcairn that floated innocent and pure over the lagoon. Only Pritchard and Moerenhout had a conscience clear enough to watch and listen.

Late on August 20th 1831, after 20 weeks of melancholy and misery, first Papeete and its house of death and then the peaks of Tahiti and Mo'orea sank below the horizon. None had wanted to stay. Most, like Mauatua, wondered why they agreed to come.

She whispered special prayers into the wind for the Pitcairners she left behind, particularly for Toofaiti and Vahineatua. Their *pufenua* might be on Tahiti and so might their bodies now. But she knew their hearts were in Pitcairn and surely that was where their spirits would want to rest.

She sent promises they would be welcome and find repose there amongst their children.

CHAPTER 69

September 2nd, 1831: return to Pitcairn Island

She knew the ship had been sighted when she spied a small crowd gathering at the bottom of the Hill of Difficulty. Younger eyes than Mauatua's told her it was the party led by the Englishman John Buffet and her daughter Dolly, who sailed from Tahiti so soon after Thursday died.

Her joy was quickly extinguished when she landed. The disease that infected and killed on Tahiti had pursued her fleeing family, too. Her stepson Robert Young and grandson Edward both died of influenza after they sailed from Papeete.

She overshadowed this with her recitation of the long list of Pitcairners left in Tahiti's soil.

John Buffet walked away from her, his hands to his head.

'There are other things you should know, Mrs Christian,' he said. 'Before you go up the hill.'

'Let me sit,' Mauatua asked, taking her time to choose a place. Surely there had been enough pain and she had paid every possible price?

She gathered the grandchildren left to her and gripped her walking pole with both hands.

'I'm ready.'

'There've been visitors.'

Her mind didn't flinch, for she couldn't imagine what was to come. She nodded to nudge Buffett to get on with it.

'Looks like some native boys were here, from Bora Bora. Wrecked fences and gardens. Broke into houses. Set hogs free. That sort of thing.'

She lifted her eyebrows and tightened her lips.

'Could've been worse,' she said brusquely.

'We've started the clear up.'

'We've missed hard work like that, haven't we boys?' Charles exclaimed with great energy. Bless him. He'd risen to the challenge of taking over from Thursday as senior Pitcairner man. Arthur Quintal was older than Charles but, as more than one had said to her, it felt right to have a Christian as leader. She saluted Charles with her pole. 'We're used to hard work, aren't we, son?'

'The Navy was here, too. The British Navy,' Buffet added.

She stood, blenching. 'What did they want?'

'A bit more revenge it seems.'

'After all this time? Go on tell me.'

'They've taken almost everything they thought came from BOUNTY or that reminded them of the mutineers.'

She angrily used her pole to force her way through the crowd to the start of the Hill of Difficulty. She hesitated, her lips trembling. It would be better if she had some warning of what to expect.

'Tell me everything,' she managed to gasp.

'Jars, they took storage jars. Casks. Copper. Bits and pieces. But the worst. I'm not sure how men could do such a thing. The worst thing . . .'

'Out with it!'

'Father Adams grave.'

She forced herself to stand as still as a statue for the half a minute it took before he could continue.

'They've taken his grave marker.'

She slashed at trees and bushes, swinging her walking pole with a fury she had not felt for decades.

Why did everyone in the world think Pitcairners devoid of feeling or emotion? What heartless beasts. And Englishmen at that.

Father Adams' tombstone was made from pieces of BOUNTY's oak salvaged from the coastline. The thick boards were wrapped in lead sheeting once in the ship's greenhouse and had an inscription laboriously made by tapping a blunt nail into the soft metal.

It took thousands of dots to make the lettering of his memorial, a task everyone old enough had helped to do.

The Navy had taken this expression of love and gratitude from their island, ravishing their most personal memories with not a word of respect or consultation or thought for its people. For what, for something that happened more than 40 years ago?

She hated England and her Navy in a way she had never hated before.

But how could she protest loud enough for them to listen? She probably couldn't she thought, and that unfairness enraged her even more.

Men and missionaries, curse them doubly, had made decisions as though Pitcairners were toys, playthings to soothe and settle their sense of importance and to stoke the bonfires of their ambitions. Pitcairners were dead on Tahiti because of their heartless follies, graves on Pitcairn had been desecrated, their possessions stolen. There had to be a way to stop this but there probably wasn't. Mutiny would be the least of her choices.

In the midst of her rage her great secret sprang to mind.

'Charles, Mary Ann . . . Help me,' she commanded.

She hardly needed her children's help and didn't stop at the top of the Hill of Difficulty.

She straightened her back and marched on, her jaw set, her pole beating time, looking neither left nor right so she was not assaulted by more than she could bear. She ignored the square, passed her house and headed into her gardens and only then gave way to tears, but they were of relief.

Tamahere was safe and everything else important to her in the gardens seemed undisturbed.

Charles and Mary Ann had barely been back to this place since the day Tamahere died and they were uncomfortable even now to see their mother standing by his grave.

'That's typical,' Mary Ann scorned. 'You go straight to a black man's grave. What about our father's grave? Why aren't you checking his? Where's his grave?'

Charles cut her off. 'Does he have one? Or did he leave the island? That's all the ship's crew wanted to know.'

'This is my son's grave, your half brother's grave. If you cannot speak with respect don't speak at all.'

She was so clearly wounded that Mary Ann didn't retort in the usual way. Might a truce at last have been struck?

'Look, this is the past. Tamahere is gone. Thursday is gone,' Mauatua said placatingly. She turned to them with her arms open.

'The difference is they both have a grave. Our father doesn't,' Mary Ann countered, her voice thin and vituperative again.

'What happens to the spirit is more important.'

'Who's that talking? The Tahitian or the Christian?'

'Both,' Mauatua said. 'Both if you know anything about either.'

'I wish my Daddy had a grave,' Mary Ann whined. There it was again, her pitiful pleading and a child's name for her father.

'You'll have to tell us sometime,' Charles agreed.

'That's rot,' Mauatua retorted. 'Other Pitcairners don't know where their first fathers are buried.'

'No-one ever asks about them,' Charles protested. 'We are always asked about Fletcher. I'm sick of it. Everyone who spoke to me in Tahiti wanted to know what happened to him.'

'I know why you won't tell us. He escaped, didn't he?' Mary Ann crowed. 'People might say he wanted to get away from you. You couldn't bear people saying that, could you?'

Mauatua walked to the foot of Tamahere's grave. Just a scatter of stones marked it these days. She was not ready for this from Charles and Mary Ann, not so soon after learning of another dead grandchild. And certainly not standing over Tamahere's grave.

Only one thing to say came to mind.

'On an island without a history there is nothing a woman might not have to do to survive,' she said proudly, yet knowing her daughter didn't have the emotional capacity to understand the profundity of such words.

'But to talk, to tell it, to have everything known, that is too hard. I don't think I can do that, I'm sorry.' She turned away, hiding tears.

Mary Ann didn't care about her distress, airing only pity for herself.

'It made me look stupid. I couldn't even tell anyone why there were no black children on Pitcairn.'

Mauatua's unhappiness was arrested. Maybe that was a question she could answer, something she could get out of her head without compromising anything else. She spoke slowly, not quite believing she was exposing such words for others to hear after they'd lived so long in her head.

'This was a new world, made by Ma'ohi women with white men and children that were both. Ma'ohi children, black children would have felt different, might have become . . .'

'What, Tahitian, like Tamahere?'

'Exactly.'

'And then be like their fathers, Massacre Day and all that, I suppose,' Mary Ann said, offensive and condescending.

'Who knows?' Mauatua snapped, anxious now to stop the revelations.

Then she appreciated something quite new to her. It *was* 40 years ago. Perhaps she had been holding too tight too long, she could let some of the story out. Perhaps someone should know before her time came?

She might even get some credit and some thanks.

'It wasn't necessarily their decision. The Ma'ohi men, killing the whites, that is . . .' she whispered.

'Then who? Who?' her children chorused. Mauatua shrugged and looked away from them.

'It was you. You got the black men to kill for you!' Mary Ann's triumph at her quick insight had to be contained.

'We voted. All of us agreed.' As her children absorbed this Mauatua slowly walked to the head of Tamahere's grave.

'If you have ever loved me, think about this.'

She methodically pushed stones together with her foot, to make more of a marker and that composed her. She dared her children to accept and understand an explanation she might have given years ago.

'What child could love a mother whose hands had killed their father?'

Charles couldn't look at her, but Mary Ann seized on her words.

'And that's why the black men had to die, too. That's the real reason, isn't it? So they never told who really wanted our first fathers dead.'

'We never knew what ship might call and what might happen if they told anyone. What if someone took all the women off Pitcairn to be punished? What would have happened to you?'

'They did your killing and then they had to die. That's disgusting.'

'No. No it's not. They wanted to be fathers.' She stopped.

She was too weary to defend herself and didn't want to tell any more of Pitcairn's secrets.

'There is nothing a woman might not do.' Charles muttered to himself, over and over again.

'There was something, one thing we women never did, Charles We never did anything that might harm our children, then or in the future,' she assured him.

'So, the black men were sacrifices, they were sacrificed for us,' Mary Ann insisted. Her sour face made Mauatua want to smack it.

'If you like.'

She took a deep breath, determined her daughter would face up to the complexities of real life rather than hiding herself in a fantasy world of biblical parables and psalms.

'Look at me, Mary Ann, and listen! It takes more than a dead man on a cross to make things right in this world.'

The insult to Mary Ann's blind faith shut her up.

Mauatua kept her advantage and stalked out of the garden. She was old, tired through lack of sleep and proper food on the sea voyage and wanted peace and quiet to adjust to Pitcairn without those she had lost.

The memories of that wet day of Tamahere's burial rushed back, of her children shouting and throwing rocks at her on this same path, half their lifetimes ago. Please God, if there was a god of any kind, let nothing like that happen. Let them leave their old mother alone.

It was hard enough to have memories like hers in her mind, but to have them brought out and spread before others, so people could laugh and point and accuse. No. Absolutely not.

Charles and Mary Ann hadn't followed. It gave her time. If she walked fast enough, she could do what she really wanted to do. Her legs were no longer used to Pitcairn's hills and bumps. Had they got steeper? She wanted to rest a few minutes to ease the pain in her hips.

She glanced behind and they'd still not followed. Good. They'd not know where she was. Instead of resting she tried to take longer steps but this hurt, so she hobbled short ones faster.

The house had only been deserted for five months but the path was already overgrown. Somehow the lushness made it more welcoming, signifying life when so much else was death.

The memories came back so vividly she had to pause. Thursday's birth there and that long, delayed first breath of Charles. Fletcher so loving and Fletcher so distressed.

More time passed than she realised. She heard their voices behind her. She crashed her way through the path with her pole. She pulled at the door and it slid easily. Bligh's books, what were left, were on the floor.

Imagine people doing this to someone else's house. But then, Englishmen and the Navy hardly thought Pitcairners human.

The table Fletcher had made, where he had eaten so carefully with his knife and fork, tottered on snapped legs. And what would they have done through there?

She couldn't go into the bedroom. That part of her life, those memories, were not to be touched. Everything else important was being ripped from her. But not those.

The single most sustaining thread of her life was still Fletcher and their shared visions. He had always found a way to come out of his depressions to make love to her, with her, to make both of them bigger and better through love.

She would never go into that room again and there was no reason to go up to the second storey so many houses now had. There was nothing important in her room up there. It would have seemed too obvious.

She listened carefully. Charles and Mary Ann must have walked past. She'd do it now.

CHAPTER 70

'What's the secret?' Mary Ann's question startled her. She lost her balance and fell from the pile of furniture she had made, banging her head hard on the floor. Her head spun but Mary Ann laughed, telling her how she'd been given away by the bushes she slashed with her pole.

Charles held his mother in his arms while her head cleared, asking her if she was alright.

'Of course I'm not. Otherwise you'd not be holding me.'

'I'm sorry,' he apologised. 'We didn't mean you to fall.'

'Of course you didn't. Say something sensible Charles or shut up.'

Charles hated that phrase, but it worked.

'What would you like me to do?' he asked.

'That's better. Help me stand. Get me off this floor.'

The memories of Fletcher and her two sons asleep on her lap on this floor were still powerful.

That was the moment she felt the last of Fletcher's determination slip away like breadfruit pulp running through her fingers.

She couldn't help looking up into the rafters and Mary Ann was quick to spot this.

'Some things I kept,' Mauatua explained, waving her hand airily.

'How mean, how spiteful. We've got nothing of him but you kept stuff for yourself. As usual.'

'Mamoo, Mary Ann. Mamoo. Those things were hidden *for* you. Almost everything from BOUNTY or its men on this island has been stolen by sailors or given to them too easily. We became a sort of exhibition for their entertainment. Except we seemed to pay for them to come and see us. I had to save something.'

'You hid them from us all this time.'

Time? Mauatua turned her back on Mary Ann's sour face. Time was running out. Could she still keep the biggest secret from her remaining children? She doubted she had the strength to tell it and wasn't certain her children were robust enough to hear it.

'Everything is you, just you,' Mary Ann flung at her, reassembling the pile of furniture so she could climb up to the roof.

Mauatua resigned herself. Perhaps it was finally time to start that long overdue journey, a journey she feared to take yet hoped would lead to a place that would bring her peace.

'Nothing on Pitcairn was ever *just* me, or ever *just* any of BOUNTY'S women. It was always *just* you, our children.'

'Hah. That's easy to say,' Mary Ann said, from the top of the pile.

'It was not easy to do. But there was no choice. If you had been a mother, you might understand.'

She'd never said such things to her daughter. Mary Ann held her tongue so she knew she'd really hurt her. But it was true.

Nothing was stronger than the determination of a mother to protect her children, born or unborn. No woman on earth knew that more than her – *'there is nothing a woman might not have to do'*.

'There are parcels tucked behind the rafters. Charles, if you could. She won't be able to reach.'

Mary Ann climbed down showing all the surliness she had countless times been told made her look old and ugly. Charles' greater height made it easier for him to reach into the corner behind a rafter, where shadows had held her secrets for so long. The parcels were blackened by the waxy smoke rising from decades of strings of spluttering candlenut lights. He threw them to Mary Ann. She pulled at the sooty wrappings. Inside each was a carved image, the sort of gods Christians were supposed to revile and smash.

'I knew you were still Tahitian,' she said with malicious triumph.

'They were in Tamahere's sea chest. Probably some of the few safe from missionaries' axes. Have reverence for them. They are your blood, too, Mary Ann.'

'They make me feel sick.'

Mauatua tossed her head. Her daughter was absurd, with no care for anyone other than Jesus and herself. She hated to be hurtful but, like throwing his *hei* back at Tamahere, it seemed another old secret would be revealed in anger.

It was wrong, but Mary Ann forced her.

'Charles, there's another.'

It took him longer to release the last parcel, blacker than the others and much bigger. Inside, were other small parcels and a big one. The smaller ones held gold braid from uniforms and shiny buttons. They were little things of Fletcher's she'd hoped to use to honour him one day.

Mary Ann's anxiety always to know first, and then to damn as unimportant, made her impatient. She grabbed the biggest parcel and tore at it like a starving dog. Inside were two officer's hats, stored brim to brim and she pried them apart.

'Be careful,' Mauatua shouted, but she was too late.

Mary Ann jumped as the ball from between the hats thudded onto the floor. It was thickly cushioned with tapa and coconut fibre and rolled until it stopped at Mauatua's feet.

'What is it? What's in there?' Mary Ann demanded.

There was still time. She could take it and never let her children see the contents. They had a way of dragging secrets from her in times of maddening anger, when she had always hoped for quiet, bonding moments.

There would be a better time than this, had to be.

She bent to pick up the package. Her fingers felt for what they could of the familiar shape, determining everything was in place.

The delay infuriated Mary Ann.

'Give it to me, I'll open it,' she said, grabbing for it. She almost had it from her mother's grip.

'It is not yours to open,' Mauatua yelled, resisting Mary Ann's determined struggle, still not certain it should be opened at all.

'It's my father's.'

'No.' Mauatua hissed fiercely. 'It is not your father's.'

She dug deep to find the strength to wrench the parcel back and turned away from Charles and Mary Ann. She yanked away the protection, much of it crumbling in her hands, until the contents were half revealed.

'It is not your father's,' she repeated. 'Not really.'

Balancing herself carefully she took a deep breath and then spun quickly to them with the skull exposed.

'It *is* your father.'

It felt good no longer to be the only keeper of her secret.

Charles gagged. Bile gushed from his mouth. Mary Ann staggered and turned to him and finding no refuge there fell to the floor in a faint. Charles followed. She had no sympathy. That's what happened when child-like minds pried into anything biblical in their lives.

The pain of grown children who fainted was nothing compared to the agony of watching two sons die, both too soon and too horribly.

She pulled them against the wall and propped them up and wiped Charles' mouth and chin.

She put Fletcher's skull on the floor in the middle of the room and then perched against the pile Charles had used to climb.

They didn't need to know everything. Probably wouldn't understand, anyway. How could they imagine it had been a year before women felt safe going back to the gardens to bury the dead men of what they already called Massacre Day. All their bones except Fletcher's were interred together. She told the women she wouldn't need any help with his.

That was the unwitting seed, the first time the men and women of Pitcairn wondered if Fletcher was dead. Jenny helped without knowing, saying she thought she'd seen Fletcher dead, but couldn't be sure.

When Jenny carried Thursday and new-born Mary Ann from the smoke-filled gardens on Massacre Day, she'd left Mauatua there. She presumed she wanted to mourn over his body. Perhaps he wasn't dead at all, she gossiped to any and everyone.

Mauatua never commented but quickly fell into a pattern of ignoring such stories or laughing at them.

Fletcher's bones had quickly been stripped and bleached by Pitcairn's weather. Some of the sea birds must have helped, perhaps even the land crabs, but she'd never wanted to think about this. She buried his bones by the pool where he'd finally lain, so she would never forget. There would be no markers, just memories. There was nothing unusual about keeping his skull. Tahitians always separated the skulls of important men and women from their bodies and kept them as sacred objects. On special occasions they were worn around the waist.

The one time the women did this Quintal and McCoy were horrified and their threats violent and angry beyond belief. Luckily, Pitcairn's last four men were so drunk they couldn't later trust or believe what they saw. Fletcher's skull went back in the rafters and the men never quite agreed if they had seen four or five. That strengthened her story more, that Fletcher might be alive and still on Pitcairn.

Adams, Young, Quintal and McCoy looked over their shoulders continually since that day. They remembered her magical touch with wounds on Tubuai. She overheard them say Fletcher really could be alive on

Pitcairn, saved by her potions. They just as easily believed he had escaped because if anyone could navigate to Tahiti or, even, South America, it was Fletcher Christian. She agreed with whatever anyone said and eventually rumours of his fate grew in number, complication and geographical location, exactly as she hoped would happen.

Her son and daughter revived but she did and said nothing. The first thing they saw was the eye sockets of their father's skull.

It shocked them into defiance rather than making them faint again. Mary Ann began, of course.

'You wanted his memory all to yourself. Selfish.'

'I put him there so he watched you grow up. I needed him there.'

'But you had children with Ned Young.'

'And I wasn't the only one. Pitcairn needed children. Pitcairn was all about children and the more there were the happier I was.'

'So you were doing your duty?' Mary Ann tossed her head.

'To the island. Yes, I thought so.'

'You must have hated Daddy. To get the black men to kill him.'

'No, I loved him.'

There really was nothing more than that to say to her children. Except neither of them would have the maturity to understand.

'That was it, was it? Three children. Then, thank you very much, Mr Christian. Off with your head, Mr Christian. Next please.'

Mauatua hid her disgust behind her hands. 'You are what they say Mary Ann, aren't you? A true bitch.'

She waited to recompose her face but couldn't. She slid her hands away and stood, feeling strong and tall again.

'Here's the truth then. The real truth if you are woman enough to understand anything other than the Bible.'

She kicked at the books and debris on the floor. She couldn't believe she had been taunted to go this far but she couldn't mourn the new dead until she'd made peace with the old.

'If your father had lived, he would have killed you before you were born. I had to make a choice. I chose you.'

'Killed me? You chose me? I don't believe it.'

Of course Mary Ann didn't believe her, that the price of her life had been so high. That's why she'd kept her secrets for so long. Whatever she told Mary Ann, it was unlikely she would ever honour her mother.

'The spade. I was there, wasn't I?' Charles hopped to his mother.

He had been introspective since kissing his second dying brother. The shock of seeing his father's skull opened deeper doors.

Mauatua didn't speak, hoping he'd remember more of the past. He'd only been two but perhaps Charles would now repay her years of love by remembering, so she didn't have to endure the telling of it.

'You were on the ground and someone was pushing a spade into you,' Charles muttered as his memory clarified. 'And then he did it hard and made you cry loud and then he pushed our face in the dirt, me and Thursday. Was that him? Was that our Daddy who did that?'

'He would have killed you, Mary Ann,' she told her daughter again. 'He didn't even want you born. He thought you would be a cripple, too.'

Charles's face contorted but Mauatua shrugged. Charles was a cripple. That was the word for it. Why pretend? A name didn't make her love him more or less.

Mary Ann whipped the attention back to her. 'He was mad!'

'Yes. He was. His conscience drove him to it. With no way of explaining himself to his family or the rest of the world, he drove himself mad. By then he really had no idea where he was.'

'Or who we were. He wouldn't really have killed me, would he?'

'I couldn't take that risk.'

Mary Ann's head shook with bewilderment.

'So it wasn't for you, is that what you are saying? You didn't murder him for your benefit.'

'Or exclusively for yours, Mary Ann, so don't bother to feel special if you please. It was for your father, too, *mainly* for him. He was suffering, broken by never-ending remorse.'

She swayed on her feet, feeling again the weight of Fletcher's anguish.

'It overwhelmed him. He believed Bligh was coming to take him back to England. Please think. What if the world knew what he was becoming? How could I take that risk?'

She looked at his skull. Even that told her Fletcher was truly the one. *E ha'apua'i te here mau, i te pua'i o na ta'ata e piti.* Love is only true when it makes both lovers bigger, she remembered.

Fletcher's love made her a bigger and better person, then and now. But this was no time for reverie. She drew on the skull for courage, just as he had called on the tattoo they had designed together.

'I knew ships would come one day and want to know what happened to him. I didn't want him remembered as a monster, a mad child killer. He didn't deserve that. Mutiny was bad enough.'

Charles hopped to her, keeping well away from the skull. Her legs were weaker again and her pole was on the other side of the room. She fell back on the pile of furniture. She expected him to crouch and take her hands.

Surely he'd understood what she had suffered and would tell her he sympathised with the agony of her decisions to protect him. He'd tell her how grateful he was that his father wasn't despised as a mad man and infant murderer. Instead he leaned over her and shouted abuse.

'This is cruel. It's self deluding fantasy. You murdered him and all the other poor sods so you could claim Pitcairn had been your doing, yours alone. It's all about what people think about you and this bloody island.'

Emotion strangled Charles's voice. He spun on his club foot, using his whole foot to propel him as he fought to find his next words.

'There is no stupid secret. You killed our father like some old dog you couldn't be bothered to look after. He needed you to love him, not to get rid of him. And then, then you stuffed him away up there. So everyone would forget all about him.'

His spittle landed on her. She wiped it from her face slowly, using the time to deflect what she wanted to shout back. It was best not to say anything until he had finished. Her eyes widened, daring him to go on.

'He's been hidden away with Tahitian idols, things you probably still think of as gods and worship as gods. What does that make him?' Charles implored, his face still too close to hers.

She put up a hand, until she judged both of them were prepared for her hushed and careful answer.

'Make him, Charles? A god, that's what. Fletcher is my *only* true god. He died because I wanted him remembered as a good man by the world.

'In Matavai I hardly dared dream about what he made possible for me here. Or for you, kindly remember.

'On Tahiti you would have been dead before you breathed. You have no idea of the pain and agony it cost him to give you life.'

This stabbed Charles as much as her jibe at Mary Ann's faith, but it would be the pain of reality and so she didn't sympathise with the way he staggered away from her at last..

She wanted the comfort of taking Fletcher's skull in her arms, their father and mother together again. No, she would spare her children that. She left Fletcher where he was.

Charles was staring, his eyes unfocussed. His head was nodding very slowly but his spine was straight as though her awful reminder about the cost of his birth had grown him. Yes, she was certain that was so.

His eyes might have been Fletcher's. They were certainly as deep and warm with wisdom and compassion. Perhaps they were his, at last released to look through his son's eyes as the old beliefs promised.

Charles had finally found his place in the world. She should have told him years ago. She judged him ready for more.

'I didn't want to keep Fletcher to myself and I don't want him to be forgotten. That's not thinking sensibly, Charles.

'If there is an afterlife it is in the minds of those who are alive. You've seen it for years. You've heard it from every ship that called here and in Tahiti and the ships we sailed on. He is constantly in other people's minds all around the world. They argue and wonder about him.

'To me, this means he is alive.'

Mary Ann scoffed. 'If he is such a god, why doesn't he have a tomb or a memorial of some kind, where we could all worship him?'

It was time to end this, time her daughter dealt with all she had done to protect her and to honour Fletcher. Charles was almost 40, Mary Ann a year younger. She was old enough to share the load.

It was nothing to what any one of Pitcairn's foremothers had endured.

'As you well know, only mortals have tombs,' she explained. 'Fletcher is immortal because he has no tomb. That's what I wanted for him, so no-one forgets what he made possible on this island.'

'I don't think so.'

She paid no attention to Mary Ann's sour rejection. Instead, she welcomed a strange word into her head. Epiphany. Fletcher explained it to her years ago but she never thought she'd realise one for her daughter. She pushed herself to stand.

'Come here,' she commanded Mary Ann.

'Think what you like about my motives, but I *have* made your father an immortal instead of a mad monster who killed his unborn child, who would have been you, you might care to remember.'

Mary Ann screwed up her face and sobbed. So, she believed did she? It was too late to give her daughter sympathy, and too late for her daughter to apologise for her lifetime of bitter mistrust.

'Your father has no grave, no tomb. So who can say he is dead? Without a tomb, he is forever immortal, just as I planned.'

She pulled off her wooden cross and held it high. At last she could say it for someone else to hear.

She said it first directly into her daughter's face.

'Just like your Jesus.'

It was days before she could bear to see Charles or Mary Ann. In spite of themselves they agreed to keep her secret, so that their father's descent into tortured madness was never known.

That also meant the world would never believe Ma'ohi women succeeded where white men failed, that she and the eleven other Ma'ohi were the true founders of Pitcairn. No one would know the unimaginable things they had to do to protect the lives and freedoms of their children.

Only men were celebrated, only men were allowed to be heroes.

Pitcairn was founded because Fletcher mutinied, and because he believed in new ways of life. Pitcairn survived through the voting he taught them. She had made his vision into reality not for themselves but for their children.

She buried Fletcher's skull with his other bones by the pool. That was one secret she would never share. And now all she wanted to do was to sit under a coconut palm and play and talk with her grandchildren.

Joseph, another of Thursday's sons, died from after effects of influenza a few weeks after he returned from Tahiti.

He was her fourth dead grandchild.

For all their sakes as much as hers, there had to be something positive to show for Pitcairn's blood and misery, something that was a greater memorial to Fletcher.

Fletcher believed even a community that voted needed a powerful uniting leader. Perhaps Mr Nobbs or Mr Buffet might become one, but until then there was no-one to unite the Pitcairners. It couldn't be her, not at her age.

And so far, Fletcher seemed loath to speak through Charles, even if his spirit was within him.

Gradually, the solution came to her. It would properly make women the equals of men, protect Pitcairn from outsiders and lessen the risk of a weak or ill-intentioned leader.

One last effort, that's all it would take.

And, please God, a ship from England while she was still alive.

Sarah Christian Nobbs was Mauatua's granddaughter, a daughter of Charles 'Hoppa' Christian, her second son by Fletcher Christian. Within the family she is said to have looked remarkably like her grandmother. From this portrait it's clear to see she has an equivalent height and determination. She married George Hunn Nobbs, one of the first white men who settled on Pitcairn and who then became its Pastor. In later life she became remarkably handsome and matriarchal.

CHAPTER 71

November 28th, 1838: HMS FLY, Bounty Bay

Mauatua let the rope slip through her hands. It wasn't that she cared much about the traded goods in the woven palm-frond basket at its end. She'd lived without flour or calico or proper candles for decades and could do it again.

No, she was slow because there was unfinished business on this ship.

She turned her head and reminded herself. FLY, that was its name, HMS FLY. The H would stand for Her, now there was a young queen on the throne back Home. Home. Funny to call it that when no-one from Pitcairn had been there. But that was what Fletcher and the others called England, and so that's what she did.

Her basket landed in the canoe below and she let the rope snake down after it. She was the last of the Pitcairners on board and the sailors were about to tie a safety line around her before she climbed down the rope ladder. She waved them away and looked back at the island. Pitcairn had been her home for almost fifty years. It was just a rock really, an isolated Pacific fortress of sheer red cliffs crowned with coconut palms that topped out a lush green covering.

From the ship the appearance of isolation was multiplied because no current-calming reef offered safe anchorage at Pitcairn. Instead, the closer you got to the tiny landing place they now called Bounty Bay, the more rocks there were. On a high-wind day like today, those not hidden beneath the Pacific swell had their jagged tops smothered by a thick cream of surf that had hurtled unhindered for thousands of miles.

Learning to read Bounty Bay's turbulence was one of the earliest survival skills a Pitcairner had to master. Some of the young men who returned to shore earlier were balanced on the broadest rocks. Powerful surges harried their calves and thighs as each man gave returning canoes and small boats safe points of reference for their final surf-powered slide to safety. On and in the sea Pitcairners were safe, sensible and skilled. It was on land they were vulnerable.

The sailors were anxious to help her off the ship but she refused. 'I'd be grateful for a little of Captain Elliott's time,' she said.

'Captain's in a meeting.' She didn't mind that the sailor's disdainful face said more than his answer.

'It'll only take a few minutes. Would you be so kind as to ask? I'll follow you.' Mauatua led the way, marking her short, shuffling steps with the beat of her walking pole.

When FLY anchored in Bounty Bay that morning, almost all the 95 Pitcairners braved heroic surf to board the sloop. A British warship was prayers answered. The island was desperate for the protection of the British monarch and of her Navy. They wanted British approval for Mauatua's idea of a system of self-government, defence against such cruel invaders as Joshua Hill.

Mauatua watched for six years as that uninvited, insane imposter ruled on the island by schism and bullying, even wanting to execute a 12-year old girl for digging sweet potatoes from the wrong patch. Hill made it impossible to unite the island under a single elected leader. If she had achieved it Hill would never have succeeded in setting Pitcairn family against Pitcairn family, never created the horror of Buffet and Evans being publically flogged or the nonsense of competing schools and churches on their tiny island.

They managed to have him taken off the island a few years ago, but ruffians from American whalers and sealers still refused to believe Pitcairn was British. Where was the proof they'd ask? Keeping the louts' drunken hands off Pitcairn's young women concerned its men and boys so much they interrupted work in the fields and the reservoirs had not been cleaned.

The younger men distilled spirits again after they came back from Tahiti but this caused so many problems everyone agreed to ban it once more. Such agreements weren't laws to visitors. There were no enforceable ways to punish a rampaging youth who brought alcohol ashore.

Who could be sure he would not share with a Pitcairner? What could they do if he did?

Until Hill everything had been voted on informally, and since him, as more of the world encroached more often, Pitcairn knew it needed laws the rest of the world would heed. For this to succeed, Pitcairn needed a framework in which the laws worked, a body that agreed or disagreed for everyone on the island.

Today she stood back to let Pitcairn's men plead again on behalf of the island, but they failed. Just as they had last year, when HMS ACTEON and HMS IMOGENE called.

She'd listened carefully as Captain Elliott told the Pitcairners he didn't have the authority to put them under the protection of the British Crown. Both the last kings, George and then William, refused to annexe Tahiti because it was too far away, the other side of the world. No navy or army could guarantee to protect it. And Pitcairn, well, Pitcairn was even further away and so small. He doubted the new queen had even heard of it.

Elliott's last comment really rankled. Every ship that called at Pitcairn since the BOUNTY mutineers' refuge was discovered thirty years ago reckoned the island's story was known worldwide. Every sailor wanted something to prove they had been here and left determined to brag about visiting Pitcairn and to speculate about Fletcher's fate.

Of course Queen Victoria would know about the island.

Last year an Englishman in a private schooner even took away a heap of Pitcairn's tapa designs, saying they were unique and he would make them famous and admired in England.

The sailor told Captain Elliott she wanted to see him, and she heard low laughter from inside his cabin. This didn't surprise her, for once she overheard a young officer describe her as 'the perfect picture of an old hag'. Well, she was very old, ancient, at somewhere around 80, making her some three decades older than any Pitcairner except Teraura, Thursday's widow and now the only other full-blooded Tahitian who had arrived on BOUNTY.

Her hair was white, startlingly so. That happened almost overnight, weeks after returning from Tahiti and her confrontation with Charles and Mary Ann. She cut it short at once and it looked like a monstrous frizzed halo when light came from behind her. The perfect teeth of her youth and prime had become discoloured and crooked and a few were missing, which emphasised the profound age and weather lines in her sunken cheeks. Age pushed her head forward too, and hunched her shoulders.

She understood why a British sailor had called her a walnut-skinned witch to her face, when he thought she was bargaining too hard for what he was selling. Words didn't matter to a woman who had seen and done what she had.

Her bare feet were splay-toed, broad and calloused from their long life of freedom. Captain Elliott's watched them as he offered her a chair.

'I speak better on my feet,' said Mauatua, turning away. Elliott coughed with embarrassment, so she had put him off balance. A good start. Mauatua kept her advantage and surveyed the cabin, balancing with her pole against the ship's slow roll and pitch.

The portrait of the child-like Queen Victoria amused her. She would look like a toy beside Queen Pomare.

They made small talk about the small, gold-framed watercolours of his family home that Elliott stood amidst his journal and charts on his work table and then she rested the pole on the chair she had been offered, braced her legs apart and faced him with her hands on her hips. The captain took this as a cue.

'So, you are who, exactly?'

'Mrs Christian. Mrs Fletcher Christian.' She was the only woman called Mrs Christian on the island. Everyone else used only first names or nick names because there were so few family names. It kept Fletcher's name alive, and that helped her get what she wanted from visitors.

'You mean, and I ask this with respect Mrs Christian, are you saying you are the wife of the mutineer?'

'He mutinied against that wicked Captain Bligh, not against his king or country. He was always British, so were we. We still are.' Mauatua held Elliott's look, knowing her eyes, at least, were as bright and vital as ever.

It was obvious Elliott couldn't think of a response and she didn't want to get into yet another argument over whether the mutiny had been caused by Bligh or by Tahitian beauties. Bligh or beauty? She couldn't imagine why there was still confusion, not 50 years later. That's one thing she'd always told the truth about, plenty of times.

She walked towards Elliott and put a hand on his shoulder. 'You know, it doesn't have to be true.'

She kept her hand on his shoulder and her eyes on his until he had to ask, 'What doesn't have to be true?'

'It doesn't have to be true we are British.' Uncertain of his attention, she kept her gaze steady.

'When you live on an island like this, so far away, truth is often . . . Well, sometimes truth has to be what is most convenient.'

'I'm not sure I understand.'

'You don't have to make us officially British.' she barked.

The man's slow thinking made her impatient. 'We don't need something signed by the new queen.' She patted his shoulder for emphasis with every word. 'We can't wait that long, what, two or three years by the time it came back to us? There are other ways to make ships think we are protected by Britain.'

She leaned closer, her eyes aspark with what she was about to say. Her voice was conspiratorial.

'If the captain of a British warship approved our laws, if a Royal Navy captain acknowledged our council was set up fairly, well then . . .'

She stood back until Elliott again felt obliged to fill the silence.

'I see. You mean, if I did these things you ask, then it would *look* as though you were British.'

She didn't dare use the word hypocriting. Every Englishman who heard it laughed. But whatever you called it she was asking him to provide a false image of the truth on Pitcairn.

Elliott picked up the papers on his desk. Once more his eyes flickered over the tight writing on the pages.

'These, these, well, they're extraordinary these rules and laws you Pitcairners want formalised. Never seen anything like them in my life, not anywhere in the world. Rules about cockerels and dogs, pigs and alcohol, about who owns which breadfruit tree or coconut palm, and who should work for the common good and when. And so on. It seems like the worst thing you can do is to kill someone else's cat. A $50 fine, is that?'

She interrupted the captain. 'You've travelled so you'll know.'

'Know? Know what?'

'Know that what is right for one part of the world is useless in another. These are what we need on Pitcairn.'

'Have you thought how members of this, this island council that's suggested here, will be appointed?'

'By voting.'

'The men have agreed to this?' She hesitated, suppressing a smile. She knew what his reaction would be to what was next.

'And the women,' she said. 'They'll be voting, too.'

'What? Women voting, too? That's astonishing.'

She stood behind Elliott and reached over him. She turned back the pages in his hand and then stabbed at one with her finger.

'It's there. Right at the start. You must have missed it.' She pulled her finger away quickly, in case its broken nail and tarnish of ingrained Pitcairn soil diverted him.

But the captain kept staring at the page, quite agog.

'This is a revolution, better than a revolution. The women of America and France didn't get the vote after their revolutions. And voting for women in Britain, well, they just don't.'

'But we do. Always have. Fletcher taught us. There's something else. Look there. Education will be compulsory, for boys *and* girls.'

'For girls, too? Compulsory education for girls, bless my soul, that's too rich to believe.'

She watched Elliott realise the full significance of what she was asking. He stood and paced around the cabin, looking back into the proposed rules and laws again and again.

'Y'know, I could be the one to enshrine such laws, both unique in the world as far as I know. There could be a book. I don't know if you realise this but these, these laws are more revolutionary than any other I know.

'And, by God, there's no blood! You've led an extraordinary revolution, and on an island like this, of all . . . By God, Mrs Christian!'

She lifted her chin and rebuked him. 'We don't use God's name to curse, not on this island.'

'Of course, I remember. My apologies.' Elliott hastened to retrieve himself. 'I congratulate you, I really do.' He sat behind his table again and fiddled with his pictures until he made his decision.

'I could come ashore tomorrow morning.'

'You'll know the surf's safe if we fly a white flag. I will send some men to guide you in. They'll carry you up the Hill of Difficulty.'

'Carry me?'

'It's been raining. You'll have pounds of red clay on both shoes in minutes. We call it the world's friendliest mud, but that's not the way a British naval captain should look.' Elliott thanked her for this valuing of his status. And then he asked if Mrs Christian might honour him further, by revealing the fate of her husband.

'The world is still diverted by the mystery,' he added.

The fire in Mauatua's eyes died. The British Navy was finally doing something for Pitcairn and yet there was a price attached.

'There are so many tales,' he continued. 'I mean, do you think he escaped and sailed back to England? Excuse me, of course, there is nothing for you to 'think'. Of course you know. But which is correct? I beg you. I've heard he was shot dead by natives 11 months or two years or three or four years after you arrived here, or he escaped to South America and then was in Spain . . .'

She copied and continued his sing-song recitation. '. . . or became insane and threw himself off rocks, or he died a natural death, or he was seen in Devonport by an old shipmate etc etc etc.'

'It is very confusing, isn't it?'

'If I could ascertain the truth, Mrs Christian, it would, well, it would help my book's success.'

She dared not speak and hoped it looked like she was considering his question. He must have thought so.

'And I'm sure the Navy would show its gratitude,' he insisted, 'of that I am most heartily certain. In the meantime, it will be an honour to ratify your bloodless revolution, Mrs Christian.'

Mauatua's shoulders dropped further and her flat hands slapped her scalp, the old Tahitian way. She retrieved her pole and hobbled to the door.

She stopped and stretched her back so she stood tall, as tall as she was so long ago in Matavai Bay, when her only name was Mauatua.

'*Bloodless* revolution, Captain Elliott?' She felt tears overflow and silver the furrows in her dark cheeks.

'Yes, I suppose it is. I suppose it is bloodless. Now.'

EPILOGUE

From November 29th, 1838, every woman over 18 years old on Pitcairn Island had her right to vote adopted into law, regardless of property she might or might not own or if she was married or single. They were the first women in history to enjoy unencumbered universal suffrage and not a single one of them was Caucasian.

On the day Pitcairn Island's women became ratified voters their daughters, granddaughters and great-granddaughters were guaranteed the same compulsory education as boys.

Only Catherine the Great of Russia had attempted this, and she failed.

Mauatua and her daughter-in-law Teraura were born on Tahiti as women with virtually no rights, not even to eat what they wanted or to be mothers when they chose.

The blinkered, two-century quest by some men to blacken Fletcher Christian and to whitewash William Bligh has overshadowed these women's extraordinary achievements for women's rights and suffrage.

Mauatua thought that day in 1838 was Fletcher Christian's greatest memorial. She'd given up any idea of recognition for Fletcher or for herself as social revolutionaries but she'd finally achieved what they discussed so long ago in Matavai Bay and on board BOUNTY.

She completed his vision of an ideal and equal community for which she had endured so much pain for so long.

Mauatua/Mrs Christian died of influenza on September 19th 1842. It came to Pitcairn from the very source that first freed her from Tahiti, a ship from a foreign land. She thought she was over 80 years old.

Teraura was the youngest Tahitian woman to sail on BOUNTY in 1789, perhaps aged 14. She died on July 15th 1850 aged around 70.

A BRIEF HISTORY OF NEGLECT

For over two centuries Pitcairn Island's self-government was slowly whittled away by British Governments that came to think of the island as a thorn in its side.

In the mid to late 20th century it was an embarrassing reminder of Britain's dead days as a colonial power and thus largely ignored.

No-one in Whitehall had the slightest interest in understanding the reality of what its remoteness meant to its inhabitants or that the difficulty of daily life got markedly worse from the 1960s. Jet planes that put us more easily in touch with the world replaced the ships that had called at Pitcairn every 10 days or so on their way to or from the Panama Canal. Pitcairn and Pitcairners were as isolated from the rest of the world as they had been in the 19th century before the discovery of radio, except that then they might be visited by over 100 sailing ships a year.

By the 1980s Pitcairn was Britain's most neglected inhabited possession, relying on charity and the illicit use of ham radio to survive. While the rest of us thrilled to the revolutionary home video, Pitcairn's official communication with the British Government was Morse Code telegraph. And yet Pitcairner Islanders of all ages were expected to know and to live by British Law . . .

The 21st century has finally seen a reverse, not least because as a British Overseas Territory Pitcairn Island is also a dependency of the European Union. Then, early in 2010 the Government of Pitcairn Island was incorporated and self-determination returned. It took seven years of wrangling, because of a plethora of objections, requirements, demands and refusals, very often by Pitcairn's determined women.

In modern parlance you might say: They were back. But it had taken almost two centuries.

One day I hope the world finds the means to discover the bones of Fletcher Christian and of Mauatua on Pitcairn Island and then to reunite them beneath a splendid memorial to love and to the birth of universal suffrage but primarily to that most powerful of all driving forces on this planet, a mother's determination to defend and nurture her children at any cost. Primal maternal instinct is what drove Mauatua and the other foremothers and is what really founded Pitcairn Island.

This remarkable 1856 photograph shows sons and grandsons of Mauatua's companions. From the right, Arthur is the son of Tevarua and mutineer Matthew Quintal; next is George only son of Teio and mutineer John Adams Far left is George's son John Adams and then Arthur's son John Quintal.

ARTEFACTS, SIGHTS AND WEBSITES:

- **Nantucket Historical Association's** museum displays two of Fletcher Christian's Chinese bowls and the camphor-lined mahogany chest that were given to Captain Matthew Folger of TOPAZ, the first ship to discover the mutineers' hideout. www.nha.org/
- **The National Maritime Museum** at Greenwich, London, displays the famed Kendall Chronometer Bligh and Fletcher Christian used on BOUNTY; it had many adventures after Mauatua gave it to Folger. They also have other artefacts not always on display and these include John Adams' stolen lead-and-oak tombstone and his pigtail. www.nmm.ac.uk
- **The white and gold Music Room of Norfolk House** from St James Square, London W1 (now demolished) in which Fletcher Christian sat with Society to enjoy Mozart's latest music is in the Victoria and Albert Museum. www.vam.ac.uk/
- **Moorland Close** where Fletcher Christian was born just outside Cockermouth in Cumbria is a privately owned working farm, but visitors are usually permitted to see the walls and battlements that abut the house, itself built just a few years before Fletcher was born.
- All that's standing of **Ewanrigg**, the Christians' mansion behind Whitehaven in Cumbria, is part of its facade and some of the luxurious quarters of dressed stone built for John and Isabella Christian's hounds.
- **Belle Isle**, the unique Grade 1 Georgian round house on an island of the same name in Lake Windemere, named after Isabella Curwen, was lived in until 1993 by descendants of she and John Christian, Fletcher's first cousin and head of the Christian family. The island and the house are not open to the public.
- **St Bridget's Church, Brigham, Cumbria**, is where Fletcher was baptised, and also has the grave of Fletcher Christian's father Charles, one of the few family graves that have survived. It's a showy table grave proudly displaying the family crest to remind viewers he was of the Ewanrigg/Milntown dynasty.
- **Milntown**, the Christians' family home on the Isle of Man since 1342 (at least) until the early 20th century now features a cafe and restaurant with views of the delightful garden. The main rooms are opened to the public during the Summer only. There is an embryonic plan to make it an inter-

national centre for the Christian family and their many amazing stories in all corners of the earth. www.milntown.org/

An extraordinary handwritten **two-volume history of more than 20 generations of the Christians of Milntown and Ewanrigg** – and of most family branches – was written over many years by the last Mrs Christian to live in Milntown. It is now in the Manx Museum, Douglas, IOM, with much supportive material, by courtesy of Ewan Christian, to whom it had come from Susan Hicks-Beach, author of The Yesterdays Behind the Door, a Christian family chronicle which is largely based on this material. www.gov.im/mnh/heritage/**museum**s/**man**x**museum**.xml

The two **BOUNTY replicas** continue to inspire, wherever in the world they might be, sailing and thrilling visitors and participating crew members. www.tallshipbounty.org offers sailing experiences in many parts of the world on the ship built in NZ for the Mel Gibson movie. The bigger 1961 version made for Marlon Brando's film is currently for sale (early 2011): www.easternyachts.com

www.fatefulvoyage.com This extraordinary site displays copies of most original documents relating to the BOUNTY story. It's an amazing resource that took an age to assemble and revolutionises BOUNTY research. Thank you James Galloway of Yuma, AZ in the United States

http://library.puc.edu/pitcairn/studycenter This takes you to the Pitcairn Islands Study Centre in California, the world's largest such centre, part of the Pacific Union College in Angwin, Ca.

The Pitcairn Island Study Group, was formed in North America and also has a very active branch in the UK. www.pisg.net/ and www.pitcairnstudygroup.co.uk/ Originally Pitcairn stamps were the focus of further study but now the groups host wider ranging conferences and meetings.

http://dir.groups.yahoo.com/group/EchosOfTheBounty is a dedicated website chat group: http://dir.groups.yahoo.com/dir/1602230387 lists other sites devoted to Pitcairn and the saga of BOUNTY, including FriendsofPitcairn, which in turn has many fascinating links.

Pitcairn Island Here are some suggestions for more information about the island today, including how to visit, or to discover what you can buy, including its sensational tropical-flower honey (also available on line or direct from Partridges of Sloane Square and from Fortnum and Mason in Piccadilly)

- www.government.pn/ is for information about visiting and residing on the island and many Pitcairners and Pitcairn enthusiasts also have websites and blogs.
- www.pitcairntravel.pn plans to run regular trips between Pitcairn and Mangareva between April and September on the 60ft yacht Committement: these will offer a ten-day stopover on the island.
- **Pitcairn News** is a free illustrated monthly newsletter published on Pitcairn and distributed by e-mail. If you'd like to be on the list, tell Kari Young: uptibi@hotmail.com.
- Dozens of cruise liners call at Pitcairn Island during their summer but only the smaller ones are usually equipped to allow passengers to land; web-surfing will find these.

- **GLYNN CHRISTIAN'S** website is www.glynnchristian.com. His biography of Fletcher Christian FRAGILE PARADISE *The Discovery of Fletcher Christian, BOUNTY mutineer* is available world wide from Amazon.com. Second-hand copies of earlier editions can often be found on ABE.com.

ACKNOWLEDGEMENTS

This book is the result of many people's generous support and suggestions. Today's amazing world of communication means this often happened while I was asleep and appeared in an e-mail in the morning.

Here are those people, in approximate order of the time they came to know Mrs Christian.

From early days, very early days, CuChullaine and Basha O'Reilly of the Long Riders Guild, pushed, prodded and cheered at every opportunity and their fascination with Mauatua's story is what gave me the confidence first to sit and write. They tell extraordinary stories of their own and are currently making the first horse ride around the world and doing astonishing things on their way. Jamie Wolpert was a priceless, staunch pioneer in Mauatua's world, David Wilson was an enthusiastic missionary for the project, and regular cakes and coffee with writer Ian Wisniewski were always invaluable, feeding much more than the belly. Chris Gaskell and Bernadette Kilroy were wonderful enthusiasts from the very start.

Distinguished Professor Dame Anne Salmond at Auckland University is a lauded and highly awarded anthropologist and the author of such subject-related books as APHRODITE'S ISLAND: THE EUROPEAN DISCOVERY OF TAHITI (University of California Press) and the forthcoming BLIGH IN THE SOUTH PACIFIC (Penguin NZ/University of California Press). Rolf DuRietz in Uppsala is the most incisive and careful of BOUNTY scholars. Both challenged my first draft and then generously told me what they would do instead. Much of this was priceless and I did it, of course.

Sally Ryder Brady in Vermont is the prize-winning author of A BOX OF DARKNESS (St Martin's Press) and the widow of Upton Brady, who commissioned FRAGILE PARADISE, my biography of Fletcher Christian. A writer of great skill and a teacher of writing at Harvard, she diplomatically steered my first steps into historical-fiction and suggested how and why I should delete 100 pages and kept a welcome stream of compliments flowing. In London the writer, editor and historical-fiction reader Gillian Stern picked up the reins and trotted out more ideas for improvement; thanks to Patrick Walsh for that introduction.

Chrissie Walker was exceptionally generous and gave me her late father's collection of BOUNTY material including large deck plans and a copy of McKay's Anatomy of the Armed Transport BOUNTY (Conway Maritime Press), all useful in setting events and people in the right place.

My sister Faye Christian knows and cares deeply about things Polynesian and womanly and was an insightful guide. Andrew Smith in Toronto was unfailingly encouraging, a true friend at the time when he was completing his excellent novel EDITH'S WAR (Axiom Publishing), about another man and woman from different countries during WWII. Everyone should have friends like Topher Russo in Baltimore, a life-long BOUNTY enthusiast and loyal champion of the book. My operatic neighbour Constance Novis, her husband Rob and her brother Tim, Chaplain at Wellington College, all interrupted busy lives to jump on board very early, for which I am truly grateful.

Louella and Robin Hanbury Tenison in Cornwall, my godson Merlin Hanbury Tenison, who was being courageous once again in Afghanistan, ever-generous Michael Truscott of Penzance, cousin Jane and Jack Tresidder in Samoens, France, Roger and Val Jupe in London, Reid Bishop in Switzerland, Noelene Gillies in Auckland and John Laflin in Edinburgh at the time, all played an important part in getting me through the obligation I felt to tell the story of Mauatua and the Ma'ohi women who are the foremothers of Pitcairn Island.

Donald Cameron was extraordinarily generous in giving me time away from domestic humdrum, first aboard LOCHEIL on the Thames and then in the amazing contemporary house he had just built in Cape Town, where these last words were written. The hospitality of cousin Gillian Reckitt, of Sally Young, of her sister Pat Redfern, of Richard Broome and Robert Mansell, of Daryl McKeown, of my dear friend the late Peter Leggatt MBE and of the late, much missed Princess Luciana Pignatelli was always timely and sustaining.

Very specific help was given by Max Cryer, Dr Kaori O'Connor, Professor Bruno Saura, Professor of Tahitian History at the University in Tahiti and M. Vetea Hart in Tahiti. Steve Pendleton was perceptively helpful in establishing that BOUNTY couldn't possibly have been run onto Pitcairn's rocks. Barbara Kuchau and others of the Pitcairn Island Study Groups, Herb Ford of the Pitcairn Islands Study Centre and BOUNTY Scribe Dennis Stephens in Florida all helped with advice and staunch encouragement.

The late Dr Sven Wahlroos' contributions to Tahiti and to the BOUNTY story are legendary. His book MUTINY AND ROMANCE IN THE SOUTH SEAS (Salem House) is without doubt the best published reference to the BOUNTY story.

His widow Eva was wonderfully kind and generously gave give me an invaluable copy of Sven's masterful TAHITIAN.ENGLISH.TAHITIAN DICTIONARY (Ma'ohi Heritage Press).

Neighbour Alastair Tewarrie was a rock, ready and willing and able to do all things IT related.

My major reference for pre-missionary Tahiti was ANCIENT TAHITI by Douglas Oliver (The University Press of Hawai'i). Much of what happened on Pitcairn in this book comes from almost 40 years of reading and then from learning to think a different way, so Mauatua's story was not yet another story told by men about men; my approach of seeing events through Mauatua and the Ma'ohi women began when I questioned why no woman was pregnant when BOUNTY arrived at Pitcairn after so many months searching for a home.

Otherwise I've relied on what I researched and wrote for FRAGILE PARADISE – the Discovery of BOUNTY Mutineer, Fletcher Christian.

THE AUTHOR

Glynn Christian is a great great great great grandson of Mauatua and Fletcher Christian. He is the author of FRAGILE PARADISE, the only biography of Fletcher Christian, which is now considered an indispensable work of reference in the enormous compendium of books, articles, films and documentaries there is about the mutiny on BOUNTY in 1789.

This new book means he is one of the few writers in history honoured to have been able to write about both partners in a pair of his great great great great grandparents.

He was born in New Zealand but has lived mainly in London, UK since 1965, where he is very well known as a pioneering television chef, journalist and prize-winning food writer.

He is the only food writer to have been honoured with a Lifetime Achievement Award from within the food industry, from the Guild of Fine Food in 2008.

Glynn has been a Fellow of the Royal Geographical Society since 1980

WWW.GLYNNCHRISTIAN.COM